T0291201

industrial **mega**projects

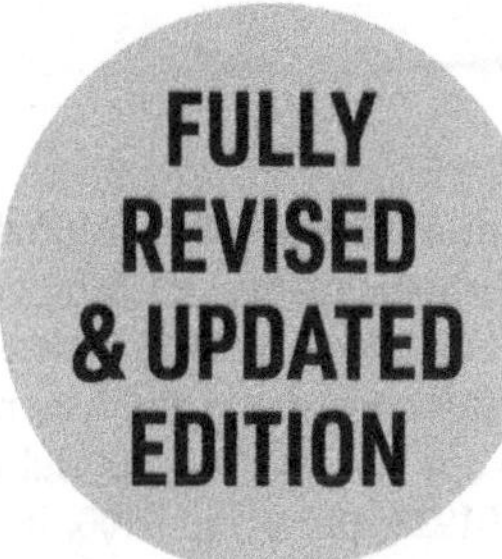

Edward W. Merrow

industrial **mega**projects

CONCEPTS, STRATEGIES, AND PRACTICES FOR SUCCESS

SECOND EDITION

WILEY

Published by John Wiley & Sons, Inc., Hoboken, New Jersey.
Published simultaneously in Canada.

For general information on our other products and services or for technical support, please contact our Customer Care Department within the United States at (800) 762-2974, outside the United States at (317) 572-3993 or fax (317) 572-4002.

Wiley also publishes its books in a variety of electronic formats. Some content that appears in print may not be available in electronic formats. For more information about Wiley products, visit our web site at **www.wiley.com**.

Library of Congress Cataloging-in-Publication Data is available:

ISBN 9781119893172 (cloth)
ISBN 9781119893189 (epub)
ISBN 9781119893196 (epdf)

Cover Design: Wiley
Cover Images: © Photocreo Bednarek /Adobe Stock Photos, © Karl Hendon/Getty Images, © WangAnQi/Getty Images
Author Photo: © Stephanie Dupuis Photography

SKY10077577_061524

For Justin

Contents

Part 5 Finishing Up 435

Preface

It seems to me that we live in a vastly more complex world today than in 2010 when I wrote the first edition of *Industrial Megaprojects*. The industrial projects landscape has changed significantly due to the need to address climate change as de-carbonization requirements add a wholly new dimension to assessing what is a good project outcome. Renewable energy projects and carbon capture projects will have to be an integral part of our immediate future in the hundreds or thousands if the warming of the planet is to be slowed. A very large fraction of those projects will be megaprojects. If humanity decides not to combat climate change in a serious and concerted way, there will be hundreds or even thousands of megaprojects to attempt to combat the damage that climate change will cause. Megaprojects will feature heavily in our future either way.

The other big change since 2010 has been the Covid pandemic and its aftermath. It will be many years before historians will be able to realistically assess the effects of the pandemic, but we already know that it changed project work very substantially. The pandemic hastened the demographic cliff that project organizations and owners and contractors were already facing. The pandemic also has changed the way teams work; the usual format in 2024 is a hybrid in-person and virtual model. That model may be working well enough for most activities, but it is not working well for projects. Projects, like many sports, is a deeply team-based activity. Teams always work better together.

In this edition of *Industrial Megaprojects*, I try to reflect how the world has changed in the new emphases in the book. I spend much more space on the role of Shaping in project success and failure because projects aimed at mitigating climate change turn out to be very "Shaping heavy." *Shaping* is the process of allocating the value of a project out to the stakeholders in a way that achieves agreement that the project can go forward. Shaping shapes "the deal" around which every major project ultimately depends. Unless society moves quickly to make the Shaping of energy transition projects achievable, we will fail this critical test and jeopardize our futures.

I also spend more space on project teams and what makes them tick. If the business case for a project is strong and the objectives are coherent, the success or failure of the project depends on the abilities of the owner team and how well it is led. If the owner team is able to do its required part to prepare a project well, the contractor teams will rarely fail.

The other major section added to this edition is Chapter 4, which addresses the mechanisms by which megaprojects actually fail when they do. This is to correct an oversight in the first edition. I realized shortly after its publication that I had only talked around the mechanisms of failure rather than fully exploring the subject. I am hoping that Chapter 4 remedies that oversight.

Since the first edition, megaprojects have improved significantly. The rate of success as we define *success* has more than doubled in the years after the first five-year period of this century. It is unfortunate that the baseline success rate was not quite 20%. For the sake of the investors in these projects, the teams that develop and execute them and the societies in which they are built, my Independent Project Analysis, Inc. (IPA) colleagues and I very much hope that this book will play some part, however small, in generating another doubling of success from here forward.

Acknowledgments

This book records some of the history of large complex industrial projects that make the things on which modern societies depend. Many thousands of people contributed in ways large and small to the projects that we have studied here. I especially want to thank and acknowledge the hundreds of owner teams that spent countless hours assembling data for Independent Project Analysis, Inc. (IPA) analysts and research staff and answering thousands of questions. Without your contributions there is no database and histories from which to assemble this book. This book is, above all, written for you.

I also acknowledge the essential role of my colleagues at IPA who visited project teams and sites in all corners of the world to assemble the incredibly rich data, information, and knowledge behind the 760 projects included in the database. By asking the right questions and asking again when things didn't make sense, the IPA staff made this book possible.

I thank my IPA colleagues who read and commented on sections of this new edition. I especially want to thank Luke Wallace, the director of IPA's Projects Research Division, and Anish Kalro, a member of Luke's staff, for their invaluable assistance in putting together the database that was essential for this book. My thanks also to Kelli Ratliff, product delivery manager at IPA, for sorting out and constructing all of the figures and illustrations that help tell the story. And last but not least, thanks to the Wiley staff for once again being patient and quickly turning around things.

Why Megaprojects Fail So Often—Seven Key Mistakes

By way of introducing the reader to the strange world of megaprojects, I am starting by discussing seven critical mistakes that I have seen most often in my 40 years of studying these projects, first at The Rand Corporation, and then for the last 35 years, at Independent Project Analysis (IPA). If you are responsible for a megaproject right now, try to ask yourself, "Am I now in the process of making one of these whopper blunders?"

After outlining how to do large projects well to the executive committee of a large company, the CEO asked me an obvious question: "Given that all of this is rather straightforward [he actually said "smashingly banal"], why can't we do it?" The answer was one he anticipated and feared: "Because you are incapable of generating the kind of deep cooperation within the company that is necessary to do these projects well." Most of the big mistakes that companies make in developing and executing these projects stem from a basic lack of being able to pursue a common goal with clarity and good behavior.

This book is mostly about mistakes, often masked with the bravado of "taking daring risks," but in the end, just plain mistakes. So, I thought it appropriate to start our discussion of megaprojects with seven whopper mistakes that doomed too many of these projects from the start. For the most part, the engineers on these projects tend to make little mistakes, although some of them occasionally cascade into disaster. Most big mistakes are made by senior business managers in the sponsoring firms. The reason they make most of the big mistakes is because they have control of the things that matter most: strategy, money, and people. In most megaproject development, the most important single relationship among the many thousands of relationships involved is the one between the business director for the project and the project manager, often called the project director.

So here are my top Sorry Seven.

1. I want to keep it all!

In days of yore, greed was considered a bad thing, even in business, because greed was liable to get us into trouble. I am pleased to report that in megaprojects, greed still works that way. When companies approach these projects with a view of trying to take as much of the pie as they possibly can, they lose sight of an essential element in making the project succeed: the allocation of the project's potential value in a way that provides a stable foundation on which the project can be executed. This will be a primary subject of Chapter 5. Working a deal that will be seen as essentially unfair to other stakeholders will tend to backfire. Greed generates an imbalance in the distribution of cost and rewards of the project.

Most commonly, a project with a greedy lead sponsor falls apart in the development (Shaping) phase, so we end up with nothing rather than all of it. In other cases, the project proceeds, but those who feel they have been treated unfairly never let go of their opposition. They then add turbulence to the project environment, giving project directors more trouble than they can manage. By their nature, megaprojects often suffer with turbulent project environments. Adding to that turbulence is a recipe for failure.

2. I want it *NOW!*

Schedule pressure dooms more megaprojects than any other single factor. When there is pressure to quickly move along a project from the outset, corners get cut and opportunists have a field day.

A classic case was a group of difficult deepwater petroleum developments that was put on a fast track when the CEO mentioned in a meeting with the financial community that the projects would go into production on a particular date. The project community's reaction within the company was "It can't be done!" but that didn't deter an ambitious vice president who saw an opportunity to ingratiate himself with the boss. He then set up a "daring and ambitious" program with an inexperienced contractor to deliver the projects in 70% of industry average time at 70% of industry average cost. The result was a program overrun of several billions of dollars, and the largest and most important project was a fully four years late and $2 billion to $3 billion overrun. (We will never know for sure how much!)

No project should ever be deliberately slow. (If it really doesn't make any difference when the project is completed, you probably shouldn't be doing the project now anyway.) But taking risks with megaproject schedules is a fool's game. Every megaproject has an appropriate pace at which the project can be developed and executed successfully. Furthermore, that pace is known with a fair degree of confidence early on if good practice is followed. If the economics of the project require an accelerated schedule, then the appropriate conclusion is that project is uneconomic and should not be done. Unlike smaller projects, megaprojects cannot be used to "fill in a gap" in your production or "meet a market window." When the calendar rather than the needs of the project drives the schedule, the project fails. We return to the issue of fast-tracking megaprojects in numerous places in the chapters to follow.

3. Don't worry, we'll work out the details of the deal later.

As a megaproject director friend of mine likes to say: "The deal drives the project; the project can't drive the deal!" I would add that the project *can* drive the deal, but it never turns out to be a *good* deal. The business deal and the project have to develop together and inform each other, but the deal governs. The deal establishes the parameters and the priorities for the project. The deal determines the relative importance of capital cost versus operating cost and cost versus schedule. The deal also determines how big the scope can be.

Many megaprojects center on a deal between a resource holder, for example, petroleum, minerals deposit, and so on, and a company with the technical expertise to develop that resource and sell the product. The basic contours of the deal between the resource holder and the resource developer must be decided quite early in the front-end development of the project. The deal is what will ultimately shape how money will be made as well as how it will be divided. In the absence of the deal, the project is directionless. If project development continues without the deal informing its shape, the chances that the deal will never be struck increase. Furthermore, if the potential partners cannot agree fairly quickly on the shape of the deal, there may be something terribly amiss. Let me cite an egregious example.

A European company was developing a large project (~$7 billion) in the Middle East with a resource holder. The idea was that the resource holder would provide the feedstock at a discounted rate to promote industrialization and job creation; however, the negotiations over the formula for this went nowhere while the project was busy being developed and defined. When we challenged the rationality of this situation with the company executive driving the deal, we were brushed aside with a "You don't understand the Middle East." Finally, the invitations to bid were issued and over $250 million of the company's money had been spent and the board of directors finally required a deal or no authorization. When there was no deal forthcoming, the company was forced to cancel the project and eat the loss. What was going on? The resource holder didn't actually have the feedstock and exploration efforts were coming up empty. Not wanting to lose face (and make their resource situation known to the world), they dragged their feet until the sponsor quit. They then publicly blamed the sponsor for killing the project and being an unreliable and untrustworthy company! And who is it exactly who doesn't know the Middle East?

4. Why do we have to spend so much up front?

Every project professional worthy of the title knows that skimping on the front-end definition of a project is stupid. When it comes to the biggest and most important projects that we do, we routinely skimp on the front-end. Megaprojects—with so much at stake—are routinely less well defined at authorization than smaller, less important projects. The primary reasons are time (see preceding mistake No. 2) and money (see preceding mistake No. 1).

Depending on the specifics of the project, doing a thorough job defining and planning an industrial megaproject takes 3% to 5% of eventual total capital cost. Let's be clear: on a megaproject, that is a lot of money. The cost, however, of *not* spending the money is much, much more.

Senior managers are understandably concerned that if they spend, say, $100 million and the project is canceled, they are stuck with the bill. Even worse, from their perspective the $100 million is expense, not capital, and is therefore deducted immediately from earnings. However, when senior managers are faced with this situation as a realistic possibility, it is symptomatic of other problems.

Sometimes managers find themselves in this risk of loss position because the resource holder has deliberately set them up. Some resource holders want no decision points between the initial "memorandum of understanding" (which has no binding effect) and the full-funds authorization of the project. This is a simple bargaining ploy: if I can get them to spend enough money, they are locked into the project whether or not they really want to be. This is a psychological example of the forward-going economics trap—that is, "throwing good money after bad."

At other times, senior managers can find themselves in this dilemma because the cost of the project was not understood at the necessary and appropriate time. As we will discuss at some length later, the eventual cost of the project should be known with a fair degree of assurance when only about 1% of total cost has been expended, not 3% to 5%. If management doesn't have the stomach for spending 1% as pure risk money, they should not play the game. Spending that front-end money well is the subject of Chapter 10.

5. We need to shave 20% off that number!

One of the most counterproductive exercises in megaprojects is the "cost reduction task force" responding to management's admonition to significantly reduce the cost of the project, usually within a few months of full-funds authorization. I have literally heard a vice president say, "You guys [meaning the project team] need to sharpen your pencils and get a billion dollars out of that estimate!" Those must be magic pencils because in the real world, the cost of a project is inextricably linked to its scope, which in turn is a reflection of its intended functionality. Unless I change the scope, which means that some functionality has to give way, I cannot really change the cost estimate. But to change the scope would require another year or two before we are ready to authorize the project, which is, of course, unacceptable because of preceding mistake No. 2.

So project teams in this situation do one of two things: (1) they change the assumptions underlying the estimate such as the cost and productivity of labor, prices for equipment, and so on; or (2) they actually cut the scope knowing that it will all have to come back later to achieve the needed performance of the project. Either way, they are headed for a big overrun and the savviest among them will be preparing to post their resumes so as not to be caught up in the scapegoating that will surely occur later.

6. The contractors should carry the risk; they're doing the project!

A majority of megaprojects in most parts of the world are executed on some form of fixed-price contracts between the sponsors and one or more prime contractors. Rather than project professionals, the preference for fixed-price (lump-sum) contracting almost always comes from the business leadership or from the banks financing the projects. Their belief is that the contractual form will transfer the cost (and often schedule) risk from the sponsors to the prime contractor(s). And every once in a while, it actually does! Most of the time, however, relatively little risk is actually passed, but a substantial premium is paid nonetheless.

There is a simple and unavoidable problem with wholesale risk transfer from sponsors to contractors: the contractors cannot actually carry the risk on a megaproject. The firms that engineer and construct industrial projects are variable-cost ones with very little in the way of fixed assets. Their balance sheets are not loaded with capital assets, and generally, the cash they have on the balance sheet is needed for working purposes. They earn by selling the services of people rather than via the production and sale of products. This simply means they cannot possibly carry the kinds of losses that can and do occur on megaprojects. As a consequence, given the preference of business leaders and banks for lump-sum contracts, the engineering and construction firms have become very adept at taking on lump sums with loopholes or bidding so high that the risk is manageable.

Most of Chapter 13 takes up the issue of how to match the contracts to the situation rather than the situation to the contracts. However, the belief that fixed price contracts establish a ceiling on what sponsors will pay for a project is to completely confuse a ceiling and a floor. No sponsor has ever paid *less* than the value of the lump-sum contract, but many, many a sponsor has paid much more.

7. Fire those #$@$^! project managers who overrun our projects!

Beating up project managers who overrun capital projects is a blood sport that certainly dates back to the Great Pyramids. However, it's a bit of fun that comes with a very high price tag for the business.

I have been looking at capital projects now for over 40 years. I have met hundreds of project directors and managers of all sorts and descriptions. I have yet to meet one who starts the day by asking, "What can I do today to screw up my project?" I have met some project directors who struck me as hopelessly incompetent, but very few of those were working on megaprojects. Large cost overruns on major projects can almost never be honestly laid at the door of the project director.

I will never forget a very long morning I spent with the CEO of a large international oil company. Much of our discussion that morning focused on why it was inappropriate and counterproductive for him to personally browbeat project managers who overran the company's projects. I finally concluded the discussion this way: "If you beat up the project managers for overruns, they will find ways to hide money so you can never find it. If they don't, you have hired a bunch of morons. And morons don't do projects well either!" As I walked down the corridor after the meeting, the vice president responsible for Exploration and Production turned to me and said, "Ed, now you see what we're up against." I left that day knowing that I had lost the argument, and 15 years later, the company's engineering department, led by a former contractor, focuses most of its effort on finding where the project directors have hidden the money.

The preceding seven mega-mistakes are not mutually exclusive; they can and do show up together in many combinations. However, any one is usually sufficient to doom a project to failure.

PART 1

Success Is Elusive

It is difficult to write a short book about megaprojects. Megaprojects have many more salient features than smaller projects. By *salient*, I mean aspects of the projects that may well turn out to be the basis for failure. For a megaproject to go well, a great many things must go well and nothing can go very poorly. Megaprojects are political. Megaprojects tax sponsor organizations and contractors. Megaprojects are usually technically complex and often innovative. Such features tend to be occasional with smaller projects. They sometimes get caught up in local or company politics, but not usually. If they are very complex technically, that is often the only respect in which they are challenging. For megaprojects, lots of challenges usually are present as a set, but often in a configuration that most of those involved have never seen before.

Part 1 does several things that are essential for understanding the rest of the book. First, I define what constitutes success and failure. Those definitions will be used throughout the book in every case in which the terms *success* and *failure* are used. In the course of defining *success* and *failure*, I also explain why I decided to define them as binary rather than as existing on a set of scales. The reason is that megaprojects tend to actually sort out in a binary way and that is quite important to understanding the projects.

Second, in Chapter 3, we will review what has changed and what has stayed the same in the 13 years since the first edition was published. Part of the impetus to write this second edition was to see if we learned anything after the disastrous first set of about 100 megaprojects we authorized in the first five years of the 21st century. We did learn; I wish that we had learned more, faster.

The third big subject of this introductory part of the book is contained in Chapter 4, which discusses the concrete mechanisms by which megaprojects fail when they do. When viewed from the proper perspective, there are actually only a few ways in which the projects fail, and one mechanism, cascading failure, is by far the most common. If practitioners can get sensitized to look for the early signs of cascade failures, the outcomes might be improved dramatically.

The final big point that I hope readers note is that a lot of megaprojects are, in fact, very successful ventures. The number of successes is far too many to be a matter of luck, and all of the analysis in this book points away from luck playing much of a role in megaproject success. One of my disappointments with the first edition was that some readers came away with the impression that I said that megaprojects were bound to fail when that was far from the truth. Yes, there are more megaproject failures than successes. But very few of the failures were inevitable; almost all were preventable by the project sponsors. But if a sponsor is passive and expects success without having to work very hard and smart, then failure is, in fact, inevitable for them. Megaprojects are bloodsport; the timid or the lazy should not apply.

CHAPTER 1

Megaprojects—Creators and Destroyers of Capital

Megaprojects are important in the grand scheme of things. Industrial megaprojects provide most of the things necessary for life on a planet with 8 billion humans and counting: energy, metals, chemicals, pharmaceuticals, seeds and food. When the projects are done well, they accelerate economic development and security. But it is also no secret that megaprojects are the most uncomfortable subject in the management of projects.

As a project management community, we have struggled to develop and execute these large complex projects with anything approaching consistent success. I first looked at these projects systematically in 1988 as a researcher at the Rand Corporation.[1] I found a story of large cost overruns on projects that were often delivered so late that their original purpose no longer existed. When I revisited the subject 22 years later, it was with a much deeper and better nuanced database that my colleagues and I had assembled through years of evaluating projects at Independent Project Analysis (IPA).[2] In that long interval depressingly little had changed. There was, however, a glimmer of hope in 2011 that was nowhere in sight in 1988: a number of large complex

[1]Edward W. Merrow et al., *Understanding the Outcomes of Megaprojects: An Analysis of Very Large Civilian Projects*, Santa Monica, CA: The Rand Corp., 1988.
[2]Edward W. Merrow, *Industrial Megaprojects*, John Wiley & Sons, 2011.

industrial projects were brilliant successes, a number far greater than two decades before. Those projects demonstrated that success was not a matter of luck or circumstance, but a product of deep and collaborative planning by the owners leading the projects.

In the 12 years since publication of *Industrial Megaprojects*, a great deal has changed. Today's world seems much further removed from 2011 than 2011 was from 1988. We have entered in earnest what promises to be a long crisis period around climate change. Renewables megaprojects have become common and will coexist with oil and gas projects and other megaprojects for years to come. All major projects in most parts of the world have to navigate the requirements of sustainability along with the mandate to be profitable. Local content requirements have proliferated and become increasingly complex in the past decade. We have lived through our first global pandemic in a hundred years, which changed both the projects landscape and geopolitics in profound ways.

The world is much more connected today than in 2011. The greater connectedness has made Shaping of megaprojects more challenging. The amount of information and disinformation available today dwarfs 2011. In 2011, the remarkable term *alternative facts* had yet to be coined, although the underlying concept was surely known. And in 2011, artificial intelligence (AI) was talked about but in much the same way we talk about space travel today.

There are more megaprojects today than ever before. Projects have increased in size and complexity for a number of reasons: easily accessed resources close to markets have largely been depleted; international oil companies must venture into deep water and other difficult environments because national resource holders control more easily developed oil and gas; chemical companies seeking lower cost feedstocks need to exploit economies of scale to compete globally, and often must go to the source of the feedstocks to make the project viable. The need for extensive infrastructure development means that many projects will have to be very large to spread the infrastructure costs over a wide enough base of beneficial production to be economic.

The efforts to control climate change, which are just beginning, have already given rise to a great many megaprojects and will give rise to thousands more if the efforts are successful. Many of the megaprojects aimed at climate change mitigation have already encountered significant problems, especially with regard to economic viability and stakeholder alignment. If, as a projects community, we do not learn quickly how to do these projects well, efforts to slow planetary warming have little chance of success.

As the projects have increased in size and complexity, they have become much more difficult to manage. Cost overruns, serious slips in completion schedules, and operability problems have all become more common. Many of these very large projects end up being disappointing to their sponsors; a fair number turn out to be massive destroyers of shareholder wealth; and a few are horrendous with respect to anything and everything involved: the investing companies, the local population, and the environment. When megaproject disasters become public knowledge, which is rarely the case, they damage reputations and even jeopardize continued existence.[3]

IPA's research program on megaprojects over the past 20 years shows clearly that most of the poor results of these projects constitute self-inflicted wounds. The sponsors are creating the circumstances that lead inexorably to failure. *And that is profoundly good news!* What we do, we can fix.

Who Should Read This Book?

Anyone with responsibility for large, complex, or difficult capital projects will find things of interest in the pages that follow. My particular goal is to help those who sponsor, direct, or work on large projects guide the projects to safe and successful outcomes. Although my focus is on industrial megaprojects, very large projects sponsored by the petroleum, chemicals, minerals, power, and related industries,

[3]The failure of BHP's Hot Briquetted Iron Project in 1999 contributed to the company losing over half of its market value. The $10 billion plus overrun of Shell Sakhalin-2 project damaged Shell's reputation and created an excuse for the Kremlin to nationalize a large portion of the project. The structural failure of BP's Thunderhorse semi-submersible platform in 2005 in the U.S. Gulf of Mexico was an important element in a series of stunning setbacks for the company. Most megaproject disasters, however, remain carefully private—while sometimes wearing a very different and well-contrived public face.

those working on large public infrastructure projects should find the discussion relevant to their work.

Anyone interested in complex projects, even if they fall far short of megaproject status, will find the story of these projects informative to their situation. Most of the basic principles of doing megaprojects well are the basic principles of doing all projects well. Small complex projects often behave more like megaprojects than their small project cousins. If the reader is interested in projects generally, megaprojects will always be fascinating.

I very much hope that members of boards of directors of companies that sponsor megaprojects will read this book. To be blunt, when it comes to the governance of large projects, most boards strike me as brain dead. They are not asking the right questions and they are not asking questions early enough in the process to deter bad decisions.

Those who finance major projects should find a great deal of interest (forgive the pun) in the book. In many respects, this book is all about large project risk, which is a key concern for banks and others involved in project finance. It is my observation that bank financing often increases cost while doing nothing whatever about project risk.

Those who are concerned about the management of the modern publicly owned industrial corporation and teach others about how it should be done will also find this book interesting, and perhaps, very disturbing. The failure of these projects is symptomatic of the core problems of the modern firm: too much out-sourcing of key competencies, poorly informed decision-making, a woeful lack of accountability for results, and a pathological focus on the short-term at the expense of the long-term health of the corporation and its shareholders.

What Is an Industrial Megaproject?

The projects that are the subject of our research are a subset of all projects and even a subset of large projects. We focus on *industrial* megaprojects. By *industrial*, we mean projects that make a product for sale, for example, oil, natural gas, iron ore, nickel, gold ingot, diamonds, high-volume chemicals, and so on. All of the projects under scrutiny were intended to make an economic profit, at least eventually, for some if not always all of the sponsors.[4,5] By confining ourselves to industrial projects, we have excluded several classes of important projects: military developments, purely public works and transportation projects, monuments, works of art, and so on. By excluding these sorts of projects we have excluded some megaprojects from our analysis. We have a couple of reasons for doing so:

- Confining ourselves to projects that are intended to make money simplifies the task of assessing outcomes, while not necessarily simplifying the range and complexity of objectives in the projects. Although it is true for almost all of our projects that *someone* wanted and expected to make money on the result, it does not follow that *all* of the sponsors expected to make an economic profit. Some were motivated by jobs creation, political ambition, general economic development, and other "public" goals. These "mixed motive" projects, as we call them, are an interesting class and pose challenges for "for-profit" sponsors.
- Having some economic profit motive disciplines and constrains the objectives of the projects in important ways. Some public works projects have objectives that are hard to fathom by mere mortals. Some military acquisition programs appear to continue almost solely on the strength of political patronage long after the military rationale has become obsolete or discredited.[6] And some "prestige projects," such as the *Concorde* supersonic

[4]A few of our projects were undertaken with the explicit expectation that they would make little or no economic profit, but would facilitate highly profitable projects later. These projects bear the dubious title "strategic," a subject to which we will return when discussing project Shaping.

[5]The term *sponsor* will be reserved for those organizations that claim formal ownership of a project by virtue of their economic investment in the project. Those investments could occasionally be in-kind or deferred, but usually indicate monetary investment in the cost of the project.

[6]For example, the U.S. Air Force B-1 Bomber program continued long after a superior option had emerged due entirely to political influence. "B-1 Problems, If Reparable, Could Cost $3 Billion," *The Boston Globe*, February 13, 1987. The V-22 Osprey aircraft program not only overran its budget colossally, but also suffered repeated crashes, but continued anyway. "Assessments Needed to Address V-22 Aircraft Operational and Cost Concerns to Define Future Investments," GAO-09-482, May 2009.

transport, have objectives that must forever be in the eye of the beholder. Who is to say whether prestige has actually been enhanced and was it by an amount sufficient to justify the opportunity cost of the project? Industrial projects tend to have at least some nicely tangible objectives.

What makes an industrial project an industrial *mega*project? Megaprojects, as the name implies, are very large. We start considering a project in the megaproject class at about $1 billion in today's terms. This is slightly more relaxed on the low side than the definition used in the first edition of *Industrial Megaprojects*. I decided to make the change because using the $1 billion threshold, there is no relationship between size and success or failure[7] (to be defined in the next chapter). If we include smaller projects, success becomes negatively related to size.

Why Study These Projects?

There are four compelling reasons to study and understand megaprojects:

- There are many more of them than in times past and this will continue for decades to come.
- These projects are important. They are important to the societies in which they are being done; they are important to the health of the global economy; they are important to the sponsors and others putting up huge amounts of money.
- These projects are very problematic. They are failing at an alarming and unsustainable rate.
- There is not much published that speaks directly and quantitatively to the types of projects considered here.

I will discuss each of these reasons to worry about megaprojects in turn.

[7]The statistical relationship is close to null (Pr.|z|<.81).

Increasing Numbers

Industrial megaprojects have become much more common. For much of the 1980s and virtually all of the 1990s there were few very large projects, even in the petroleum industry. The Norwegian and U.K. North Sea had been home to a number of megaprojects in the 1970s. These projects had a very difficult go, and without the rapid rise in crude oil prices in the wake of the overthrow of the Shah of Iran, almost none of the megaprojects in the North Sea would have been profitable ventures.[8] Most of the megaprojects that had been in planning stages in the late 1970s died abruptly when commodity prices fell in the early 1980s.

However, a number of factors have converged to make megaprojects much more common in the first decades of the 21st century, and these factors give every indication of being enduring drivers of very large projects. The first factor driving the current wave of megaprojects has been the rapid rise in the demand for almost all major commodities; iron ore, coal, copper, and petroleum have all experienced very rapid increases in demand (and therefore, price) since 2003. Previously, most prior commodity price fluctuations had not been synchronized; prices might rise for one or two metals, oil and gold prices might rise for political reasons, but not all at the same time. The underlying common driver this time was the rapid industrialization of China and India in the context of reasonable overall global growth. None of the major commodities are actually facing imminent global depletion; however, most are facing upward sloping long-run marginal costs.

The different commodities have had somewhat different drivers for large projects:

- Opening up a new major mineral ore body has long been expensive. Most major new mines today are in places that require major infrastructure development to be practicable. When a good deal of infrastructure is needed, the production volume must be very large to spread those infrastructure costs across a broad enough

[8]G.R. Castle, "North Sea Scorecard," Society of Petroleum Engineers Paper 15358, October 1986.

base for the venture to be profitable. This makes large size the only avenue to development, not an option. Today, a good many megaprojects in mining are driven by the "energy transition metals," that is, those required to sustain efforts to mitigate climate change: copper, nickel, cobalt, lithium, and rare earth metals.

- Crude oil is a special case, at least partially. A large portion of oil that remains relatively inexpensive to produce is held by state companies.[9] In order to stay in the oil business, international companies have been pushed quickly into places where oil is difficult and costly to develop, usually deep water. International companies also have gained access when reservoirs are difficult to produce, for example, offshore heavy oil production in Brazil, very heavy oil onshore in Venezuela, the very sour oil and gas reservoirs in the Caspian area, or the very harsh climate off the eastern Russian coast, or in inaccessible areas such as central Africa. As a consequence, the marginal capital costs of production have increased very rapidly for these companies. This translates into a dramatic increase in the number of international oil company megaprojects.
- Rapid changes in the global economy have driven basic chemical companies to shift more of their manufacturing to fast-growing Asian economies. They have also sought to gain feedstock cost advantage by moving manufacturing to countries offering feedstock at below world open market average prices to attract production facilities, mostly in the Middle East.[10]
- A wide variety of megaprojects are being spawned by climate change action: carbon capture and sequestration, nuclear reactor projects, including small modular reactors, wind and solar renewable power, and various forms of hydrogen and hydrogen-to-carrier projects.

[9]Estimates of world reserves held by national oil companies range between 75% and over 90%. See, for example, *Wall Street Journal*, May 22, 2010.

[10]High natural gas prices continue to push much basic chemical manufacture out of Europe and into the United States where natural gas from shale provides low-cost feedstocks. Natural gas prices control the prices of ethane and propane, which are feedstocks for building block commodity chemicals such as ethylene and propylene.

Megaprojects Are Important

Without the industrial megaprojects in the extractive and manufacturing sectors, global competition for resources, which is already very intense, would become unmanageable. While one can reasonably question whether extractive projects have been a net boon for less developed economies that hold large supplies, one cannot doubt that the overall megaproject effect on global economic growth has been substantial. Megaprojects are responsible directly and indirectly for millions of jobs around the world, and without the many megaprojects we have seen over the past decade, global prices for virtually all major commodities would be much higher with all the attendant economic dislocation.

For the sponsors of megaprojects, success or failure of the project can mean the success or failure of the company. For all except the largest oil companies, a serious failure of a megaproject puts the company's future in jeopardy. Megaprojects are increasingly seen as essential to being competitive, but in many cases, the skills needed to effectively develop and control these projects have not developed in tandem with the need.

It is also important to remember that the success or failure of these projects is often critical to the societies in which they are developed. Megaprojects place a good deal of stress on local communities. When they fail, and especially when they fail completely, the local communities suffer irreparable damage.

Megaprojects Fail Too Often

Megaproject results are frequently seriously short of the expectations of the sponsor-investors. Their cost overruns are often so significant that the whole project becomes NPV negative.[11] Their schedules often slip and early-year operability, which has a disproportionate effect on profitability, is frequently very poor. Occasionally, the projects produce environmental disasters as well. As we will show, these results are not

---

[11]*NPV*, of course, refers to *net present value*, which is a measure of the economic returns from an investment with future profits discounted for the effects of time.

inherent in the nature of the activities. They are, instead, caused by human decisions, ignorance, and uncontrolled but controllable human failings. These projects can be fixed.

The Literature Is Sparse

This book is needed because, despite the many thousands of pages written on the management of projects, very little of the literature addresses the peculiar nature of very large and complex projects as a class. There are some notable exceptions. Morris and Hough explored a set of eight very large public and private projects in 1987.[12] Like me, they concluded that the success rate is quite disappointing. I build on their path-breaking work. Miller and Lessard[13] and their colleagues explore what they call "large engineering projects," focusing on the development of new institutional arrangements. Their discussion of the process by which turbulent project environments might be settled is a key starting point for our own discussion of the Shaping process in Chapter 5. We focus much less on the creation of new contractual forms, such as build-own-transfer (BOT) simply because we have seen very few of these "new institutional arrangements" actually function as advertised. Our data, which are considerably deeper than that found in Miller and Lessard, flatly contradict the effectiveness of certain arrangements, such as incentivized contracts, which they tout as successful.

Flyvbjerg, Bruzelius, and Rothengatter make the most recent major contribution to the megaprojects literature, focusing primarily on very large infrastructure projects executed by the public sector around the world.[14] Although I share some of the same conclusions about these projects, public infrastructure projects are, in many respects, quite different than the projects explored in this research. Public infrastructure projects share many of the pathologies common in other publicly funded projects, such as military acquisition. They are frequently beset

[12]Peter Morris and George Hough, *The Anatomy of Major Projects*, John Wiley, 1987.

[13]Roger Miller and Donald R. Lessard, *The Strategic Management of Large Engineering Projects*, Cambridge, MA: MIT Press, 2000.

[14]Bent Flyvbjerg, Nils Bruzelius, and Werner Rothengatter, *Megaprojects and Risk: An Anatomy of Ambition*, Cambridge University Press, 2003.

by a phenomenon known as "buy-in and hook" in which low costs are promised early, knowing full well that the eventual costs will be much higher. While this sort of deception is not unknown in private sector ventures, it is not very common, simply because there is usually no taxpayer available to foot the bill later. As we will discuss later, many of the core conclusions of the "Oxford School" of megaprojects are highly inaccurate when applied to industrial projects.

The Organization of This Book

I have organized this book into five parts.

- Part 1 introduces the IPA megaprojects database and describes the research process that underpins this book. I seek to provide enough about methodology to satisfy the methodologically oriented reader without boring others to a stupor. I then present the track record of industrial megaprojects, summarizing the 760 large and complex projects studied to date and exploring trends in megaproject performance in the 21st century. To conclude Part 1, I describe the mechanisms by which projects fail and the narrower pathway to success.
- Part 2 is devoted to the three streams of work that must be completed and synchronized successfully by the sponsoring companies to produce a successful project. I devote three chapters to various aspects of the "Shaping" process, which is the least well-articulated and understood of the work streams. This section deals extensively with what Miller and Lessard[15] call the "Shaping" of megaprojects. It focuses on some brilliant examples of business leaders making an inherently unstable environment strong enough to permit a successful megaproject to be executed. But it also focuses on the decisions that business managers make that have devastating consequences for their projects without their ever fully understanding what went wrong. The business sponsors of large projects should really focus on the Shaping discussion

[15]Miller and Lessard, 2000.

because it should be their work stream. Project professionals need to read about Shaping to understand how they got into this mess and what they might do in the future to elevate problems to corporate management when mischief is being created by their business bosses.

Then we turn to the acquisition of the Basic Data, that is, the technical information underpinning design of the project in Chapter 9. Errors in the Basic Data are the quickest route to a project that does not operate as intended. As I was tallying up the causes of failure in these projects, I was surprised to see the number of times that Basic Data problems occurred. Because the Basic Data development often needs to start long before the project gets fully going, the Basic Data chapter should be read by the business professionals who often control the funding for Basic Data development, and by the R&D and technical specialist community that often do not consider themselves part of "project management" but who usually do the Basic Data development.

The project work stream up to authorization, which I call front-end loading (FEL), is discussed in Chapter 10. The discussion of the project work stream is written more for the project professional. It focuses not just on what needs to be done to make these big projects successful, but *why* those things are crucial. Many of the practices required to generate successful megaprojects are resisted by business management because they are apparently expensive and time-consuming. When the project team understands why certain practices are critical based on the actual history of megaprojects, they are better able to persuade reluctant managements to do the right things.

- Part 3 is all about people. First, we discuss the key players on the owner management side. Owner teams and owner team organization models then follow. I have also added some discussion of desirable attributes of own project organizations to support megaprojects.
- Part 4 is entitled "Getting It Done" and focuses on contracting for the engineering and construction services that will be essential to executing the megaproject, and then I discuss the control of risk in execution.

- Part 5 discusses the critical role of governance in making successful projects and then some summary conclusions about where to go from here.

Respecting Confidentiality

Some of the readers (I sincerely hope) will have been directly involved in the megaprojects that underpin the conclusions of this research. When I have offered examples, I have tried to select cases that are not unique, and in some cases, I have masked them enough to ensure that no individual project for which we have conducted a closeout evaluation can be identified conclusively. This is necessary to meet our obligations of confidentiality to the people and companies involved. When any project is mentioned by name, it is based solely on publicly available information.

If you are certain that I am discussing your project in a particular example, let me offer this caveat: several years ago, I wrote a volume of 20 case studies of new technology projects for the DuPont Company. Many of the projects had disastrous outcomes and some were brilliant successes. In the introduction, I carefully explained that *none* of the projects summarized in the volume were DuPont projects because the DuPont new technology projects would be covered in a separate volume. Nonetheless, for the next six months I had DuPont business and project professionals stop me in the hall while I was visiting the company and comment something like this: "You did a pretty good job summarizing my project, but you got a couple of the details wrong. . . ." This reflects a well-known fact: we humans have been making a hash of projects for a long, long time.

CHAPTER 2

Data and Methods

Research on capital projects, especially in the private sector, is sorely hampered by the researcher's lack of access to data and the people who created those data. In these regards, Independent Project Analysis (IPA) is enormously fortunate; we have access to both the written record of projects and the people who developed and executed the projects as part of our normal project evaluation work. In the course of a year, we evaluate 700–800 capital projects in the process industries. There are typically 40–60 megaprojects in that set of evaluations.

The Timing of Data Acquisition

IPA's data collections are mostly synchronized with a company's staged and gated project work process. The typical arrangement of such a work process is shown in Figure 2.1. The usual work process is arranged into three to five phases prior to full-funds authorization (sanction) of the project. The three-phase front-end arrangement, which is the most common, is shown in Figure 2.1 along with the various names that are widely used by different parts of the industry.[1] More and more

[1]Occasionally, companies have a formal and systematic "Phase 0" during which background work is performed for potential projects. Megaprojects in locations new to a company benefit greatly from such an "FEL-0" process because it is an opportunity to familiarize the company with the peculiarities of the locale. We will discuss "country advance teams" in more detail in Chapter 5. Some companies also divide the scope development phase into two parts: the first selects the general scope or "concept" that will be employed for the project, and the second refines and completes that scope. We believe the two-part Phase 2 is a best practice.

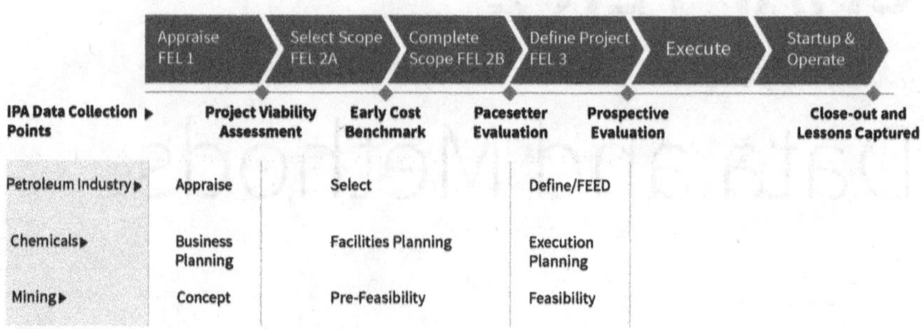

FIGURE 2.1 Project Work Process

companies are inserting a "check gate" in the second phase to improve the chances that all scope elements will be accounted for prior to moving into the "define" stage of the front-end. The first row of names below the figure is mostly used by the oil industry, with the second and third used commonly by the chemical and minerals industries, respectively. For the most part, the meanings of the stages are very similar, even if the names are not.

IPA's data collection points are shown beneath the stages. We collect the status of a project as often as four times prior to full-funds authorization (also known as final investment decision [FID]). As the project moves into scope development, data are collected on the completeness of the business case. Sometimes this is done in the form of a Business Engineering Alignment Meeting (BEAM). When a basic scope is available at the FEL 2A check gate, an early assessment of cost competitiveness is often completed, followed by a complete evaluation at the end of scope development. A final evaluation before the start of execution is performed to establish the final set of promises and commitments the project is making to the business and corporation. That evaluation then forms the baseline against which success and failure are measured.

We call the whole period prior to sanction of the project "front-end loading" (FEL). I will provide a quick overview of the "stage-gated" project work process now in order to ground the reader. The subject will recur multiple times in much greater detail in other parts of the book.

FEL-1 is devoted to the development of the business case and sorting out the basic feasibility of a capital investment. Among more disciplined (read, better managed) companies, the paramount issue for this phase is whether the type of investment contemplated in the locale envisioned is consistent with the company's overall business strategy. FEL-1 should be used to winnow down the range of possible projects to a manageable few to be explored in the next phase. The issue of whether a particular project is consonant with the company's strategy is very important for megaprojects. To be successful, megaprojects require much deeper corporate support than smaller projects. Sometimes this is in the form of technical support; sometimes it is in the form of senior management willingness to intervene on behalf of the project when difficulties arise.[2] Companies sometimes have IPA evaluate the completeness of the business case package as the FEL-1 phase is drawing to a close.

The gate monitoring passage from FEL-1 to scope development is the least well managed of all the gates. In too many companies, what would constitute an acceptable package for this gate is not well established. Too often, the businesses that staff the gate do not hold themselves to particularly high standards. This weakness in the FEL-1 stage foreshadows the weakness we see in the Shaping process for megaprojects that is a greatly expanded and enriched version of the FEL-1 work process.

FEL-2 is the scope selection and development phase of a project. If it was not already commissioned during FEL-1, a core technical team is now formed. The team seeks to translate the proto-project as envisioned in the business case into a real project with a defined physical scope, albeit all on paper (or in electrons) at this point. The definition of all elements of the scope with completed flow diagrams for all facilities marks the end of the FEL-2 phase. This is a critical juncture for the project because it is now, for the first time, that a reliable cost estimate can be developed for the project. The reliability of that estimate hangs heavily on the completeness of the scope developed. IPA usually evaluates a project at this point to assess whether the scope is actually

[2]Some companies take pride in being "highly entrepreneurial," which often translates into every business unit for themselves. Such companies, even if they are very large, often find it very difficult to develop and execute megaprojects successfully because they lack a center strong enough to provide deep support to their very large projects. The tendency to organize the company in a highly decentralized fashion is normative in minerals and a few oil and gas companies as well. Decentralization makes most aspects of megaproject management and control more difficult.

closed, and to benchmark the competitiveness of the cost estimate and preliminary execution schedule. For the great majority of projects—both large and small—the sponsor's decision to actually undertake the project is made at the end of the scope selection phase. The final phase of the front-end is expensive, usually costing 2% to 4% of eventual total project cost. The final phase is typically capitalized. Therefore, sponsors need to be in a position to make a decision at the end of phase 2, despite the "authorization" or "final investment decision" label given to the end of phase 3.

The third phase of the front-end process involves advancing engineering to a point where detailed design can be fully mobilized and advancing the execution planning to the point that execution can proceed without changes. This final phase of FEL is quite expensive for any project and very expensive for megaprojects. As a consequence, very few projects are halted once they begin the FEL-3 phase. IPA typically conducts a full evaluation of a project at the end of FEL-3 just before full-funds authorization.

Each of the IPA front-end evaluations is designed to support the management decision about whether a project should proceed to the next phase; continue in the current phase; or be stopped, shelved, or canceled outright. The final IPA evaluations of a project occur after the completion of commissioning and startup of the project and then 12 to 18 months later to assess production performance. If an evaluation is not performed at any point, we collect the data that would have been collected at the skipped stage at the next evaluation point.

The Data Collection Process

We collect all data except production information with a series of face-to-face interviews with members of the extended project teams augmented with a large number of documents. We employ a set of standardized electronic data collection protocols and train project analysts on the use of the protocols and interpretation of the questions in an extensive classroom and on-the-job program. By the time a project is complete, depending on the complexity of the project, we will have collected the answers to between 2,000 and 5,000 questions about the development, execution, and startup of the project facilities.

The training programs for project analysts are key to ensuring the greatest possible consistency of data. Trained analysts can explain what the questions mean to those providing the answers. We train analysts for particular types of projects, for example, minerals mining and processing, petroleum production, chemical process facilities, and so on. Senior and highly experienced analysts evaluate the megaprojects because they often pose significant data collection problems. Unlike smaller projects, megaprojects are frequently highly political in the general sense of that term. Careers can be made not only by bringing a megaproject to a successful conclusion, but also by merely getting a megaproject successfully to authorization. Because of the political nature of the projects within the companies, we are more likely to encounter "gamesmanship" in the data collection process for megaprojects than other types of projects.

The IPA Megaprojects Database

The database consists of 760 projects.[3] The industrial sectors involved are shown in Table 2.1. Over 40% of the projects are oil

TABLE 2.1 Types of Projects Represented in Database

Industrial Sector	Number	Percent of Sample
Oil & Gas Production	360	47
Fuels Processing (incl. biofuels)	107	14
Chemicals	97	13
Mining	93	12
LNG	42	6
Power & Renewables	17	2
Pipelines & Terminals	44	6
Totals	760	100

[3]We also draw on a number of projects that never went forward. These projects are very instructive. Sometimes not going forward was a major success because the projects would have been disastrous. In other cases, the failure of the projects to proceed represents a failure to effectively Shape and control the project environment, the subject of Chapters 5, 6, 7, and 8.

and/or natural gas production projects. Just over two-thirds of the oil and gas projects have their primary production facilities offshore, often in deep water areas. Many of the offshore projects also had a substantial onshore component. This is important because the construction of onshore facilities and offshore projects present different challenges. Offshore environments heavily penalize failure to complete work in the fabrication yards. If far from land, they pose significant logistics challenges. However, offshore projects benefit from being out of sight, and therefore not constantly in public view. The second largest group of projects involves the processing of hydrocarbons. These include both petroleum refining projects and large oil or gas processing facilities that were not executed in conjunction with a new production project. Minerals and metals projects constitute about 12% of the sample. Most of these include both a mining and a processing facility. In general, those that involve only mining and transportation of the ore to shipping are technically easier than those that also process the material. Basic chemicals, liquefied natural gas (LNG), long major pipelines, and power generation including renewables round out the set.

Locations of the projects are shown in Figure 2.2. The projects are fairly well distributed around the globe. The sample in Central

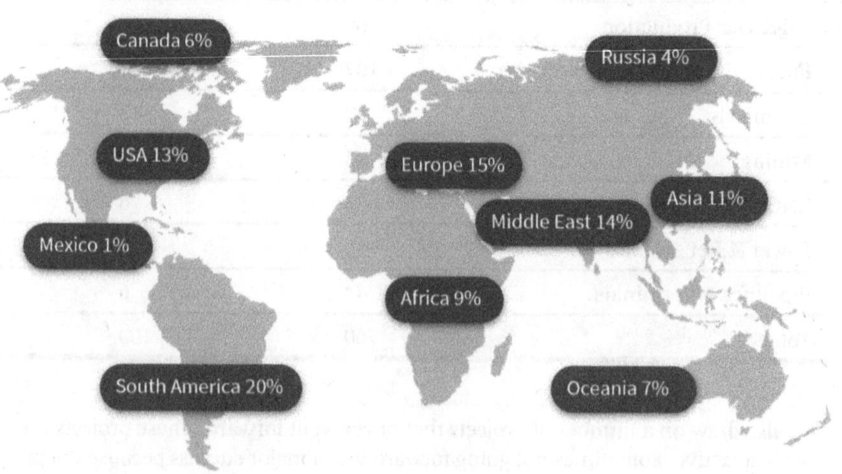

FIGURE 2.2 Global Distribution of the Project Sample

Asia (including Russia) is relatively small, but the projects themselves tend to be very large and are centered around the Caspian Sea. The U.S. projects are primarily oil and gas developments in the Gulf of Mexico and Alaska. We have a very good sample of South American projects drawn both from a number of national companies and the private sector. All of the industrial sectors are represented in the South American sample.

The only area that could be described as seriously underrepresented is China. Although there are a good many Chinese projects in the data set, almost all are joint ventures with Western companies rather than Chinese firms acting alone. The sample of projects in Africa includes oil and gas developments from both North and West Africa, and predominantly minerals projects from the southern area. Similarly, the Australian/Papua New Guinea sample is mostly a split between minerals and petroleum development with just a few chemicals projects.

The projects range in size from just over $1 billion to almost $70 billion, measured in 2023 U.S. dollars. The average project cost about $4.9 billion and took 49 months to execute, which is measured as the period from full-funds authorization to mechanical completion of all facilities required to make product. The average cycle time, measured as the start of scope development through startup, averaged 77 months and took over 10 years in a number of cases. In the case of petroleum production projects, the first phase of drilling may not have been complete when we stop the clock on the project.

Company Representation

The 114 companies represented in the database are a good cross-section of the process industries. The sample is described in Table 2.2. The oil, chemicals, and minerals industries are very well represented with both national and international oil companies in the mix.

Sixteen companies were represented by more than 10 projects. Not surprisingly, the companies in the best represented groups include almost all of the leading companies in their particular sectors. Not shown are a number of single-project joint venture companies. Perhaps quite surprising to some, company size is not a good predictor of success and failure of projects. Large and powerful companies fail at

TABLE 2.2 Industrial Sector Representation

Industrial Sector Category	Number of Companies Represented
Integrated International Oil Companies	10
National Oil Companies	14
Non-integrated Petroleum Producers	22
Petroleum Refiners	14
Chemical Companies	19
Mining, Minerals, and Metals	20
Power & Renewables Companies	12
Pipeline Companies	3

least as often as smaller firms. Of course, that may reflect the fact that a failed megaproject can be the end of a smaller firm, while it merely wounds the largest companies.

Use of New Technology

Our most general scale describing the degree of technological innovation embodied in a project is shown in Figure 2.3.[4] Over half of the projects in our sample employed technology that had been used before in similar applications, which we dub "off the shelf." To describe technology as "off the shelf" does not imply that the project was in any sense a clone of another. Only a handful of projects were approaching clones. And being off the shelf does not imply that the technology is simple. Many of the standard technology projects employed the technology at a scale that had never been attempted before. However, using technology with a track record of successful application does remove one source of risk and challenge for the project teams.

Another 12% of our projects used standard technology but in a mix that was novel, that is, the integration or mix of technologies was new

[4]Testing for whether the greater use of technology in megaprojects is statistically significant, we find $Pr.|X^2| < .0001$.

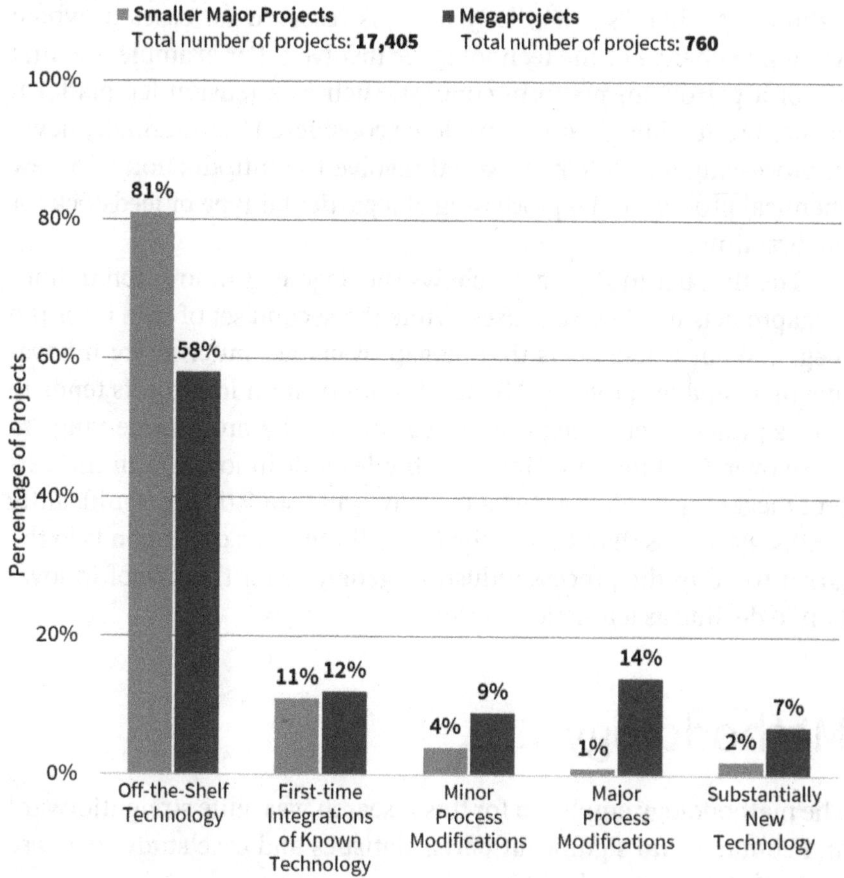

FIGURE 2.3 Technological Innovation Embodied in a Project

in commercial use, but not the individual steps. These new integrations increase the engineering challenge associated with the projects and add appreciable risk, especially when practices are not strong.

The remaining 30% of the projects introduced at least some element of technology that had never been applied before. We call an innovation minor if it affects only a single step in a process and the step is not core to the functionality of the technology. Minor modifications are genuine improvements, but with relatively little risk attached because they are isolatable.

The projects in the last two categories took on substantial new technology risk. Major process modifications involve a change to the core technology while "substantially new" is reserved for cases in which wholesale change of the technology is involved. For example, the first use of a petroleum platform concept, such as a tension leg platform or spar production platform, would be considered "substantially new." In processing technology, it would involve the introduction of a new chemical process or the processing of a particular type of feedstock for the first time.

The first bar in Figure 2.3 shows the degree of innovation in non-megaprojects in IPA's databases, while the second set of bars is for the megas. What it tells us is that megaprojects are much more innovative than smaller projects. The level of innovation in projects tends to rise as projects get larger, even if we confine the project size range to those over $500 million. However, the level of innovation in the current megaprojects data set is noticeably—and statistically significantly ($Pr.|t|<.04$)—less than that in the first edition. This corresponds to the larger trend in the process industries generally for the rate of innovation to decline as a function of time.

Methodology

The methodology employed for this research was quite straightforward and contains two significant parts: statistics and case study root case analysis. I discuss each in turn.

The Conceptual Model and the Role of Statistical Analysis

In this book, I will lay out a conceptual model (*theory* is too grandiose a word) of how and why megaprojects succeed or fail. In presenting the model, I support the argument with empirical analysis of a set of industrial projects. Although only industrial projects are used in the analysis, I see no reason that the results are not fully generalizable to all megaprojects regardless of type or purpose.

I hope that the pragmatic reader looking for applicable lessons will not be disappointed. There are a good many lessons to be learned.

I would also encourage that pragmatic reader not to dismiss the importance of the conceptual model. All imputations of causality flow from the conceptual model, not from the data and not from statistics. If the conceptual model is flawed, the implied causality is, at a minimum, partially incorrect and possibly wholly so.

The conceptual framework that we employ to understand the high rates of failure is critically important because that framework will tell us what to change in future projects to secure better results. The framework developed in this book can be summarized as follows:

> *The development of a megaproject is a complex process that folds together the assembling of the Basic Data, the Shaping process that aligns the stakeholders through the allocation of value, and the Project Development process that progressively defines and refines the project scope and execution planning. Because it is a complex process with lots of unknowns and fallible people doing the work, there are lots of opportunities for things to go wrong. Complexity creates fragility. However, things do not go wrong inevitably; owners actually have a great deal of control over the outcomes if they know how to develop and exercise that control. That control is called project governance.*

The reader will see this conceptual framework develop and take shape over the course of the book. This is not the only conceptual framework by which we might seek to understand megaproject outcomes. But for a number of reasons, I believe this framework is the best currently available:

- It accords with available systematic empirical observation.
- It explains both successes and failures with equal authority.
- It fits with known and established patterns in smaller, less complex projects while accommodating the additional requirements that megaprojects often bring.
- It satisfies the requirements of Occam's razor.[5]

[5]Also known as the Law of Parsimony, Occam's razor states that the simplest explanation that fits the data is to be preferred.

Competing frameworks—plural because more than one has been offered—come from Professor Bent Flyvbjerg and associates at the Oxford Business School.[6] I will use the term *Oxford School* to delineate this group of scholars. In its first formulation, the Oxford School's explanation of megaproject failure can be summarized thusly:

> *The primary cause of megaprojects producing disappointing outcomes—cost overruns and schedule slips—can be understood as a result of "strategic misrepresentation" by project sponsors. Sponsors, who are very desirous of securing funding and other support for their venture, use the uncertainty inherent in projects to understate the cost and schedule, while perhaps exaggerating the benefits to make the project go. By the time reality sets in during execution, it is too late to recoup the situation and cancel the project.*

For public infrastructure projects, in particular, this conceptual approach has some appeal. I have little doubt that sponsors—both private and public sector—sometimes downplay risk while pitching their projects; it would be foolish to believe otherwise. But a number of objections can be made against this theoretical approach. The most obvious is that it fails to explain success. Over a third of the projects in our database are brilliant successes. Are we to believe that simply reflects the percentage of honest sponsors? Second, the framework assumes that there is a conspiracy of silence among the many people involved in the project in the preparation phases. Although conspiracy theories are very much in vogue in politics these days, conspiracies involving large numbers of people remain far-fetched among serious people.

A more appealing formulation of this approach incorporates the notion of the "optimism bias" in human decision-making. The optimism bias, of course, is Daniel Kahneman and Amos Tversky's[7] brilliant reinvention of the ancient Latin phrase *fere libenter homines id quod*

---

[6]Bent Flyvbjerg, Nils Bruzelius, and Werner Rothengatter, *Megaprojects and Risk: An Anatomy of Ambition*, Cambridge University Press, 2003.

[7]D. Kahneman and A. Tversky, "Prospect Theory: An Analysis of Decisions under Risk," *Econometrica*, *47*, 1979a: 313–327.

volunt credunt.[8] Humans tend to screen out and underappreciate negative information and overweight positive information. The result is that decisions are biased in a way that does not accurately reflect available information. For example, if an estimator says to the business sponsor, "This project could double in cost," the sponsor will tend internally to hear the "could," which is to say also could not, more than the "double."

The conceptual framework for megaprojects offered in this book in no way disputes the reality of people sometimes lying (*strategic misrepresentation* sounds so much better) nor the reality of the optimism bias. (The optimism bias may even be necessary to getting any of these difficult ventures off the ground.) But strategic misrepresentation and the optimism bias can only cause failure—cost overruns and schedule slip—when the sponsoring organization lacks an effective governance process. That deficiency is the norm in many government organizations, which are the sponsors of much of the Oxford School data.[9] Governance is much less often absent in industrial organizations because a complete lack of capital project governance will ultimately cause an industrial firm to disappear.

A deeper problem with the Oxford School's approach to understanding megaprojects is that its notion of what constitutes success and failure is far too narrow. The school focuses almost completely on the *predictability* of cost and schedule. Predictability of cost and schedule are indeed important, but they are probably less important than (1) whether the eventual asset produces the stream of benefits promised, (2) whether those benefits were provided at a reasonable cost, and (3) whether the time taken could have been materially shorter.

If cost and schedule predictability were the key problems with megaprojects, inflating the cost estimates and plumping up the schedules would fix the problem. In keeping with its focus on predictability, the Oxford School suggest that "Reference Class Forecasting" will fix

[8]"Generally, people gladly believe what they wish to," attributed to Julius Caesar in *The Gallic Wars, Book 3.*

[9]The horrid track record of nuclear power projects in much of the Western world can be understood as a combination of the problems presented in this book, plus the compounding problem of rate-based utilities lacking an incentive to economize on capital, which is known in economics as the "Averch-Johnson Effect." Lacking an incentive to economize on capital, many utilities also lack competent capital project organizations to develop and execute projects, which compounds the problems.

the problem.[10] As discussed in Chapter 4, some of our projects actually took the fat estimate route to "success." They inflated their cost estimates by about 50%, underran those estimates by an average of 6% and would be defined by the Oxford School as successful megaprojects. But they overspent what was needed to execute the scope by over 40% and destroyed huge amounts of shareholder wealth in the process. To describe such projects as successful defies common sense.

Leaving those projects aside, which only constitute about 10% of our sample, we do not really have a significant estimating problem for industrial megaprojects by the time the projects reached authorization. The projects that overran spent too much during execution because they contained fundamental flaws in some aspect(s) of the front-end work—Basic Data, Shaping, or front-end loading. If the Oxford School's interpretation of megaprojects were correct, we would routinely see smoothly executed megaprojects with large overruns. Instead, what we actually see are overrunning projects that are a shambles in execution. We see this same phenomenon across all types of megaprojects. When infrastructure projects overrun, the execution of those projects were routinely plagued by problems that should have been addressed in the front-end. Misrepresentation and optimistic estimates should not have such effects.

Underestimation of project costs early in their development is a universal problem and affects projects of all sizes and types. The primary cause of such bias (in the mathematical sense of the word) is that estimators find it difficult to estimate what is not yet seen. As discussed in Chapter 10, scope is cost and cost is scope. Until FEL-2 is complete, the scope is not complete and arriving at centered estimates is a challenge. That is why effective governance processes focus heavily on the decision gate at the end of scope development; estimates and schedules made prior to that point are notoriously inaccurate and tend to be biased low and short because the cost of that which is unseen is zero and takes no time to complete.

It is in this context that reference class forecasting—conceptual stage benchmarking—is potentially enormously helpful. If the right benchmarking observations are available and correctly identified,

[10]We, at IPA, know "reference class forecasting" by the rather more mundane label of "conceptual stage benchmarking."

which requires skill as well as data, early estimates based on incomplete scope can often be substantially debiased. But the core problem is neither misrepresentation nor optimism, but incomplete scope. The incomplete scope makes room for liars and optimists to do their worst. The business sponsors that we see pushing industrial megaprojects are just as optimistic as the politician or public official pushing a marvelous new rail line or superhighway project. And they are probably not more or less honest as well. However, their optimism and misrepresentation are checked by a project work process and the governance process that accompanies it.[11]

Misplaced causation in the Oxford School's conceptual model has consequences. Those who see the primary problem with megaprojects as an issue of underestimation caused by misrepresentation or the optimism bias will never address the core problems: inadequate project Shaping, errors or late arrival of Basic Data, and deficiencies in the sponsors' front-end preparation of the projects. These are the true causes of failure in execution. In Chapter 4, I describe some of the actual mechanisms by which these failures play out.

IPA has been exploring what makes projects succeed and fail for almost 40 years. That research provides the conceptual framework from which we proceed to establish and test hypotheses about the relationships between project characteristics and project development practices on the one hand and project outcomes on the other. The overall purpose of the effort is to provide our customers with the basis for using statistical process control as the primary method with which to manage their capital project systems. Almost from the beginning of our research,[12] we have explored the relationships between project size and complexity, and project outcomes, noting that outcomes tend to deteriorate as a function of size and complexity.

[11]Although I would describe successful megaproject directors as an optimistic lot in general, it is very unusual in my experience to have them misrepresent their project to management. The reason is not, I believe, that they are more honest than business folks. The reason is that they are much more likely to be held accountable for any such misrepresentations later. The accountability systems for business sponsors, however, tend to be much weaker.

[12]See Edward Merrow, Kenneth Phillips, and Christopher Myers, *Understanding Cost Growth and Production Shortfalls in Pioneer Process Plants*, Santa Monica, CA: The Rand Corporation, 1981; Merrow, et al., op cit., 1988.

The conceptual understanding as it exists at any point in time guides our statistical analyses. Most of our "Aha!" moments come not from statistics, but from seeing something occur in an individual project, recognizing a pattern with other projects, and only then checking our supposed insight with the data. If the data support the pattern, we pursue it further. If not, we move on. Humans are evolved to look for patterns and humans often see patterns where none actually exist. Statistics are quite useful to debunk patterns that we thought we saw but are not really there.[13]

The testing of hypotheses is one key role for statistics. The other is building statistical models that enable us to compare project outcomes in a meaningful way. If one seeks a reasonably high degree of precision, comparing projects is actually quite difficult. No two projects are exactly the same, and across any large database of projects, the projects will usually be very different along a number of dimensions that are important to project results. Statistical models facilitate valid comparisons, even for quite disparate projects. Using statistical controls, we can control for key characteristics such as size, technical complexity, the degree of technological innovation, process type, and so forth while comparing cost, schedule, operability, or even construction safety. Statistics enable us to "hold constant" inherent project characteristics while exploring the effects of practices, including both business and project management practices, on project results.

A variety of statistical techniques have been used to test and demonstrate that various relationships are not likely to have been generated randomly. We use ordinary least-squares regression, *t*-tests, and logit and probit regression when binary dependent variables are involved, and Pearson product-moment correlation and the Pearson chi-square for testing differences in tabulation tables.

Table 2.3 shows how the various test results will be noted in the text and footnotes as we proceed. We show the results of the statistical test that supports a statement and indicate the type of test performed. For example, "Pr>|t|<.001" means that the probability of generating the result randomly with repeated tries is less than 1 in 1,000 based

[13]Ironically, when misused inductively, statistics can become part of the problem of seeing patterns that are not really there. This is the problem of spurious correlation and misplaced causation.

TABLE 2.3 Test Results Noted in Text and Footnotes

Technique	Test Statistic	Notation
OLS or *t*-test	*t*-ratios/*t*-test	Pr>|t|<.0XX
Logit or probit regression	z-ratio	Pr>|z|<.0XX
Pearson correlation	R	Pr>|r|<.0XX
Tabulation	Chi-square (X^2)	Pr>|X|<.0XX
Regression	R^2	Denotes portion of variance explained by model

on a *t*-test or coefficient *t*-ratio from a regression. This enables the methodologically sophisticated reader to judge the basis on which the conclusion is reached. Fortunately, in most cases common sense works as well as the statistics. Following standard procedure, we only call results statistically significant when the probability (using a two-tailed test except where noted) is less than or equal to .05.[14]

Root Cause Understanding from Cases

The typical megaproject in our database has thousands of variables that have been coded from our completed interview protocols and supporting project documents. These supporting documents often include the "lessons-learned" developed by the project team. The strengths and weaknesses of those lessons learned will be discussed in later chapters.

The preceding information is augmented and fleshed out by case study write-ups by our analysts for every project collected, large or small. For megaprojects, the case studies are quite extensive and focus on what happened and why. These case study notes are based on in-depth and wide-ranging discussions with members of the project teams and the business leadership of the projects. Much to our continual surprise and delight, project directors and managers

[14]In many cases, the argument for using a one-tailed test would be persuasive. Most of the hypotheses being tested have very strong priors. However, we almost always elect to use a two-tailed test anyway.

are overwhelmingly forthcoming and forthright about their completed projects. Without their cooperation, this book could not have been written.

Some Methodological Notes

Escalation Adjustments

Unlike many project researchers, IPA measures capital cost and cost growth in costs in constant currency terms. If the effects of inflation on costs are not removed, it is impossible to really understand project results. When it comes to measuring cost and cost growth, most project researchers fail to follow basic sound practice.

A simple example will clarify how important this is. Let's say a natural gas processing facility is estimated and authorized on January 1, 2004, for exactly $1 billion dollars. Included in the cost is $50 million for inflation. The project is completed on schedule on January 1, 2008, for a cost of $1.4 billion—a massive 40% overrun of the costs, right? Well, yes and no. In the period between 2004 and the beginning of 2008 the costs of the items going into a gas plant increased by 52% on average around the world. The cost of the equipment, the pipe, the engineering, and in most places, the craft labor increased quite rapidly during this period. Was the estimator's inclusion of "only" $50 million for inflation the problem? Yes, but the $50 million was entirely reasonable; for the 15 years prior to 2004, project inflation had only been averaging 1% or 2% a year. When measured correctly, the project actually came in just about where it should have. On the other hand, if the product being sold from this gas plant has not escalated along with the cost of the plant, the sponsor is going to earn a significantly lower return than expected. From a methodological viewpoint, the problem of reporting our gas plant as having suffered a 40% overrun is clear: there is absolutely nothing that the project team could have done differently to prevent an overrun. In the same vein, there is no reason to think that those making the decision to invest in the facility should have been able to anticipate the sudden change in the project's marketplace. Therefore, if we are trying to explore the relationships between investment decisions and project practices and outcomes, failing to correct for escalation will leave us forever bewildered. It is very unfortunate that too many researchers studying capital projects do, in fact, fail to do so.

In addition to adjusting cost for the effects of inflation (usually called *escalation* in the project business) we also adjust for the effects of location when we are measuring cost-effectiveness. For example, building a plant in China is generally cheaper than building the equivalent plant in the United States or Europe. Not only is craft labor less expensive, almost all items that are purchasable in China will be less expensive than in the United States or Europe. Specialized equipment that must be imported is not subject to extraordinary taxes in China and so can be purchased on the open world market. Only the costs of any expatriates sent by a foreign sponsor will add to costs in China relative to most other parts of the world. Therefore, in order to make "apples to apples" comparisons of cost, we adjust the various input costs up or down depending on the location in which they must be purchased. We are careful not to overadjust as well. If a project chooses to purchase items locally that can be purchased for less on the world open market, that added cost is not adjusted unless the local purchases are formally mandated.

Finally, we correct for changes in foreign exchange relationships as they apparently change the cost of a project. Almost all megaprojects buy things from all over the world. When the final estimate before authorization is prepared, a set of assumptions must be made about the value of the different currencies in which things will be purchased. Unexpected changes in foreign exchange can make a project substantially more or less expensive unless the currencies are hedged, which is an uncommon practice.[15] Like escalation, however, currency fluctuations are notoriously difficult to predict. If they were easy to predict, they would always be hedged or hedging would never be necessary.

[15]The sponsors could also seek to "fix" the currencies by passing all foreign exchange risks to the vendors and contractors. As we will discuss later, however, this approach is highly problematic. Many industrial owners with worldwide sales decline to hedge the project currencies, arguing that their sales footprint mitigates the risks anyway.

Sample Bias

Is our sample of 760 industrial megaprojects really representative of all industrial megaprojects executed over the past 25 years? That question is important in some contexts and less important in others. If we are discussing what all recent industrial megaprojects look like, then the question is very important and the answer, alas, is no. We are not particularly concerned about any potential effects of the mix of industrial sectors represented for a very simple reason: the industrial sector in and of itself appears to have little if any effect on how the projects turn out. Differences between sectors can be accounted for by differences in practices. However, we have a couple of reasons to suspect that our sample of megaprojects is, on the whole, *better* in terms of outcomes and management than industrial megaprojects as a whole.

First, companies that subject themselves to systematic benchmarking are generally more capable project companies than those that do not. We can infer this in many ways. For example, we know that the companies that benchmark their projects with IPA suffer about one-tenth of the number of construction accidents as the overall construction industry norms. We know that companies first starting benchmarking have project outcomes that are significantly poorer than those that have benchmarked for more than a few years.

Second, we know that even the companies with which we have worked for many years will sometimes find excuses not to close out a project with particularly horrid outcomes. The excuses range from the specious "That project really isn't representative!" to the lame "We fired all the people on the team so there is no one to talk to." And, of course, our favorite: "We can't provide the data because the project is in litigation." Conversely, we are aware of no megaprojects whose final data were withheld from us because the projects went embarrassingly well!

The fact that we have a known "positive" bias in the data should make the outcomes presented in the next chapter all the more sobering because, even with the assistance of the bias, we are not doing very well.

CHAPTER 3

Project Outcomes and Trends

In the world of normal-sized projects, how well they turn out distributes in the usual way: there is a big group of mediocre projects in the middle, a smaller group of good projects, and a slightly larger group of poor projects. When we, at IPA, first started examining very large projects as a separate group, we almost immediately noticed an odd phenomenon. The projects seem to fall naturally into exceptionally good projects and exceptionally poor projects with only a very few in the middle where the bulk of smaller projects would be found. For this reason we separate our megaprojects into two groups: successes and failures.

To separate the wheat from the chaff, we use the five dimensions of project effectiveness shown in Table 3.1 along with the thresholds shown to establish what would constitute failure.

If a project fared more poorly than our threshold on any one of these five, we classified the project as a failure. However, very few projects failed on only one dimension. If they did fail on only one, it was overwhelmingly likely that it was the most economically important criterion: production versus plan.[1]

[1]Peter W.G. Morris and G.H. Hough (1987) defined *success* and *failure* along three dimensions: "functionality," which is only partly captured by my measure of production versus plan; "project management," which they define as delivery on cost, schedule, and technical specification; and contractors' commercial performance. I consider their final criterion irrelevant. I believe that my criteria for success and those of Morris and Hough would come to the same conclusion in most cases. Their project set included some very difficult to deal with projects such as the *Concorde* supersonic transport, which I consider a prestige or monument project rather than a commercial venture.

TABLE 3.1 Five Dimensions of Project Effectiveness

Type of Outcome	Threshold for Failure
Cost Overruns[2]	>25%
Cost Competitiveness[3]	>25%
Slip in Execution Schedules[4]	>25%
Schedule Competitiveness[5]	>50%
Production versus Plan	Significantly poor production first two Years

If a project does not experience one of the serious problems listed in Table 3.1, we call it a success. By *success*, we mean that the project basically performed as promised at authorization or better. It was built close to budget, close to on-time, it was reasonably competitive on cost and schedule, and it made on-specification product as intended.

Success, then, is defined as a lack of failure. While this may seem rather unsatisfying, it works for these projects because very few were merely mediocre; overwhelmingly, the successes are outstanding projects in every respect. The very small mediocre group could easily have been great projects: they were planned and executed well. However, they set conservative targets and then executed on lump-sum contracts that locked themselves into mediocre results. Most of these projects were sponsored by government-owned companies in regions where failure to be predictable is heavily penalized.

We were sometimes missing one or two of the measures on any particular project. For example, a few projects do not yet have enough operational history to judge whether they have failed or succeeded in that dimension. Some of the projects are so peculiar in scope that we

[2]Cost overruns are measured as the ratio of the actual final costs of the project to the estimate made at the full-funds authorization (sanction) measured in escalation-adjusted terms.

[3]Cost competitiveness measures how much the project spent (in constant dollars adjusted to a common location) relative to other projects with similar scopes.

[4]Execution schedule is measured from the start of production (sometimes called detailed) engineering until mechanical completion of facilities. *Slip* is defined as the actual schedule divided by the schedule forecast at full-funds authorization.

[5]Schedule competitiveness is the length of the execution relative to similar projects.

could not measure cost competitiveness. Whenever we are missing a measure, we assume the project succeeded on that measure. What this means is that a few more projects will end up in the failure category when the final data become available.

Cost

The thresholds for success and failure are less arbitrary than their round numbers would suggest. If you overrun a project by more than 25% in real terms, the project manager and project team will likely be considered a failure (and may well receive a career-limiting flogging).

It is also true that the original business director of the project will probably not suffer adverse consequences of that overrun. It is very likely they will have moved on to another, usually higher, position and any connection with the project will have been forgotten. The tendency in most companies to move business directors rather quickly (three years is a long stay) fosters a lack of business accountability for project results. This is especially true for megaprojects because their gestation and execution periods are so long. The probability of a turnover in the business sponsor position jumps markedly as projects overrun their sanctioned budgets by more than 10%.

A 25%-overrun substantially damages the economics of many megaprojects.[6] If you overspend in competitive terms by 25% or more, the business is spending itself into oblivion. As we look back over the past 35 years at IPA companies that have disappeared, all but one of them grossly overspent for their capital assets.[7] (The exception was a large oil company that could never seem to find any oil.)

---

[6]This anticipates an issue that we will take up in the next chapter: the relative importance of cost versus schedule for the typical large project.

[7]Too many senior business decision-makers in commodity industrial sectors fail to realize the disastrous effects of overspending on projects. When a company overspends on its capital projects relative to the competition, even by a relatively small amount, it is systematically disadvantaging itself. The effects show up when a serious downturn hits its industry. In commodity businesses, cycles are a fact of life. Part of the reason for business indifference to capital effectiveness is that the effects are insidious and long-term rather than dramatic and immediate. Some, I fear, understand the effects but simply do not care—because the effects are long-term and their personal horizons are not.

One of the ironies of large projects around the world is that most of them are executed on fixed price (lump-sum) contracts. And yet many of those "fixed price" contracts end up anything but fixed.[8] The reason that lump-sum contracts offer only the weakest insurance against cost overruns is changes made after agreement on the contract is reached. It doesn't make much difference where the change comes from; if there is substantial change, the cost of the project will go up. Sometimes, we can point to new technology as the source of change, but that just begs the question of why the technology was not ready when the project was sanctioned. And many large overruns, some up to 350%, are in projects with entirely standard technology. Sometimes the source of change is lack of sponsor familiarity with the region, although again, we will have to ask why. Some of the large overrun projects were caught up in a downward labor productivity spiral. I will discuss how and why these collapses of progress in the field occur in Chapter 14.

Schedule

The execution schedule is the forecast of the time that will be required from full-funds authorization until the project is ready to start up. If the schedule was developed properly, the time requirement is intimately linked to the scope, and therefore, the cost of the project. If you slip your schedule by 25%, you are usually a year late, which is very damaging to the economic value of the project. Being late in execution is associated with stretching out the period in which you are heavily invested in the project (most of the money is already spent) with no revenue stream to show for it. We set the threshold on being slow higher (50%) because if you *plan* to be slow, the economic damage is less because the spending is back-end loaded and you tend not to plan to be slow in the construction portion of the project. However, there are limits to that strategy and we set them at 50% over industry average time.

Large schedule slips are a little less common than large overruns, and some of the projects with large cost overruns had only modest schedule slip. The underlying reason that schedule performance looks

[8] I will discuss the merits and demerits of lump-sum contracting in Chapter 13.

somewhat better than cost is also one of the core pathologies of very large projects: they are frequently highly schedule-driven from the earliest point right through to startup. Because we end the execution time when the facility is in principle ready to operate, we are not capturing with this measure whether the project operated successfully. Executing a project rapidly that also operates is much more compelling than merely executing a project rapidly. Startup and operability are captured separately.

Some very extended construction schedules had their proximate cause in engineering. As mentioned in the last chapter, industrial megaprojects are very engineering-intensive. For a typical project, 25% of total cost will go to engineering and project management services. A good many of the projects with severe slips and cost growth in construction suffered from late and/or shoddy engineering. Late and poor-quality engineering make the construction in the field or fabrication in the yard much less efficient. Late engineering and poor-quality engineering tend to happen together; as engineering gets late, it gets progressively rushed and quality control is bypassed to get engineering to the constructors. When engineering slows to mobilize early in the project, it drives late and out-of-order equipment and engineered bulk materials, such as pipe spools. Construction/fabrication then waits until the right materials arrive. Engineering problems were common in the failed projects, but they were usually proximate causes, not root causes of failure.

Some of the large schedule slips occurred when the projects got crosswise with the host government. One of the time-honored ways politicians have of intervening in large projects is to withdraw a permit on a technicality. For example, the Russian government withdrew the construction permit for the Sakhalin-2 project when it was deep into construction, knowing that the project was very vulnerable economically at that point because the investment is large and irreversible—you can't get your money back!

A few of the large slips in schedule occurred when the sponsors acknowledged that the project was going so poorly that it needed to be slowed down while errors were corrected. That is a very painful, difficult, and courageous decision to make, which is why it is made so rarely. Ironically, two of the successful projects were rescued by running into government trouble. Both projects were about to be authorized, but were nowhere near ready for execution; their failure was ordained when government delays in approvals held them up for 18 months in one case and 2 years in another. They used the time to get ready for execution. Both project directors said they could never have otherwise succeeded. Their good fortune was to encounter the government problem early rather than in mid-execution.

Production

Finally, production versus plan is the most economically leveraging outcome. When we assessed operability, we did not penalize a project if there was insufficient demand. (One could justifiably argue that is the worst outcome of all. I built a great project that nobody wanted! Lack of demand, however, is not something on which project management per se can have much effect.) We classified a project as a failure in this dimension only if it was experiencing severe production problems that continued well into the second year after startup. We did not set an absolute production threshold because the importance of poor operability is different for different projects. For example, for an oil production project, production of 70% of plan is not terrible—the industry's average is just over 80% of plan.[9] By contrast, 70% of plan for LNG is abysmal. LNG is very capital-intensive, which exacerbates the effects of poor operability. LNG is almost always forward-sold, and if you cannot produce the LNG, you have to go into the merchant market and buy it from competitors to fulfill your contractual commitments. The result is that you hemorrhage money. The actual production of the projects that failed in this dimension averaged a miserable 34% of plan in the second six months after startup.

Even worse, however, when a project suffers significant production shortfalls, a great deal of money is spent trying to rectify the problems. Although we lack the systematic data we would like, my guesstimate, based on limited data, is that 25% to 50% added cost over the initial capital is common. Most of this is not actually capitalized, and in many

[9]Yes, that does raise the question about why the industry, as a whole, is so optimistic, but that is not an issue for us here.

cases, there are no reliable records of the amount spent at all—because nobody actually wants to know.

Production shortfalls in petroleum production megaprojects were common among megaprojects early in this century at over 40% of projects with significant operability problems. A few were caused by facilities that did not operate properly or facilities that were incorrectly matched to the characteristics of the oil and gas being produced. The most common problems were associated with reservoir surprises that limited the production from the intended wells.[10] This almost always resulted in additional wells that were often more complex than the original wells planned. We almost never were able to capture the cost of these additional wells. So once again, we are perforce underestimating the true economic costs of production shortfalls.

The effects of production problems can be debilitating for a business. One global chemical company client had a $9 billion-per-year business earning 22% return on capital employed (ROCE)—a very nice commodity business. A single megaproject that failed to produce as planned reduced the ROCE from 22% to 16% for the five years after the project was supposed to have started up. They ended up divesting the business. Another example is a metals project that was to debottleneck and expand a major processing complex by 90%. After a 39%-overrun (76% nominal) and an 85% schedule slip, the complex actually produces 10% *less* than before the project. This project managed to achieve the unachievable: negative production!

When megaprojects fail, the results are rarely publicized unless the failure is spectacular. When the failures do make the press, they are damaging to a company's reputation. Large overruns and delays in cash flow due to schedule slippage or production shortfalls jeopardize the sponsor's ability to fund other projects in its portfolio. Megaprojects are by nature lumpy investments. Only a handful of companies in the world are large enough to be able to support a genuine portfolio of these projects to spread the risk internally, which is why most industrial megaprojects are joint ventures.

[10]As we will discuss in Chapter 9, the reservoir problems could often have been anticipated and addressed prior to the start of the project if the basic technical data development had been better.

Trading Outcomes

Making trade-offs among cost, schedule, and quality (measured by operational performance in our case) is as old as projects and a feature of everyday life. How trade-offs are made tells us a lot about how decisions around major projects are made. I find the patterns in megaprojects interesting. Figure 3.1 summarizes the trade-off picture for our megaprojects. The figure reports only cost and schedule competitiveness rather than cost or schedule predictability. We create the quadrants not by success or failure, but simply by greater than or less than/equal to industry median values for the indices. Also provided is the percentage of production failures in each quadrant, which is a measure of quality.

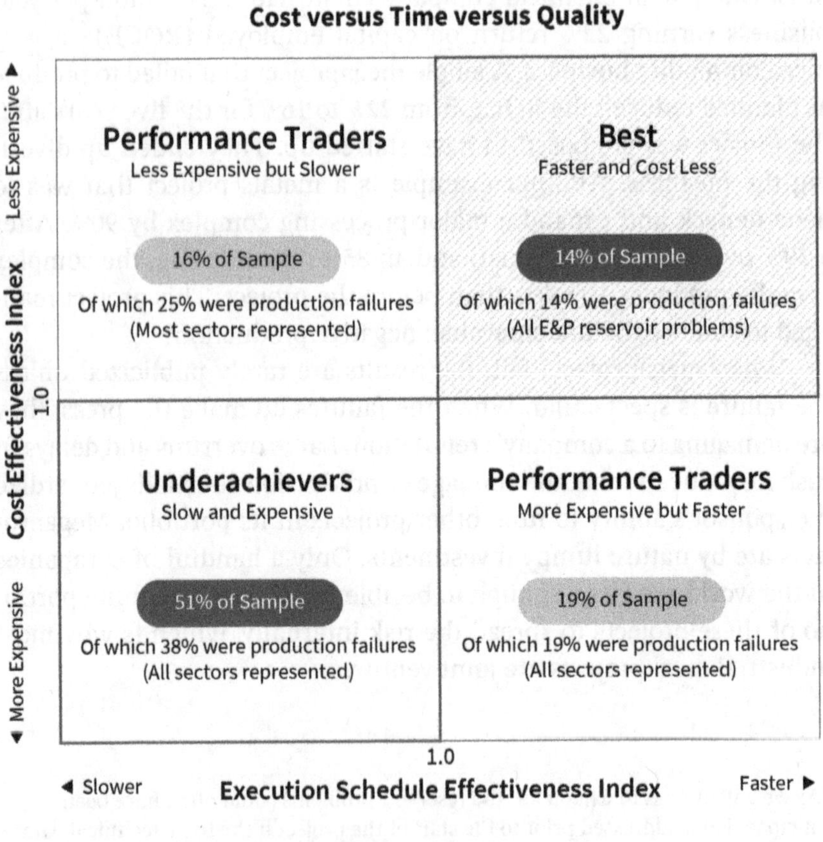

FIGURE 3.1 The Trade-Off Picture for Megaprojects

The northeast quadrant is the best-in-class projects. They achieved fast schedules along with excellent cost performance. The projects are drawn from every region and a great many companies with only one company overrepresented in this group.[11] This set of projects is quite remarkable: the projects averaged 88% of industry average cost, they underran by 4% on average while achieving very fast schedules with no slip. Only 14% of projects in the northeast quadrant—the smallest of any group—suffered significant production problems in the first two years. All of those production failures were offshore petroleum production projects and all suffered unhappy reservoir surprises rather than facilities faults. In other words, all of the facilities built for the projects were fully operable, but the reservoir the project was seeking to tap was more difficult to produce than expected. Such projects are very disappointing but very difficult to avoid completely. The set of fully successful projects is of interest because it demonstrates that it is possible to generate low-cost, fast, and high-quality megaprojects.

Just over half of our megaprojects are found in the southwest quadrant: expensive and slow. Only one company is significantly overrepresented in this group of failed projects, a large international oil company. That company is also without any representation in the northeast quadrant. To provide some context, collectively, the projects in the southwest quadrant overspent relative to their "should" cost by nearly $600 billion. The slow and expensive quadrant also has a higher percentage of production failures than any other group—38%. Taken together, the northeast (best) and the southwest (worst) represent 65% of our total sample. These projects suggest that good things stick together and bad things stick together. Now let's explore the other 35%.

Of all the projects, 19% traded cost for speed (the southeast quadrant). Most of these projects were explicitly schedule-driven, that is, the teams were directed to spend more money to achieve better schedules if needs be. These projects, on average, saved about four months relative to industry average for a cost of 29% above industry average. They set very fast schedules—less than 85% of industry average—and generous (+24%) Final Investment Decision (FID) cost estimates, which

[11]That company is a national petroleum company and not an international major company as might be supposed.

were nonetheless overrun. These projects deliberately spent a lot of money to get a little speed. Of course, the project teams hoped to get more speed than they actually achieved; the projects slipped their FID schedules by 9%. About one project in five in this southeast quadrant was also a production failure. Unlike projects in the northeast quad, most of these production failures were caused by poor facilities quality, not by Basic Data problems. These rather disappointing results are to be expected. Megaprojects are by their nature very hard to accelerate. This is not to say that megaprojects have to be slow to be successful. But when they are successful, speed is a product of how the project was put together on the front-end. When projects are designed with lean and efficient scopes, they can achieve both good cost and faster schedules. But if the objective is to go fast by spending more, it is very likely that a little speed will be achieved for a lot of money. The typical project in the southeast quadrant lost a great deal of NPV by adopting a go-fast strategy. The southeast quadrant also had the largest concentration (22%) of projects that padded the cost estimates for no purpose other than to prevent overruns. That set of projects in the southeast quad overspent industry average by 44% while underrunning their estimates by 6%. As we discuss elsewhere, this pattern has become more common in recent years.

Why were the go-fast strategies adopted? A few of the projects in the southeast quad had explicit business reasons for attempting speed, such as filling a gap in production that was recognized too late. Most, however, were told that speed was the goal without business justification for speed. This is not unusual in projects large and small.

Our final quadrants are the projects that traded speed for lower cost. This set of projects planned to be slow (+13 on planned schedule) and planned to be low cost (−5%). They actually ended up even slower (+36%) but also even lower cost (−10%). This northwest quadrant had about 25% production failures, most of which were quality related rather than Basic Data related. This group of projects made the most use of EPC-lumpsum contracting, with two-thirds on EPC-LS and lump-sum turnkey. When EPC-LS contracting is used, owner project controls, especially quality controls, are very important. When controls were strong, the speed of these projects was reasonable, but when controls were less than good, the projects were very slow—56% longer than industry average. The strategy of trading speed for lower cost is a reasonable one, in most cases, for megaprojects. All of the projects in this quadrant were producing pure commodities, that is, products that sell only based on price. Unless one has forward-sold product, which none of these projects had, speed has relatively little value, while low capital cost makes one competitive long term—provided, of course, that facility quality is good, which is again a controls issue.

What about Construction Safety?

Normally, when IPA evaluates a project, the first outcome discussed is whether the project was completed without seriously hurting anyone. We have three basic safety statistics for about 70% of the megaprojects:

- The recordable incident rate, which measures the number of injuries and work-related illnesses that require assistance beyond first-aid.
- The number of DART cases—injuries and work-related illnesses that require **D**ays **A**way from work, **R**estricted work duties, or job **T**ransfer.
- The number of fatalities.

I have elected not to incorporate the safety results in the assessment of success and failure for a very simply reason: too many of the safety numbers for megaprojects are simply not credible. Some of them are ridiculous on their face; we had one project with 36 recordable injuries in over 20 million hours . . . and every one of those recordable injuries was a fatality. We only got the fatality number because we had monitored the local press.

Injury rates in construction follow a reasonably predictable pattern: there are many more recordables than DARTS, and many more DARTS than fatalities. This is classed the "safety pyramid." For megaprojects, that relationship *appears* not to work. In particular, there are a lot of fatalities and too few recordables. This leads us to believe there is a reporting problem; fatalities are generally very hard to hide.

The third reason to doubt the data makes us sure that underreporting is going on: there is a very strong regional bias to the numbers and that regional bias is completely counterintuitive. Projects with higher skilled, more experienced, and higher productivity workforces

TABLE 3.2 Location Is Important in Reporting of Construction Safety

Incident Type	Europe and North America	Middle East, Central Asia, Asia and Africa
Recordables[12]	1.20	0.43
Dart Rate	0.50	0.12
Fatal Incident Rate	.009	.006
Projects w/ Fatalities	18%	39%
Field Hrs. per $Million	7,300	21,500

will, on average, experience fewer accidents. The higher productivity effect alone helps greatly because it reduces the number of laborers on site. Congestion is a known safety hazard. However, as one can see in Table 3.2, none of this appears to hold for megaprojects.

If we believe the numbers, which we do not, megaprojects in Europe and North America where skill levels and productivity are high are about three times more dangerous than those in areas where the average skill level is much lower. They even have more fatalities per 200,000 field hours worked, although the probability of having at least one fatality is much higher in the second group. What we also know about Europe and North America is that there are substantial penalties for underreporting injuries and that the legal systems are geared to ensuring that reporting occurs. Those safeguards are much weaker in many other areas.

There is one final clue that the safety numbers are not entirely legitimate. For North American and European projects, the DART rate is correlated with the thoroughness of the project execution planning, just as it is for projects generally. (This is a subject we take up in Chapter 10.) For projects in the regions in the second column in the table, there is no relationship whatever.

In low productivity environments, keeping track of safety and getting reporting done accurately are much more difficult. Each million

[12]The rates in the first three rows are calculated per 200,000 field hours. For readers more familiar with the per million hour formulation, multiply by 5.

dollars (2003 U.S. dollars) of investment in North America and Europe consumes about 7,300 hours in the field. In the low productivity regions, about three times as many hours are needed, and the projects in those regions are among the largest in our database. Further, the labor force is often drawn from numerous nationalities and cultures so language and custom must be overcome as well.

Nonetheless, the underreporting is systematic. The problem starts at the craft level. The workers know that when injuries are reported they will get into trouble. Sponsors try to fight against the problem (although sometimes not too much), but the problem is deeply endemic from the work face level up. The pattern of safety results from the regional difference paints a clear picture of underreporting.

It is very unfortunate that construction safety numbers in some parts of the world are underreported. Honest reporting is necessary to genuinely safe projects because it provides the incentive structure for strong safety systems to be viewed as good business. It also must be very disheartening to those project professionals who have driven genuinely safe projects in places where the numbers are suspect. Their accomplishments tend to get denigrated along with the liars and the cheats.

There are things that sponsors can do to improve safety reporting even when the governmental apparatus does not support honest reporting. The first and perhaps most important step is to discontinue all monetary incentives to contractors and subcontractors for meeting safety goals. *For projects as a whole there is absolutely no relationship whatsoever between safety-based monetary incentives paid to contractors and better safety performance.* That result is only logical: if a contractor has strong safety systems and culture, they will always carry them to the job. If they lack the systems and culture, there is no chance they can acquire them in time to be of any use on your project. Safety incentives paid to contractors encourage underreporting whenever and wherever it is feasible to do so. Safety incentives to contractors were so ubiquitous on the megaprojects in our sample that we cannot even prove our point with the data here. It is a mindless and counterproductive practice.[13]

[13]Properly structured recognition awards at the craft level can be quite effective in promoting safety. Where it is easy to hide accidents, however, even these incentives can encourage underreporting.

Having eliminated bonuses to contractors for meeting safety targets, sponsors need to recognize and reward incident reporting when incidents could have been made to disappear. Modern safety programs are all positive reinforcement centered; this is just another application of that approach. There should be no penalties and no penalties allowed by contractors to subcontractors for safety outcomes. The penalties must be centered on failure to cooperate fully with the project's safety program. In this area, as in so many others in projects, it is impossible and counterproductive to try to manage by results rather than practices.

The Jemima Principle

Most of us in the English-speaking world grew up with a nursery rhyme by Henry Wadsworth Longfellow, the first verse of which goes like this:

There was a little girl who had a pretty curl
Right in the middle of her forehead.
When she was good, she was very, very good
And when she was bad, she was horrid!

Like Longfellow's "little girl with the pretty curl," whose name was Jemima, megaprojects are rarely mediocre; they tend to be either very, very good, or they are horrid. Figure 3.2 tells the story: the 32% of the projects that succeeded were genuinely excellent projects. On average, they underran their budgets by 4% while delivering highly competitive (98% of industry average) costs. They were completed on time with schedules that were faster than industry average. None of them (by definition) could be classed as operational failures, and the average project exceeded planned production in the first two years.

By contrast, most of the failures are truly miserable projects: they averaged a 33% constant currency overrun while being very expensive in absolute terms—45% more than the industry average to produce the same product(s). Overwhelmingly, the failed projects make commodity products, just as most industrial megaprojects do. Spending 45% more capital than others to make a product means the project returns will never be competitive.

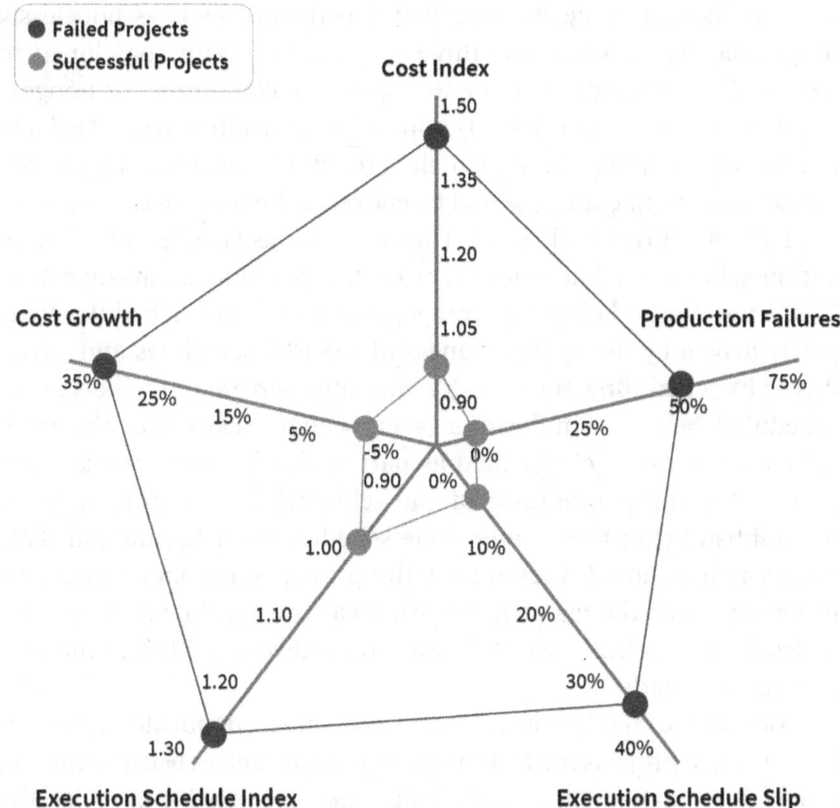

FIGURE 3.2 Failed versus Successful Projects

Half of the failed projects were operability failures. That means that they experienced severe operational problems for two years after startup. The failed projects that had good operability tended to fall into two classes: first and largest were a group of petroleum production projects in which the reservoir produced at much higher rates than expected. Second were a group of projects discussed in the next chapter as the super-padded projects—projects that stuffed so much money into the estimates that they ended up overspending by more than 25% (our threshold for failure) while *underrunning* their estimates. As mentioned earlier, those projects are becoming more common. When I exclude those two groups of projects, the median production of the failed projects as a group was 38% of plan. Fifteen percent of the operability failures had no production whatsoever in the first two years after startup! Six more projects were abandoned completely as hopelessly inoperable. There were also three projects that were abandoned in the middle of construction due to implacable community or nongovernmental organization (NGO) opposition that ultimately translated to governmental opposition, which is the death knell for any project. Those projects, of course, would be classed as Shaping disasters.

Last, we turn to schedule. The failed projects slipped their execution schedules (time from FID to completion) by an average 35%. That translates to being, on average, over a year late. Schedule slip is partly driven by the aggressiveness of the FID schedules and partly driven by scheduling practices. Twenty-four percent of projects never scheduled beyond a milestone level, which means that the critical path was never established as part of the front-end work. Even more astonishing, one-third of the schedule-driven projects failed to establish better than a milestone schedule prior to sanction. This means that although they were willing to spend money to achieve faster schedule, the teams never established what they most needed to accelerate to obtain speed because they never established the project's critical path.

Most of the failed projects were unprofitable, but not all. In particular, some bad projects made money despite themselves because market prices shot up after completion. Sometimes, the manner in which the operator was compensated by national resource holders made it possible to make money even with massive cost overruns or large shortfalls in promised production. Some of the projects with highly padded estimates were profitable, but at much lower rates of return than they should have achieved.

Success and Industrial Sector

Figure 3.3 summarizes the percent of operability failures of the five best populated sectors in our sample. LNG had more successful projects than any other sector at 48%, followed by chemicals, refining, and petroleum production in that order. Mining came in worst with a success rate of only 29%. Only LNG stands out at all and that result is statistically marginal (Pr.|X|<.07).

For readers conversant with the first edition, you will note that the overall production performance of megaprojects has improved.

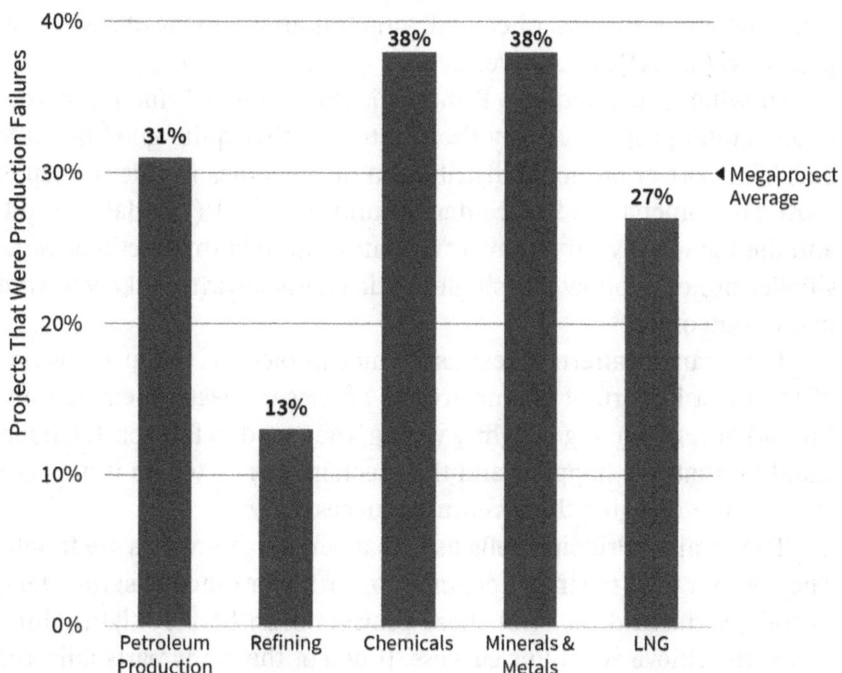

FIGURE 3.3 Operability Failures

The improvement is especially notable for petroleum refining[14] and petroleum production.[15] Chemicals and mining improved slightly, and LNG production failures actually increased—the only sector to see that result.

[14]The very good 13% production failure rate for refining should be viewed with some caution. A good many of the refining projects are excluded because they do not have adequate operating history at this time to establish success or failure in this dimension. However, refining projects experienced more cost growth and schedule slip than average, and both of those measures correlate strongly with operability problems later. Therefore, we should expect some downgrade of refining production success when all project data are available.

[15]Some (but only some) of the improvement in production performance of petroleum production projects is driven by the remarkable performance of wells in Bazil's presalt developments.

If we compare the two groups—successes and failures—shown in Figure 3.2 against a pro forma 15% real internal rate of return base, what results? The returns of the successful projects increase to almost 18%, while the returns of the average failure fall to 5%, which is significantly less than the cost of capital, which is another way of saying net present value (NPV) negative.

So what is the Jemima Principle? The Jemima Principle is that large capital projects are, by their nature, either quite good or quite bad. This sort of bi-modal distribution of outcomes is quite unusual; most phenomena tend to center around a typical ("modal") result, and then gradually vary away from that result in both directions. Most smaller projects follow this single-mode character with a skew toward poorer outcomes.[16]

The strange pattern of results for megaprojects is produced by one of the most important characteristics of megaprojects: their fragility. Instead of tending to go slightly wrong, they tend to fall apart. Understanding that this happens and the mechanisms by which it happens are keys to managing these ventures successfully.

The Jemima Principle tells us is that very large projects are fragile. They do not tend to simply degrade toward poor outcomes; they tend to collapse instead. Most of these projects must be very tightly integrated to achieve economic success. If one of the many parts fails, the whole effort fails. So we have a lot of failed megaprojects, even if many of the failures are carefully covered up.[17] As the reader will see as we move forward, this is not a necessary outcome. It can be fixed.

---

[16]The skew is to be expected: there are more ways for things to go poorly than well. Good outcomes tend to be strictly bounded, while poor outcomes (except operability, which is bounded at zero) are not.

[17]When a company has experienced a particularly poor megaproject, it is not uncommon to see a glowing article in the trade press about what a wonderful project triumph it was. Perhaps the most amusing example of this was in *Offshore Magazine* touting BP's Thunderhorse development in the Gulf of Mexico as a "Top 5 Project of the Year 2009." Thunderhorse was supposed to be operational in 2005 and was about four years late and far over budget after suffering a series of well-publicized major technical problems, including nearly sinking to the bottom of the ocean—none of which were mentioned in the article (*Offshore Magazine*, Volume 69, Issue 12, December 1, 2009). The point is an old one: be careful about what you believe.

Trends: What Has Changed Since the First Edition?

One of the important questions that I hoped to address with this second edition of *Industrial Megaprojects* is whether we have improved on the rather disappointing outcomes that we documented in 2011. Are we, in fact, learning anything from the losses suffered in the first decade of this century?

The short answer is that megaproject performance has improved markedly from a very rocky start at the beginning of this century as shown in Figure 3.4. We measure the timing of projects by their date of full-funds authorization, also called FID. Before going into the

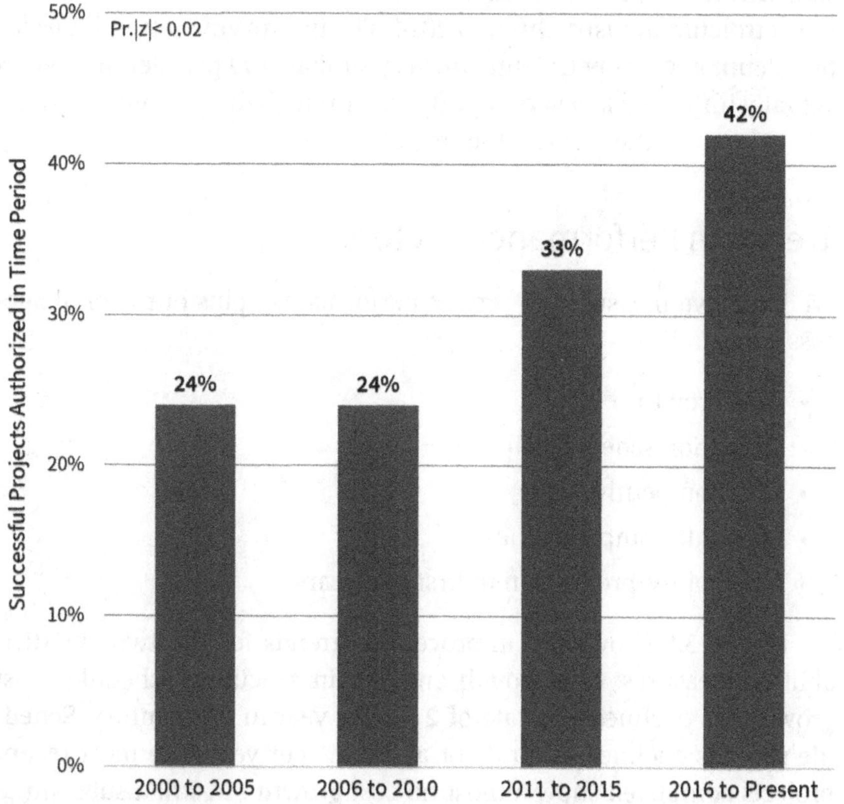

FIGURE 3.4 Success Is Trending Upward

improvement numbers, I need to revisit some conclusions from 2011. Using the criteria just reviewed, we saw an overall success rate for the projects of 35%. When I "closed the books" on the database in 2010, there were a great many projects that had been authorized in the 2005 through 2010 period that were not completed and some dating back as far as 2003. Those projects have now been completed and the data closed and the picture that emerges is actually worse than it looked in 2011. Of the projects authorized in the first five-year period of the 21st century, only about 24% were successful projects. That number rose in each successive five-year window and now stands at over 42%. The trendline is clearly reliable from a statistical viewpoint.

One cannot attribute the improvement trend to market conditions. IPA normalizes the effect of market changes to the greatest extent possible. Furthermore, market conditions continued to deteriorate substantially in the 2006 through 2010 period and continued to worsen for the petroleum industry through 2014. The improvement trendlines for petroleum and nonpetroleum are very similar, and petroleum projects actually improved at a very slightly faster rate than megaprojects overall. (Of course, they had further to go!)

Trends in Performance Factors

We have five measures of project performance, plus our overall success measure:

- Cost growth
- Execution schedule slip
- Cost competitiveness
- Schedule competitiveness
- Operability/production in first two years

Figure 3.5 shows the improvement trends for the two "predictability" measures: cost growth and slip in execution schedule. Cost growth has declined at a rate of 2.2% per year in this century. Schedule slip has declined at a rate of about 1% per year. The most recent projects completed show almost no cost growth but still a substantial slip in schedule, albeit considerably better than years past. What is

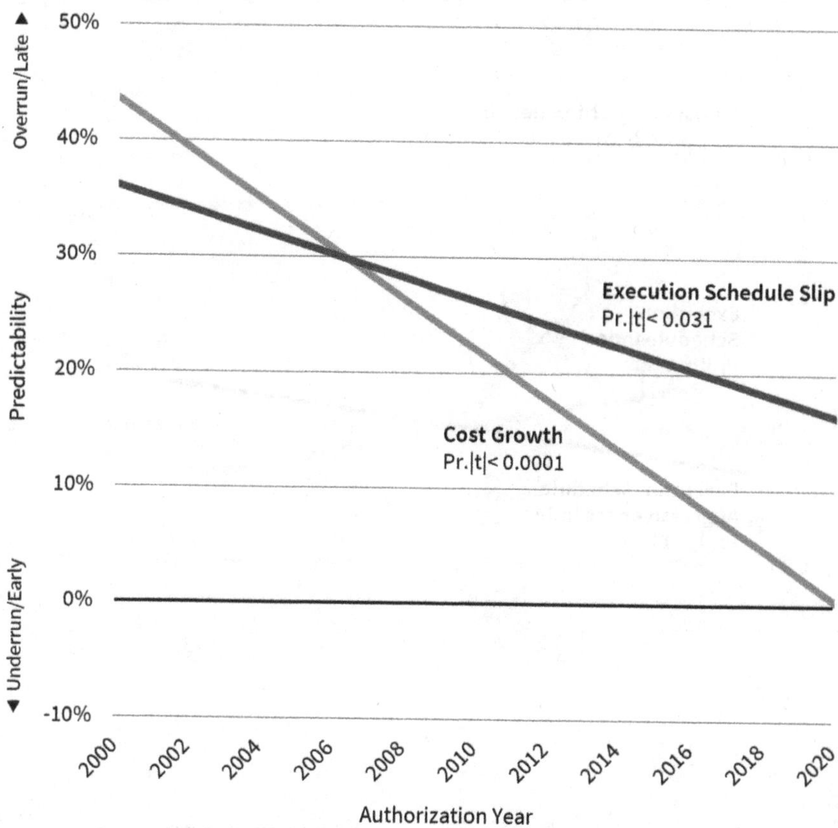

FIGURE 3.5 Cost Growth and Schedule Slip Are Declining

remarkable about the decline in schedule slip is that slip in smaller projects generally has been increasing during this period, driven primarily by increases in slip in engineering.

The improvements in predictability of cost and schedule are accompanied by improvement in cost competitiveness. As shown in Figure 3.6, the cost competitiveness of megaprojects improved by almost 3% per year in the 2000 through 2020 period. The slope is very strong statistically as shown by the probability. By contrast, the improvement in schedule competitiveness is very gradual at less than .5% per year and not statistically significant. Even of more interest, the forecast schedule competitiveness at FID actually increased during the 2000 to 2020 period. This means that schedules gradually became less aggressive as we moved through the first two decades of this century. These data

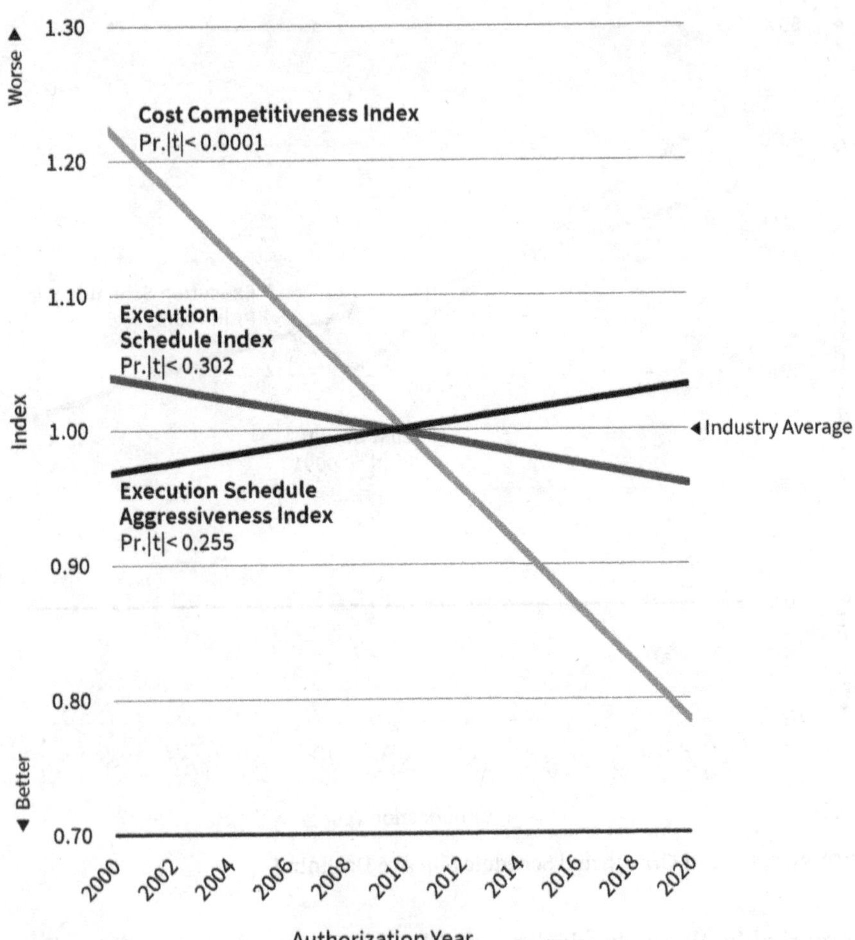

FIGURE 3.6 Cost Competitiveness of Megaprojects

suggest a modest improvement in the rationality of megaproject strategies as we responded to the poor results of the first decade. The percent of schedule-driven projects remained about constant at 35% until 2015. Only 22% of projects authorized and completed since 2015 were schedule-driven, which has combined with other factors to make those projects more successful. Driving the schedule on a complex megaproject is a fool's errand. We will discuss the reasons for that at length later.

The final performance measure, and the one that is most leveraging for profitability of a project, is operability (production over time). After controlling for technology innovation and the implementation

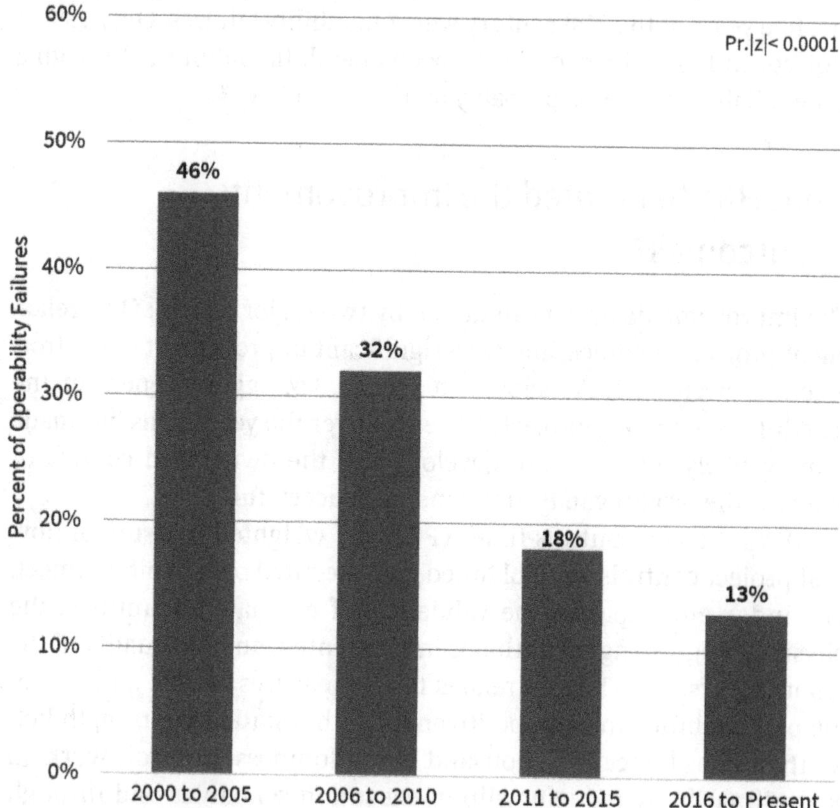

FIGURE 3.7 Operability Failures Are Declining

of a late cost-reduction exercise,[18] operability of facilities has improved by almost 2.5% per year (Pr.|t|<.04) from 2000 to the present. As shown in Figure 3.7, the rate of what we define as *operability failures*, that is, projects with significant problems keeping facilities running in the first two years, has declined very significantly over the past two decades. Almost half of industrial megaprojects in our sample authorized in the

[18]It is necessary to control for the level of technological innovation in the projects because the level of innovation affects operability and the level of innovation has declined over the 20-year time period covered (Pr.|t|<.04). Controlling for cost-reduction efforts late in front-end loading or early execution is also required because their use has increased (Pr.|t|<.05) during the period, and like innovation, cost-reduction efforts damage operability. We will discuss the "Cost-Reduction Exercise problem" in Chapter 4. Without these controls, the rate of improvement in operability would appear to be greater than it really is.

first five years of the 21st century were operability failures. Only 13% of projects authorized recently have been operability failures, although a more reliable number is probably about one in five.[19]

What Has Generated the Improvements in Outcomes?

The improvements have been driven by two major factors: (1) a relaxing of project schedules, and (2) a significant improvement in controls practices over time. As shown in Figure 3.6, aggressiveness in the schedules set on megaprojects has eased over the years. This has made it more likely that the plan developed by the owner and contractor team for the project can be implemented successfully.

IPA's Project Controls Index (PCI) is a weighted measure of how well project controls were planned and executed on a capital project. The index encompasses the validation of estimated quantities, the physical progressing effort that is implemented, and the quality of the reporting system. The PCI relates to all measures of cost and schedule predictability and competitiveness with a statistical strength better than one chance in a thousand of randomness. Controls work on cost primarily by reducing slip in execution schedules and through improving productivity in the field. The PCI is strongly related to slip, to execution schedule competitiveness, and to faster construction times. During the two decades covered, the PCI improved from *Fair* on average to *Best Practice* on average for megaprojects. The improvement in controls was the most important practice improvement by far.

[19]Our sample always contains some degree of bias for projects in the most recent period. The projects that slip their schedules the most slip out of our sample. It is a fact of project life that as slip increases, the chances of being an operability failure increase ($Pr.|z|<.0001$), and of course, cost growth increases as well ($Pr.|z|<.0001$). Almost all of the megaprojects that we evaluated on the front-end that were authorized in the 2011–2015 period are completed, with only a few exceptions that will likely be disasters. Projects authorized in the 2016–2020 period are less likely to be completed. Those authorized early in that period that are not completed are more likely to be slipping their schedules, growing in cost, and are less likely to operate as planned. Even considering those caveats, the improvement trend is clearly real.

There are three key practices that set behind and drive the quality of project controls: (1) clarity of objectives, (2) functional completeness of the owner project team (which we call "team integration"), and (3) front-end loading. The three practices work both independently and interactively to facilitate controls by suppressing the need for major late changes. Major late changes are very disruptive of the controls process. During the 20 years covered, clarity of project objectives has not changed significantly and front-end preparation (as measured by the IPA FEL Index) has not changed at all on completed projects and may have even degraded slightly, which is disappointing. But team integration has improved very substantially ($Pr.|z|<.005$), from just over 50% of projects in the first decade of the century to over 70% in the last 200 projects authorized. That improvement in team integration facilitated the improvement in project controls ($Pr.|t|<.001$).

So, megaprojects are improving. It appears that at least some learning has occurred, especially with regard to the need to integrate the owner project team, putting a controls process and team in place, and relaxing schedule. Perhaps the progress has not been as fast as one might have hoped, but it is substantial.

Why Do We Learn So Slowly?

It is a rare company that actually wants to learn from its failed megaprojects and knows how to do it. That is very unfortunate because deeply understanding failure is the most profound and effective way to improve. It is sometimes almost amusing to hear the "company line" that develops around a failed project. For example, we had one large chemical complex expansion and modernization that overran by about $2 billion. The overrun was quite unnecessary as it was caused by lapses in practices on the front-end. However, despite the overrun, the project was profitable because the complex was able to take advantage of a low-cost feedstock. Rather than actually learning anything from the failed project, the standard company line is "the project had some problems but was a great business success." The company did not even have an internal closeout of the project. We only got the overrun amount by talking to (the quite demoralized) members of the project team after the project was finally completed. It is all quietly forgotten. The problem is that the company does much the same on *every* disappointment, including the cases that are business disasters.

There are two reasons to carefully explore and deeply understand failed megaprojects. The first is for the benefit of the individuals who were involved in the development and execution of the project. Even those who were involved only early in the project development, such as the original business sponsor, should be required to be part of the learning process. It is well understood that learning from the experience of others is difficult and less likely to effect change than learning from one's own experience. When a properly structured lessons-learned exercise is skipped in the wake of failure, those involved with the project are deprived of a golden opportunity to become far better at their professional work. In a learning organization, having learned from past failures is a badge of honor, not one of shame.

The second reason to do a lessons-learned exercise is to understand whether the failure of a project was a systemic failure—that is, rather than a failure of individuals to do what the system says should have been done. This sort of learning can only occur if the lessons-earned process is accompanied by a strong conceptual framework that knows where to "park" the lessons and can also do something about what was learned. Many more failures are systemic than recognized. For example, one of our oil industry clients does most of its major projects, including most megaprojects, quite well. But when projects get to about $10 billion, its performance disintegrates to almost no successes. The company's lesson was that the "gigaprojects" are too complex to do and should be avoided. In fact, however, all of those projects were deemed so "corporately important" that they circumvented the company's normal governance procedures and became very political within the company. That fact, rather than their size, caused the projects not to follow sound practices, which in turn, caused failure.

CHAPTER 4

The Roads to Ruin—The Mechanics of Failure (and Success)

In the first edition of this book, I discussed at length the factors that are the precursors for a failed project:

- Hazy and inconsistent objectives
- Inadequately staffed teams
- Teams missing one or more key owner functions
- Incomplete or poor-quality front-end loading
- Weak project leadership, including the business lead as well as the project director
- Missing, late, or incorrect Basic Data
- Poor Shaping

Nothing has changed in that regard; these things are still precursors to failure. What I did not do in the first edition, which I realize was a failure on my part, is describe and categorize the *mechanics* by which the projects fail. This is important because, if one understands the mechanics, it may be possible to see the earliest signs of failure and stop the process before it becomes unmanageable.

Sometimes the relationship between an oversight or error and project failure is simple and direct: for example, we had a project in the North Sea in which the owner neglected to examine the seafloor conditions to ensure that the oil production platform they intended to install could be effectively anchored. They had installed many prior platforms in the area without incident and felt that there was little or no risk that the seafloor conditions would be materially different for the chosen location. They were wrong; the platform could not be installed, and the entire project became an embarrassing fiasco.

Those simple examples are relatively rare. Often the relationships between causes and results are not obvious. In the following, I discuss four mechanisms by which megaprojects can fail in declining order of frequency.

- Cascading failure, usually from an omission in the front-end
- Basic Data failures
- Failures from fear, being so risk-averse that failure is built in
- Cost-Reduction Exercises (CREs) as a route to fail

I will close with a discussion of execution schedule slip, which is what I call "the slayer of megaprojects." Sometimes slip is an effect, sometimes it is a cause, but it is always bad. And finally, I will review the narrow road to success, which is easy to define and hard to travel.

Cascading Failures

Most failures result from errors and omissions on the front-end that would never appear to be project killers, but clearly were in retrospect. The most common mechanism involved in these stealthy project killers are oversights on the front-end that trigger what is known as a "cascading failure" in execution.

A cascading failure occurs when a single element of a network fails and triggers failure in adjacent dependent elements, which in turn trigger the failure of those around them, and so on until the entire network has failed.[1] The more tightly a network is integrated, the more likely it is that a cascade will occur and that the cascade will have devastating effects on the whole. Failures of electricity grids are an oft-cited example of sometimes devastating cascading failures. One common characteristic of cascading failures is that they start with something small and go unnoticed until they become obvious and recovery is difficult or impossible.

Projects are networks—a set of interconnected activities—some of which are necessarily sequential and some of which can be done in parallel. As projects get larger, and especially as projects have more elements or subprojects, the complexity of the network that is the project increases rapidly.

Cascading (or cascade) failure is a concept that is well known in design of complex networks, such as electricity grids, but not much talked about in projects. I believe the lack of discussion of cascading failure in projects is because small projects rarely fail by cascade. If an error is made in a relatively simple project, there is ample capacity to fix the problem and proceed without further incident. In complex megaprojects that is not the case. The more closely coupled a network is, the more it is subject to cascading failure.

I have tried to illustrate a network and cascading failure in Figure 4.1. Along the bottom of the figure is the project work process stages. The number of nodes and activities in FEL-1 and FEL-2 is quite limited, and the coupling (how close together they are) is not onerous. We can make changes relatively quickly and without having to back up very far to do so. As soon as we move into FEL-3 (front-end engineering design, or FEED), however, the number of activities jumps and they become closely coupled, and there are more connections from each node to others up and down as well as forward. This change occurs because the work goes from being largely sequential to massively parallel. By the time we are in execution, the network has become incredibly dense and complex. What that means is that any failure that is allowed to propagate becomes unmanageable very quickly from FEL-3 forward.

[1]Lucas D. Valdez, et al., "Cascading Failures in Complex Networks," *Journal of Complex Networks, 2,* 2020.

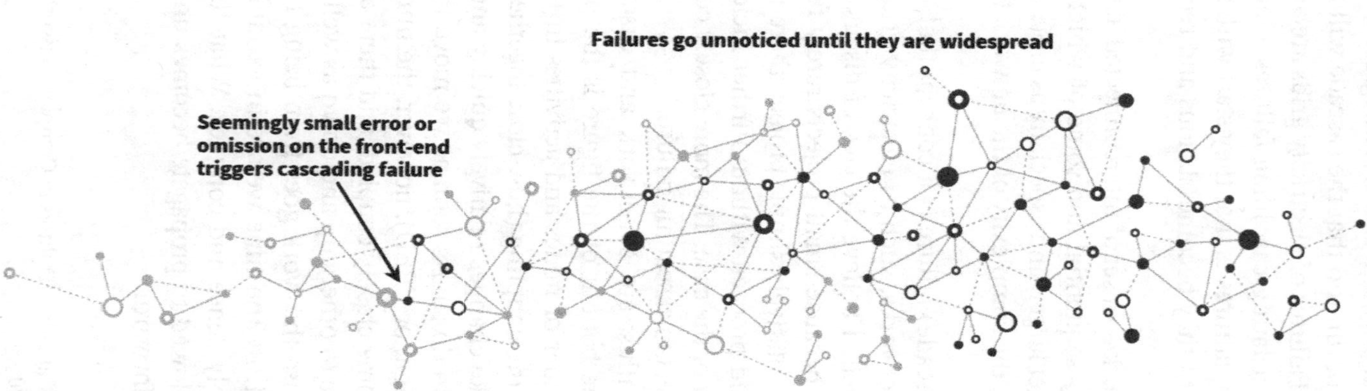
Complex network of interconnected project activities with a cascading failure
Failures go unnoticed until they are widespread
Seemingly small error or omission on the front-end triggers cascading failure
Failed activities shown in black
FEL 1
FEL 2
FEL 2
Execution Phase
Startup & Operate

FIGURE 4.1 Cascading Failure

Be clear that the network in a large complex project must be closely coupled or the project duration would render the effort uneconomic. The typical billion-dollar project with a well-defined schedule has defined over 4,000 individual major tasks that must be completed during execution. If the cost is $3 billion, the number of defined activities averages over 7,000. If we insert time (float) for checking and reducing the risks of knock-on effects behind every element of a project, any megaproject would take decades to complete and could not possibly be profitable.

In the first edition of this book, I put a good deal of emphasis on aggressive schedules as being a primary root cause of project failure. That is still true. In retrospect, however, I realize I did not actually explain the processes by which aggressive schedules translate into failure beyond the rather banal point that schedule aggressiveness makes schedule slip more likely. When we think about aggressiveness of project schedule, we think in terms of how tightly packed the network is. The megaproject with a good—that is, achievable—schedule is a tightly packed network. The same project with an aggressive schedule that might be 20% faster in theory is an incredibly densely packed network. More activities are on the critical path. There are more activities that are close to critical path, which means they can easily become critical path with even small delays. There is no time to fix problems before damage has been done to the next activity and so forth. The effect is that the aggressively scheduled megaproject is very vulnerable to network failure via cascade. Once a cascading failure has started in execution, it is extremely difficult to stop because it is occurring quickly on multiple fronts. Often the only step that would actually stop the cascade would be to shut down the project execution. That is the one step that is almost always totally unacceptable.

The Most Common Cascade

The most common cascading failure that we see starts back in scope development, which we label front-end loading stage 2 (FEL-2). Often in the interests of moving the front-end process along faster, the team leaves some elements of scope open in FEL-2 and the governance process fails to catch the omission. The open scope then hugely complicates FEL-3, which is when the engineering is progressed to the point where detailed engineering can be started in earnest in the next phase and the project execution planning should be completed. As a consequence, the front-end engineering is only partially completed and again the governance process fails at the authorization gate.[2] The execution schedule, which would be reasonable if the front-end engineering design (FEED) had been completed, is now hopelessly optimistic, but of course, the schedule remains unchanged. The project starts execution six months behind in terms of work actually accomplished and has, in effect, already failed.

A variant of this cascade is when some critical path event prior to authorization did not happen, but no one is willing to blow the whistle. I recall one project in which the schedule required access to the site 15 months prior to authorization, but access was not gained because the landholder was a competitor who saw no point in being helpful, which just might have been anticipated. No one mentioned the site access problem when the project was authorized on a schedule that assumed site access had occurred as planned. The project cost almost doubled, and the completion date slipped two years on a project that had forward-sold its output.

Project Types Most Prone to Cascading Failure

Projects that require a great deal of bespoke engineering appear more prone to cascading failures than other projects. Projects exist along a continuum of how much new project-specific engineering is required. Process plant megaprojects require the most engineering, particularly if no attempts at standardization are being made. These projects include chemicals and refinery process facilities and complex minerals processing such as hydrometallurgical processing. On the opposite end

[2]Governance almost always fails to stop a project at the authorization gate even when defects are glaring, *and that should be expected.* By the time we get a megaproject to authorization, lots of binding commitments have been made to partners, governments, customers, and shareholders. To refuse to authorize at that point is viewed as a catastrophe, but a bigger catastrophe usually awaits. We are all familiar with that too-human failing of avoiding immediate pain in the hope that something miraculous will bail us out later (or we will be off the scene).

of the spectrum are megaprojects that consist primarily of installing standard equipment, such as solar photovoltaic installations, wind farms, and simple minerals processing such as crushing and beneficiation. Offshore petroleum production projects generally fall somewhere in the middle.

The engineering-intensive projects are more prone to cascading failures for several reasons.

- They are less forgiving of change at an earlier point in the project's evolution than other projects. When scope development is complete, the design must be effectively frozen whether or not the business is ready or the project must pause. That requires a level of discipline and project knowledge that are frequently not present.
- The out-of-pocket cost of the front-end in heavily engineered projects is considerable and the time requirements substantial. If money or time is not available, it is less likely that the project's scope will be fully appreciated. When elements of scope are overlooked or not fully understood, cascading failure is very likely.
- Heavily engineered projects have work sequences that are rather rigid because so many elements of design are progressive and cumulative in nature. When the work sequences are disrupted, for example, by stakeholder alignment issues, the front-end engineering can easily get thoroughly fouled up. Engineering work during FEED is usually being executed in multiple locations by several—sometimes many—engineering organizations. If work is paused, it is very difficult to restart. If engineering work across several organizations becomes unsynchronized, getting the work back in sequence is quite difficult.

The other type of project that is particularly vulnerable to cascading failures are projects with unusually complex logistics in execution. In particular, remote location projects in which transportation to and from the site is difficult and easily subject to disruption are very vulnerable to cascading failures in execution. Complex logistics require the same sort of disciplined in-depth planning on the front-end as engineering intensive projects. Any temptation to skimp on the front-end, for whatever reason, is likely to result in a cascading failure later for these projects.

Preventing Cascading Failures

In his wonderful book on the Dow-Aramco megaproject, Sadara, Joseph Brewer poses a fascinating question: why don't we as project professionals pay as much attention to schedule as we do to the cost estimate?[3] We worry about the right amount of contingency and the accuracy of the labor productivity assumptions endlessly, while giving only passing glance at the schedule. Very few owners believe they can survive as projects organizations without estimators, but a majority of capital-intensive companies have no significant scheduling expertise.

I raise this issue because I believe that the failure to take schedule and scheduling of megaprojects seriously is the largest single source of cascading failures in the projects. A project schedule is much more than a timeline or even a set of networked activities, although it is both of those things. A schedule is our opportunity to *simulate the execution of a project* and see if it works. It is our chance to ask hundreds of "what-if" questions. "If this is late, what happens to the adjacent activities?" "If this activity has to be done out of sequence, what else would have to be rearranged? Is that doable?" "If items from this source/country are systematically late, what risks does that pose for the project?" Good scheduling prompts questions about sourcing risks. "Does it really make sense to put all of our pipe into the same fabricator?" "Why are we getting such a good discount?" Using the process of developing the schedule to simulate the risks of the project is an opportunity that is routinely lost.

A good master schedule for a megaproject also incorporates potential Shaping issues, such as government approvals, joint venture partner approval processes, community relations, and finalizing the details of the commercial deals. A good master schedule will always incorporate the timing of any missing Basic Data inputs. As we will discuss in Chapter 9, Basic Data are frequently missing during scope development for resource development projects and new technology using projects as well.

The primary discussion of the schedule for a megaproject is usually "Why does everything take so darned long?" and not "What could

[3]Joseph C. Brewer, Jr., *When Mega Goes Giga: The Rocket Ride on Dow & Aramco's Record-Setting Project*, Lulu Press, 2019, pp. 45–46.

trigger a series of failures from which we could not recover?" In my experience, business executives often view project schedules as negotiable and pliable. That is often true for smaller projects, but is almost never true for megaprojects. One of the brilliant observations that Brewer makes about Sadara—a project that built 27 integrated chemical plants—is that the project had to be understood "as a parade, not a symphony." Organizing the project such that subprojects could proceed along playing a different tune than the others made the project less prone to cascading failure; a symphony has no such forgiveness. Like a parade, there needed to be some space between the bands. The *overall* pace of all the subprojects was very important, but the precise pace at any one time was not.

If we are going to see a significant reduction in megaproject cascading failures, owners will have to substantially change the way they approach schedules for the projects. The schedules for megaprojects cannot be viewed in the same fashion as for simpler projects. Schedule development cannot be viewed as a contractor task, but as a core owner team task. That, in turn, will require that owners beef up their scheduling disciplines within the companies.

Basic Data Failures

Errors and omissions associated with Basic Data can trigger failure in very different ways depending on how the problem is addressed. Sometimes Basic Data are late or incorrect during front-end development, and that fact is known and attempts are made to work around the problem. If this disruption to the work flow occurs during FEED, it may well trigger a cascading failure as previously discussed. This usually occurs by the FEED work not getting done, which results in a project with an unworkable plan. Sometimes the disruption occurs even during detailed engineering, and an engineering intensive project is now very likely to become a victim of cascading failure.

However, sometimes Basic Data errors are not recognized during the front-end, or if they are recognized, a decision is made to try to "fix it later." These projects are subject to what we at IPA call the "bookend failure": the very first thing we do on the project—the aggregation of the Basic Data—affects only the very end of the project—startup and operation. The project can, from cost and schedule perspective, be a great success only to be an operational catastrophe. Such projects are analogous to that cliché about the surgery was a great success, but alas the patient died.

Failure from Fear

Most of the first decade of the 21st century was a boom period for capital spending in the industrial world. For petroleum production, this "super cycle" period, as it was called, continued until 2014. During those boom years, the cost of equipment and materials rose rapidly. Contractors went from being in long supply to short supply almost overnight starting in about 2003. The result was that a great many projects large and small overran their cost estimates due primarily to escalation. As discussed earlier, when IPA assesses overruns and underruns, we remove the effects of escalation (project-specific inflation). That does not mean that escalation may not be quite damaging to the business—if product prices do not escalate as well, it is damaging to the business case. But it is also something about which a project team and organization can do very little.

The one outcome that business folks hate above all else in projects is a cost overrun, regardless of the underlying cause of the overrun. Indeed, *under*running cost is the most important single factor governing what businesses think about project outcomes.[4] It is far more important than schedule, safety, operational effectiveness, and cost competitiveness in shaping business judgments about project quality. In some companies, an overrun of even 10% is career limiting for a project director.

What followed the rash of overruns due to market forces was a process of stuffing way too much money in the cost estimates of a good many megaprojects. As we discussed in Chapter 3, IPA carefully distinguishes between cost deviation—overruns and underruns—and cost competitiveness, which measures how much capital a project is

[4]See Ed Merrow, *Contract Strategies for Major Projects*, John Wiley, 2023, Table 3.1, p. 64. This finding was made in a brilliant research study by my colleague, Paul Barshop. Experienced project professionals already know this ugly secret, but it needs to be digested by business professionals as well.

spending relative to others to create a unit of product. When estimates are padded, project costs can be *under*run while *over*spending. The effects of padding on corporate health are enormous. When a cost estimate is padded, it is very likely that the project will overspend. Contractors, which often make the estimates, know when there is extra money to spend and usually oblige by spending as much of it as possible. Most industrial companies are measured in terms of performance by return on capital employed (ROCE). Padding cost estimates depresses ROCE.

After the start of cost overruns in the middle of the first decade of this century, the number of projects that overspent while not overrunning doubled. Post-2007, 13% of projects fell into this category. The padding of the estimates on these projects averaged 49% (43 median)! The average FID cost estimate was $3.2 billion in today's terms, meaning that, on average, an extra billion dollars was hidden in the estimate.

The padded estimate projects often had strong front-end loading. They were more likely than average to have a fully staffed and fully integrated owner team. Nonetheless, the projects set very high cost estimates and sometimes followed with contracting strategies that invited high cost, such as sole-source contracts. The projects were slightly more likely to be schedule-driven but ended up no faster in execution, which is an old story in megaprojects because going fast in execution is so difficult.

The extra money was not in contingency: the padded estimates had contingencies of 8.6% versus 9.1% for other estimates. Padding is rarely put in the contingency account because it is too visible and easily removed by those reviewing the estimate. If FEED contractors were making estimates against which they would perform, the padding would mostly be in the bulk materials accounts. The average such project finished was with a competitiveness index of 1.41, which is 40% expensive, while underrunning their authorization estimates by 6%. The projects were generally viewed as highly successful (as they were quietly bankrupting the shareholders).

A Prototypical Example

This was a $1.5 billion, multi-unit chemicals project in an existing complex in a project-friendly region. Coming into scope development, the project charter from the business designated capital cost effectiveness as the No. 1 priority for the project. Schedule was stipulated as the least important among capital cost, operating cost, operational effectiveness (uptime) and schedule. The project was not designated as schedule-driven at authorization. Given that the project makes only commodity products, this is the expected configuration of objectives. During scope development, the team decided to run a design competition (aka a FEED competition) to select a firm to execute the project on an engineering, materials procurement, and construction (EPC) lump-sum basis. The design competition was chosen because it is both low-cost and highly predictable contracting approach.

The design competition was started with three competing firms (the ideal number) at the start of FEL-3, and then abruptly canceled and replaced with a sole-source EPC reimbursable contract. The rationale offered by the venture manager was that "Contractor X did a pretty good job on our last project and why spend all that money on the design competition thing." The result was a well put-together project with good practices that cost over 30% more than it needed to.

The Estimating Scam

One of the ways that FID estimates can end up as very conservative is via the "estimating scam." On EPC-reimbursable and engineering, procurement, and construction management (EPCm) contracts, the FEED contractor is usually the EPC/EPCm lead contractor. That contractor is then responsible for preparing the project's authorization estimate, or at least a large portion of the authorization estimate.[5] Unless the contractor knows that the project is economically marginal and may not be authorized with a high estimate, the contractor will generally overestimate the project relative to a "50/50" estimate.[6] That is not the scam, that is just normal economically rational behavior.

[5]Sometimes the estimating role is taken by the project managing contractor (PMC) who is filling many of the owner roles. The PMC has every bit as much incentive as an EPC-R or EPCm contractor to inflate the authorization estimate.

[6]An *estimate* is defined as "50/50" if the estimate (including contingency) is intended to provide an even chance of an overrun or and underrun. In general, 50/50 estimates provide best value for the investing companies' shareholders. Estimates are sometimes aimed at a lower chance of being overrun, such as 70/30 estimates. From time to time, some companies have attempted to set "stretch targets" with 40/60 estimates, but the practice is never, in our experience, successful.

The scam part is withholding the estimate from the owner(s) as long as humanly possible so there is insufficient time for validation of the estimate by the owner or a third party. At IPA, we see this play out, especially in large projects, and sometimes do not get the FID estimate until authorization has actually occurred. Then noting that the project benchmarks as very expensive is beside the point. Sometimes, the withheld estimates result in no benchmarks at all, which from the ethically challenged contractor's perspective is even better.

Cost-Reduction Debacles[7]

It is a simple fact of life and human nature that by the time a megaproject is well into FEL-3, doing front-end engineering and planning execution, it is very difficult to accept the bad news that the project is too expensive to be a good investment. The business folks who have championed the project and the project folks who have spent years developing the project are loathe to give it up. Many commitments may have been made to governments, customers, financial markets, and partners. So, the "solution" is to cut costs, which means making the cost estimate go down.

As defined here, a CRE is a mandated attempt to reduce the estimated cost of a project in late FEL-3 (FEED) or just after full-funds authorization. Most CREs occur very late in FEL when the intended authorization estimate appears and is deemed too high to authorize. Sometimes approval itself is conditioned on a CRE being successfully implemented. The most common triggering event for a CRE is when the authorization estimate is substantially higher than any previous estimate and higher than management (either business or corporate) expects. Significant cost growth can occur in FEED either because scope was incompletely defined in FEL-2, critical Shaping issues

[7]The cases in which the estimates have been significantly padded are indeed opportunities for cost reduction. In practice, however, they rarely are because estimate padding does not occur where it will prompt outrage and trigger a Cost-Reduction Exercise. It is rather the high rate of return projects where estimate padding is most likely.

remained unresolved, new Basic Data arrived during FEED, or due to major changes in market conditions for project inputs.

It is important that we are clear about what we do not consider a CRE. Value engineering performed in late FEL-2 or very early FEL-3 is not a CRE. That is a normal part of the project development process for some companies. Value engineering done late in FEL-3 is often a cover for what is actually a CRE. Sometimes during detailed engineering, opportunities to reduce cost are identified and implemented. While it is true that those opportunities were identified later than we would wish, implementing cost savings ideas during detailed engineering is not a CRE; it is just an example of a late change.

Usually, cost reduction is deemed necessary because at the estimate cost the project is not economic or does not meet the corporate hurdle rate (internal rate of return) requirements. (Because hurdle rates are often set higher than economically justified to account for risk, well-developed and properly estimated projects are sometimes subjected to CREs.) Softening product markets sometimes cause companies to defer final investment decision and attempt to reduce costs.[8] On still other occasions, cost reduction becomes necessary because one of the venture partners does not have the cash needed and financing of the project had not been set up. No matter the driving rationale, projects subjected to a CRE are usually disappointing. They often end up much worse than they would have been had the original estimate simply been approved. About 6% of megaprojects go through a CRE. Of those, only 17% of projects were successful using the criteria for success and failure laid out in Chapter 3.

Figure 4.2 shows the relative outcomes of projects with and without a CRE.

Every outcome is worse than the overall megaproject averages when we subject a project to a cost reduction effort, although the cost growth delta is not material. Because of the disruption associated with

[8]Softening markets as FID approaches is usually a poor reason for a CRE or deferment of authorization unless the company is worrying about cash flow availability to keep the project going forward at an appropriate pace. Megaprojects take so long to execute that immediate market outlooks at authorization are largely meaningless. If the long-term market fundamentals are sound, the short-term has little meaning for large projects.

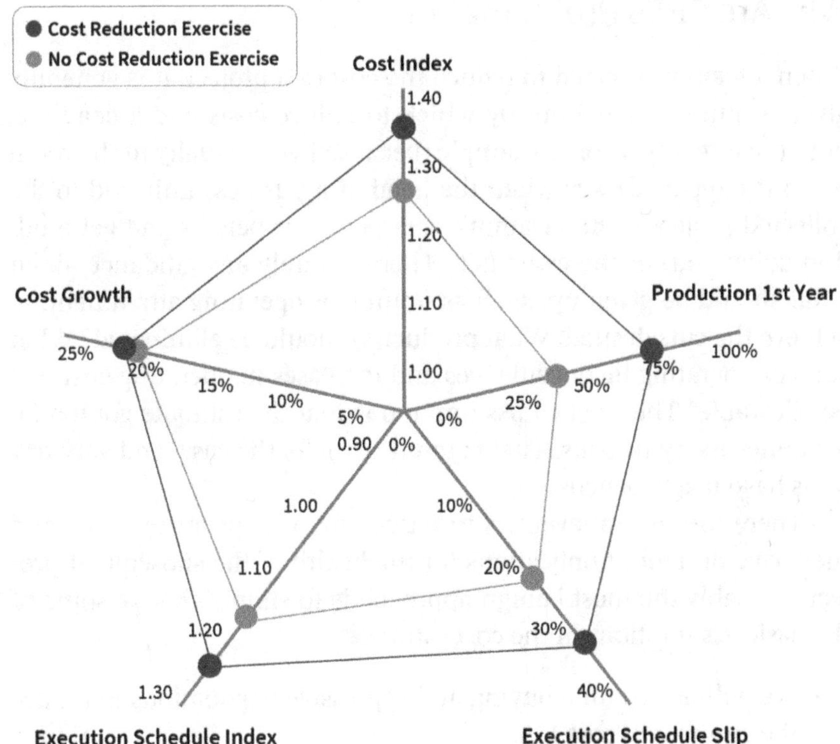

FIGURE 4.2 Relative Outcomes of Projects with/without CRE

a CRE, we are much less likely to be able to use lump-sum contracting as our primary vehicle. The use of EPCm jumps from about a quarter of projects to 56% of projects when we do a CRE. EPCm is among the most problematic of contracting strategies for megaprojects, but EPCm and EPC-reimbursable are often the only fallback strategies left after a cost-reduction effort. In a number of cases, the project was paused when the EPC lump-sum bids came in higher than expected. A CRE was implemented and then no contractors were willing to bite on the re-issued invitation to bid.

The loss of production in year 1 is especially problematic as it materially affects cash flow and NPV. The loss holds up at about 37% of nameplate production even after controlling for technological innovation and rises to 40% when we also control for the completeness of FEED.

Why Are CREs Problematic?

When a team is directed to reduce the cost of a project, it is generally given a minimum amount by which to reduce costs and a deadline, but little else. My favorite example (because I was actually in the room when it happened) was when the head of a business unit said to the collected project team: "Dammit, sharpen your pencils and get a billion dollars out of the estimate!" There is rarely any guidance about what should be given up, such as uptime or operating attainment, to achieve the cuts desired. What product(s) should be eliminated? What sorts of operating inconveniences and increases in operating cost will be allowable? The implicit assumption is that the estimate got too fat for unnecessary reasons. That is rarely actually the case, and very few of us have magic pencils.

There are several avenues to reduce the size of an estimate and they have different implications for the health of the subsequent project. Probably the most benign approach is to simply change some of the basic assumptions in the cost estimate:

- We will use volume buying and aggressive negotiations to reduce the equipment cost 15%.
- Labor productivity, which was assumed to be half the U.S. Gulf Coast base will actually be 80%.
- We will reduce overall construction costs by 10% by increasing the use of preassembled units.
- We will reduce or eliminate all design allowances in the estimate.
- We will increase the nameplate by 10% to match the hydraulic capabilities of the FEED design.
- And so forth.

The great advantage of "reduction by assumption" is that no violence is done to the scope of the project. The material quantities baselines are unaffected, so controls are still viable. As long as construction planning is not changed to match the lower number of hours apparently needed, there is no real change. Of course, the disadvantage of reduction by assumption is that costs were not actually changed and I see an overrun in your future.

A second approach to reducing the estimate is to change the execution strategy. For example, we will drop our EPC-lump-sum strategy and go to EPCm to remove the risk premiums in the lump-sum bids. We will tighten up on the schedule, reducing float, executing more in parallel, and thereby, reduce all time-related costs such as the cost of the project management team. "Savings by strategy" usually produces worse outcomes than reduction by assumption because changes in strategy made at the last minute are almost impossible to execute.

The third approach to cost reduction is the most honest and the most problematic: cut scope. Often, cutting scope is explicitly off the table, but any significant cost reduction that does not change scope is probably illusion rather than reality. Some projects lend themselves to scope reduction. For example, a project with a complex product mix can reduce the number of products and usually save money. Sometimes, real scope cuts can be traded for increased operating cost.

The problem with scope cuts is a lack of time. Significant changes in scope are akin to major surgery for a person: wounds are created that take time—often a lot of time—to heal. All of the scope elements that are affected by the scope reductions, such as the utility requirements, have to be redesigned. The heat and material balances have to be reevaluated and thoroughly checked. If we follow the prescribed work process, which is there for almost all companies these days, when we significantly modify scope, we should back the project up all the way to FEL-2, come through the FEL-2 gate again, and then do a modified reduced FEL-3, and then and only then, proceed to authorization. We almost never do that because there is not nearly enough time provided.

When we carve up the scope of a megaproject over the course of a few months and then move through to final investment decision, things can be made to look okay, but underneath all is chaos. Nothing is really as it seems. A project that might have been well prepared is now a shambles: the design is not as good as all the work that has gone into it; the controls baselines are now more fiction than reality, which invites contractors to get rich. It is very likely that some of the elements of scope we thought we could do without were actually essential to an operating asset. And as in a recent case, now is the perfect time to hire a predatory contractor as project managing contractor (PMC) who will clean up any and all money that isn't nailed down.

Can Cost Reductions Be Done Well?

The simple answer is yes, but . . . it isn't easy and it isn't common. To execute a cost-reduction effort late in front-end loading successfully requires:

- Discipline to not resume project activities until all of the damage done is fully restored
- A coherent strategy and plan for how the cost reduction exercise will be run, who will run it, how it will be governed and what constitutes success
- A fully involved and functionally integrated owner team with strong leadership
- Enough time to complete all of the work.

If any one of these is missing, the effort fails.

Table 4.1 details the differences in inputs between the unsuccessful CRE projects and the small group that beat the odds.

An Effective Example

In his book on the Dow/Aramco Sadara Project, Joseph Brewer discusses the wholesale reworking of the project late in front-end loading.[9] The project was originally developed to be an integrated chemicals/petroleum refinery at Aramco's Ras Tanura Refinery. The chemicals

TABLE 4.1 Drivers of Success and Failure in Projects with CREs

Success Driver	Successful CRE Projects (17%)	Unsuccessful CRE Projects (83%)
Fully Integrated Owner Team	100%	55%
FEL Index post-CRE	4.73 (Best Practical)	6.64 (Fair/Poor)
Status of Engineering	All Best Practical	50% Best Practical
Project Controls Index	5.4 (Good)	3.9 (Fair)

[9]Joseph Brewer, *When Mega Goes Giga*, op. cit.

complex was greenfield with lines connecting to the refinery. Major new port construction would be necessary along with a number of refinery units that would be constructed with the chemicals complex, which was a 400-hectare site that required extensive fill. Just before the EPC bid were to be placed, the total cost estimate arrived and the project was suddenly impracticable: it was too big and too expensive. The project would either move sites and be reconfigured or it would die. As Brewer put it, "If they proceeded, I was convinced the rocket would blow up on the launch pad."[10] Before agreeing to come in on the project as Dow's lead, Brewer required that the project be paused, that all gaps created by a change of site and reconfiguration in the FEED work would have to be fully closed, and that the commercial deal between the partners had to be finalized.

For Sadara, a plan for how the reconfiguration work was to be done was created. A very strong team was put together, help was recruited by the project leadership, and the work was completed in the space of 12 months, including sorting through 50 possible new product configurations as well as a new site at Jubail and filling almost all of the gaps in FEED.[11] The final complex was 27 integrated chemical plants, down from about 35 in the prior configuration.

From the Sadara Project we can learn both how to do cost reduction well and a critical lesson for avoiding the need for a CRE to begin with. If the Shaping work, which of course, includes finalizing the deal, had been done in the manner discussed in Chapters 5, 6, 7, and 8, this crisis in the project would never have happened. As soon as the deal was being hammered out, the project team would have known that the estimate would never fly.

A second example, which I cannot identify because it has not been discussed in print, is an offshore petroleum development project that was in FEL-3 in 2015 as oil prices were in free-fall. The project was ready to authorize, but corporate cash flow was declining rapidly and the project's break-even cost was $20 more than the price of a barrel of oil. The CEO asked the team to spend an extra year in FEL-3, delaying authorization by a year, and look for ways to reduce capital cost by

[10]Ibid., p. 67.
[11]Ibid., Chapter 6, pp.111ff.

at least $600 million. (I think it is significant that the CEO personally *requested* the team to try to do this despite the fact that this is a very large company.)

Knowing that they had a year to work with, the team members put together a very comprehensive plan of attack to reduce and rework the scope of the project. They revisited the internal standards and switched to less costly U.S. Gulf of Mexico standards. They reworked the subsea scope to decrease the amount of revamp work that would have to be done on an existing platform. (That sort of work is about the most expensive work one can do in the oil industry.) They reworked the drilling strategy as well. At the end of the year, with all gaps in FEED healed, they had reduced the project cost not by $600 million, but by $1.3 billion. Yes, they got some help from declining prices of inputs, but it was a remarkable achievement.

When the team was describing its work, a couple of things stood out for me. First, the team members recruited help from wherever in the company expertise existed. There was no exclusion of good ideas. And second, they said that one of their major "wins" was being able to persuade management to allow them to do things differently. With a good deal of effort and education, they got the company's technical authorities to sign off on things that had not been done by the company before.

What Should You Do?

Generally, going forward after the CRE wrecking ball has hit the project is a bad idea. Proceeding with a commodity megaproject that will cost 25% to 40% more than the average competition is simply to dig a capital cost hole from which it will be difficult for the business or the company to dig out. However, if a CRE is necessary and appropriate, it will take at least a year to yield a solid result. It appears that the decisions to order a CRE are way too fast and not given the sort of deliberate calculation they need. Around FID time, the project already has a great deal of momentum—as it must. But the decision about whether to do a CRE and *how* to do a CRE are very important.

Schedule Slip Is the Slayer of Megaprojects

When we think about bad outcomes of projects, there are lots of measures: cost overruns, poor operability, high cost, long schedules. But it turns out that the most telling of all measures is slip in execution schedule. In Figure 4.3, we have used a schedule slip of 10% as the cutting point. A slip of less than 10% is three or four months in a typical megaproject. The average project with a small slip is comfortably a success by our criteria. More than 10% slip almost always means failure.

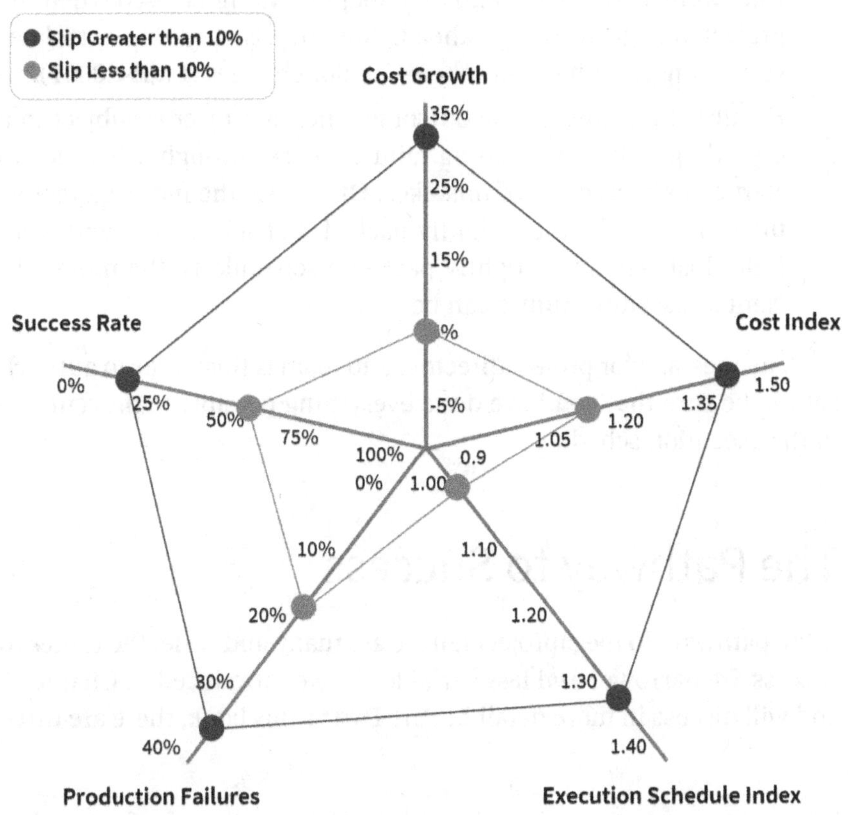

FIGURE 4.3 When Execution Schedule Slips

No other outcome measure so clearly distinguishes success and failure. So why is execution schedule slip so telling? There are several reasons.

- Schedule slip often reflects that the execution plan for the project was a setup to fail. Many megaproject schedules are simply unachievable, but the attempt to meet the achievable damages the overall project. Realistic, achievable schedules reflect deeper execution planning.
- Slip is often a symptom of a poor front-end. Not only are project practices poorer (clarity of objectives, team integration, front-end loading, and planned controls), but it is more likely that Basic Data were incomplete[12] and that Shaping was not closed when the project was given the go-ahead. Not surprisingly, slip correlates very strongly with the number of major changes ($Pr.|t|<.0001$).[13]
- Finally, slip is always the outcome when a project is subject to a cascading failure. Cascading failures work through schedules to start a chain reaction of mistakes. Of course, the more aggressive the schedule, the more tightly packed that schedule is with very little float. The more tightly packed a schedule is, the more efficient a cascading failure can be.

The message for project directors and team is this: prior to authorization, be sure that you have done everything possible to prevent slip in the execution schedule.

The Pathway to Success

If the pathways to megaproject failure are many and wide, the routes to success are narrower and less variable. As we introduced in Chapter 1 and will discuss in more detail in Part Two of this book, there are three

[12]In petroleum production projects, the IPA index of the completeness of appraisal (the key Basic Data for the project) reflects less appraisal completed on projects with more execution schedule slip.

[13]A major change involves a cost of more than one-half of 1% of estimated total cost and/or one or more months of schedule.

streams of work on the front-end that must be completed well to ensure a high probability of success: the Basic Data must be in-hand by mid-FEL; the Shaping process that allocates the value of the project out to the stakeholders must come to closure with the project work stream's scope completion; and the front-end loading should be complete and of good quality at final authorization. That whole complex process starts with clear and consistent business objectives for the asset.

A defect in any of the three work streams can result in project failure. However, defects in the different streams tend to play out in different ways. When the arrival of Basic Data slips into FEL-3, cost and schedule and FEL quality suffer with all of the known knock-on effects from there. When Basic Data errors are not seen until execution (or at all), operability suffers. As we discussed in Chapter 3, we have projects that were great successes except for the unpleasant fact of not operating due to a Basic Data error. Failure to close Shaping usually results in projects being canceled late in FEL. Relatively speaking, that is a good result; the only projects that were canceled in mid-execution were projects with unresolved Shaping problems. Poor work in the project stream—front-end loading—results in cost growth and schedule slip, and less often but too often, poor operability.

So what is the path to success?

1. If Basic Data needed for scope development are not available by mid-FEL-2, slow the work until they are!
2. If stakeholders are dissatisfied and the deal is not complete by the end of scope development, do not pass through the FEL-2 to FEED gate until the Shaping situation is resolved.
3. In the project stream, close the scope fully in phase 2 so the FEED work has a reasonable chance of being completed before execution starts; complete the execution planning and be prepared with controls.

I am sure that every experienced project director reading these three points is saying, "Yes, obviously, and of course." It may be quite simple, but clearly it is not easy. We will now dive into the three work streams in Part 2, and then move on to people in Part 3.

PART 2

The Three Work Streams

Almost all of what creates success or failure in megaprojects happens before the projects are formally authorized by sponsors. By the time a project starts execution, it is too late to fix most of the problems that will eventually result in failure. For a number of reasons that we will explore later, that is less true for smaller and less complex projects.

One of the fundamental lessons about megaprojects is that the work done prior to formal authorization is more complex and difficult than the equivalent work on smaller projects. When project professionals think about the process of getting a project done, it is usually in the context of the front-end loading, execution, commissioning, and hand-over to operations that comes to mind. However, as shown in the figure there are actually three work streams that have to be accomplished for a successful project:

1. A business work stream, which we call *Shaping*, that assesses the rationale for the project and whether a project would likely be a net benefit to the company; Shaping addresses whether the deals necessary to make the project a business reality are feasible.
2. A *Basic (technical) Data* stream package that includes all the information that will underpin the design.

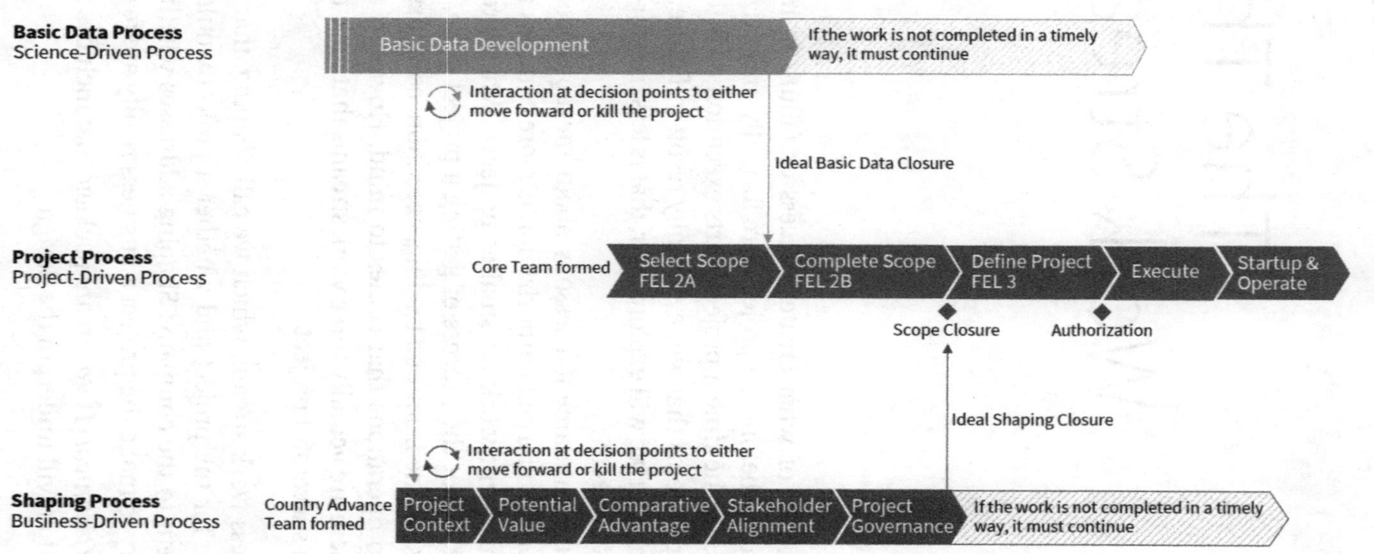

Basic Data Process
Science-Driven Process
Basic Data Development
If the work is not completed in a timely way, it must continue
Interaction at decision points to either move forward or kill the project
Ideal Basic Data Closure
Project Process
Project-Driven Process
Core Team formed
Select Scope FEL 2A
Complete Scope FEL 2B
Define Project FEL 3
Execute
Startup & Operate
Scope Closure
Authorization
Ideal Shaping Closure
Interaction at decision points to either move forward or kill the project
Shaping Process
Business-Driven Process
Country Advance Team formed
Project Context
Potential Value
Comparative Advantage
Stakeholder Alignment
Project Governance
If the work is not completed in a timely way, it must continue

3. A *project work process* stream, which will take the business objectives and the Basic Data and fashion a real project that can be executed.

In most (but not all) medium-sized and smaller projects, the Basic Data stream is not particularly prominent unless new technology is involved. There is Basic Data work to do even on mid-sized brownfield projects, but it is understood and often performed by the project team.[1] Putting together the business case is usually done by an opportunity manager or perhaps by the site at which the project will be located as almost all mid-sized projects are executed at existing sites.

In megaprojects, the Shaping and Basic Data work streams are routinely large and complex. Each will be handled by a separate group of people who sometimes know relatively little about how projects work. That makes the integration of the work more challenging. The relationships among the three work streams—their synchronicity or lack thereof—become critical to a megaproject's outcomes. I have tried to illustrate this in the figure. What the figure cannot show effectively is that constant interaction and communication must exist among the three streams of work. Any work pursued in isolation of the other two streams is likely to be wrong or irrelevant to moving the effort forward.

The Three Work Streams

The Basic Data stream often starts the work, especially on resource development projects such as petroleum and minerals production. A discovery is made and the process of characterizing that reservoir or orebody proceeds at least to the point at which the discovery is considered commercially viable. When new technology is involved, the Basic Data development process may start many years before the project opportunity is even identified. In other cases, the Shaping work starts the process.

[1]For example, on a revamp project, the Basic Data that require de novo development are usually around the state of the existing facilities that will be modified. Those data are critically important, but are usually assembled by the project team.

There are a number of challenges associated with successfully navigating the three streams of work. First, the fact that there are three big and difficult streams of work is often not clear to everyone involved. Yes, the Basic Data developers know they are hoping to feed a project, but it is difficult for them to know exactly when particular data will be available with sufficient certainty to allow project scope development to proceed. Those responsible for Shaping know that they are trying to develop a project, but often have no work process for Shaping and no strategy for how they will proceed and only guesses about how long things will take.

Each stream of work must continuously inform the other two and be informed by them. If the Basic Data are taking longer to firm up than expected, the other two work streams must be slowed or even stopped until Basic Data catch up. If Shaping is not going well—for example, if significant unanticipated opposition to the project is mobilizing—project work must be slowed because major changes in scope may be required to satisfy opponents. For each stream to move along as if it exists independently of the other two is to ensure failure. The way I think about it, the three streams have to be braided into a strong rope. Weakness in any stream will cause the rope to fail—sometimes quickly as when failure to Shape effectively results in abandonment before FID, sometimes slowly as when Basic Data errors cause operability failures at the end of the project.

In the best case, Basic Data development is complete with respect to scope and design requirements by the middle of FEL-2. That ensures that the scope is unlikely to harbor errors that will cause major changes later. When the data are not complete, the work normally continues and is fed to the scope development team as quickly as possible. The implications of late Basic Data are discussed in Chapter 9. Closure of the Shaping process should best coincide with the closing of the scope. As we will discuss in the Shaping sections that follow, scope closure without Shaping closure is not real; the deal that emerges from Shaping must reflect and govern the scope. Scope changes may unstick the deal and deal changes may unstick the scope.

Most capital projects are developed and executed as a normal part of a company's ongoing business: a facility is expanded, a new manufacturing line added, a refinery unit refurbished, a mine expanded, a new reservoir tied back (added) to an existing producing petroleum asset. These business-as-usual projects are rarely megaprojects, and if they take on the characteristics of a megaproject, it is usually an unwelcome surprise.

The discussion of the three work streams is not balanced by design. I devote much more space to Shaping than the other two work streams for a simple reason: Basic Data development and the project work stream are much better understood and accepted among those who put together megaprojects than the Shaping stream. Shaping is the orphan of megaproject work.

CHAPTER 5

An Introduction to the Shaping Stream

A defining characteristic of megaprojects is that they are, to a substantial extent, unique endeavors. They are not necessarily unique technologically, although they often are, but they are always unique in terms of the combination of context, partners, stakeholders, and the precise business deal that sits at their center. Even in the case of large petroleum companies, which often have a few megaprojects authorized each year, the projects present their own unique configuration of problems.

The challenges that make megaprojects unique are what we call "Shaping." *Shaping* is the owners' work that takes an opportunity and fashions it into a business venture and asset. It is the work to understand the context in which the asset will be developed, assess whether there is economic value in pursuing the asset, and then align all of the people and organizations claiming part of the asset's value (stakeholders) so that the execution of the project can be accomplished in a stable environment.

Unlike the other two big work streams in a megaproject (the development of the Basic Data and definition of the scope and execution plan, which we call front-end loading [FEL]), Shaping is not a well-defined and fully articulated workstream in most industrial companies. But Shaping is critical to megaproject success. When

Shaping is done poorly, most potential megaprojects never make it to authorization. When poorly Shaped projects do get authorized, the sponsors eventually will wish they had not.

Opportunity Shaping[1] is a business-led process by which sponsors evaluate the key attributes of a potential project, develop and gather information that is needed for key decisions, and then allocate the value to the various stakeholders to make the project environment stable enough for successful execution while holding enough of the project's value for themselves to make the venture worthwhile.

Money spent on and during the Shaping process is not capital investment; it is *not* project money and must not be perceived as such by any concerned. Money spent in Shaping is for purposes of information acquisition only, not capital investment. One must be prepared to walk away from a bad deal without any negative repercussions. Think of it this way: you were engaged in information acquisition and you acquired enough information to understand that this deal was not going to benefit the company. That is a good result; now move on. One of the keys to a successful Opportunity Shaping process is to be looking for reasons to *kill* a project, not reasons to continue. The more clearly you can view the process as information-gathering for decision-making, the less likely you are to become so invested in the project that you are unable to negotiate successfully, and are only able to extricate yourself (and your company) at considerable personal loss. During this same period, the project management team will be busy developing the scope for the project in tandem with the businesses Shaping efforts. Those expenditures are also for purposes of information development only. All money and effort up to the Shaping closure point, which we will discuss in the next three chapters, are not capital investment; they are the cost of information and the price to play the game!

Megaprojects don't come ready-to-go right out of the box from any perspective—technical or business. A good many megaprojects are

[1]I owe the term *Shaping* to Roger Miller and Donald Lessard, *The Strategic Management of Large Engineering Projects: Shaping Institutional, Risks, and Governance*, Cambridge, MA: MIT Press, 2000. Their ground-breaking volume is largely devoted to this subject. My use of the term is somewhat broader than theirs. Their focus was mainly on institutional structures around large complex projects, for example, the use of public/private partnerships and the like. My use of the term is more generally around the deal and allocation of value.

not even the result of a systematic corporate search for opportunities. The exceptions to that rule are oil and gas development projects, which generally result from a corporate exploration strategy. Even then, I often get the clear impression that the company was not really prepared for the success of that exploratory process, especially in regions that are new to the company.

In an ideal world, megaprojects would be the result and expression of strategies to sustain and grow the corporation.[2] Extensive analysis would have preceded a search for opportunities that fit with the comprehensive vision.[3] However, there are distinct limits to how far eschewing opportunism will carry companies in the current environment. International petroleum companies are facing rapid depletion of opportunities for new black oil developments. Similarly, minerals companies have long since discovered and developed rich ore bodies in easily accessible venues. European and American commodity chemical company assets are mostly far from rapidly growing markets and far from low-cost feedstocks. Repositioning requires gaining access wherever an opportunity arises. And repositioning often requires megaprojects because large size is an essential element in cost effectiveness when opening up new areas.

The result is that we are often, perhaps usually, facing challenges in our large projects for which we are ill-prepared. Shaping is an essential response to that reality. We must take the project opportunity that has arisen and subject it to sufficient scrutiny that we understand the implications in terms of risk, resources, reputation, and preoccupation that will be involved in trying to turn this possibility into an asset. The Shaping process requires an open-minded approach because so many aspects of the process will be new.

Shaping must not be confused with the project work process prior to full-funds authorization. That process, which we call front-end loading, partly overlaps Shaping in time, and is both informed by Shaping's progress and informs the Shaping process in turn. Shaping and

[2]Peter W.G. Morris and Ashley Jameison, "Moving from Corporate Strategy to Project Strategy," *Project Management Journal,* December 1, 2005.

[3]There are notable exceptions. For example, the Kerr-McGee Corporation (later subsumed by Anadarko, and subsequently, by Chevron) systematically searched for petroleum development opportunities that suited the deepwater development technology, production spars, that it had perfected.

the project work process must be aligned. Shaping never substitutes for front-end loading; the two processes are symbiotic, not substitutes.

Why Is Shaping Essential?

Project management is the science of project planning combined with the art of reacting to surprises during execution. I describe planning as a science because we know how to do it and what needs to be done. It is a repeatable process. If the planning is thorough, the project is appropriately staffed, *and the project environment is stable*, surprises will rarely overwhelm the ability of project managers to react appropriately. If the planning is inadequate, or if the owner staffing is too lean to identify problems, or the project environment is unstable, the art of project management almost always fails for complex projects.

As the name implies, the role of Shaping is to configure a project in such a way that it is profitable for the stakeholder-investors, and at the same time has stabilized the project environment. These two objectives—profitability for the investors and a stable project environment—generally compete. The more of the pie that you as the leader of the Shaping process attempt to keep for yourself, the less likely you will be to have a stable platform from which to execute the project.

Unlike project planning, Shaping remains substantially an art at this point. Though there are many common elements from case to case, each megaproject poses its own Shaping challenges. The effective management of large projects requires a stable environment. The requirement to make major changes in the objectives, scope, precise location, or any other major element after the start of the detailed definition phase[4] can result in an unmanageable project. Turbulence in the

[4]We call this phase of the front-end work front-end loading phase 3 or FEL-3. It is also often called FEED—front-end engineering design. I don't like the term FEED (but use it anyway) because much more than engineering design is involved in the phase. In particular, the execution plan must be perfected in this phase and that is a major activity. In the minerals world, this project phase is often called the "feasibility study." I like that term even less. The economic and other dimensions of whether a project is feasible should have been largely settled before the *beginning* of FEL-3. FEL-3 is expensive, consuming 2%–3.5% of eventual total cost. We cannot be getting to the full-funds authorization point at the end of FEL-3 and then deciding the project is not feasible.

project environment translates to changes and disruptions in execution that render projects failures. We often blame the project managers for these failures, but they are actually failures of Opportunity Shaping, not project management.

The Five Steps in the Shaping Process

Whatever the underlying source of the possible opportunity, in the beginning the project is nothing more than that—a possible opportunity. In the usual case, 6 to 12 years will pass from the first identification of a potential project until something of value is produced, and sometimes no project ever results from the effort. Sometimes, the company that was the potential lead sponsor initially is no longer part of the sponsor group when the project starts up.

What determines how often a company ends up with the prize—and whether that prize is valuable or a booby prize—is the company's skill at Shaping a raw opportunity into a valuable project. We are not aware of any company in the process industries that has developed a work process specially designed to meet the challenges of the Shaping process for megaprojects. There is no standard practice here within the industry, which helps explain the considerable variation in the practices and procedures followed. Only a handful of companies in the process industries have sought to develop and train a cadre of personnel that is particularly skilled and trained in the activities needed to Shape a megaproject and those developments are quite recent. Whether these efforts have succeeded is an open question. These factors contribute to the failures of Shaping that later result in failed projects.

The steps in Shaping are:

1. Understand the Context
2. Assess the Potential Value
3. Identify Comparative Advantage
4. Identify, Understand, and Align the Stakeholders
5. Establish the Rules with Partners

These steps and their order are normative rather than empirical. These are things you *should* do, not necessarily the things that have been done in any systematic fashion in the past. The order of the steps is important because each builds on the prior steps. It is important to remember that Shaping is an artificial construct, not a naturally occurring process that we are observing. Indeed, often when we observe the front-end of many megaprojects, no one on the lead investor side seems to be aware that a stream of work is proceeding at all. Instead, Shaping appears to be a series of demands and reactions and emergencies without any over-reaching strategy guiding the effort.

The next three chapters will address Shaping. The first of these will focus on understanding the context in which the asset will be developed. The next will address taking that knowledge of the context and fashioning a project with a solid business case, coherent objectives, and aligned stakeholders. The third chapter will discuss the development of a strategy for how Shaping will be accomplished so as to improve the chances that a good outcome can be achieved. Before diving into the Shaping process, I will relate a very real story about how poor Shaping can damage a project, a community, and a company. It is a story that has been played out in many places by many projects over the years.

A Shaping Nightmare

One of IPA's clients—a really smart one—bought a small independent oil company, and with it, an offshore project in a developed country. The independent company had developed a basic scope and had purchased land for the onshore processing facilities. The acquiring company had never worked in the country as a project developer, but the situation appeared benign. The country has a strong institutional environment, clear regulations, no problems regarding adherence to law, and a reasonably welcoming political environment. Indeed, the central government was a strong supporter of the development. Like the great majority of industrial companies, the company had no explicit process for Shaping. (It does now.) The very small local business organization of the sponsor was responsible for dealing with the government and local communities. The company had no experience in the part of the country affected by the project, which was a rural and pristine countryside and seacoast.

The scope of the project was routine: an offshore scope to produce the petroleum, a marine pipeline, and then an onshore facility to process. Processing offshore would have been much more expensive because it would have required much more substantial offshore facilities and the field was large, but not so large that processing offshore would not damage the economics. The small company acquired had appraised the reservoir, purchased an onshore processing site, and set a route for the pipeline to bring the petroleum from the wells to the processing facilities. The project was expected to cost less than a $1 billion and provide solid returns over at least a 15-year life while providing a measure of energy security for the host country. The reservoir was well appraised and there were no issues with respect to the Basic Data. The scope was simple, elegant, and low cost. No new technology was required and there were no issues around supply chains. Sounds like a successful project in the making.

However, as the project began to take shape, local opposition began to form, principally around the route of the onshore portion of the pipeline and the onshore processing facility. The pipeline was less than 6 miles but passed close to a number of homes. The consultation process started after the scope was fully developed. A number of changes to the scope were suggested and recommended, all of which would have increased cost, and a few of which would have increased cost very significantly. (Along the way, several scope changes were made to accommodate local concerns, but the basic scope remained unchanged.)

Very quickly, the opposition spiraled out of control with national environmental groups joining and misinformation spreading rapidly. Protest groups blocked the site of the processing facility, resulting in a number of arrests and incarcerations, and claims of police brutality. Company security personnel were accused of joining police in abusing protestors. The project was stopped repeatedly and costs increased rapidly. Local anger was directed both at the authorities and the sponsoring company in equal measure. Security firms were employed to keep protestors away from the site and more rounds of arrests followed. The project generated international condemnation from NGOs.

Eventually, the opposition ebbed, but never fully disappeared. Over a decade after the project was authorized, it finally started production. By that time, however, several times the original budget had been spent and the project was deeply NPV negative. Our client divested the project soon after at a considerable monetary loss. The loss of reputation, however, was far worse.

What are the lessons from this debacle?

1. Shape first, scope second; the Shaping of the project and the scoping of the project are inextricably linked.
2. Shaping is essential, not a nice-to-do.
3. Shaping is like politics; it is always local. Central government support may be necessary, but it is rarely sufficient.
4. To ensure that Shaping will be done, a mandatory process is needed.
5. In order to Shape a project, you have to know the players.
6. In order to Shape a project, you have to know the capabilities of the players: who can really hurt us and who might really help us?
7. Taking over a project that has been started by another is fraught with danger. You do not know exactly what they have done, what they have not done, who is in their camp and who is deeply unhappy.
8. It is far better to deal with potential opposition early than try to cope with it later.
9. Know when it is better to give up rather than solider on. With organized opposition, this project could not make sense economically or reputationally. Kill criteria should be an essential part of any Shaping strategy.

Before a megaproject can be successfully Shaped, a good deal of information is required, information that was sorely lacking in the preceding example. The first step in the information acquisition process is to understand as much as possible about the context of the project. As the old song goes, "You gotta understand the territory!" That is the subject of the next chapter.

CHAPTER 6

Shaping Step 1—Understand the Context

When thinking about what makes megaprojects especially difficult, the first consideration is the project context, which is to say, the environment in which the project will have to be executed. It is the interaction between the context and whether it is relatively robust or fragile, and the size and characteristics of the project that determine whether this will be "just another big project" or a project of considerable difficulty.

The interactions between the project size and the context might be considered this way: if the project is a rock and the context is a body of water into which that rock will be dropped, then what happens when the stone hits the water is a function of three things: the size of the rock, the size of the body of water, and who is standing nearby when the splash occurs. A very small rock will rarely cause anyone to get wet, even when dropped in a small puddle, while a large rock dropped into the ocean will usually disappear without a trace. However, even a medium-sized rock dropped into a puddle with lots of people standing around will cause a fair amount of distress to those getting soaked.

Like every other organization, all projects have a context, an environment, a milieu.[1] That context may be relatively stable and robust with respect to the things that affect capital projects, such as regulatory regime, labor relations, and so on. The context may be stable, but fragile, which is to say unaccommodating of major changes. The milieu may be turbulent and even chaotic. The relationship and interaction between the context and the project help us decide whether a project is merely large or a megaproject. One of the key tasks of the Shaping process is to assess the context, decide whether the intended project will be feasible in that context, and then seek to fashion the project and the distribution of its value in a way that will render the milieu stable enough for the project to be successfully completed.

The context for a project should not be conceptualized as merely or even primarily local, although the local project context is important. The context includes the global markets for project inputs: materials, engineering and project management resources, and finance. The context includes what is happening regionally, and finally, the nature of the local situation. Context assessment is also time-bound and in turbulent times may have a short shelf-life.

The context is also subject to change through time. A context that was very difficult to deal with when the first megaproject was introduced may become progressively more benign and hospitable to projects over time as local players adjust to the presence of the projects. Contexts that have been stable and accommodating for many years can suddenly become extremely turbulent. Examples include the U.K. North Sea regulatory context for petroleum production immediately after the Piper Alpha disaster and the change to the deepwater U.S. Gulf of Mexico's regulatory climate in the wake of the Macondo blowout.

The context does not *cause* project failure, although it is often used as an excuse for failure. Failure results when the context is not adequately or correctly assessed or when major changes are unanticipated. In the last 20 years, one of the most important changes in the

---

[1]Emery and Trist in their seminal article, "The Causal Texture of Organizational Environments," *Human Relations, 18*: 21–32, 1965, explain the profound importance of the nature and stability of the environment (which they call "texture") to the difficulty inherent in organizational management. Projects are, of course, organizations as well and are quite sensitive to their context.

global context for megaprojects was the turn in the contracting market in 2003–2004 from a generation of being a buyer's market to a decided seller's market. That change caused a good deal of disruption and some significant cost overruns, although many of the overruns were due entirely to escalation rather than fundamentals. After correcting for the effects of escalation, however, we cannot point to a single project in our database for which the turn in the market was the root cause of failure. Many projects weathered the market change with discomfort but without major damage. The projects that were hurt seriously had other crucial vulnerabilities that were exacerbated by the market chaos. The next big change in market fundamentals for megaprojects occurred with the Global Financial Crisis. The crisis cooled the market in chemicals and minerals, but had little or no effect on the petroleum sector because oil prices remained high. When oil prices finally came down in the 2014–2015 period, project demand fell very quickly and significant deflation occurred in projects. That period of relative calm ended in 2020 with the global Covid pandemic. The current period is one of considerable uncertainty, which is likely to continue for at least a few years.

If the context does not *cause* failure, what it does do is outline the magnitude of the task that lies ahead. If the context presents major challenges, the sponsor's strategy for Shaping should be different. The need for staff resources may increase very substantially. The amount of time that sponsors expect for both development and execution should increase.

An ever-present danger in the early days of Shaping is an abundance of optimism. We humans are always quick to believe what we wish to. When we are ignorant of the difficulties because they are new and unappreciated, optimism is very easy. Sponsors need to have clear objective criteria established in advance in order to keep realism in play.

Country Advance Teams

The assessment of the project's context needs to start as soon as the project possibility arises or even earlier.[2] If the project is in a new

[2]Companies with an FEL-0 phase are exploring the context before any particular project has been identified. It is an excellent practice.

venue for the company, or if the company has not done a project in this location for several years, a country advance team needs to be formed immediately.[3] The team needs to be staffed with specialists trained to assess the nine problem areas described in this chapter. This prescription applies equally to companies doing their first offshore oil and gas project in a country as well as those working onshore. The country advance team provides critical information about the context for any project.

The country advance team should include marketing and sales, supply chain, purchasing and logistics, public relations and government affairs, and human resources. The country advance team should always have at least one experienced megaproject director on the team. It can be a great job for an experienced senior person who will retire within a year or two and cannot therefore take on a new major project.

An effective advance team will consist of 12 to 15 members, plus locals, who speak the language and can assist in introductions. *In most cases, the lead sponsor should not depend on a local partner to do this work.* A local partner may be very helpful in the process of investigating the context, but the local partner may not share the same objectives or concerns as the lead sponsor. The local sponsor may be anxious for the project to proceed whether or not it makes sense for other partners. *In far too many examples, the local partner lacked the needed expertise or objectivity to assess and weigh the issues.* The local partner may not know what to look for, especially if they have little megaproject experience.

Sometimes a sponsor makes the classic mistake of relying on their FEED contractor to supply the needed expertise in the local setting. There are a number of reasons why contractor expertise cannot substitute. First, the contractor is usually brought on board far too late in the project's evolution to be discovering how much of a mess you are getting into. Second, the contractor looks at projects from a distinctly different viewpoint than an owner. The contractor's focus will be on

[3]The need for an advance team is equally pressing if the project is in a new region of a large country, for example, the United States, Russia, China, Brazil, and so on. Local governments are routinely very important in geographically large countries.

execution issues, while the sponsor's focus needs to be on whether the project is a good idea at all. Finally, contractors and owners have different interests, and to put the contractor in this role is a conflict of interest. Owners need to do this work.

1. The Physical Location

The physical location comes first, and the first question about the location is the weather. It is surprisingly difficult to take a proven technology and design and move it from a temperate climate to a harsh climate. This is true both onshore, where it should be obvious, and offshore, where sometimes it is not. For example, the first projects executed west of Shetlands off the United Kingdom encountered ocean conditions that battered one of the vessels almost to pieces, leaving it with a serviceable life of about half what was expected. For many process-type facilities, including liquefied natural gas (LNG), the ambient temperatures are extremely important and have a dramatic effect on facilities cost. Facilities designed for a very cold environment for the first time are very prone to high levels of cost growth because the difficulties both with the design and the construction have not been anticipated. Process projects being placed in very warm climates have to be able to deal with much greater cooling requirements than the "standard" design. Projects in or near desert areas will have to design for blowing fine sand, which is quite difficult. Four of our megaprojects failed only because they got the implications of the weather wrong and for no other reason. One failed because of the cold and three failed because of the heat! The weather may be obvious, but that doesn't make it easy.

The second element of the location is remoteness, which affects infrastructure, logistics, human resources, and the supply chain. If a site is remote or otherwise requires significant infrastructure development, the prize involved in the development of the project must be much larger than in nonremote locations. We call an onshore project remote if it is more than 93 miles from a population center and there is little or no project-related infrastructure at the location. For projects labeled "remote," the average distance from a population center was over 258 miles. Remoteness may change over time. The first or early projects in a location may be considered remote, but as experience and project supply chains develop around the site, the effects of location decline. Offshore, a project is considered remote if the project opens a new province. A project is considered semi-remote if it is among the first projects in an area and the infrastructure is still in development. About 23% of our sample projects were done in remote locations.

Very few petroleum refining and chemicals facilities are constructed in remote locations (<10%). Few petroleum offshore locations were considered remote (19%). Of course, for offshore projects, most construction is actually done in fabrication yards rather than on site anyway. But over 60% of mining projects were in remote locations. About the same percentage of pipeline projects had at least some portion in remote sites, and over two-thirds of the renewables power projects were in remote locations. About 30% of LNG project sites were remote.

Figure 6.1 shows the relationships between remoteness and key project outcomes. Remote projects fare less well on all five measures of project quality. They have much worse cost growth, averaging over 40% in real terms. And their cost-effectiveness is also materially worse. Remote projects achieved a success rate of less than one project in four, a result that probably does not surprise many project managers. Although the result does not quite reach statistical significance, semi-remote projects fared better than nonremote projects.

If being in a genuinely remote location is really difficult, and the paltry 23% of successful projects would support that, being in a more heavily populated area can also present some serious challenges. When you are close to population centers, projects are very visible and more likely to become politically difficult. Densely populated areas also create serious logistics problems because moving people and material in and out of the site is often difficult.

One of the very important changes since the first edition of this book is the improvement of operability in remote projects as a function of time. Two-thirds of remote megaprojects authorized in the first five years of this century were operability failures. There was marginal improvement in the second five-year period and dramatic improvement after that. Part of the explanation is the distribution of projects by industrial sector, but even taking that into account, the improvement has been substantial.

A project may need infrastructure additions whether or not it is remote. In fact, we know one example of a project in a nonremote

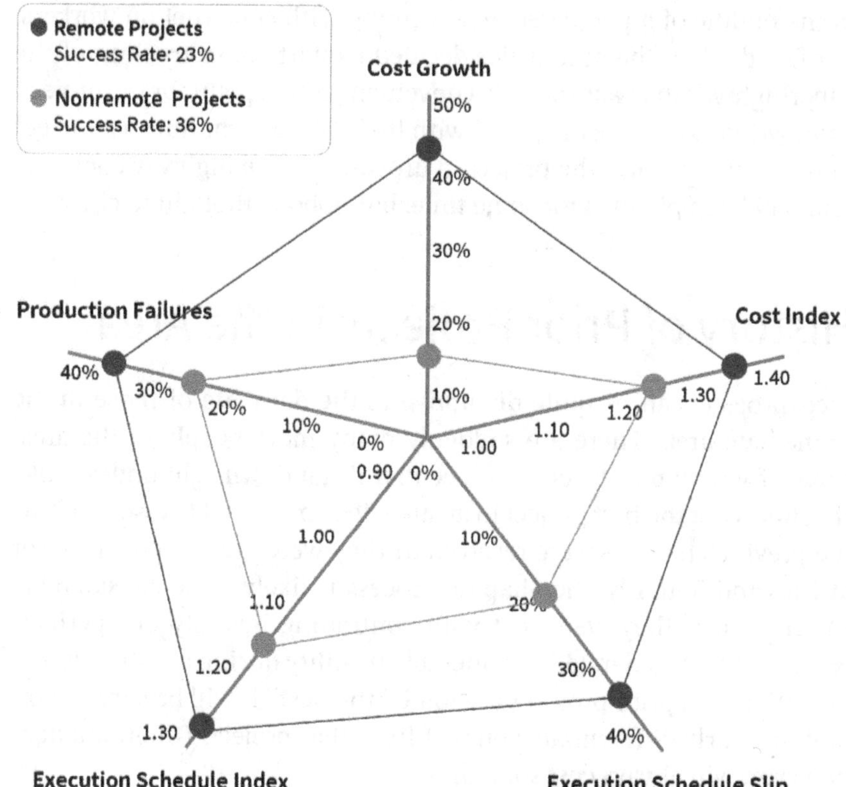

FIGURE 6.1 Remote Projects Suffer Worse Outcomes

location that will require at least $8 billion in infrastructure additions. When substantial additions must be made to infrastructure for a project to be practicable, substantial new risks are added. If the infrastructure being added serves only the project, the project usually pays the cost. However, paying the cost does not always translate into controlling the infrastructure projects. If the infrastructure will be used by others and over a long period of time, the central or local government may be responsible for paying the cost and often for controlling the infrastructure project. This now means that your project is dependent on the timely and successful completion of a third party's project. Consider this a major risk because governments are notorious for being late with projects and there isn't a great deal you can do about it.

Not being in a remote location should not encourage complacency, even about a simple thing such as access. One of our failed projects was in the middle of a populated area teeming with construction workers, but failed when the authorities decided to start reconstruction of the superhighway that was the only convenient access point for the project. Craft workers became disgusted with their 60- to 90-minute wait to get into the site and quit the project in droves. Yes, the highway construction had been planned for some time, but nobody thought to check.

History of Prior Projects in the Area

Megaprojects can be quite disruptive to the daily life of those in the immediate area. There are suddenly many more people in the area, some of whom may be deemed peculiar if not downright undesirable. If yours is not the first project in an area, it is important to discover how the previous projects were received. If they were greeted positively, or at least indifferently, the Shaping process is likely to be considerably easier than if they were met with continuing hostility or—perhaps worse—if they generated considerable hostility during construction or operation. If a prior project has "fouled the nest" it will be very important to clearly differentiate yourself from that project. Differentiation, however, will always cost something.

Understanding the local reaction to a new megaproject absolutely requires local presence and local presence for a substantial period of time, not just a few weeks. As a sponsor that may be bringing huge amounts of money to a local area, what you are told by the community boosters, who are often the first ones you meet, and what is true can be very different. Local presence is required.

The Nature and Perceived Value of the Physical Environment

If your project involves disruption to an area that is considered of substantial value from an environmental standpoint, be prepared for a long Shaping process that must be carefully orchestrated. Being in such an area does not necessarily doom the project. After all, the Chevron-led

Gorgon project in Western Australia built three LNG trains on Barrow Island, which is a nature preserve. That said, the Shaping process was long and tortured for the project. Key to success in such cases is to genuinely accept that the environmental value of the area will have to be carefully, if not fully, maintained. Remember that the environmental value of an area is always, to some extent, in the eyes of the beholder. Appreciating how the local population views the area is also not enough. How the area is viewed more broadly in the society is often what counts. In the United States, for example, many residents of Alaska strongly support opening the Arctic National Wildlife Refuge to oil and gas exploration and development. But national environmental groups almost uniformly oppose it.

Where prior projects have done considerable environmental damage, the Shaping road is likely to be a bumpy one. It is likely that a tightening of environmental regulations will take place or is under way. You can deal with tight regulations; dealing with changing regulations is a real problem.

2. The Political and Institutional Environment

The strength of the institutional environment is measured by the extent to which business in the country, including projects, is controlled by rules that are clear, codified, agreed to by all key players, and enforced by the appropriate authorities. One simple measure is the extent to which the political authorities are controlled by the rule of law. If laws can be bent or ignored to suit the wishes of those currently in power, the institutional framework that will surround your project is weak.

No institutional environment is perfectly predictable and under control. Officials can drag their feet on your requests or expedite them in the most rule-bound of societies as they see fit. However, if the institutional environment is weak, the Shaping process is both much more difficult *and much more important to the success* or failure of your project. One way of thinking about the Shaping process is that it is intended to shore up, from the project's perspective, those areas where the institutional environment does not provide much assistance. In a strong institutional environment, most stakeholders in your project will be bound by the institutional rules not to renege on promises they have made. Contracts have clear and enforceable meaning. In a weak institutional environment, players in your game have to be bound in non-institutional ways. Usually, this means they must be bound by self-interest to meet the commitments they have made.

Consideration of the political environment should inform the sponsor's basic strategy regarding investment in the country. The most important political consideration is whether the political authorities are controlled by the courts or vice versa. If the politicians control the courts, the value of the project is never fully secure at any point. The project will always depend on the sufferance of the political authorities and whether they see your presence as beneficial to their interests, which may or may not coincide with the country's national interests.

There are a number of ways that sponsors have tried to hedge or lay off political risks, but none of them are entirely satisfactory. As Exxon learned with its Chad experience, even World Bank involvement in the financing, which was seen as the gold standard of reducing country risks, doesn't always work.

Sponsors also need to remember the late U.S. House Speaker Tip O'Neil's admonition: "Politics is always local." It is not sufficient, in most cases, to have the central government on your side if local officials are not. As many a company moving into China has learned the hard way, the local mayor may be more important to your project's prospects than the premier in Beijing. Access to land, water, power, and people may be controlled locally, even in countries that appear to have strong central control.

Political instability is an obvious source of significant risk, and again, both the national and local levels need to be reviewed and understood. Political instability is not a problem confined to the so-called Third World. When a project becomes politically contentious, even orderly changes of political party in charge can spell serious trouble for the Shaping process or execution in the worst case. Even in orderly political climates, politicians will weigh whether killing your project will buy or cost votes. How one is treated may depend on where you are from, and therefore, how many votes you have. For example, in "resource-development-friendly" Queensland, Australia, the state premier had no trouble throwing a bone to Greenpeace by killing an oil shale development venture sponsored by Americans. Welcome to Queensland; now go home!

If there is substantial political opposition to a project, the greatest virtue is often patience. Trying to push forward in the face of serious opposition will be costly and usually ends up being futile. Smart companies will keep a constant eye on project opportunities in areas with political opposition because times do change.

3. Regulatory Climate and Stability

The regulatory climate is defined by whether the regulations are clear and strictly enforced. The regulatory climate in the State of California, for example, is widely viewed by industry as being very difficult. But from the viewpoint of planning a project, the climate is stable and reasonably predictable: it's going to be difficult. Problems are most likely to occur when the regulations are unclear or in transition. (Of course, if the regulations are not thoroughly investigated by the sponsor, they will be unclear.)

About one megaproject in five encounters a significant permitting problem. We define a *problem* as when one of the following occurs:

- A permit is seriously delayed or withheld such that it causes slippage in the overall schedule.
- Permitting requirements change repeatedly during front-end loading.
- Permits are made contingent on nonpermit related issues, such as allocation of ownership rights.
- Permits are withdrawn for nonpermit related reasons.

Although only 20% of our projects encountered such problems, those that did really suffered. Permitting problems were most common in Russia and the Caspian area. Nearly three-quarters of projects in that area encountered difficulty. Asian and African projects encountered more problems than average, while permitting problems were less common in North America (United States and Canada) and Western Europe. Permitting problems were almost nonexistent in the Middle East.[4] Permitting problems were also more common among

[4]This result may be affected by the fact that the governments in the Middle East were partial or complete owners of almost all the projects.

TABLE 6.1 When Permitting Problems Occur

Success Factor	No Permitting Problems	With Permitting Problems
Cost Overrun (%)	16	67
Execution Schedule Slip (%)	15	30
Serious Operability Problems (% of projects)	32	56

projects in remote areas; 40% of projects in remote areas suffered permitting problems, twice the overall average.

The effects of permitting problems are shown in Table 6.1 but with a caveat: in some of the cases in which permits were withheld, it is because the sponsor-investors did not understand the permitting requirements. Simply put, occasionally permitting problems were caused by sponsor sloppiness and nothing else.

Projects with permitting problems suffered crippling cost overruns. Some of these cost overruns can be attributed directly to the permitting problems, but a good deal of the overruns can be attributed to the problems that were only indirectly related to permitting. These projects were much more likely to have problematic relationships with the host government on a range of issues, not just permits per se. There were disputes over local content, contracting, importation of equipment, and movement of labor.

Permitting problems also correlate strongly with measures of corruption of government officials. Transparency International[5] has developed a measure of reputation called the Corruption Perceptions Index (CPI). The 2009 CPI for most countries of the world is shown in Figure 6.2. Every country is given a rating based on a series of surveys and the countries are divided into 10 groups. Low numbers indicate that corruption is perceived to be worse. We assigned the CPI value to our projects based on the CPI measured in the year of authorization of the project. The CPI correlates with permitting problems as well as

[5]See www.Transparency.org.

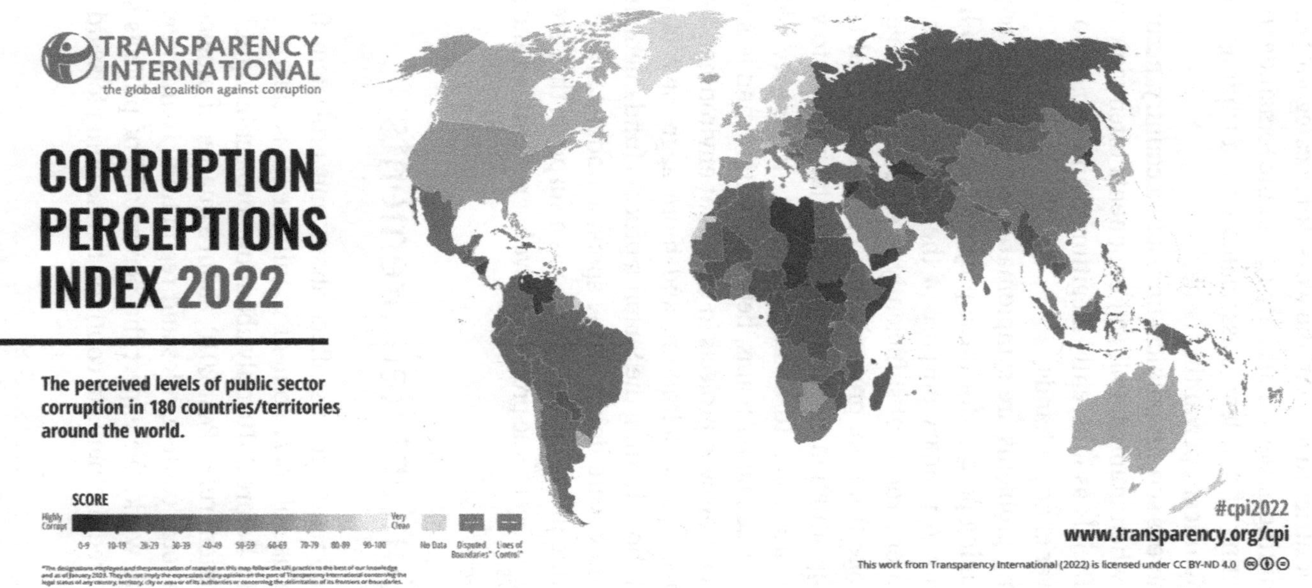

FIGURE 6.2 Corruption Perceptions Index © Transparency International

problems with the host government.[6] Even more starkly, 37% of the projects in countries that fall in the worst three categories experienced serious permitting issues versus only 12% in the remainder of the sample. A CPI rating of 3 or less is associated with a tripling of the probability of a significant permitting issue.

When there is serious political unrest in a country, permits may be at risk even when granted. Political opponents often view the actions of current officials as inherently illegitimate and subject to reversal if political power changes hands.

Permitting problems are symptomatic of a turbulent project context. The Shaping process for these projects can be said to have failed fundamentally. A primary purpose of the Shaping process is to calm the turbulent environment sufficiently to execute the project without serious damage from the project's environment. Careful attention to the permitting situation can alert the potential sponsor to what kinds of challenges are going to be faced. Projects to be executed in such environments need better teams, better definition, and less aggressive targets. In fact, however, projects in turbulent environments often had weaker teams, poorer definition, and more aggressive targets. This suggests that those leading the Shaping process fundamentally did not know what they were doing. If the sponsor understands the context well, permitting problems rarely come as a surprise; they are expected and strategies to overcome problems have been identified and executed.

Local Content Requirements

Local content requirements affect about one project in five in our sample. The use of local content requirements is clearly increasing. (Pr.|z|<.0001). Before 2010, only about one project in eight had to deal with local content rules. Post-2010, about a quarter of projects find that dealing with local content rules and regulations is an integral part of their Shaping work. We expect the percentage of projects subject to local content requirements to continue to rise going forward.

[6]Using logit regression, Pr>|z|<.02 for permitting problems and .0001 with problems with host government.

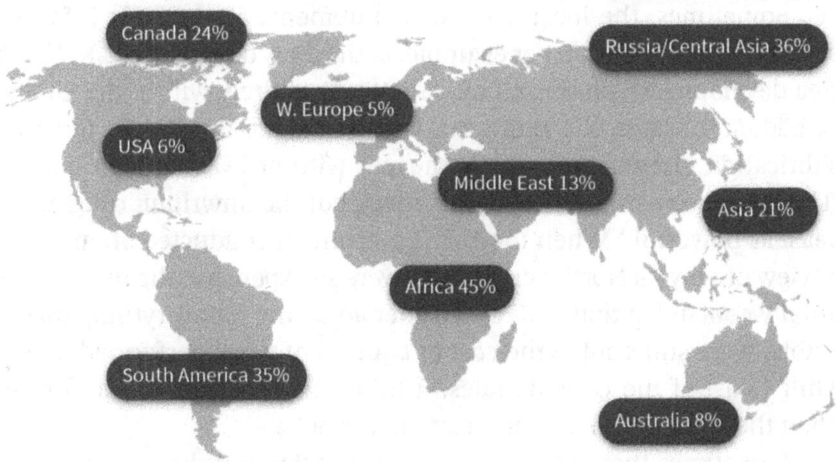

FIGURE 6.3 Percent of Projects with Local Content Issues in Shaping by Region

Virtually everywhere in the world where capital projects are executed, there are formal or informal requirements that some portion of the procurement for the project will come from local vendors, contractors, craft laborers, or whatever. No country is exempt from these practices no matter how vehement their protestations of being adherents to free open market principles. For example, in the U.S. Gulf of Mexico, only U.S. flag carriers are allowed to operate in the offshore oil fields.

Figure 6.3 shows the frequency of local content related Shaping problems by area of the world. Local content is least prominent as a Shaping problem in Western Europe, the United States, and Australia, although when it does create problems in Australia, they tend to be big problems. Local content issues are most common in Africa, Russia/Central Asia, and South America. The frequency of problems in Canada, Asia, and the Middle East falls between those two groups.

When local content issues arise in Shaping, they are associated with poorer project outcomes everywhere in the world except Russia and Central Asia. Project outcomes are so poor on average in Russia and Central Asia that local content issues are lost in the noise.[7]

[7]Project outcomes in the region are, on average, the worst in the world. The projects average cost index is 1.50, schedule slip averages 33%, and cost growth averages 47%.

Sometimes, the local content requirements are entirely informal but very consequential. For example, in the early days of the U.K. North Sea development, platform fabrication was entirely within the United Kingdom, or later, the European Union, despite the simple fact that fabrication elsewhere is much cheaper with at least as high quality. There are no written rules to that effect, but the unwritten rules are at least as powerful.[8] When the U.K. government conducted an in-depth review of why its North Sea projects were so expensive, the researchers finally concluded that U.K. costs, after adjusting for everything imaginable, were still double the cost of equivalent work performed on the Gulf Coast of the United States.[9] I think they had to look no further than the closed market to understand the delta.

Sometimes there are no local content rules, but the actions of the government authorities have the same effect. For example, in Alberta, Canada, there are no requirements for the use of only Canadian craft labor. Actually getting foreign workers into the country is so sufficiently difficult that very few projects have even tried. For some projects, the financing approach includes purchase requirements, such as when government credit facilities are used.

In some countries, mostly in the developing world, the local content requirements are formal, and that draws a lot of criticism from economists and international companies. The requirements are, of course, intended to encourage the development of local industry, and of course, tend to be politically popular in the host countries.

There is a great deal of misunderstanding about local content requirements beyond the pretense of developed nations that they do not have them. As most megaproject managers will attest, securing local content is often just plain good business. The local content is often less expensive than material procured in the world open market, and the use of local content is an important part of building a local supportive constituency for the project that pays dividends all the way through execution and into operation. Nonetheless, local content requirements are viewed very negatively by many sponsor-investors and are almost universally disliked by international contractors.

---

[8]Written rules would invite an unwanted challenge in the World Trade Organization.

[9]*Crine Report: Cost Reduction Initiative for the New Era*, United Kingdom Offshore Operators Association, Energy Institute, 1994.

The contractors' concerns are entirely understandable, especially on lump-sum contracts. The contractors feel they have very limited control over local suppliers, which are sometimes connected in murky ways to the government, but are nonetheless on the hook for both cost and schedule. Cost overruns come out of their pocket and there are often liquidated damages for delay. I have yet to see a contract in which there was an "out" in the event that local suppliers did not deliver on time with quality.

The quantitative effects local content requirements vary substantially depending on how the rules are written and implemented. The local content rules in large developed economies, such as the United States, United Kingdom, and Germany, tend to be little more than an annoyance to projects. The rules increase costs somewhat (if the costs were no higher the rules would be moot) without causing serious delays or quality problems. The large developed economies can supply what is needed; the issue is cost. The local content rules shrink the supplier side, but only modestly.

In small developed economies (e.g., Australia, Canada, and Norway), the local content rules have a dramatic effect on the cost of megaprojects simply because these are thin local markets to begin with. Developing an offshore oil or gas reservoir in Australia, controlling for reservoir characteristics and water depth, is about 75% more expensive than in the United States. That difference is not entirely due to local content rules; Australia is, in some respects, an isolated market as well. Developing large projects in Canada in any industrial sector is at least 20% more expensive than U.S. counterparts. The local content issues for Canadian megaprojects are particularly onerous in the maritime provinces. Those areas are economically disadvantaged and the federal and provincial governments often stipulate and then negotiate local content requirements on a project-by-project basis. This slows the Shaping phase of these projects substantially, and the local content provisions are often extremely difficult to meet in practice because the needed local industrial infrastructure does not exist. Project cancellations in the Maritimes after the negotiations have been completed, such as the Equinor cancellation of Bay du Nord, carry a heavy political cost.[10]

[10]See "Bay du Nord Bombshell: Equinor Pull-Back Puts Spotlight on the High Cost of E&P," *Upstream*, 7 June 2023.

Developing large oil and gas projects in Norway is about 40% more expensive than the U.S. Gulf Coast benchmarks after controlling for reservoir characteristics.[11] Norwegian local content requirements are mostly unwritten at this point. They are effectuated, however, through the Norwegian state petroleum company, Equinor, and through regulatory treatment when non-Norwegian sourcing is used when in-country equivalents are available. Every company operating in the Norwegian petroleum industry is aware of the situation, although few wish to discuss it on the record. There is little doubt, however, that Norway's local content initiatives have resulted in building a strong and effective local infrastructure for offshore projects.

4. Local Content Requirements Interact with Contracting Strategy

In the petroleum world, there is a strong preference among owners for EPC lump-sum (LS) contracting. Part of the reason for the preference is that owners want one contractor to be responsible for integrating design, various aspects of fabrication (hulls, topsides, risers, and flowlines), and installation. Most of the pieces of work are done by specialty contractors and fabrication yards, but the EPC firm does much of the knitting together of the project. Even if owners would prefer another contracting strategy, the host governments making the local content rules also often require EPC-LS contracting either as a matter of rule (e.g., Indonesia), or a matter of practicality (e.g., Nigeria, where each spending decision requires government approval down to a low level).

Local content requirements are often inconsistent with the needs of EPC-LS contracting. Local content requirements are viewed by potential EPC-LS bidders as risky unless the required levels are so low as to be easy to meet. When the level of in-country purchase is high relative to the country's industrial base, the contractors will add a substantial risk premium to their bids. For reasons that will

[11]The cost penalty in Norwegian offshore projects also results from required Norwegian standards as well as local content. But the delta versus the world open market is very substantial.

be discussed later in Chapter 13, contractors price risk at levels considerably higher than owners. Therefore, it is quite easy for a local content requirement to render a project uneconomic unless very high profits are anticipated, as is sometimes the case for oil developments. However, the effect of the local content requirements is to transfer value from the project and its stakeholders, which of course, includes the host government, to the winning contractor(s). In most cases, very little value is transferred to local suppliers and there is considerably less rent (surplus profit) available to the host government to receive in the form of royalties or taxes. Any attempt to have both high local content and high rates of royalties and taxes will result in no developments.

5. Percentage versus Prescriptive Local Content Rules

Local content requirements usually take one of two forms. The rules either stipulate a percentage of the total project cost that must be in-country, or they prescribe particular items or services that must be purchased in-country, for example "75% of FEED engineering costs, 50% of equipment and all bulk materials, etc." From the investing owner's perspective, the percentage buy formulation is greatly preferred. As long as the percentage is not so high as to be impracticable, the percentage buy provides a great deal of flexibility. But the percentage approach does not work well if the contracting strategy is EPC-LS because the bidding contractor firms still see the project as very risky. It is easier to accommodate a percentage of buy in-country in a mixed contracting form where local suppliers could be prime to the owner. But that, of course, creates a much larger project management challenge for that owner.

The prescriptive approach provides a number of problems for projects. First, the prescribed buy may simply not be available in-country. In some cases, this has caused project teams to redesign the project into a less efficient configuration that could be supplied in-country. In other cases, projects simply stop in the front-end until a solution is found or a compromise reached. Even more problematic, the prescriptive approach often ends up directing the contract to a single in-country contractor or set of contractors. In those cases, the contract terms can be largely dictated by the contractor rather than the owner. This sort of contracting problem is common in Nigeria and Malaysia, for example.

In Malaysia and Nigeria, local content is associated with a substantial cost premium (in excess of 30%) but a much larger time premium. Cycle times, which include the front-end time for working through the problems associated with local content, are on the order of 40% longer when local content is difficult to meet. It is not unusual for projects that would normally take four to five years elsewhere to take 8 to 10 years or more in Nigeria. Nigerian local content requirements are among the most prescriptive in the world.[12] There is very little doubt that onerous local content requirements and the associated problems contracting for project work have played a major role in Nigerian oil output falling from well over 2 million barrels per day at its peak to less than 1.2 million barrels per day in 2023. This has led to a budgetary crisis for the Nigerian government as foreign direct investment in the petroleum industry dried up. Nigeria finds itself unable to meet its OPEC production quota.

Brazil has imposed some form of local content requirements on the offshore petroleum industry for about 20 years. Unlike Nigeria and Malaysia, however, Brazil has used percentage requirements. While Petrobras had a monopoly on petroleum development, most of the local content rules were not formal government requirements but were worked through the government's ownership role in Petrobras, in much the same manner as Norway. As petroleum development was opened up to international firms, the local content rules became formal, but remained percentages rather than prescriptive. Sometimes the percentage requirements have been very high—65% is not uncommon.

In the early days of local content in Brazil, some very poor projects resulted from the imposition of local content requirements and a strong push by Petrobras to fully fabricate floating platforms in-country. Both the government and Petrobras realized that such outcomes achieved nobody's goals. As a company, Petrobras was striving for Brazilian energy independence. Local content requirements jeopardized that goal.

[12]See Gary Clyde Hufbauer et al., *Local Content Requirements: A Global Problem*, Peterson Institute for International Economics, 2013. Appendix 8A provides the detailed prescriptive requirements for oil industry projects in Nigeria. Virtually every aspect of the work is covered by prescriptive mandates.

Later, Brazil tied local content requirements to particular field developments. In practice, the requirements have been negotiations rather than simple mandates. That has worked as one would expect: longer cycle times (about +35%) but almost no effect on cost—less than 5% and not statistically significant. By contrast, local content in Southeast Asia and West Africa has been associated with *much* higher costs—about +30%–35%. When one considers that the average new offshore project costs over $5 billion, a 35% penalty is a great deal of money.

Local content requirements continue to grow in popularity in developing economies with significant numbers of large projects. Some countries in the Middle East, Saudi Arabia, and the Emirates, in particular, are pushing for higher local content in extractive industry projects. Projects in the Gulf Cooperation Council area have been generally competitive in cost using EPC-LS contracting strategies with large-scale importation of inexpensive labor from South Asia. I would safely predict that hard pushes for prescriptive local content will fundamentally change that competitive picture for the worse.

So, when you are exploring the project context, what aspects of local content requirements should worry you and what aspects should not? The answer depends, in part, on the relationship between the magnitude of the local content requirements and the current capabilities of the local industry. If the local markets are strong in the areas required by your project, local content requirements should not be a big concern. Second, it makes a great deal of difference if the local content requirements are specific and prescriptive rather than general percentages. The more exactly the local content requirements tell you what must be procured in-country, the more the business is being directed to specific firms in-country and they know it. These cases will trigger very sizable risk premiums in bids from international contractors for the work. Their concern is understandable: in these situations, the local suppliers are notorious for being late with low quality. When work is, in effect, guaranteed, one does not have to be good to be successful.[13]

Sometimes local content requirements are little more than vehicles to expedite bribery. There is over a full two-point difference in the CPI between countries that have formal local content requirements

[13]We will return to the issue of contractor risk premiums in Chapter 13 when we discuss contracting.

and those that do not.[14] The use of local "consultants" will satisfy the requirements, or in some cases, the local content requirements may not be enforced in exchange for "consideration." These situations are fraught with difficulty.

Your country advance team needs to be careful and nuanced as it assesses local content requirements and free of ideological bias. Yes, local content requirements can complicate the Shaping process and if not properly dealt with can cause projects to fail. However, the development of local industry is a normal and legitimate aspiration of governments. The danger in local content is worst when the rules are murky and enforced in seemingly random ways.

Local content can be a huge advantage for a project. Local content helps build support both short- and long-term for the project. Politicians who might be tempted to jeopardize your project will be much more careful if there is strong local support generated by a successful local content program.

But when local content rules are used to "create facts" by forcing the use of local contractors and suppliers regardless of their competence, the resulting megaprojects are often mega-catastrophes. It is very difficult to find instances in which this has worked. The problem is not the intent; the intent is entirely understandable. It may not even be that the problem is the form or approach that is taken, although it may be. The core problem is that there are too many ways in which local content rules can go wrong and be undermined without generating any significant degree of local industrial supply activity. If the local content involves a penalty for failure to meet the rules, the penalty will be paid because of the degree of angst that local content requirements create in the contractors.

6. Do Local Content Requirements Work? Are They a Good Idea?

The project cost and schedule penalties for stiff local content requirements are easy enough to quantify. The benefits are considerably more

[14]The mean CPI for countries with formal local content requirements is 5.1; it is 7.1 for countries without. Lower numbers indicate more perceived corruption. The difference is significantly different at less than 1 chance in 10,000 of being random using a z-score on a logit regression predicting formal local content requirements.

difficult to measure. In a few places with local content requirements, a sizeable local industry has developed to support capital projects. Nigeria, Malaysia, and Brazil are cases in which such an industry has developed. However, cause and effect are not entirely clear. Would the industrial capability have developed whether or not local content rules were in place? In the Brazilian case, for example, the most successful aspects of industrial infrastructure to support offshore projects are found in subsea facilities and in operational support. Neither have benefited much from local content requirements.

In some countries with long-standing local content requirements, such as Indonesia and Kazakhstan, it is very difficult to see any pay-off from the large project penalties incurred. I was recently working on a megaproject in Indonesia where the owner team concluded that local contractors could not even do the site preparation, one of the most basic project assignments.

I believe there is an implicit belief on the part of governments with local content programs that the requirements transfer wealth from the companies investing in the projects to the country and that the alternative is to allow very high foreign profits at local expense. That belief is simply mistaken. The resource holding country can reduce the profitability of projects to the point where the risk-weighted returns are just high enough to permit investment to continue through taxation and concessionary methods. If those mechanisms were tied to the global price of the commodities involved, those mechanisms would be considerably more efficient than local content at ensuring that the host country is not being fleeced.

Host governments should also remember that, in a good many respects, construction projects are not makers of a great many "good" jobs. Projects are temporary and involve surges and falls of employment. The best jobs developed by manufacturing and other industrial assets tend to be the operating positions and all of the businesses that support the operating facilities. Those jobs will be there as long as the facilities are operating, which is several times the years of project execution.

Economic development is clearly the responsibility of governments, and local content rules are seen as part of that remit. The issue is not one of legitimacy as free-market ideologues would argue; it is simply one of efficiency and effectiveness in achieving economic development goals. There are examples in our data of local content done well, by which I mean significant substantive development was promoted by the project and venture activities. However, the clearest examples were not a consequence of government-required mandates, but were a result of investor efforts to build community support for their project. Prescriptive requirements in particular create an enormous amount of disruption and added cost for projects with very little to show for it at the end of the day.

7. Social, Religious, and Cultural Considerations

Over the past 15 years or so, there has been a sharp focus by companies sponsoring megaprojects on not running afoul of cultural differences as they execute their projects. This awakening to cultural issues followed a series of notorious projects in Sub-Saharan Africa and Asia Pacific that justifiably damaged the reputations of both sponsors and contractors.

After reviewing the records of several hundred recent megaprojects, I am pleasantly surprised to say that this focus on understanding the importance of social and cultural differences appears to have paid off. Few in our project sample got into serious trouble in this area. Of course, this doesn't mean that we should not worry about such things. It simply means that when we pay attention, it makes a difference.

In some countries, Australia and Canada most notably, but some Andean nations as well, indigenous peoples have gained considerably more control of natural resources on their lands and access to their properties than has been historically the case. In effect, indigenous peoples in these cases have been able to gain stakeholder status on projects that affect them. Negotiation will be essential, and additional time to conduct Shaping of the projects will likely be necessary. The legal frameworks in which negotiation will occur are often unique to the particular indigenous group involved and will need to be thoroughly understood.[15]

The one area that was problematic for our projects was dealing with craft labor cultural and religious issues. The juxtaposition of imported

[15]See Ciaran O'Faircheallaigh, *Negotiations in the Indigenous World*, New York: Routledge, 2016.

and local labor caused serious difficulties in the field for some of the projects, particularly in Central Asia. In areas in which imported labor was the norm and expected (e.g., the Arabian Gulf area), there were relatively few issues. The combination of substantial amounts of relatively unskilled local labor with imported labor is a difficult mix to manage. It is also very difficult to have in-country national laborers who are managed at the foreman level and above by foreigners. Wherever possible, foremen should have the same ethnic, cultural, and national background as the labor they directly manage.

8. Local Labor Availability and Quality

When in-country labor is going to be used for construction, its availability and quality are one of the most important Shaping issues. These situations are usually ones in which the mass importation of labor is forbidden or actively discouraged by the host governments. This issue is so important that it should often prompt decisions not to proceed with projects or to proceed very carefully.

During the last decade, the megaprojects in northern Alberta, Canada, suffered from a thin labor market and found that even the slightest imperfections in their development and definition led to enormous problems. Thin labor markets are most damaging to megaprojects under two conditions: (1) the labor requirements for the project, and particularly, the labor peak were underestimated and (2) the schedules were too aggressive. These two conditions are not entirely unrelated: projects with resource-loaded schedules prior to authorization tended to get the labor requirements right, and generally had longer planned schedules than those without resource-loading. The projects in Alberta that suffered the worst overruns would have all underestimated the base labor requirements even if they had been in a benign labor market.

Megaprojects fail in a fairly small number of ways. One of those ways, however, is the downward labor productivity spiral. This occurs when engineering deliverables are late and/or incorrect, which in turn, causes field construction to fall behind and get out of sequence. When field management responds incorrectly, which is quite easy to do, a collapse of labor productivity results. Problems with the availability and quality of local labor almost always accompany this scenario. We will discuss this failure process in considerably more detail in Chapter 14 as we discuss project execution.

9. Competing Projects

Part of the context assessment should be real or likely projects that will compete for resources. Competing local projects exacerbate potential labor shortages previously discussed. One must be very cautious about assumptions that a neighboring project will provide labor for your project as it ramps down. Neighboring projects often slip.

The crucial engineering services component of megaprojects is a global, rather than local, marketplace. When that global market is overheated, as it was in the 2004–2009 period, megaprojects are more prone to fail, but the overheated market *does not cause* failure. Rather, the overheated market renders the project more sensitive to errors. The market increases fragility of the project, and if the Shapers of the project do not understand that, the projects fail.

Again, the competing projects themselves do not trigger failure; the root causes are found elsewhere. The competing projects render the projects more vulnerable to mistakes and errors of omission. When the global megaprojects market is hot, there is very little resiliency. Contractors will not have the personnel "on the bench" that can be brought in to help rescue a project experiencing difficulties. Similarly, sponsors usually find themselves understaffed in a hot market environment as they attempt to do too many large projects. As I write this in 2023, the global projects market is not particularly hot, but it nonetheless lacks resilience because major contractors in many parts of the world are suffering with demographic problems.

Once the context for the project is understood and its implications digested, one is ready to move on to the next steps in the process: making what will be the first of many economic assessments; understanding whether we have comparative advantage to do the project well; aligning all the stakeholders around the deal, that is, the allocation of project benefits; and finally, making the rules of the game with our investment partners so that things do not come unstuck later.

CHAPTER 7

The Next Steps—From Context Knowledge to Project Shape

In the previous chapter, I introduced the first step in the Shaping process—understanding the context. This chapter will cover the remaining four steps from assessing the project's potential value to establishing the governance.

Step 2: Assess the Potential Value

The Early Economic Assessment

The potential value of a project is the total net gains that could be developed as a product of the project if it goes forward and is developed and executed well. The potential value of the project should not be confused with the value that may accrue to your firm. Furthermore, the potential value should not be confused with just immediate short-term economic returns. For example, the number of short- and long-term jobs created by the project may be considered a prime benefit by the host governments, one of the critical stakeholders in most megaprojects. Downstream or secondary employment should also be assessed. In addition to the cash costs associated with the development of the project, social costs associated with the project should also be assessed as well. In other words, a full benefit-cost analysis of the venture should be developed.

There are a number of compelling reasons for a company considering a megaproject to do a comprehensive benefit/cost analysis early in the Shaping process:

- Megaprojects that survive the Shaping process to sanction will almost always appear to be very lucrative ventures at the start of the Shaping process. Projects that appear economically marginal at the outset are likely to look submarginal quite quickly and should be discarded from the portfolio.[1] Does the venture offer enough possible value to make it worth the effort?
- The Shaping process is all about the allocation of the project's value out to various claimants, also sometimes called stakeholders. If you do not understand the value that can be produced, you lose control of the process very quickly. If, for example, the government doubts the value of the project and you are in a position to counter with the number of primary and secondary jobs to be created, your bargaining position is much better. If environmental or other social cost objections are raised, you are in a position to respond. If you are going to be the lead sponsor of a complex megaproject, you must be in a position to control the conversation about the project's worth. If you surrender that position to another stakeholder, your interests will suffer.
- The potential value needs to be weighed against the assessment of the project environment. If the environment looks difficult, the project is not nearly as valuable as it may first appear. For example, if there are infrastructure requirements, the nonvalue-adding portion of the project's cost will balloon. If the geography is environmentally valuable and fragile, the costs will increase dramatically, and so on.

[1]Opportunities are rarely fully discarded from the portfolio. Instead, they are shelved. Capital portfolios often accumulate a good deal of debris that is very hard to dispose of.

- The potential value will also have to be weighed in light of the other stakeholders. If there are a large number of claimants on the project's value, there may not be enough left to justify proceeding.
- A thorough benefit-cost analysis strengthens the negotiating position of the lead sponsor enormously. When you come to the negotiating table with all the facts, when you can articulate the benefits that can flow to other stakeholders and honestly acknowledge their costs, you are much more likely to come out with a valuable result. Being surprised when opponents point out unacknowledged costs—and they will—is a good way to lose.

Making that first assessment of whether there is enough potential value to proceed is quite difficult. Our standard tools tend not to work well and good data are hard to come by. As discussed later, those facts alone will tend to create a positive bias in the assessment. When combined with the human psychological tendency toward optimism, some early assessment can, in retrospect, look positively naïve.

The first assessment of a project's potential value will reverberate throughout the life of the venture. If the initial assessment is unduly optimistic, which is the case most of the time, the echoes of that first assessment will always be negative. The element of the economic assessment that is most likely to be optimistic—often by breath-taking amounts—is the capital cost of the asset. Every veteran project director knows that when the first estimate is highly optimistic, one is fighting against perceived failure from the outset. When the first assessment is solid, it provides a meaningful backdrop against which to develop the asset and gauge one's success. An unduly optimistic first assessment often creates a dynamic of mistrust between the sponsoring business folks and the project leadership.

It's All about Capex, Stupid!

Of the factors that make up a potential value assessment, the one that tends to have the strongest optimistic bias is capital cost. Counting the benefits side of a project is intrinsically easier than the cost side. Product prices for most megaprojects are well established in markets. Yes, market prices can go up or down, but no project-specific information is needed to project the product revenue stream.

Why are initial capital cost assessments usually optimistic? There are a number of causes, some of which are present in projects of all sorts and some of which are peculiar to megaprojects.

The Missing Scope Problem

The most common reason that early capital cost estimates are low is that estimators cannot easily estimate what they cannot see. This problem bedevils projects large and small, but is more acute for complex projects. Large complex projects, in part by definition, tend to have more scope elements. It is more likely that one or more of the scope elements will not be identified and accounted for correctly in the estimate. It is more likely that the estimators involved have little or no experience with one or more of the scope elements, which often also means they have little or no data available.

For onshore megaprojects, the most commonly missed or underappreciated scope elements are infrastructure elements. Because details of the site and associated logistics are not fully known, the estimator makes assumptions about the infrastructure situation. Those assumptions often turn out to be incorrect. Remote sites, which are common in resource development and renewables megaprojects, offer particularly challenging situations. It is one thing to understand that a water supply will have to be provided, but securing rights to a *particular low-cost* water supply may not be forthcoming. At remote sites, every aspect of logistics may become part of the project's scope. Roads, port enhancements, rail infrastructure, and even airports can appear as essential elements of the project's work. Sometimes governments or other third parties promise to be responsible for those items, but that becomes another element of risk. Urban sites have their own infrastructure scope peculiarities. At urban sites, site access may require major transportation improvements in order to get community approval for the project. All of these infrastructure scope elements are potential sources of Shaping problems as infrastructure is usually political.

The Assessment Tools Problem

The most commonly used economic assessment tools for projects are *net present value* (NPV) and its close cousin *internal rate of return* (IRR). Both of these tools incorporate *time* into the assessment of a project's value. A basic tenet of economics is that a unit of product is more valuable today than tomorrow and *much* more valuable than the same unit of product 10 years from now. The amount by which a unit of product is said to decline in value is the *discount rate*. The discount rate is influenced by the cost of capital, which in turn, is related to prevailing interest rates. The cost of capital is not a single universal rate, but is influenced by the credit worthiness of a particular company.

The higher the discount rate, the more rapidly value declines as a function of time. Figure 7.1 shows how different discount rates affect value over time. Note how the value curve for the 15% discount rate has

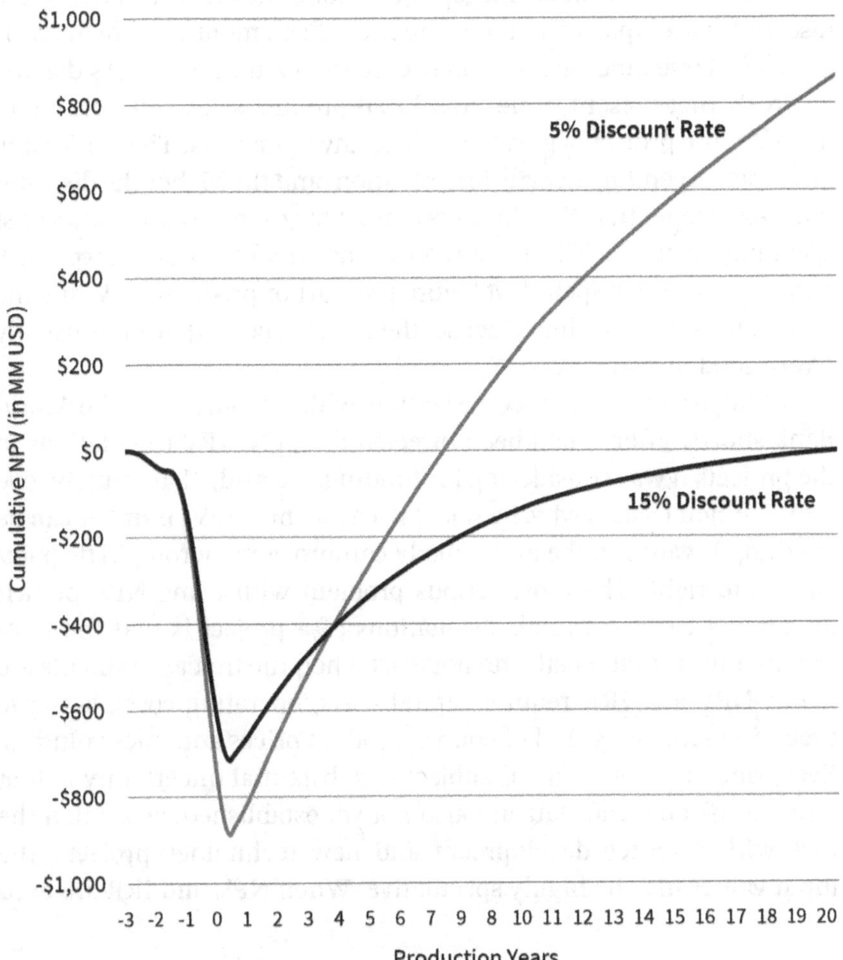

FIGURE 7.1 High Discount Rates Discourage Long Projects

a slower ascent than the 5% case. This is because the higher discount rate makes outyear product less valuable much faster than the 5% case. It is interesting that most government investments, many of which are multigenerational in character, typically use a much lower discount rate, often on the order of 3%, relative to private investments. If high social discount rates were employed, very few government projects could be economically justified.

One of the central characteristics of megaprojects is that they take a long time to develop and execute. They then tend to have a long period in which they make product, often 20 years or more. Their long execution durations make megaproject economics very sensitive to the discount rate employed in their valuation. Each month in which one is spending large amounts of money executing a megaproject is digging an "NPV [net present value] hole" that product sales will have to fill in before the project begins to produce any net profits. The earlier one has to start spending heavily for execution, and the higher the discount rate,[2] the deeper that NPV hole becomes. One of the arguments against spending money early is that it reduces the NPV of a project disproportionately to money spent just before the start of production. While the argument is true in a literal sense, the money spent up front is usually a very good investment.

I will never forget a conversation with an official at the World Bank shortly after it had been directed to apply NPV calculations to the projects it was considering for funding. He said, "I absolutely love NPV!" When I asked why, he said, "Because the [NPV] number can be anything I want it to be and nobody can prove me wrong." His point was quite right. The most serious problem with using NPV or IRR to conduct early economic evaluations of a project is that the tools require inputs that usually do not exist when the first assessments are made. NPV and IRR require capital costs, operating costs, accurate execution schedules, and of course, product prices and sales volumes. Every one of these inputs is subject to substantial uncertainty at first forecast. If the Basic Data are also not yet established, as is often the case with resource development and new technology projects, the input values may be highly speculative. When NPV and IRR are used

[2]The discount rate is the rate at which money becomes less valuable as a function of time.

for early economic assessments, the values of a great many of the inputs—sometimes all—have to be guessed.

This is the point at which human nature enters the equation: if one has to guess an input value, are we more likely to guess an optimistic number or a pessimistic number? Of course, an optimistic number is more likely. This is when my friend Bent Flyvbjerg will say, "Aha! Merrow finally agrees with me; the source of unrealistic cost and schedule projections is the optimism bias!"[3] But optimism is *not* the problem. Optimism around projects is a given and is actually essential to ever getting anything done.[4] The problem is the use of tools that provide far too much room in which optimism can operate. That problem, in turn, is a part of the larger governance problem that we will discuss in Chapter 15.

Consider Endowment and Context Together

Early economic assessments of projects, in general, and of megaprojects, in particular, need to be based on knowable inputs. Those knowable inputs are often *comparative rather than absolute.* Figure 7.2 illustrates this point. When taking a first look at the potential value of a megaproject, two key dimensions must be considered: (1) the size and nature of the "endowment," and (2) the ease or difficulty of the context.

The Endowment Dimension

The endowment is a primary driver of project value. In resource development projects, such as petroleum and mining, the endowment is described by the Basic Data package that often starts the project. The Basic Data answer questions such as: How big is the oil reservoir? The appraisal of the reservoir may be incomplete, but do the seismic data show complexity or simplicity? What is the quality of the oil? Do we

---

[3]See Bent Flyvbjerg, "Curbing Optimism Bias and Misrepresentation in Planning: Reference Class Forecasting in Practice," *European Planning Studies, 16*(1), January 2008.

[4]Note that optimism is a key element of high emotional intelligence; see Daniel Goleman, *Emotional Intelligence*, Random House Publishing Group, 10th Anniversary Edition, 2006.

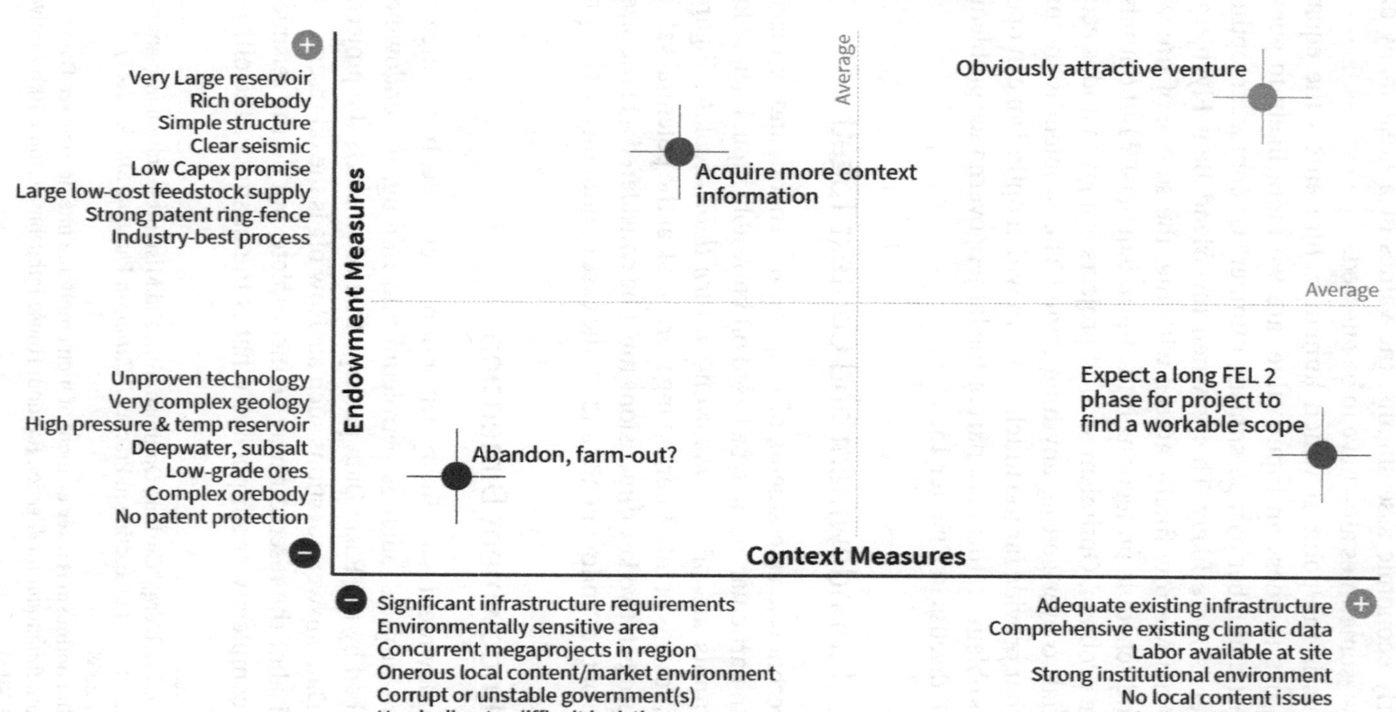

FIGURE 7.2 Endowment and Context Establish Approximate Value in Early Shaping

have good analogue reservoirs to use as a basis of comparison for recovery? For mining projects, the questions are similar: How large is the orebody? How rich is it? Note that all of the questions are actually comparative. *Large* is only meaningful as compared to other reservoirs and orebodies, and so on.

Standard bottom-up approaches to cost estimating, which will be essential later on, are of little or no value at this point. At this point in project evolution, if we ask a cost estimator to develop a standard estimate of the project, we are, in effect, asking the estimator to fake it, to imagine a concept and fill in so much missing information that the result may be unreliable in the extreme. Despite the thousand caveats that the good estimator puts on the number, if the number is treated as though it is the "real" and correct number, we are already on the path to failure. (We will address this problem of bogus cost estimates later.)

In nonresource development megaprojects such as chemicals or pharmaceuticals, the endowment questions are different. In a biofuels project, the endowment question may be: How good relative to competitors' situation is the feedstock position that we can secure for the project? In pharma, the endowment question may be: How large is our intellectual property (IP) (read: patent) lead over competitors for this product? In chemicals, the question may be: How much better is our proprietary technology versus the rest of the industry? In commodity chemicals, the cost of feedstock and any feedstock cost advantages that we can secure relative to others in the same market are key elements of the endowment. The endowment should always be considered in comparative terms because making or not making money is always a comparative issue. If your company makes 10% return on capital while your direct competitors average 15%, you are on your way out of business; that 5% gap will lead to shareholder flight and eventually to corporate collapse.

The Context Dimension

We have already discussed the context dimension for megaprojects in the previous chapter. Like the endowment dimension, context should be evaluated comparatively. The question is not "How difficult is it to develop an oil project in Nigeria?" but "How much more or less difficult it is to develop a project in Nigeria than elsewhere?" If a company has worked extensively in a region or has access to good benchmarking data, the cost of context can often be quantified in monetary terms.

The biggest challenge in considering the context portion of an early economic evaluation is getting decision-makers to take the context difficulty seriously. Business folks will often give great weight to the endowment dimension, but insist that a difficult context "just has to be worked." In fact, however, context is often more intractable than a low-grade orebody or technically difficult reservoir. Dealing with a corrupt government or an environmentally fragile site or lack of adequate infrastructure is often a challenge of the first order.

Referring again to Figure 7.2, where one's project sits in the two dimensions should be a guide to deciding whether to proceed with a project and whether to proceed aggressively or cautiously. Each area in the figure gives rise to different considerations when trying to decide whether the economics are sufficient to continue working on the opportunity.

The **northeast** and **southwest** corners *should* be easy decisions. Excellent endowment in an easy context demands to be pursued. The problem with the northeast corner is that it is rarely well populated. If it were, portfolio management would be a breeze. Weak endowment with a difficult context should be easy—don't do it! Either abandon the opportunity or "farm out" (i.e., sell it) to someone else to develop if you can. Surprisingly, quite a few southwest-corner projects actually get developed, and they almost always disappoint. Some business folks fall deeply in love with any opportunity. In a company with a thin portfolio, southwest-corner projects are more common simply due to desperation. In business-decentralized companies, southwest-corner projects happen more often because each regional business unit is strongly incentivized to try to survive, even if it is with poor projects. Even companies with reasonably disciplined portfolio management will often move southwest-corner projects into scope development because their gatekeeping is weak between business case development and scoping, or because business development cadres are incentivized on *numbers* of projects placed into scope development rather than *quality* of projects passed into scope development. The reality is that each southwest-corner project moved into scope development has some chance of moving to authorization even though it should have been killed or sold.

Most megaproject opportunities are found along the **middle diagonal**. They are large projects, but do not promise extraordinary returns. Industrial companies do these projects because they are necessary to maintaining market share and because, when completed, these projects can produce substantial free cash flow. The danger in middle-diagonal projects is that they generally offer little upside potential unless product prices move substantially and unexpectedly upward. In the same vein, middle-diagonal projects should not provide significant downside risk because the context is in the manageable range. Misjudging the context dimension can be very damaging. This occurred in a number of the chemicals megaprojects pursued on the Gulf Coast of the United States in the second decade of this century. Because all producers were looking at the same advantaged feedstock situation for ethane- and propane-derived petrochemicals, there was a stampede to start megaprojects. The resources needed to do the projects well did not exist, and many of them suffered large to massive overruns depending on how well or poorly managed they were. Only the few companies that got in early managed to make unusual profits because the rents were quickly eroded by everyone responding to the same signals.

The **southeast** corner is home to technically difficult in hospitable contexts. The reason that technically difficult projects are clustered here is simple: undertaking a technically very difficult project in a difficult context situation is viewed as a nonstarter by most sponsor companies. It is no surprise that offshore U.S. Gulf of Mexico has been the home of many innovations in the petroleum industry. The infrastructure for doing projects there is very strong, governments are cooperative, and both engineering and construction labor are reasonably plentiful. In chemicals, technically innovative projects done at the home base of the companies' R&D organization are much easier than trying to do a technically challenging project far from home.

The problem with these technically difficult projects is that they often have an incomplete Basic (technical) Data package, which will be discussed in depth in Chapter 9. The most important feature of technically difficult projects is that they require patience. Time is required to complete the Basic Data to an adequate degree. Time is required to find and perfect a workable scope for the project. Patience is always in short supply.

The **northwest** quadrant—great endowments in terrible places—features many of the biggest megaproject disasters in modern industrial history. Some of these projects have cost overruns in the tens of billions of dollars. For reasons of confidentiality (as well as decorum), I cannot name them, but readers familiar with projects in the petroleum and mining sectors will be able to list a few with ease. The failures are projects with excellent endowments in very problematic contexts. Sometimes the projects were very remote; sometimes, in environmentally fragile areas with intensive scrutiny; sometimes, in countries with corrupt or merely very chaotic governments.

Northwest-quadrant projects tend to be very large because the endowments are large and because many of these projects require extensive infrastructure development. The need for infrastructure development, in turn, requires that production must be very large to carry the infrastructure cost. The northwest-corner disasters should remind us all to take context issues seriously. In my experience, there is a pervasive tendency for business managements to underplay the importance of context, especially when the endowment prize appears big. Both ignorance and hubris are at work.

Finding the Right Economic Indicators

For industrial firms, overcapitalization is an economic millstone around the neck. If a firm spends more capital per increment of product than competitors, the company has to be significantly lower in operating costs than competitors or it is disadvantaged long term. Most operating cost advantage must derive from low feedstock costs in commodity projects because feedstock makes up the lion's share of operating cost in commodities.

By definition, megaprojects are major assets. Even for large companies, each megaproject adds a significant increment to the firm's capital base. Megaprojects are also, with few exceptions, long-life assets, typically 20 years or more. Asset size and life should guide the choice of early value indicators. In most cases, the indicator should point toward a competitive capital cost.

For resource-development projects, the size and quality of the reservoir or deposit form the key indicators on the endowment side.

Large petroleum reservoirs with average to good producibility promise low capex per barrel equivalent. If a reservoir is of moderate size, higher than average recovery needs to be indicated or the cost per barrel of oil equivalent (BOE) will be higher than average (holding context measures constant). For mining projects, a large orebody with average to better than average ore quality is the key endowment measure. The smaller the orebody, the higher the grade will have to be to make the endowment attractive.

For nonresource development megaprojects, the endowment dimension of the business case is less obvious, and therefore, in even greater need of scrutiny. The endowment may be an advantaged feedstock situation, which is the most common driver in commodity chemicals and petroleum refining because feedstock cost and capital cost are the two principal drivers of value in commodity chemicals and fuels. In specialty chemicals and pharmaceuticals, unique product characteristics and IP (e.g., patents) form the heart of the endowment dimension. In a few chemical product areas (e.g., titanium dioxide), the IP and know-how associated with manufacturing may form the endowment.

What is different about endowment in the nonresource projects is that the perceived endowment may not be independent of the context dimension. For example, a national oil company offers a discounted feedstock price for a petrochemical facility if built in-country, but the national government (of which the company is a part) is known for always trying to drive a "hard bargain." Now the presumed endowment and the context are inextricably linked and subject to a common mode failure. This is a real, not hypothetical, example and has been replayed many times.

An IP endowment such as a superior technology is a very concrete endowment. But it, too, may be subject to being linked with context. For example, if the government where a project would be placed is eager to misappropriate the technology, the context and endowment are again subject to a common mode failure.[5] When endowment and

[5]For example, see "Two Individuals and Company Found Guilty of Conspiracy to Sell Trade Secrets to Chinese Companies," U.S. Department of Justice press release, March 5, 2014. DuPont, the company victimized by the conspiracy, had previously announced and then abandoned plans to build a titanium dioxide plant in China using its best technology. Shortly after that decision was made, the "front" company was established to misappropriate the technology to China.

context are cross-linked in this fashion, risks are much higher, and a meaningful economic assessment of the possible venture is difficult to fashion.

How Much Potential Value Is There?

If the combination of endowment and context point to a valuable project, it is very likely that the project will happen, but the project may not end up being owned by the first company to identify and assess the potential asset. That will depend on whether the company has comparative advantage for the project and the needed skills to Shape the opportunity into a real project. When assessing potential value, a sponsor should have a process by which to challenge the accuracy of all input information and to challenge the realism of every assumption that has to be made. It is far easier to slow or stop the train now than it will be later when stopping will be disappointing to many and embarrassing for a well-placed few.

While assessing the project's value, you must also ask whether the project fits with basic corporate culture, commitments, and strategy. If it does not, you will probably fail in the Shaping process, and if you are unlucky enough to get the project sanctioned, it is likely to fail during execution.

Let me provide some real examples of disconnects between company policies and projects:

- Your company has a strong and deep safety culture, but your strategy to make the project sufficiently low cost is to have the locals with their terrible safety culture control the project.
- Your company is genuinely committed to Responsible Care®[6] or some other set of promises vis-à-vis environmental protection, but you would like to follow weaker local codes.

[6]Responsible Care is a program of the Chemical Manufacturers Association that promises to maintain the highest environmental standards regardless of location of facilities.

- Your business is built around a strong IP position, but you would like to put your flagship technology in a country that practices routine technology theft. In the last example, we saw something that is almost unknown in project circles; the project team rebelled against the business because a substantial portion of the team was convinced the project would destroy the global business by ceding their leading technology to competitors.
- You have set ambitious carbon abatement goals, but the project you are promoting will use an extraordinarily carbon heavy feedstock.

The company's geographical strategy may also be important. If your project is to be located in an area that had not been targeted for entry by the company, you have a problem that must be addressed immediately. Entering a new geography is a basic strategic decision for a company. It implies a major corporate commitment of money and leadership resources. If your proposed megaproject is not an outgrowth of the corporation's regional strategy, it will be very difficult to win support as the project moves toward authorization. Even worse, when the inevitable difficulties arise, you will not have easy access to additional corporate resources to push through the problems. If your project would expand a business from which the company is beginning to withdraw, you will likely encounter headwinds all the way. Even if the CEO supports your efforts on a project that is running counter to strategy, others will actively seek to undermine your progress by starving you for resources and withholding information whenever possible.

The potential value of a project at this first assessment point needs to be weighed against the challenges that will be associated with the Shaping process and the internal resources of the company sponsor. This is where comparative advantage, our next step in the Shaping process, is key.

A Note on NPV and Long-Life Assets

One of the drawbacks (I am sure many economists would call it a feature) of NPV and IRR as project evaluation tools is that long-life assets are discouraged by the valuation methodologies. NPV and IRR, especially if high discount rates[7] are used, strongly discourage investment in assets that take a long time to develop but produce for many years. What this means in practice is that very few long development/long-production assets will pass an NPV/IRR test.

An example of the NPV/IRR challenge is the Olympic Dam copper and uranium deposit in South Australia. Olympic Dam is the fourth largest copper deposit and largest known uranium deposit in the world. Both copper and uranium are key metals in the fight to limit climate change. After buying the company that owned Olympic Dam, BHP Billiton intended to develop a massive open pit mine that would have had a life of at least 60 years, probably far more. The NPV problem was that the deposit is under about .2 mile of overburden that would have taken a number of years to remove. Once removed, the deposit—which includes gold, silver, and rare earths as well as copper and uranium—would have been inexpensive and highly profitable to operate. But the time required to remove the overburden weighed down the NPV to the point that the project was rejected. A far less efficient underground mining scheme was adopted instead that will leave much of the deposit in the ground.

Step 3: Identify Comparative Advantage

One of my favorite questions to ask the business director on a megaproject is: "Why do you want to do this project?" "To make a lot of money" is a common but meaningless answer. Some megaprojects, usually at

[7]The discount rate is the percentage that money is to be devalued per year from any base year. A 10% discount rate would mean that a dollar earned a year from now is worth only 90 cents relative to a dollar earned today. The minimum required rate of return (discount rate) for a project to be authorized by a company is usually called the "hurdle rate." Companies often set the hurdle rate high to account for risk. The companies do not actually expect to make the hurdle rate on average, but believe it helps protect them from poor project results. A high hurdle rate, however, will often kill a megaproject because megaprojects are, by their nature, modest rate-of-return projects. A high hurdle rate will almost always kill off a megaproject with a long development time.

the smaller end of the spectrum, are extensions of normal business. The development of another oil reservoir in a province in which you are already active is an example. It does not mean, by the way, that the project will be easy, but (other things being equal) it should be easier than, say, opening in a new area. Many megaprojects, however, are path-breaking for the lead sponsor in at least some dimensions and sometimes in a number of ways at once.

When considering whether to entertain a path-breaking project, some key questions need to be addressed:

- Why is this project fundamentally better than alternatives? For example, does it provide an enduring low-cost basis for the product? How?
- If this is a new geography for the company and do we really want to be here for a long time? Is the long-term political outlook stable? Is there really enough enduring business or resource base to make the area interesting long term? For example, when planning the path-breaking petroleum project in Chad, I have to wonder whether the sponsors asked themselves these questions, and if they did, how they came up with affirmative answers.
- What are the characteristics of the eventual venture and project that will be important to success? For some projects, maintaining or developing a strong relationship with the local community is as important as correctly designing the project. Some projects depend on keeping a very low profile, while others are best served by prominence.

Unfortunately, in too many cases, the question of why the company wants to do this particular project in this particular place and at this particular time is never fully addressed. When we lack convincing reasons, we often label a project "strategic." *Strategic*, in this context, is another way of saying "we are going to lose money but we want to do it anyway." I was once in China evaluating a megaproject one of my Western clients wanted to do there. At the end of the first day with the business team, I could not see any way that the venture could turn a profit. When I said that, they immediately shot back, "This project is strategic!" So, I quizzed them about what that really meant, and it finally came down to this: "Yes, we may lose some money on this project, but the Chinese will be grateful and it will pay dividends later." That prompted two more two questions: (1) "Who exactly are 'the Chinese,' as it is a country of 1.5 billion people," and (2) "Are you aware of a single instance in 4,000 years of recorded Chinese history in which 'the Chinese' had been grateful to a bunch of Westerners for losing money in China?" They built the project; they lost money; they have never done another project in China. Too many "strategic" projects lead to bankruptcy.

Comparative Advantage Helps Define Business Objectives

Comparative advantage exists when a company can uniquely do something of value better than others and can hold that position over time. The key reason for defining comparative advantage is that it needs to be central to the business objectives for the project. If we gain comparative advantage with the project because the long-term prospects for business are excellent and we are in first in the market, then the objectives will need to mirror the permanent presence in the area by, for example, including objectives around community relations and community development. If comparative advantage is generated with low feedstock costs, the objectives must be consistent with maintaining a low cost of goods sold (COGS) throughout the supply chain for the project. Otherwise, the low-cost feedstock advantage will be lost in other areas. If comparative advantage is to be generated by being the first to develop in this geography, this will ultimately translate to a time objective for the business objectives and schedule objective for the project, and a larger program of projects will need to be planned to follow on from the first project to realize the full advantage. If comparative advantage flows from being a great manufacturing company, then manufacturing excellence needs to be reflected and nurtured in the project objectives.

Comparative advantage becomes the core of a bundle of business objectives that will ultimately translate to project objectives and into the complexion of the finished project. If you are not clear about what generates the comparative advantage, the business objectives will not

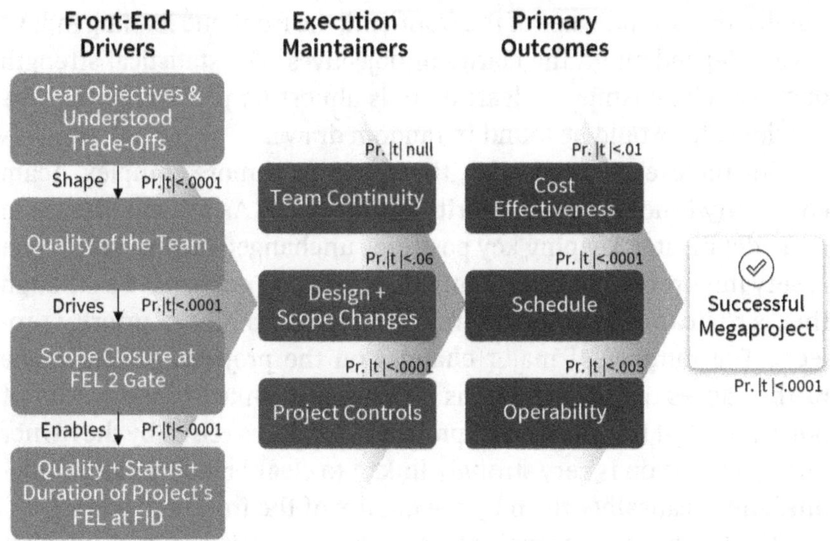

FIGURE 7.3 Clear Objectives Start the Causal Path to Success

reflect all that is important or the priorities among the many objectives that make up a project.

It is difficult to overstate the importance of clear and coherent business objectives to megaproject success. Figure 7.3 illustrates the relationships between clear objectives and the elements that engender project success in our megaprojects set. The probability measure above each box depicts the strength of the statistical relationship between clear business objectives and that element of the casual path to project success. Clear objectives drive the quality and completeness of the owner team during front-end loading. When the objectives are not clear, the owner team is missing one or more key people during the front-end 60% of the time. The missing functions mean that errors and omissions are very likely during the front-end work. When the objectives are clear, the percent of fully integrated teams jumps to 70%. Clarity of objectives and trade-offs also drives whether or not the scope is fully closed at the end of the scope development phase (FEL-2). This is not a surprising result; scope is developed as a direct response to the business objectives of the project. If those objectives are unclear, scope development is slow and difficult, and subject to repeated change.

Finally, the key indicator of the front-end, the front-end loading index,[8] is very dependent on the clarity of objectives. The statistical strength of these relationships is clear: there is almost no probability that the relationships would be found in random draws.

For the execution metrics, the situation is more complex. Team continuity is not driven by clarity of objectives. As we will discuss in more detail later, keeping key positions unchanged during the project is very important, but some companies often do not behave as though that is the case and transfer project directors to higher priority projects. The number of major changes on the projects, which is one of the causes of cost growth, is only weakly linked to the clarity of objectives. But the measure of project controls exercised by the owner during execution is very strongly linked to clear objectives and trade-offs, and is causally driven by the quality of the front-end work.[9]

The primary outcomes of cost effectiveness and cost growth, schedule effectiveness and schedule slip, and operational performance have varying strengths of relationship to clarity of objectives. Cost effectiveness and cost growth are reliably related to objectives, but the relationship would be considerably stronger if we excluded projects that set very conservative cost targets. Setting conservative cost targets is more common among megaprojects authorized after the commodities super-cycle of 2004–2009. (We discussed this phenomenon at some length in Chapter 4.) Schedule and schedule slip tie closely to clarity of objectives. Projects with clear objectives take less time to develop on the front-end and are executed faster as well. They experience, on average, 23% less execution slip. Clear objectives are related to asset production in the early years, but that relationship is somewhat mitigated by hidden errors in Basic Data. The role of Basic Data in project success and failure is discussed in Chapter 9. Finally, employing the same definition of *success* defined in Chapter 3, clear objectives and trade-offs are strongly associated with successful projects. The objectives set the table for success or failure most of the time.

[8]Front-end loading is the subject of Chapter 10.

[9]The quality of the front-end work creates the quantities baselines that are the prerequisites to effective controls.

The Business/Project Team Interface Requires Attention

Successful megaprojects require an extraordinary degree of trust, cooperation, and communication between the business sponsoring the project and the technical functions developing and executing the project. Too often, we encounter the precise opposite. Project team entreaties to fully understand what the business is trying to accomplish are treated as a challenge to business prerogatives. Requests for the economic model of the project are sometimes treated as a threat to confidentiality. And protests that the objectives appear blatantly conflictive are classed as whining. The all-too-frequent result is that project teams are attempting to meet business expectations they do not fully understand.

The interactions between the business and the core project team, especially the project director and direct reports, are critically important during the Shaping process. Too often the business professionals pursue the commercial aspects of the venture and the project team pursues the engineering aspects of the venture, and the two streams fail to align. The business leadership and project leadership need to be inseparable until the Shaping process can be closed and the scope development is complete. Good alignment means full and complete access to business information by the core project team, and project information by the core business team. It means models are shared, progress and setbacks are honestly shared, and at the end of the day, success is shared. It means that business director and project director report project progress and problems up the ladder together without any possibility of blame-shifting.

Team Development Depends on Clear Objectives

We must not overlook the psychological dimension to the relationship between clear business objectives and high-performance teams. If the objectives are unclear, the project leadership's task of building a strong team is hopeless. Figure 7.4 tells a stark story for our megaprojects. Almost all of the projects with the strongest teams were cases in which the objectives were clear. By contrast, poorly developed teams

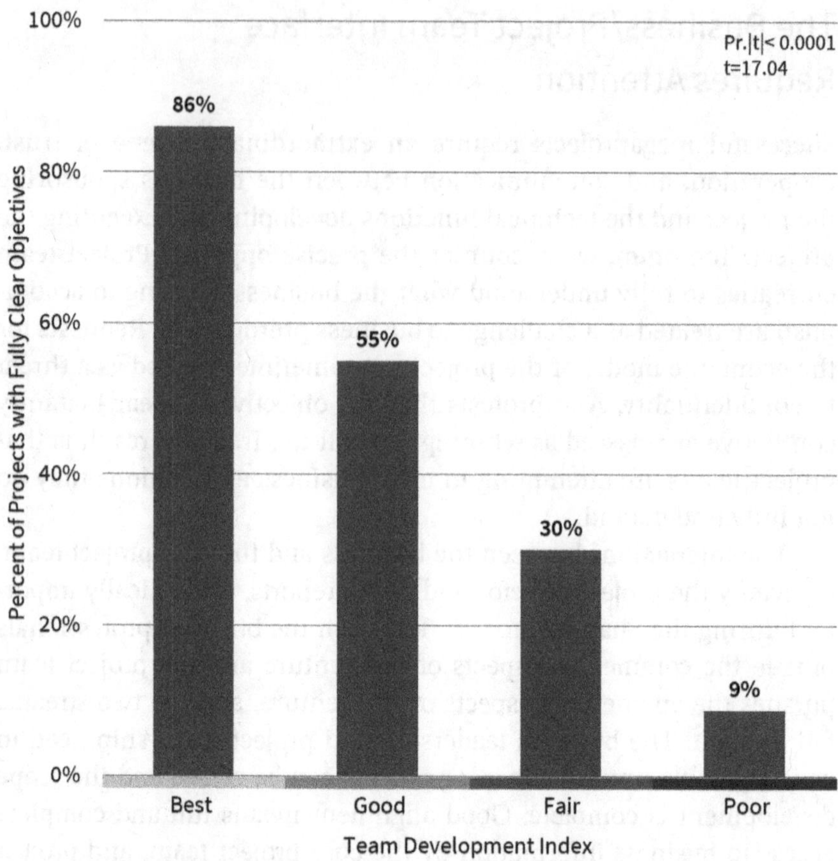

FIGURE 7.4 Clarity of Project Objectives Drives Team Quality

had unclear objectives almost 70% of the time.[10] When there was any fuzziness around the objectives, the chances of developing a strong team were very poor indeed.

We should be unsurprised by this result. Consider the situation from the prospective team member's point of view. I am being asked to spend a large portion of my career, move my house at least once, and possibly leave my family for several years, but the project leadership

[10]The TDI is a weighted index composed of the documentation of project objectives, team composition, a set of questions around assignment of roles and responsibilities to team members, and the availability of a structured and documented project work process.

can't even explain what the objectives are much less why I should consider them important! The relationship between clear goals and team effectiveness is echoed in virtually every study of team development. Of course, the exact same dynamic applies to the business team.

So, if comparative advantage gained via the project is understood and clear business objectives are communicated to the project team, then the next step in the Shaping process—identification of the stakeholders and defining the boundaries of the project—can proceed.

Step 4: Identify, Understand, and Align the Stakeholders

We define a *stakeholder* as any organization or person (in the odd case) that asserts an *enforceable* claim on some of the value of the project. Asserting a claim on the value of the project does not necessarily mean that a stakeholder is an owner in any normal sense of the word. When an environmentalist objects to a project's potential effects on the natural environment, they are, in effect, staking a claim on the value of the project. They want at least some of the project's value spent on mitigating the effects of the project on the environment. When a community group demands funding for a hospital from the project, they are doing the same. When a politician sees an avenue to winning more votes by increasing jobs or economic development via the project, the politician is claiming some of the value for themself. Even a public official demanding a bribe is a stakeholder, and like any other stakeholder, will have to be addressed, like it or not.

We define a *stakeholder* as a claimant on value because we see the Shaping process for a megaproject as a process of allocating value in a way that renders a project feasible. Stakeholders must be bought-in or bought-off. Either way, a piece of the value is allocated because nothing is free. Some stakeholders are unable to make a successful claim. Usually, that will be because they are not strong enough politically. However, the sponsors of a project need to understand that anyone who is affected negatively by a project is likely to assert a claim. Furthermore, we live in an age in which information moves so easily that claimants who would have had no voice in the past may be able to find that voice effectively today. The losers will attempt to widen the sphere of conflict until they either fail or create a winning coalition.[11]

It is generally much better to anticipate who the stakeholders are likely to be and devise one's approach to them early than to wait until they have developed into implacable opponents of the project. The failure to correctly identify those who will be negatively affected by a project can have tragic consequences, ranging from tens of thousands of cases of bilharzia around African rivers from dam impoundments to destroyed livelihoods in Papua New Guinea due to pollution.[12]

If any third-party projects will be needed for your project, be sure that the sponsors/responsible parties of that effort are included among the stakeholders for your project. Sometimes this will be local or central government bureaus responsible for infrastructure development, such as transportation, water supply, electric power, and the installation of the grid. Sometimes local universities will have a role in the development or certification of part of the scope. They, too, should be included in the mix. While it is tempting to try to put these players to the side, it is a mistake.

Getting all of the stakeholders identified early, and the size, strength, and realism of their claims evaluated in at least a preliminary way is essential to sponsor decision-making. Knowledge of the stakeholders will inform and guide their strategy toward Shaping the project. It may even cause sponsors to withdraw if they believe that the size of the prize cannot justify the number and size of the enforceable claims that are sure to be made. Sometimes the strategy will involve getting legislation passed that defines who is and who is not a stakeholder, or at least establishes a process in law by which claims can be pursued.[13]

---

[11]This process was described nicely in Elmer E. Schattschneider's *The Semi-Sovereign People*, Collier, 1962.

[12]See William R. Jobin, *Dams and Disease*, New York: Routledge, 1999; Richard T. Jackson, *Ok Tedi: The Pot of Gold*, University of Papua New Guinea, 1986.

[13]One prominent example of this route was passage of legislation in the United States that made the Supreme Court the court of original jurisdiction for suits opposing the construction of the Trans-Alaska Pipeline System, the megaproject that eventually carried oil from the North Slope to market.

Many of those making decisions that affect the success and failure of these projects are not acting out of a desire to make the project economically successful. In many cases, that is altogether appropriate behavior given their underlying goals. For example, in some cases (but certainly not all) environmentalists may aim to kill a project they believe is too damaging to the environment. Politicians may be interested in maximizing the number of local jobs and economic development at the expense of profitability. Project success is merely instrumental for them; whether sponsors make money is not their concern. In some cases, political opposition groups or even nongovernmental organization (NGO) interest groups may want a project to be canceled so the proceeds of the project will not be available to strengthen the government or provide an avenue for corruption. Nonsponsors often have entirely understandable goals that damage a project's value or even render the project economically unacceptable. That is why sponsors' decision-makers need to be very cognizant of the incentive structures of nonsponsor stakeholders.

In many democratic societies, it is often quite easy for groups and individuals to make claims on project value via the court system. Moreover, the lawsuits sometimes appear to be timed to cause significant monetary harm to the sponsors regardless of their merit. For example, a $12 billion gas development in Australia was recently halted by a suit brought by an indigenous individual claiming that seismic data acquisition would bring harm to whales. But this suit was brought *after* the completion and approval of the environmental plan for the project, which included a very extensive public comment period in which the objection could have been raised and adjudicated. Interestingly, the court halted the project, not because it found that whales would be harmed, but because the sponsor had "failed to consult" with the individual who brought the suit. This case and many others like it make clear the importance of sponsors actively finding potential stakeholders rather than waiting for claims to be made later.[14]

[14]Amanda Battersby, "Court Ruling Threatens Delay to $12 billion Australian LNG Project," *Upstream*, September 29, 2023.

A final concern: when there is a time constraint on getting the Shaping process completed, one of the stakeholders put that constraint in place for their benefit, not yours. Ask yourself who controls the rules by which this process will unfold? Obviously, to the greatest possible extent, you would like to make the rules, but often that is simply not possible. If you are playing someone else's game, then be sure you understand the rules and carefully assess whether your company can reasonably live with those rules. If your company culture is careful and systematic rather than daring and entrepreneurial, you may not be able to function in an environment in which break-neck speed in decision-making is going to be essential.

When Banks Are Stakeholders: Challenges of External Finance

Only about 5% of the megaprojects in our sample sought outside financing. Liquefied natural gas (LNG) production, chemicals, and pipeline projects are the most likely to be bank-financed. *There are no obvious links between bank financing and any project outcome.* This is not surprising when one observes that there is also no relationship between bank financing and any of the drivers of project excellence. Clarity of objectives and trade-offs among objectives are not clearer; front-end definition is no better; team development is no better; planned and actual controls are no better. Directionally, the quality of key drivers tends to be slightly poorer on a bank-financed project. The instance of EPC-lump-sum contracting is higher, but that is not a driver of success because, unbeknownst to many bankers, EPC-lump-sum contracting does not bear on the intrinsic riskiness of a project.

The null results for bank financing force one to the following conclusion: those doing due diligence for banks and lending syndicates for projects have no clue about what they are doing when it comes to seeking to ensure that the financed project will be completed on time and on budget, and will produce as planned. Those doing due diligence do not even insist that *planned* controls are sound, much less actual controls!

Early in the Shaping process, the lead sponsor needs to address the issue of where all this money will come from. If the lead sponsor *or any partner* will need to seek nonrecourse[15] bank financing, a new set of issues is introduced and these issues need to be addressed earlier rather than later.

If all of the sponsors have strong balance sheets, and one or more simply want to increase their gearing with the project, financing may be reasonably straightforward, although in my experience, it will still be late. If one or more of the sponsors have weak balance sheets, the inability to finance the project may be a killer, at least to that sponsor.

When the bank's guarantee of the loan is the project itself without the ability of the bank to attach other corporate assets (i.e., nonrecourse financing), then the bank will have a considerable say in how the project will be developed and executed. And that's the problem. In my experience, bankers know less about major capital projects than any other group of humans on the planet. Quite understandably, bankers seek to take on as little risk as possible when they lend money for a project. But their actual behavior often actually leads to higher costs without any corresponding decrease in project risk. Bankers will almost always seek to force EPC lump-sum contracting on the project, regardless of the contracting market situation, because they believe that a lump-sum contract actually imposes a ceiling on what the project will cost. Except in periods of very low demand for EPC services, attempted risk transfer on megaprojects via lump-sum contracting is expensive in terms of the bids received and ineffective in terms of risk actually transferred.

The banks do focus—as they should—on the cash flows that will be generated by the project. But they need to focus on the core elements of risk to project execution when they fund. Those risk elements that will be discussed are Basic Data reliability (discussed in Chapter 9), the owner's project team (discussed in Chapters 11 and 12), and project preparation (front-end loading), discussed in Chapter 10.

---

[15]*Nonrecourse* means that the lenders cannot seek to be repaid from the cash flow or balance sheets of the borrower, but will have to depend on the cash flow produced by the project to repay their loan. Recourse financing is based on the credit worthiness of the company, not that of the project.

Finally, financing usually is a very slow process. It takes the banks time to syndicate the loan, and there may be a good deal of negotiation about the details of the loan agreements. An agreement in principle between the sponsor(s) and the banks should be in place before Shaping closes. Once the project moves into FEL-3, the rate of spending will increase dramatically, and the funding to actually execute the project needs to be assured even though the first tranche will not occur until a year or more later.

Step 5: Getting Rules Straight with Partners

Having *partners*, defined as other formal sponsor-investors in the project, is a bit like having children: it is often rewarding, but only occasionally a lot of fun. Usually, your partners are one of the first elements you know. If you are partners in a petroleum field lease, for example, you knew your expected partners before the discovery well was drilled because you bid jointly on the lease. If the project involves working with a resource holder, such as a national company, you already know that the resource holder will be a critical partner in the venture. Before making even the most tentative decision about moving forward, some basic partner issues need to be addressed:

- What kind of partnership is this (probably) going to be? If you wish to be the lead or operating partner, do your partners accept you in that role? Do they get actively engaged in projects in which they are not the lead operator? Is this project big enough, prominent enough that they will require direct involvement this time? It is generally preferable to have a lead partner in a venture because it simplifies decision-making, at least a bit. The worst arrangement is to have three or more equal partners. Then decisions tend to get made by committee very slowly. A dual 50/50 partnership is workable as long as the companies are compatible in terms of project outlook, but again, it is best to have a clear lead sponsor.
- What does your partner want/need out of the project? Your partners *never* want *exactly* what you want. Partners can want all

sorts of things. If they are host government company partners, they may need a whole set of social objectives met by the project. How they will be met is likely to become an issue for the partnership. Private-sector partners also have mixed objectives, by which I mean things other than just money. For example, they may want to understand/acquire/steal your technological expertise. Is that going to be acceptable to you? Partners do not have to derive value from the same aspects of a project. But they have to derive value from the same result for the project. If they do, the goals are complementary; if they only get value from a different result, a collision is inevitable.

- Does your partner have an (equity) interest in a competing project or in a venture that will be a supplier to your project? This is a recurring problem in petroleum production projects, and we are seeing it in renewables projects as well as when one of the partners is pushing its technology. Your partner may own a production platform adjacent to your planned project into which production might be tied. Or your partner may own interests in adjacent fields that are competing for customers, which is a particular problem for natural gas projects. Your partner may own or have an interest in an engineering and construction firm that they want employed on the project. Conflicts of interest can abound!
- Who is the champion of the project within the partner organization? How well positioned are they? Are there opponents to the project within the partner organization? (If you don't know, start devising a strategy for finding out.)
- What are your partner's capabilities to assist in the project? This can be critically important if your resources are thin. But it can also be a source of enormous risk for the project if you are relying on the partner's resources and they turn out not to actually have the capabilities they have promised. This is very common problem with local partners who will "smooth the way with the host governments." When the relationship is just forming, it is easy to promise things that will be very difficult to deliver later on.
- What is your partner's approach to capital projects? It is compatible with yours? For example, do they have an approach to front-end

development and definition that is compatible with yours? Are they willing to pay for the FEL work that you insist is necessary for a successful project? Do they want to contract everything on an EPC lump-sum basis while you prefer reimbursable?

- Is your partner cash-flow constrained? Are they going to be able to fund their portion (including overruns) easily or will they need financing? Are they able to borrow from commercial banks?
- Is there balance and consistency among your role, your risks, and your potential returns and those of the partner?
- Finally, if your partner has a history in the country, how are they viewed by the host governments, and if relevant, by the will-be neighbors of your project? If their reputation is poor, you may want to either look elsewhere for a partner or get them as far in the background as possible.

Partners are supposed to be a way of laying off some of the risk on a project, not the source of added risk. When you can choose, choose wisely.

About one joint venture project in four has serious Shaping problems associated with JV partner misalignment. Partner misalignment is associated with significantly longer front-end durations (+4 months) and slip in front-end engineering design (FEED) (+10 months) and with slower execution (+14%). Getting the "rules of the road" sorted with partners early is clearly best practice.

At this point, you have as much information as you are likely going to get to devise your Shaping strategy. You have a good grasp of the context for the project. If all goes reasonably well, you have an understanding of how much value the project could produce overall. More importantly, you have a clear understanding of why this project is the right one for your company. All of the stakeholders who are claimants for some of the pie you want to bake have been identified, and you have learned as much about their motives and goals as possible. And finally, you have thought about your partners who will be investing in the effort with you.

Before we move on to Shaping strategies in the next chapter, I want to discuss the particular Shaping challenges in renewable energy projects.

Shaping Challenges in Renewable Energy Projects

As I sit here in North America in the fall of 2023, we are living through what may well become the most destructive year of weather in modern history. Fire and extreme cyclone events have become commonplace. Seawater temperatures in excess of 100°F (38°C) have been recorded in the U.S. Gulf of Mexico, and hurricanes intensify from Category 1 to Category 5 in a matter of hours. Only the lunatic fringe continues to deny that the climate is changing and that greenhouse gases have to be curbed if the process is going to be mitigated.

Virtually all of the 100 or so major industrial companies that IPA works with have recognized that they will have to play a role in the mitigation process or risk their social license to operate. This has led a number of companies to develop megaprojects in offshore wind, green and blue hydrogen (with or without a hydrogen carrier),[16] solar, low-carbon commodity chemicals, electrification of facilities and product transport, bio-based fuels, and even nuclear power projects. Every industrial sector except perhaps pharmaceuticals is engaged.

Companies are finding, to their chagrin, that "green" projects are not only not immune to Shaping problems, they are often subject to more severe Shaping problems than their prior megaprojects. An example can illustrate the challenges involved.

I am currently working with an owner seeking to develop a world-scale wind-to-green hydrogen-to-hydrogen carrier project. The following is the list of stakeholders and interested parties:

- Two owner companies: one, a majority owner, and the other, a minority owner that also brings an unproven but interesting technology that partner is seeking to promote
- Two national governments with very visible politicians involved directly trying to turn green energy into votes

[16]A hydrogen carrier is a chemical (such as ammonia) or a liquid organic hydrogen carrier (such as methylcyclohexane) that is used to make the hydrogen more easily transportable. Because gaseous hydrogen has very low density, it is perhaps the most difficult of all molecules to transport.

- A regional government that has local content goals
- A host of local governments and indigenous communities, all of which have local content wishes and demands; some are very supportive, and some are uneasy and potentially opposed
- Regional power companies that could play key roles in the economics for better or worse
- Financiers:
  - At least three import-export banks
  - A private banking syndicate that must be formed
- Potential off-takers (buyers) and their national governments that will have to provide subsidies in order to make the purchase economically justified as green hydrogen is currently uneconomic

All of these stakeholders have the potential to change the scope of the project at a time when the sponsors are working to freeze the scope so they can reasonably establish the capital and operating costs. Establishing those costs is essential to setting the prices for products because there is no established market price. That price will in turn govern the amount of the subsidies that will have to be negotiated by off-takers with their respective governments. And of course, buyers' commitments (off-take agreements) are a necessary condition to make lenders willing to provide the necessary finance. Many renewables projects will be similar to the preceding one: lots of moving parts in Shaping that require well-conceived strategies to succeed.[17] That is the subject of the next chapter.

Direct Government Involvement

Like the preceding example, a good many renewables projects involve government subsidies or other forms of direct government involvement in the venture to have any chance of success. Governments are always involved in megaprojects, but usually in the role of regulator, resource holder, or cheerleader rather than investor, lender, or guarantor. Looking across the full range of megaprojects, when governments

[17]Note that many of the Shaping challenges for renewables projects would disappear if effective carbon pricing were in place.

are directly involved, Shaping is usually long and extraordinarily messy. Whenever a government program is supporting a project, there are a host of requirements that would otherwise not be there. There are public notice requirements. There are waiting periods. Sometimes, there is even the need to appropriate the promised money for project support, which creates uncertainties about the economics that make planning difficult. Direct government involvement means delay, and often delay of entirely uncertain magnitude.

Ironically, when governments are involved, NIMBY[18] is a bigger problem rather than a smaller one. This is because government programs often carry greater citizen involvement requirements than the normal regulatory procedures. Being a green project does not provide much, if any, protection from NIMBY. Even the most environmentally conscious communities often object to even minor inconveniences. Opposition to offshore wind farms in eco-friendly Cape Cod, Massachusetts, in the United States is a great example.[19] In some countries, some groups of citizens, such as indigenous peoples in Canada and Australia, have special stakeholder status that amplifies their leverage as stakeholders in projects. Being a green project does not even ensure that environmentalists will not oppose the project!

Early Commitment Businesses

Some governments, especially in the European Union and United Kingdom, have set up renewables projects as reverse auction businesses in which commitments to undertake a project—usually a megaproject—have to be taken before any substantial definition work has been completed. These "early commitment" megaprojects are quite risky. The reverse auction process caps the upside of a project while providing no protection against the downside risks.

Reverse auctions may be a viable business model when the technologies that underpin the business are fully mature and when project

[18]"Not in My Back Yard."

[19]See, for one example among many, "Cape Cod Residents Voice Concerns on Offshore Wind Transmission Lines," *CommonWealth Journal of Politics, Ideas, and Civic Life*, June 26, 2023.

supply chains, logistics, and operating and maintenance costs are fully understood. But in offshore wind, the technology is evolving rapidly, the supply chain situation is risky (and increasingly concentrated), and operating costs are turning out to be considerably higher than expected. Taken together, these factors have caused major oil companies, which were expected to play leading roles in the development of offshore wind, to pull back. Even the previously established players in offshore wind are finding the Shaping challenges daunting.

Early commitment business models are difficult under the best of circumstances. The normal progression of a project from business opportunity through scope development on to FEED and full authorization is disrupted as an irrevocable business commitment must be made when scope development is still incomplete. That disruption causes a host of work process problems for projects, which have been adequately explored elsewhere.[20] In megaprojects, the out-of-normal sequence business commitment threatens more serious disruption because the Shaping process is rarely ready for the commitment to be made. As we discuss in the next chapter, Basic Data completion, Shaping closure, and the closure of project scope need to be synchronized to generate a successful project.

When industrial companies, mostly petroleum companies, venture into "green" renewable energy projects, they often treat those projects differently than other elements of their project portfolio. In doing so, they create additional risks that are unnecessary and certainly undesirable in projects that are already often low-returns projects. Rather than governing the projects in the usual way using stage-gate processes with required levels of definition at each gate, the projects are given dispensation from the rules. Those rules, as we will discuss, are the most important element of risk reduction in large complex projects.

[20]See Pamela Wertz, "Mitigating Risk of Early Commitment in New Energy Projects," *Journal of Petroleum Technology*, January 31, 2023.

CHAPTER 8

Devising the Shaping Strategy

If ya don't know where you're goin', you might end up some place else[1]

As I talk with business leaders of projects that have bogged down in the Shaping process, I am often struck by their saying things like, "We need to put together a game plan for getting this thing going." I think, but try not to say too often, how much easier it would have been if you had put that game plan together two years ago before the effort landed in this mess! The Shaping strategy is your "game plan" for getting this idea turned into a project with a real scope and ready to authorize.

Now, imagine yourself as the lead project executive on a megaproject that is just getting put together by your company. It's a first-time assignment for you and a big opportunity. You finally persuaded your frugal (read: cheap) boss to spend some money on the country advance team and they have given you a good reading on the project context. You have an idea of what this venture could be worth overall and a pretty clear idea of why you want to do it and what the business objectives will be. You have cast your net to understand who the players will be and you have resigned yourself to dealing with a difficult set of partners and other stakeholders.

[1]Attributed to Yogi Barra, American baseball player, coach, manager, and philosopher.

How do you lay out a process that will help everyone understand (1) where you are at any particular point in the development of the project, (2) what critical activities, decisions, commitments, or events have not happened, and (3) how all this should be synchronized with your usual project work process and with any Basic (technical) Data that have yet to be completed?

A good deal of what determines how clear the Shaping process is going to be is the strength of the institutional environment for business, in general, and capital projects, in particular. When the institutional context is very strong (e.g., petroleum development in the Norwegian or United Kingdom North Sea), what needs to be done to make one's way through the process is clear. That does *not* necessarily mean that the path will be easy. If your particular project poses unusual environmental risks, for example, the strong institutional environment may actually hurt your chances of getting the project approved. If your project falls outside permissible boundaries, the answer may well be a polite, but firm, "no." When institutional environments are weak, everything is negotiable. While that may appeal to the entrepreneur in you, it also poses real problems.

When I look out over the industrial projects landscape, it seems clear that Shaping is becoming progressively more difficult for large projects almost everywhere in the world. Climate change is one element of the increasing difficulty. Industrial projects, even green industrial projects, are viewed with considerable skepticism, especially by young people in advanced economies. Unless one can demonstrate that the project is part of the solution rather than part of the problem, there is likely to be nongovernmental organization (NGO) opposition.

Climate change concerns, however, are only part of the growing Shaping challenge. Local content requirements continue to ramp up in many developing countries. Too many of the local content programs are poorly designed, which will inflict substantial damage both to projects and the host countries. The rise of social media has made the formation of stakeholder coalitions considerably easier than in the past. When stakeholder coalitions form, they do so for the purpose of extracting a larger share of the value allocation for the coalition than the sum of the members could get by themselves. And social media have also made the rapid spread of misinformation and disinformation easy as well.

For project sponsors, these changes mean that smart Shaping strategies are more important than ever before.

Conceptualizing Shaping

The goals of Shaping are to arrive at a point in time when the following have been accomplished:

- All of the stakeholders—claimants on project value—are either content with their allocation from the project or have been rendered unimportant (i.e., they are no longer stakeholders).
- The project environment has thereby been stabilized sufficiently that you will not be fighting battles and skirmishes with disgruntled stakeholders while trying to execute the project.
- With these things accomplished, there is still sufficient value in the project for your firm that your board will ratify going forward without serious qualification.

There are several different ways of conceptualizing the process you will have to follow. My preference is to think about Shaping in terms of *the theory of games*.[2] The theory of games explores how value is allocated in situations requiring bargaining—negotiation. Game theory provides a mathematics of "strategic interaction." Strategic interaction is when the best course of action for me is dependent on what you decide and vice versa. All negotiation processes are strategic interactions. Game theory provides a taxonomy of types of games that describe different situations:

- A game against nature is against a random, nonrational, nonpurposive agent.
- A two-person zero-sum game is where any gain for Player A constitutes an equal loss for Player B. Some Shaping games are, in essence, two-person zero-sum games. When Greenpeace is implacably opposed to your project, they are playing a zero-sum game—a

[2]I have always felt that the use of the term *games* was somewhat unfortunate because the word tends to connote trivial pursuits. A better name might be *Theory of Strategic Bargaining*.

game of perfect opposition. Chess and checkers are two-person zero-sum games.

- There are also two-person collaborative games or mixed-conflict cooperation games, such as the famous prisoner's dilemma game.[3]
- Most Shaping situations are what the original developers of game theory, John von Neumann and Oskar Morgenstern, called n-person games.[4] These games involve the allocation of value out to three or more players, which we can simply call stakeholders.

In n-person games, coalitions of stakeholders can form. Coalitions will only form when a stakeholder can get a larger share of the value by cooperating with other shareholders because the combined group has more enforcement power than the sum of the coalition's members individually. A central concept of game theory is that coalitions can only form when that "greater than the sum of the parts" situation exists; this is called *coalitional rationality*. Game theory does not predict that a coalition will always actually form whenever coalitional rationality exists; there must be a flow of information between the stakeholders for that to happen. Sometimes even if information flow is adequate and coalitional rationality exists, a coalition does not form because the potential members of the coalition cannot agree on the allocation of value among themselves. This constitutes a game within the game.

A critical concept in n-person games is the notion of *the core*. The core of a game is the allocations of value out to the stakeholders

[3]See William Poundstone, *Prisoner's Dilemma*, Penguin Books, 1993. The prisoner's dilemma can be explained this way: two bank robbers who made the heist together are apprehended separately and put into separate cells with no communication possible. Both criminals understand that if they both refuse to cooperate with the police, they will end up going free because the evidence is not strong enough to convict them. But they also know that if the other robber turns state's evidence, that person will get a light sentence while the other will get a very long sentence. What is the rational thing to do? This simple game highlights a number of important points about situations (like Shaping) that involve both the potential for conflict and the potential for cooperation. It also makes clear how important communication among players is and the role of trust in negotiating situations. By the way, although it is often called a two-person game, the prisoner's dilemma is actually a three-person game: Robber 1, Robber 2, and the police.

[4]John von Neumann and Oskar Morgenstern, *The Theory of Games and Economic Behavior*, Princeton, NJ: Princeton University Press, 1953.

(players) such that no further coalitions can rationally form because no stakeholder can achieve more value by breaking away from their current coalition. In many games, there can be more than a single allocation of value that satisfies the conditions for the core. When a core allocation is achieved, the game is over. In other words, Shaping is complete. There are game situations, however, in which no core exists, and therefore, a stable result cannot be expected. When the core of a Shaping game is null, Shaping closure may be impossible without an imposed settlement from a powerful third party such as the government.

Now all of this may sound terribly theoretical, but the concepts are actually quite practical in their application to project Shaping. The formation of stakeholder coalitions is a very real issue for projects. A coalition of landowners, for example, seeking to get higher rents for crossing their land with a pipeline is much more powerful than an individual landowner in the usual case. It may be easy to circumvent an individual landowner holding out for a larger payment, but it is virtually impossible to circumvent the coalition. Sometimes environmental NGOs form coalitions to stop or modify a project. Sometimes the NGO coalition combines with local community members to oppose, which then can become a very powerful coalition of coalitions. The theory of games provides guidance on what coalition will form, which coalitions are likely to be stable (and therefore, more formidable), and even a method for assessing the bargaining power of different players.[5]

In the simple case with a strong institutional environment, a straightforward partner situation (including no partners), and no NGO opposition, the Shaping process can be viewed as a game against nature.[6] In a game against nature, there are no other players who are intent on either blocking you or taking some, or all, of your share of the spoils. In games against nature, the problems that you confront

[5]See the discussion of the "Shapley-Shubik Index of Power" in Morton D. Davis, *Game Theory*, Garden City, NY: Dover Publications, 1997, pp. 204ff.

[6]In game theory, a game against nature involves dealing with threats that are random in character rather than a game against (or with) intelligent and purposive players. There is no requirement that the players be rational in any normal sense of the word. In fact, sometimes being (or being seen to be) irrational is a considerable advantage. See Thomas C. Schelling's landmark, *Strategy of Conflict*, Harvard University Press, 1960.

are random, not purposive, that is, deliberately caused by others. For example, if you carefully follow the prescribed rules, you will receive your permits in a timely and predictable fashion subject to some variation. When you are playing games against nature, you should only fail in Shaping if you encounter very bad luck.

The most common megaprojects Shaped in a game against nature are petroleum development projects in areas with very strong institutional environments. For example, for petroleum development projects in the U.S. Gulf of Mexico and in most of the North Sea, allocation of ownership rights among partners rarely arises as an issue. Ownership rights, and usually the issue of who can be the lead operator, have been decided as part of the bidding process for leased blocks. When discoveries span more than one block, rules require unitization, which prevents disputes and inefficient developments. Although governments are the resource owners, they rarely exercise their ownership rights in the form of renegotiating the allocation of rewards, and in most cases, would find themselves blocked by the court systems if they attempted to make retroactive changes in provisions.

However, even contexts that are usually benign can be disrupted. For example, the U.S. Gulf of Mexico context became very turbulent and problematic in the wake of the Macondo disaster. The U.K. North Sea context has been made considerably more difficult by climate change politics. Even Conservative governments in the United Kingdom have pulled environmental permits to stop projects (e.g., Shell's Jackdaw Project prior to COP26 [2021 United Nations Climate Change Conference]) in an attempt to appear "green."

Sadly, many megaprojects for which Shaping was a game against nature did, in fact, fail. But they usually failed for reasons outside the Shaping process. For example, there were Basic Data errors, the project process was not followed, or the level of internal cooperation needed within the sponsor was not forthcoming.

In the more difficult (and interesting) cases, imagining oneself in a game against nature is a recipe for disaster. When a project has active opponents or partners vying for more and the allocation of project value is in play, the sponsors find themselves engaged in a set of often complex negotiations, complete with threats, promises, feints, and posturing. Mostly, the game is a mixed-conflict/cooperation game. Only occasionally will the game be zero-sum. A zero-sum game is one in which every gain for me is an equal loss for others; it is a pure conflict game. In some cases, Shaping is a zero-sum game against those who oppose the project under all circumstances. These may be unhappy neighbors opposing your project in their backyard. It may be environmental groups that see no way in which your project could be made acceptable.

If you are in a zero-sum game with strong, well-resourced opponents, the usual course is to try to transform the game into a cooperation game by making changes to the project that seek to accommodate opponents' concerns. If this is not possible and the opponents are strong, the size of the prize will have to be quite large for continuation of the effort to make sense. Sometimes you lose; it is best to recognize that situation early and withdraw gracefully. Game theory helps one understand when that situation pertains.

The most common scenario is one in which all of the stakeholders want the project to go forward under some circumstances, but the issue is what those circumstances should be.[7] When that is the case, you are playing a conflict-cooperation game. You are in a negotiating situation that may range from straightforward to very complex. In our experience, the key to success consists of creating an intellectual framework that is made up of milestones for commitments, kill criteria, closure criteria, and close coordination of project progress with the Shaping framework milestones.

The various sponsors and other stakeholders must agree about what constitutes progress toward a deal. It may be, for example, a formula that will govern pricing arrangements. Very often the government approval process is used to provide milestones for sponsors. The environmental permitting process often provides the milestones for the NGOs. Agreement in principle by the bank for syndication of loans may be a milestone for sponsors. For some projects, LNG, for example, sales agreements covering a certain portion of the output may signal a key milestone.

As the lead sponsor, you have to establish what needs to happen by when, and what the consequences will be if the date passes and nothing

[7]There are certainly instances in which some of the stakeholders do not want the project to go forward under any circumstances. That renders the Shaping game zero-sum vis-à-vis those stakeholders, and the goal may be to neutralize (defeat) them rather than placate.

has happened. It is in this context that careful alignment between the project's development and Shaping development is critical. The overall deal—that is, the allocation of value among all the stakeholders—must control the engineering scope of the project. If the scope development gets out in front of the Shaping development, it is very likely that the scope development work will turn out to be incorrect. As more and more project money is spent without a deal, the sponsors paying the bill will find themselves falling into the forward-going economics trap: we have invested so much in this thing that we can't turn back now.

A common ploy used by some resource holders trying to entice investor sponsors into development is to try to remove any decision-points in the development process until the full-funds sanction point. At that point, 3%–5% of eventual total cost may have been spent and another 10%–15% has been committed, some which would be lost if the venture is canceled. A large number of sponsor-investor people have been working on the project for many months and expectations may well have been formed in the financial community that the project will go forward. Withdrawing from the project at this point will likely be a serious embarrassment to the sponsor company. This tactic seeks to create a closure point for the Shaping process that is later than most stakeholder-investors would prefer. The tactic makes withdrawal from the project more expensive and therefore less likely. We have seen this tactic employed a number of times, but we have yet to see it work from the resource holder's point of view. The sponsor-investor either insists that an interim closure point be established or ends up withdrawing after FEED with all of the costs associated.

Kill Criteria

One of the questions I routinely ask of business leaders and project directors during the Shaping phase of a megaproject is what would cause them to pull the plug on the project. Even after years of receiving the answer, I am shocked when the response is "Nothing. This project is going forward!" Of course, part of this response is just cheerleading and bravado, but it also tells me that the sponsor has not carefully thought through what its minimum necessary conditions are for the project.

It really isn't a question of whether there *are* kill criteria for the project; there always are points beyond which no potential sponsor will go. The real question is whether you have worked through what the killer issues are and whether you have shared those with all members of your negotiating team.[8] To ever convey to other stakeholders that you will proceed no matter what sends a message that you are willing to take whatever they decide to leave you. That means the Shaping game will always yield less value for you than it should have.

Achieving Final Closure

Final closure occurs when the stakeholders are satisfied with the configuration of the deal and project and agree to proceed with final definition and execution. In game theory terms, one has found an imputation (outcome) that is in the core. The closure may or may not be accompanied by a signature ceremony or some other ritual. Except where the institutional environment is strong, a ceremony closing the Shaping phase is probably a good idea.

In weak institutional environments, reaching an enforceable closure point is often difficult. That is one of the reasons that weak institutional environments are inherently economically inefficient. The problem is not so much agreement, it is whether the agreement means anything. In some situations, as often in China, for example, a written agreement (i.e., a contract) is merely a document that defines the *minimum* that you will bring to the deal. The other side doesn't feel bound in the slightest, and because the institutional environment is weak, that piece of paper is only enforceable against you. Shaping games in weak institutional environment are less likely to have a core, and when the game does have a core, there are fewer allocations of value that are feasible.

A deal is only enforceable if the other side(s) believes that you will walk away if the agreement that has been reached is not honored. In several cases among the projects in our database, this has meant that

[8]The project professionals working on the development of the scope of the project must also be privy to this information. If you are communicating to all that the project will go forward "no matter what," that (lack of) position will leak to the other stakeholders.

the lead sponsor has halted all work on the project and demobilized its team in order to send the message that the failure to reach closure is not acceptable or that the breach of the closure agreement achieved will not pass. Some companies have developed enviable reputations for being willing to immediately walk away if there is any attempt to breach the closure agreement. For example, ExxonMobil's decision not to agree to the Venezuelan government's demand that they renegotiate the ownership and financial terms of the Cerro Negro "association" joint venture and to take Venezuela to court sends a message to others considering similar action with Exxon that a price will be paid. The more one develops a reputation for being willing to walk away, the less often the situations will arise. Some companies have developed reputations as vacillating and unsure, which means an attempt to get more at the last minute may well pay off. It is worth a lot to a company to develop a reputation as "saying what it means and meaning what it says" both verbally and in the contracts that it executes.[9]

When dealing with government stakeholders in weak institutional frameworks, the most important enforcement mechanism for closure agreements is reputation. A reputation for not abiding by agreements increases the risk profile of investment in the country and makes future investors demand higher returns. When Russian President Vladimir Putin used an environmental permit as pretext for forcing Royal Dutch Shell to relinquish a large portion of its equity in the Shakhalin-2 venture to Gazprom, he reminded every global investor that the institutional environment in Russia remains weak and investments are risky. When Hugo Chavez expropriated the heavy oil ventures in Venezuela, he thereby increased the cost to Venezuela of future investment. Because reputation is valuable to governments as well as private firms, the smart sponsor may wish to be sure that the closure of a deal for a venture and its terms are well publicized. By doing so, the cost to the other side of reneging is increased.

The theory of games provides a comprehensive intellectual framework in which the Shaping process can be seen. Within a game theoretic structure, a sponsor can develop a strategy for the Shaping process, complete with a series of moves, anticipated countermoves,

[9]I thank my friend Judge T. Rawles Jones, Jr., for that dictum about contracts.

and finally, closure of the game. The strategy may be progressive closure, locking in the value allocation of one stakeholder after another, or it may be a grand closure in which the deal is struck among all of the stakeholders at the same time.

Real Options: Another Way of Thinking about Shaping

Thinking about Shaping as a mixed-conflict/cooperation game and creating a framework and scenarios (moves) for playing the game is a strong and perhaps necessary way of thinking about megaproject Shaping. There is, however, an alternative or additional method borrowed from the world of finance: real options and real options analysis (ROA). It is not my purpose here to attempt a discourse on ROA, but I will briefly describe it and the reader can pursue study *ad libitum*. Unlike Miller and Olleros,[10] I doubt that a rigorous application of ROA is feasible or even the right approach to Shaping. I am suggesting that the core idea of real options captures some of the key elements in a successful Shaping process.

A real option is a right to do something or decide about something at a later point.[11] One has to pay for real options—nothing is free, and the point at which the option is to be exercised is defined—in our previous parlance, a milestone. ROA is an approach to valuation that explicitly treats and incorporates uncertainty and recognizes that uncertainty changes over time. Traditional valuation techniques such as net present value (NPV) and discounted cash-flow rate of return fix uncertainty for valuation purposes. ROA produces a tentative expected

[10]Roger Miller and Xavier Olleros, "Project Shaping as a Competitive Advantage," in Miller and Lessard, op. cit., pp. 109ff.

[11]The biggest difference between a real option and a financial option is that the latter can be traded while the former cannot. That is important because when something is traded in markets, its value is thereby assigned in the form of a price, which is publicly available. Valuation of a real option, which, by its nature, cannot be traded, is much more difficult and subjective. That means you can "overpay" for a real option and you can undervalue, and therefore, be unwilling to pay a "fair" price as well. Tradable options cost what they cost.

NPV but allows adjustment to one's view of project risk at each real option point.[12]

The appeal of this approach to making Shaping decisions should be obvious. It demands that we establish decision-points with the creation of options and it acknowledges that circumstances change as we progress. A project that looked excellent when we started may look quite anemic when that first option (milestone) comes due and our chances of securing our mining permit (or whatever) look bleak. Even better, ROA is all about buying information. An option, after all, is a statement that "I am not yet ready to decide; I need more information." As outlined right at the outset of this section, Shaping must be viewed in that context if it is to be successful. The key aspect of an option is its expiration date. The expiration date for a Shaping option is what I call a "kill point," and ultimately (we hope), a successful closure point.

I was recently in Manhattan meeting with a couple of investment bankers who were considering supporting a very large, new technology energy project. As we were discussing their decision-making process, I said, "It's like a real options exercise." To which one of them replied, "No, it *is* a real options exercise!" Even though ROA is not a commonplace notion for most industrial company personnel, it is a very powerful way of conceptualizing the Shaping process. It is worth the effort to learn it, especially if one is already well versed in finance.

When Should Shaping End?

The Shaping process comes to final closure when all of the stakeholders—investor sponsors, regulators, NGOs, local organizations, and governments—agree to the project proceeding as planned and outlined. There is no single document or activity that defines the end of Shaping in all cases. Sometimes it is a set of formal contracts. Sometimes it is a so-called "memorandum of understanding" (MOU). It could be a ceremonial handshake. What is critical for a successful closing of the Shaping process is that all stakeholders have a common understanding of what the closure means for them.

[12]There are many good books on ROA. My favorite is Lenos Trigeorgis, *Real Options*, Cambridge, MA: MIT Press, 1996.

Regardless of the activity that signals the end of Shaping, things may come unstuck later; the end of Shaping is not the end of risk, after all. However, usually the Shaping closure agreements do not come unstuck unless the project as outlined is not the project that eventually takes form. For example, if 10 months after Shaping is closed, the estimated cost of the project has risen 40%, the Shaping agreement may well dissolve. If the schedule has slipped two years or the environmental footprint is very different, some of the stakeholders may well feel cheated and will seek redress. For example, the schedule slip experienced by the massive Kashagan oil field development in Kazakhstan opened up the project's value allocation for renegotiation. This is why the last step of the Shaping process—synchronization with the project process—is so important.

Linking Opportunity Shaping with Project Development

While the business leadership has been busy fashioning this opportunity into a stable deal, the technical teams have been busy as well. One team or set of teams may have been busy developing the needed Basic Technical Data from the earliest days of the Shaping process. Another team or set of teams may have been working on developing the contours of the actual physical scope that will, if all goes well, constitute the project when it is complete. If the effort is being properly managed, all of these teams have been talking to each other very actively, and sharing progress and difficulties every step of the way.

The communication is necessary because the various processes at work affect each other. In complex partnership situations, it is common to withhold resources for the project side while bargaining for better value allocation on the Shaping side. Surprises from the Basic Data development may change the understanding of the project's potential value either up or down by large amounts. Vitally important, the project work process requires input about the business parameters of the project at certain times or the project work may need to stop or it will be working in quite the wrong direction. For example, if as a result of the Shaping activities, one of the partners sets a cap on the total

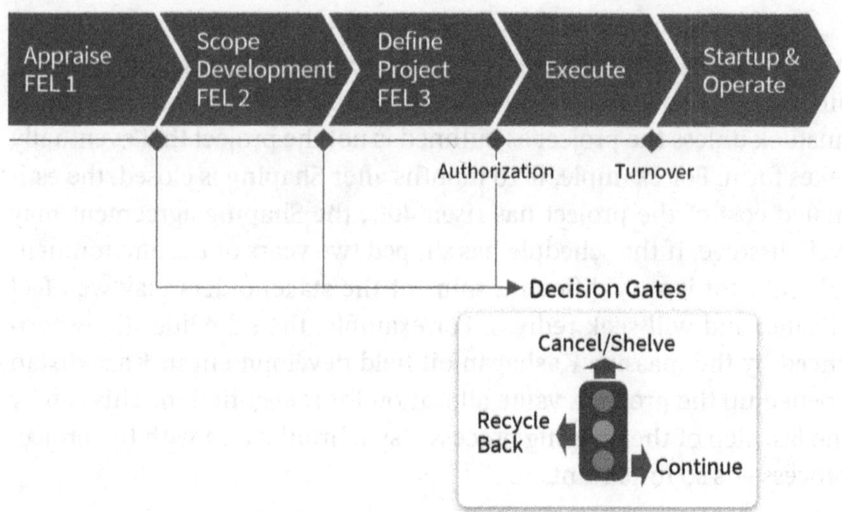

FIGURE 8.1 The Typical Phased and Gated Project Work Process

cost of the project due to financial limitations or other commitments, failing to inform the project team of this is borderline criminal—and it happens all the time.[13]

One of the things that is helpful in discussing the need to synchronize, and to some extent, integrate the Shaping and project work processes is that virtually all modern project systems are organized using a work process that consists of a series of stages with a set of defined products ("deliverables" as they are awkwardly called) at the end of each stage. The most common form of this process is shown in schematic form in Figure 8.1.

The phase prior to the first formal gate is spent trying to define the business opportunity and decide whether a capital project is the appropriate solution to the business need.

One should remember that projects are not the only way to acquire production and manufacturing capability. Merger and acquisition is an alternative; tolling of manufacturing is another alternative.

[13]I believe the reader will see the appeal of the real options approach to thinking about the Shaping process here. Uncertainties about the project are very dynamic during Shaping with the expected value of the project changing up and down multiple times. A traditional DCF IRR/NPV approach, which is inherently static in each assessment, fails to capture this important part of the process.

Occasionally, there is even an operating change that can meet a need that would otherwise consume capital. Often, a capital project solution is chosen before nonproject solutions are fully explored.

In well-managed systems, FEL-1 results in a business case package that reflects an assessment of the extent to which a business opportunity actually exists and whether a capital project is the appropriate vehicle for realizing that opportunity. As a typical project passes through Gate 1, a technical team is formed to start the assembly of a project scope that will meet the business requirement as defined in the Gate 1 package. Some of the Phase 1 activities are very similar to the overall Shaping process, but at a much-reduced scale for most nonmegaprojects.

Phase 2 is devoted to scope development. Provided that a business opportunity does, in fact, exist, Phase 2 is the most important stage in any project's development. If the scope development phase is working correctly, it will also make clear when a business opportunity does not, in fact, exist. At the end of scope development, if conducted appropriately, it is possible to generate a reliable cost estimate and schedule for the project. By *reliable*, we do not mean highly accurate. Rather, we mean an estimate with a *meaningful* range placed around that most likely value.[14] If the project looks attractive economically at the high end of the range, it will likely be approved to enter the third phase of front-end loading: detailed definition and execution planning.

Although Phase 3 is formally part of FEL and full-funds authorization of the project will not be granted until the end of this phase, projects, including megaprojects, are actually approved from a business standpoint at the end of FEL-2. If there is significant real cost growth between the nominal end of FEL-2 and the end of FEL-3, it is almost always due to FEL-2 being inadequate such that significant amounts of scope had not been identified and estimated. In that event, the FEL-2 phase has failed along with the gatekeeping that was supposed to prevent projects that are not fully defined in terms of scope from passing through to FEL-3.

FEL-3 (FEED/Feasibility) should take the completed scope and advance the design to a point that all piping and instrumentation

[14]We will return to this subject later and attempt to sort out some of the endemic confusion about this topic.

diagrams (P&IDs) and electrical single-lines are complete. It is during this phase that the execution plan, which was only sketched out at a high level during FEL-2, is brought to completion.

Every lead sponsor of every project examined in this study had a work process similar to the one very briefly outlined earlier. That is not to say that every project *followed* such a process, and relatively few of the projects followed the previous process in a way that IPA would describe as best practice. This just underscores the reality that no work process or business system creates advantage; only the disciplined execution of the work process creates advantage. We will return to this subject in detail in Chapter 10.

The synchronization of the Shaping process with the project work process should ideally proceed in the following way:

- The Shaping framework—which the lead business executive for the project has developed with the advice and counsel of all participants, including the country team, the core technical teams, and the corporate management—establishes a set of decision-points, milestones, or options points (as you prefer) as discussed earlier in the chapter.
- The business and project core team agree on how far the project work will be allowed to advance versus each milestone. The usual problem is that the Shaping progress lags the project progress, not vice versa. However, either one is a problem.
- The contours of the overall deal need to be available to the core project team when it starts its work on Phase 2, Scope Development. Both financial and time constraints need to be articulated. Artificial time constraints are particularly important because they may render the project undoable or doom it to failure. We will come back to this issue shortly. The contours of the deal then should Shape the scope development process.
- The closure of Shaping should coincide with the completion of the scope development phase of the front-end loading. Until scope development is complete, Shaping closure should not be attempted because the cost of the project is still an unknown. Conversely, *until Shaping closes, FEL-3 should not commence.* Beginning FEL-3 (FEED, Feasibility, Define) before Shaping is closed will quickly

start to affect the relative positions of those involved in the Shaping process. For example, if there is an important government approval that was supposed to be granted to close Shaping and FEL-3 starts without it, the sponsor-investors are progressively disadvantaged in their negotiations with the government about that approval. They are progressively overcommitted.

- The closure of Shaping must also mark the start of *no further changes of scope*. This is necessary for both the business and project side. Significant changes coming from the project side jeopardize the finality of Shaping closure. Significant changes from the business side will cause the work in FEL-3 (FEED) to be seriously disrupted and its quality to decline. If major changes must occur either for business or project reasons after the closing of Shaping, the project is at risk, and unless it is materially slowed down at this point, it will surely fail.

The data clearly and strongly support the importance of bringing the business issues to closure in conjunction with the completion of FEL-2. Over 40% of our megaprojects had changes in business objective in FEL-3, which means that Shaping process had not closed. Only 22% of those projects ended up as successes at the end of the day.[15]

If one is thinking about Shaping in a real options context, it is critically important to understand that all flexibility in decision-making ends with Shaping closure. Shaping closure is when the option period expires and a final, and essentially, irreversible decision to move forward must made.

How Shaping Errors and Omissions Lead to Failure

Projects fail for reasons having nothing to do with Shaping, but not very often. Shaping errors and omissions are the most common root

[15]The difference in the rate of success is statistically significant at less than 1 chance in 10,000 based on the chi-square test.

cause of megaproject failure. These errors and omissions fall into four groups, with the last one being by far the most common:

- Failing to achieve full stakeholder alignment
- Ceding too much value to other stakeholders
- Failing to develop coherent objectives
- Setting impracticable cost, schedule, or quality trade-offs

We will discuss each of these in turn.

Failing to Achieve Full Stakeholder Alignment

When the Shaping process has not been properly articulated, projects can blow right through the appropriate closure point at the end of FEL-2 without alignment. Sometimes these projects die after FEL-3; sometimes, unfortunately, they are sanctioned. Lack of partner alignment on issues such as owner staffing, completeness of FEL-3 (FEED), contracting strategy, financing strategy, and schedule ultimately result in late cancellation of the project or project failure.

The failure to properly identify all of the stakeholders can result in late NGO intervention on environmental or other grounds. In some cases, the failure to identify a set of stakeholders can be tragic as, for example, there are serious illness ramifications for the local population of a project that were not identified and mitigated.[16] Sometimes there is a failure to identify the sponsors of "third-party projects" on which your project depends as stakeholders. In one recent example in the Middle East, a third-party project tied up a $5 billion investment for 18 months by being completed late. If the sponsors of the third-party project had been viewed as stakeholders in the larger effort, they would have either been fully incorporated into the project or the project would have been reconfigured to eliminate its dependence on the third-party project.

[16]A particularly sad example of this occurred in a hydroelectric project in Africa that accelerated the growth of a bacterium in the still water in the impoundment, which caused widespread blindness in the local population. The sponsors missed the effect because they failed to consult local health officials who were aware of the potential problem. The local population was not viewed as a stakeholder in this regard until enormous damage had been inflicted.

If there are disgruntled stakeholders in projects, government officials, either politicians or bureaucrats, are the most common. When political or bureaucratic stakeholders are not fully bought in to the Shaping of the project at the closure point, they have many ways to disrupt your progress. In a recent project in Central Asia, the government withheld a permit while wanting to renegotiate the allocation of value that had long been established by and agreed on with the sponsor-investors. The sponsor-investors finally shut down the entire project just prior to what would have been authorization and disbanded its team in order to bargain credibly with the reneging government. The government finally did relent and the project went forward, but the disruption caused by the shutdown, plus a late government change in the local content rules, generated massive overruns.

Ceding Too Much Value to Other Stakeholders

As previously discussed, the Shaping process has to balance the stability created in the project environment via value allocation with the value created to the sponsor-investors. If a stable project environment comes with too high a price, there is insufficient value left to the sponsor-investors to make a good investment. The analogy that I like to draw is that you are the host at a large dinner party. A beautiful roast of lamb is the centerpiece of the dinner, and you are very much looking forward to enjoying a nice portion of it yourself. Your guests, however, turn out to be a surprisingly hungry lot, and you find yourself cutting slice after slice, handing them along, until it is, at last, your turn . . . and only the bone remains.

If the running out of lamb were obvious, you could have tried cutting smaller portions. Or you might have simply said, “This isn't going to work.” Often times, however, the loss of value to you is insidious and will occur in ways you did not anticipate. Let me relate a classic example, which is also a case of local content run amok.

The owner project team had worked with an excellent contractor team to develop the scope of this technically difficult megaproject. The contractor had done an excellent job and brought a good deal of technology know-how to the project. Because the market was softening, the contractor offered an attractive lump-sum price to execute and start up the project. The host government, which was not an equity investor, but a royalty stakeholder, objected that it wanted a local contractor to have an opportunity to bid on the work. (The host government also made clear that the license extension and royalty relief the sponsor was looking for would depend on the local contractor winning. In other words, the government rigged the contest.)

So the project was put out to tender and two bids came back, one from the FEL contractor and the other from the local contractor. The local contractor's tender offer was abysmal. To quote from our close-out report on the project, [the local contractor's] "tendered design was unacceptable for both Health, Safety, and Environment (HSE) and operational reasons; it did not even comply with government regulations." And it was higher than the bid of the competent firm. Surprise! The local contractor received the award anyway and proceeded to completely foul up the project: 100% cost overrun, 18 months late to mechanical completion, and then it was an operations disaster. Now, you know this sort of thing does happen from time to time in the Third World. But . . . this particular example was in Scandinavia! The business executive who yielded on this critical issue had no idea that he had just given away more than the total value of the project.

Failing to Develop Coherent Objectives

Shaping is a process of successive approximations leading finally to a stable "platform" of stakeholders aligned around a set of understood and coherent objectives. Too often, the sponsor-investor's business leaders do not understand that the process of adjusting objectives must stop at some point. Again, the real options analysis conceptualization of the process is useful. At a *defined* point the option must be exercised or dropped. That point for projects is the end of scope development (FEL-2). The problem is that all too often objectives continue to be "improved." (This is one of many examples where business education and capital project effectiveness collide. "Dynamic adjustment of objectives to a changing business environment" sounds nice, but it isn't.) Large projects are, by their nature, clumsy. Once finally set in motion, they cannot respond rapidly to changes in direction and attempts to make them do so result in chaos.

Changes in objectives after the end of FEL-2 take many forms but are almost always problematic. One project, for example, increased the capacity of an LNG complex by about 10% just prior to sanction to take advantage of a strong LNG sales market. The change, which was to be made without significant change in design, used up all design margin in all the facilities. When it was discovered at startup that some of that design margin was needed, the facilities would not operate. The sponsor-investors have bled money profusely because all of the output was forward sold on take-or-pay/provide-or-pay contracts. Of the projects that made changes to business objectives during FEL-3, a stunning 82% failed. They were significantly poorer in every outcome dimension.[17]

Incurring Impracticable Cost, Schedule, or Quality Trade-Offs

One key product of the Shaping process is a constellation of expected results, among which are how much the project will cost, when it will be done, and how much product it will reliably produce over time. As everyone familiar with projects knows, these three outcomes—cost, schedule, and quality—can trade off against each other. The three outcomes actually constitute a fairly complex optimization problem. This optimization problem is complicated by several factors. The three outcomes do not trade smoothly. There are some regions[18] in which outcomes can be improved without effecting any trade, provided that practices are appropriate. More vexing to the decision-maker, the trade-off functions are uncertain, although far from entirely so. And finally, the trade-off functions are different for different projects and at different times. For example, the cost/schedule trade-off is clearly different as a function of market conditions for project inputs.

These targeted results are important because, together, they establish the expected direct economic value of the project. Obviously, the targets need to be established at points in which all three outcomes are, at least in principle, feasible, and taken together, will constitute a valuable outcome. Unfortunately, this is not always the case.

As discussed earlier in this chapter, discounted cash-flow rate of return (DCF rate of return) calculations are not particularly useful

[17]All differences were statistically significant at .01 or less.
[18]Regions in the sense of mathematical functions, not geography.

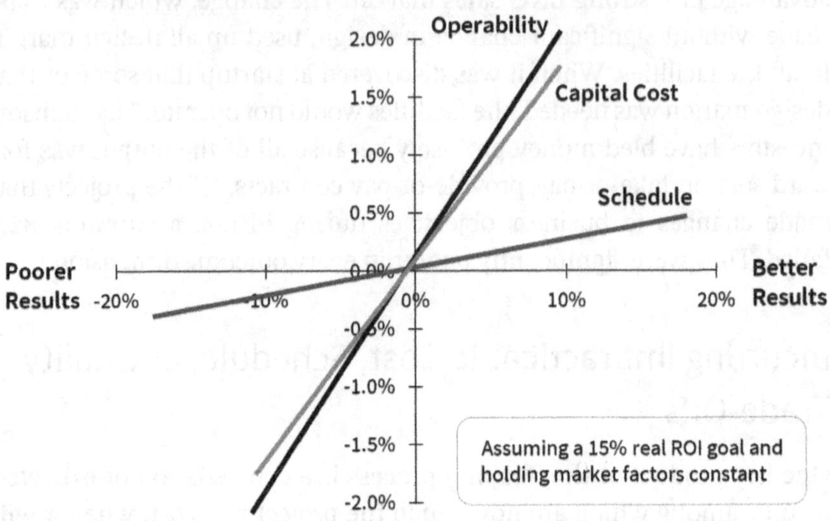

FIGURE 8.2 Sensitivity of Rate of Return to Changes in Capital Cost, Schedule, and Operability

during the Shaping process because it is a period in which uncertainty remains high and flexibility is essential. However, when we reach Shaping closure, DCF is useful because maintaining flexibility in the form of making changes has a very high price in megaprojects.[19] In Figure 8.2, you see the results of a standard DCF model in showing the relative effects of changes in capital cost, schedule, and operability (production).

We selected an inflation-free rate of return of 15% because that is about the average long-term return on capital for the commodity industries that do the sorts of megaprojects we are examining. Most of these firms calculate their cost of capital on a risk-free basis at between 9% for the very strongest to about 11% for the typical firm. If the return on investment realized falls below the cost of capital, shareholder

[19]The cost of changes after closure is reached in megaprojects appears much larger than for small projects. Because megaprojects have so many interconnected pieces, changes are very difficult to implement in an efficient way. In megaprojects, we also have the added problem that the Shaping agreement among the stakeholders can easily come apart if one of the stakeholder-investors wants to make a change.

wealth is being destroyed by the project. In other words, doing nothing would have been preferable to making the investment.

It is important to realize that most megaprojects are relatively low rate of return projects. By that I mean they typically aim to earn 4% to 8% over the cost of capital. There are exceptions, such as oil projects in countries, like the United States, with low royalty and tax regimes. In general, smaller projects have more potential to be high returns projects. They are more flexible, they can be completed faster, and they can be reconfigured more easily. The great business purpose of megaprojects is to produce large cash flows. Even though the returns are relatively low, the NPV is large because of the size of the investment. Cash flow from megaprojects funds smaller higher return projects.

Referring to Figure 8.2, you see that the most leveraging outcome is production. Production is actually even more leveraging than it appears here because we cannot easily parameterize the losses associated with higher maintenance and "fix-it" projects that are needed when operability is poor. It should not be a surprise that operability is the most leveraging result. After all, a project that produces at half the intended rate has effectively doubled its capital cost per unit of product, and the operating costs may have gone up even more.

What may be more surprising to some readers, especially business professionals, is the modest effect of schedule—either acceleration or slip—on the rate of return. Capital cost is actually considerably more important to the rate of return than the amount of time needed to execute the project. What this does not show, of course, is that the value of schedule changes as the project progresses. When the project is approaching completion, schedule becomes quite important to the returns because almost all of the investment is in place and earning nothing. But the value of schedule in the early days is extremely modest because almost none of the investment has yet been made.

The elements of schedule value that cannot be shown on a chart like Figure 8.2 are the effect of commercial agreements. Schedule promises have some value when forward selling product in competitive situations. Once product has been forward sold, the cost of being late can be quite substantial. That means that the downside of making delivery promises that cannot be met or cannot be met without substantially higher investment costs is very large.

Note also how leveraging capital cost is. A 10% increase in the capital cost of the project decreases the return from 15% to 13.25%. This means that with 30% cost growth, our investment returns less than 10%, which means that the NPV is likely negative.

Setting Overly Conservative Targets

Sometimes targets are set so conservatively that value of the project is hugely diminished from the outset. This occurs when sponsors are extremely risk-averse with respect to cost and schedule overruns. These megaprojects are most common in the Middle East among national companies.[20] For reasons cultural and historical, poor outcomes vis-à-vis promises are viewed extremely negatively within the sponsoring companies. As a result, all risks associated with cost, schedule, and often even operability[21] are transferred to the engineering, materials procurement, and construction (EPC) contractors. During periods when project input markets are soft (buyers' markets), these projects are successful, even though they are generally 10%–15% above industry average cost and 10%–20% lower than average. In heated markets, the contractors require such large premiums to accept the transfer of risk that these projects end up as failures on our cost competitiveness measures. We will discuss the reasons that wholesale risk transfer to contractors is economically inefficient in Chapter 13.

Misguided Trade-Offs

Cases like those previously described are relatively rare and mostly confined to a few locales. The much more common problem with the configuring of targeted outcomes is that one or more of the targets is set so aggressively that the project is more or less bound to

[20]The national companies may be using discount rates that are much lower than their commercial counterparts, in which case, the projects remain NPV-positive even while overspending by large amounts. That does not, however, in any way mitigate the loss of sponsor-investor value associated with the economically inefficient risk transfer.

[21]In the form of a "turnkey" contract in which the contractor is responsible for starting up the facilities and achieving the intended production rates.

end up being a major disappointment. There are four forms of these misconfigured projects:

- Quality is sacrificed for low cost
- Cost is sacrificed for fast schedules
- Quality is sacrificed for fast schedules
- Safety is sacrificed for speed, killing projects
- Safety is sacrificed for speed, killing people

Quality Is Sacrificed for Low Cost

Trading poor quality, which translates into poor production relative to plan, for lower capital cost is almost always unintentional. It is not, however, truly accidental. Trading quality for low cost is usually an unintended byproduct of accepting a very low lump-sum bid. There are a good many examples of this kind of trade-off in the database, often involving government owner situations in which taking the low bid is a legal necessity. This sort of trade-off is not supposed to happen if you do things properly: prequalify the bidders, only allow bidders who can actually handle the risk they are taking on, and so on. But, in fact, winning in such situations is very problematic.

Let me cite an example, and I select this one because the project team did everything correctly and the result was still poor. This was a joint venture project in the Middle East with a U.S. firm taking the leadership role. Four bids were received from four of the biggest and most competent EPC contractors in the world. The low bid was $175 million below the other three bids, which were tightly grouped. There was no legal requirement to accept the low bid. The schedule was also bid four months faster than the other bids and four months faster than the owners' schedule and our benchmark. After selection but before award, the lead sponsor offered a longer schedule to the winning contractor that demurred that it was not necessary. The sponsor set the onset of liquidated damages later than the contractor stipulated anyway because the project director and all of our benchmarks said the project could not be done on the contractor's schedule. The project director warned the business that the bid was too low to be real, but the business leadership overruled the project director's preference to take one of the other bidders.

A couple of months into execution, the contractor realized they had made a horrendous estimating error. The estimate was originally prepared based on their home office location and then would be translated to the Middle East setting. (This is normal enough procedure.) The translation of the estimate to the Middle East in terms of hours required never occurred, although the wage rates were adjusted. The effect was that the estimate was 16 million field hours short. That single error explained the schedule difference as well as the cost difference. So what ensued?

First, the contractor's project leader quit. He did not want his career sullied by a bad project. Second, knowing they were in a huge loss position, the contractor cut every corner imaginable. The owners' controls organization was excellent, but they had no hope of catching everything. Equipment and engineered bulk materials were sourced from incompetent, but low-cost, vendors. Engineering costs were reduced by farming out some of the utilities work to other firms. Despite the fact that there were performance guarantees, startup took 20 months, and finally, a major fix-it project was necessary to make the facility run adequately. It will never be a good quality facility.

The company "saved" the $175 million. It didn't pay the contractor anything more because it made no changes that would open up that opportunity. But at the end of the day, the company lost several times that $175 million and didn't meet its customers' demands either. The project was mechanically complete right on the benchmark schedule, four months late.

One of my reviewers reminded me that he had a megaproject that looked very much like the preceding example, save for one critical difference: his company put enough money in its authorization to make the contractor whole. The company then allowed the contractor to increase their costs to ensure that the right people were put on the job. It was completed slightly below the internal estimate (and our benchmark) with excellent quality and safety. The company had also made a friend of the contractor for many years to come. Cost and value are not always the same thing.

Cost Is Sacrificed for Fast Schedules

The most common misconfiguration is trading cost for schedule. Referring to Figure 8.2, you can see that, in the normal case, one would have to gain over 5% schedule advantage for every 1% of added capital to be return on investment neutral. However, for lots of reasons, most of them bad ones, this is not how the businesses tend to see the cost/schedule trade-off.

In the normal course of things, when a project experiences a large real cost overrun, it overruns its schedule substantially as well. The reason is that most large overruns are caused by the discovery of considerably more work to do than expected, which takes time. For those relatively few projects that collapsed in the field, that too is normally associated with slips in schedule.

However, over 20% of the failed projects combined large overruns (greater than 25% in real terms) with very little schedule slip. These projects averaged an overrun of 51% of their authorization estimates while slipping execution schedule by a mere 5%. Almost 90% of these projects were oil development, far more than would be expected from a random draw. These projects threw heaps of money at the schedules.

There are several forces at work encouraging oil projects to behave this way. In a few cases, there were weather windows that meant that slipping installation by more than a month or so would result in a slip of six to eight months as installation during the winter season is not possible. In another couple of cases, the scheduling of installation vessels was so difficult that again a very long delay would have resulted if the project missed its tow-out and installation date. Most of the cases, however, result from the strange, even perverse, structuring of many oil leases and concessions with national resource holders.

Two types of contracts distort outcomes. One involves lease concessions that are too short to develop the petroleum resource in a way that would maximize the total value from the reservoirs. When a company is given a 15-year concession to develop a resource that would take 25 years to develop optimally, it wants to spend as little time as possible on the project and as much time as possible in production. The sponsor-investor is therefore willing to overspend substantially to get the production started if they believe it can be done faster with a higher spend. Ironically, for reasons described in the next trade-off area, the break-neck speed often results in very poor production rates relative to plan. We also strongly suspect that these arrangements sometimes result in attempts to produce oil so rapidly that the reservoirs are permanently damaged and the eventual total recovery is reduced.

The second type of distorting concession agreement involves repaying the sponsor-investors' capital immediately from the proceeds of production in a way that makes capital nearly free. This produces a tendency to overcapitalize in much the same way that public utilities that earn returns on their capital rate base are known to overcapitalize.[22] The effect can be quite extreme, inducing companies to spend much more than necessary to develop the resource while effecting large wealth transfers from the resource holder to the developers.

These deals involve a Shaping allocation that increases the value generated to sponsor-investors while reducing the amount of total value created. The residents of the resource-holding countries lose a great deal in these sorts of arrangements. These arrangements could only make economic sense if the social discount rates of the resource holders were much higher than that of the sponsor-investors. In fact, however, quite the opposite should be true.[23] Generally, private-sector investors need a higher return than governments to be willing to make investments. Public sector investors have objectives such as jobs creation or security enhancement that have no value for private sponsors.

Quality Is Sacrificed for Fast Schedules

Like sacrificing quality for cost, this result is almost always unintended because it degrades the asset value very substantially. It is, however, very common. The desired schedule outcome is one of the products of the Shaping process. The schedule strategy is generally among the first outcomes "fixed" in the Shaping process. The outcome is generally fixed in the form of "production will commence first of December of _______ (year)." In other words, we will decide when it will start producing before we have figured out what "it" is! Schedules developed in this way have only one thing in common: they are almost always too short to get all of the needed work completed.

[22]This is called "Averch-Johnson effect" by economists. See Harvey Averch and Leland L. Johnson, "Behavior of the Firm Under Regulatory Constraint," *American Economic Review 52*(5), 1962: 1052–1069.

[23]Of course, the personal discount rates of government officials making the deals may well be extremely high.

Under these circumstances, there are several paths to quality degradation. One is that the front-end loading schedule is so rushed that the scope is not appropriate and the project suffers operability problems. Sometimes execution is so rushed that corners are cut to meet a first-production date target. But the most common problem is that some of the background technical data, which are essential to correct design, are never fully developed. As we will discuss in Chapter 9, incorrect Basic Data create problems from which it is usually impossible to recover.

Safety Is Sacrificed for Speed, Killing Projects

The drive for unattainable speed in megaproject development and execution is a symptom of serious pathology in the modern industrial firm. It has been responsible for the sheer vaporization of many hundreds of billions of dollars of shareholder wealth. That speed destroys megaprojects has been widely known within the IPA customer base for many years. And yet the push to develop and execute these projects too quickly has seen no relief. If many industrial firms aspire to be learning organizations, there is precious little evidence of it here.

There are a number of compelling reasons that megaprojects cannot be effectively speeded up that will be discussed in detail in later chapters of this book. What I want to discuss here is why the drive for speed continues despite the overwhelming evidence that it destroys project outcomes.

One reason surely is ignorance on the part of the business decision-makers who control the Shaping process for megaprojects. They simply do not understand why these projects are fragile and why speed kills the projects because they lack enough knowledge of how these projects work to be able to "connect the dots." This reason, of course, simply begs the question of why those who are ignorant of the process are in charge of the process or fail to listen to those who do understand how the projects work. I believe that in order to explain the ignorance, one has to look to the dramatic weakening of technical expertise and influence within industrial firms over the past 30 years.

Starting in the early 1980s, we saw a systematic dismantling of technical organizations inside industrial firms, first in the United States, and later, throughout the OECD. There is no doubt in my mind that the technical functions needed reformation. Rather than being reformed, however, they were largely dismantled. Outsourcing of technical expertise was sold by consultants, business schools, and contractors as a modern and necessary approach to making the industrial firm leaner and less subject to cyclical swings.

The 1990s made the outsourcing seem viable. This was a decade of very low spending on capital projects. The oil industry was depressed by very low petroleum prices. A huge capacity overhang depressed minerals spending, and the chemicals industry continued to be highly cyclical with prices overall trending down. The result was a period of overcapacity in engineering and construction management services throughout the Organisation for Economic Cooperation and Development (OECD) area. The companies were also left with a residuum of very talented and experienced Baby Boomers. The result is that projects, even large projects, did not suffer too much during this period. But there was in most companies almost no renewal of technical personnel with young people. When there were demands for unachievable speed in large projects, the technical organizations used to be strong enough to say "no." Now you do so at your peril.

Ultimately, the problem comes down to a simple matter of a lack of accountability. Business executives who set in motion a process that will destroy huge amounts of shareholder wealth are rarely held accountable for their errors and omissions. In the usual case, not the extraordinary one, the executive that championed a bad project at the outset has been promoted out of any line responsibility and accountability for the poor result long before the depth of the problems becomes known. This same lack of accountability for long-term results is the curse of the modern corporation. This problem of accountability goes to the heart of corporate governance. The relationship between governance and megaprojects is the subject of the next section.

Safety Is Sacrificed for Speed, Killing People

Not one of the 150 industrial firms for which IPA works would admit to sacrificing anything for safety, often not even to themselves. Yet many of them do actually sacrifice safety quite regularly and it is almost always for speed, not for cost. Almost all of our customers are willing to pay to improve safety and most consider the costs a good investment. But it is actually the drive for speed that causes most accidents and injuries both directly and indirectly. Speed causes accidents directly by making the construction workforce less sensitive to safety protocol and hazards. Speed increases the amount of construction rework, and rework is known to be much less safe, on average, than primary tasks because it is often unplanned work. The drive for speed is associated with long work hours, and fatigue is a primary precursor to accidents.

When speed is of prime concern, the underlying foundation of a safe project is put at risk because project preparation suffers. Statistically, the largest driver of accidents is poor front-end loading. Poor front-end loading means poor preparation to execute the project. It means more undisciplined and chaotic work sites. It means more people will be injured or killed to create the company's capital assets.

An Example of Successful Opportunity Shaping

The project consisted of three large pieces: a new metals processing complex, a new port, and the utilities infrastructure. The third part of the scope was a government-sponsored third-party project. Total investment was about $3.6 billion.

The Challenges

The project had been kicking around for over 20 years in the country because the availability of the resource was well established. However, the project would disturb a large area (>380 square miles) of pristine wilderness, and in this environmentally concerned nation, that made the project highly controversial. Environmental NGOs from around the world were aware of the project and mostly opposed.

The company that ultimately sponsored the development had considered attempting to get the project going several times before, but felt that the opposition to the project made it too risky to pursue. On the other hand, the resource situation promised the holy grail of manufacturing: an enduring low-cost producer status. While the sponsor watched, competitors had tried twice to get approval for the development, but were either denied outright or found the opposition too daunting. The government was also the resource owner and had been holding out for a resource price that would have eroded the economics significantly.

The project geography was remote, but with harbor and port development could be accessed from the ocean.

The Strategy

The first and most important element of the sponsor's Shaping strategy was old-fashioned patience. They understood that unless or until there was the makings of a constituency for the project, it would never fly. The project would require passage of legislation enabling use of the resource and access. An economic downturn and a change of government that had promised jobs development was the tipping point in the project's favor. When the political change came, the company was ready to respond to the opportunity. It had been researching the issues in-country for several years.

The second element of the strategy was to be all over the environmental aspects of the project. The sponsor had in-country teams on air quality, water use and quality, land disturbance, and community relations and development. The in-country teams very actively engaged the environmentalists and made a number of changes that the environmentalists wanted. It didn't eliminate the issue, but it blunted it substantially as some groups dropped their opposition.

The third element was interesting and clever: the actual resource development, rather than the processing facilities, carried the highest environmental risk and opposition. So the sponsor strongly supported the government developing the resource, which it owned after all, and selling the feedstock to the company on a long-term take or pay contract.

This was an admittedly risky approach, but it had some advantages. The downside risk was that the government would not get the resource developed in a timely way. The upside was that the cost of capital was lower to the government and the company's contract made the terms available to the government to borrow the money very attractive. Furthermore, the government could take the credit for the jobs creation and take the heat for the environmental opposition. It was also very important to the sponsor's risk profile that the government be solidly and actively in favor of the development.

This last point turned out to be extraordinarily important because a politician seeking to reinvigorate a fading career launched a legal challenge to the permit on procedural grounds. (Interestingly, the NGOs did not join the suit.) The suit was ultimately successful, but because the political support was strong, the relevant ministry allowed work to continue while the environmental impact statement was reworked to meet the court's decision. Bureaucrats will not normally subject themselves to such criticism without very strong political support.

One other element of the Shaping strategy needs a mention. Because there was substantial unemployment in the area in which the processing facilities were constructed, local politicians were demanding of the sponsor that local labor be used for construction and that a quota be set. Normally, a business person would agree to such a demand without much thought, but in this case, he did the right thing: he checked with the project director. The project director explained that, given the nature of the construction, the local workforce completely lacked the needed skills and experience. Because in-country labor could not possibly meet the project requirements, higher skilled foreign labor would have to be imported anyway. In that event, we would mix high-quality labor with low-quality labor, which depresses the productivity of the more skilled workers, and we would have a cultural mix as well, another complicating factor. Instead, he decided to promise the permanent jobs and denigrate the advantages of construction jobs as being temporary and unsustainable. Furthermore, he emphasized that the local service industry would provision the labor camp. While there was grumbling throughout the project about no local construction jobs, the project director believed the execution would have been a nightmare with them. As it was, modules were used wherever possible, and a highly skilled labor force was imported without incident.

Project Results

The project had a 5% cost overrun, slipped its schedule by four months, and had a flawless startup. The government was indeed late getting its project completed by six months, but a work-around strategy had already been developed that enabled the time to be used for commissioning and startup without difficulty. It was a successful megaproject.

Why Were They Successful?

The venture was fully aligned at the top of the company. It fit with the company's strategy and was a potentially attractive development, but not at any price. The company worked out internally what its requirements were and then was willing to wait. No one was allowed to attempt to force the project, which would have surely failed. The sponsor worked through conceptually what the Shaping process was supposed to look like and was therefore in a position to respond flexibly when necessary. The front-end development of the project was not rushed. FEL took two and a half years, and no authorization was going to be made until the political commitment to the project was made by the government and the legislature. There were no cowboys on the project.

An Example of Unsuccessful Opportunity Shaping

If the preceding project explains how to approach Shaping an opportunity in an environmentally sensitive area appropriately, this example shows how to do it exactly wrong. This was an oil production project in an environmentally sensitive area. The project was to develop a reservoir of moderate size, estimated at less than 200 million recoverable barrels. The reserves estimate was based on high recovery rates so there was very little upside potential to the reservoir. The project had both onshore and close-in offshore components. The project was expected to cost $900 million for both facilities and drilling. There were two partners making the investment. The lead sponsor was an international oil company with lots of experience developing and executing megaprojects around the world. The other partner, also an oil company, was almost entirely silent in all aspects of the project, except to provide additional money when it was required.

The Challenges

The project location is remote and environmentally sensitive. The area has very active and savvy NGOs and other citizens groups that oppose selected developments. Because this project posed some particular environmental risks to marine life, environmental groups staked out a position of opposition early on. The institutional framework for petroleum development is, at best, moderately strong. Court decisions are respected but are often circumvented by officials. Projects are intensely political, and both central and local political authorities can derail a project if they wish. Projects are routinely used for political advantage and have been known to generate cash above and below the table for politicians who offer support.

The project posed no great technological challenges outside the need to minimize environmental disruption in a fragile area.

The Strategy

There really doesn't seem to have been a coherent Shaping strategy for the project, which is quite surprising given that the sponsor had worked in the area before and expected to do so again. The sponsor knew the project to be contentious. Soon after permit applications were filed, a citizen's group filed a lawsuit, not on environmental grounds, but claiming that the local residents should get a bigger share of the proceeds. This suit stopped the project dead for 18 months and should have been the best thing that could have happened for the sponsor.

In the hiatus, the project team continued to work on the definition of the project, which was decidedly poor when the $900 million authorization estimate was made. When the problem regarding the citizen suit had been settled, a new cost estimate was available, which now showed the cost to have risen to $1.65 billion in constant dollar terms! Recoverable reserves had also been revised downward and operating costs had been revised upward. The project economics, which had never been very robust, now looked very poor. So the obvious route would be to abandon the project.

Not so fast! During the hiatus period, the company had aligned itself with the political groups seeking to crush the influence of the NGOs. Indeed, one of the stated business objectives of the project was now to "crush the environmentalists." Having expended a great deal of political capital to "align" the needed politicians, the lead sponsor would look weak and foolish if it abandoned the project. So the sponsor now found itself in a very difficult position: the project cost too much but was now too high profile to abandon. Because the project was now marginal economically, a couple of truly stupid steps were taken to keep costs down. First, the owner project team size was kept small, and second, a very complex incentivized contractual form was employed with a very large number of contractors, some that were qualified and some that were not. So the project soldiered on under very difficult circumstances.

Project Results

The project was finally completed at a cost of over $1.8 billion, more than double the original estimate. The project has produced as planned, but was an NPV-negative development that destroyed a good deal of shareholder wealth.

Why Did They Fail?

There were several flaws in the lead sponsor's approach to the project. First, the sponsor never created an overarching framework for the Shaping process. It was therefore always in a reactive mode. The various stakeholders were never aligned or mollified because there wasn't a plan for doing so. Because the project was very poorly defined when the sponsors decided to proceed, cost growth was almost inevitable. The cost growth occurred while the sponsor's business folks were busy getting the company over-committed to what was at the same time becoming a poor venture. Because Shaping was not planned, there was no closure point where the project scope and the Shaping process would come together to yield the information needed for a rational decision.

The nonoperating sponsor of the project completely abdicated any role that it might have played in preventing this mess. If the second player had exercised even basic due diligence, it would have required that the project development and execution be properly synchronized with the open Shaping issues.

Finally, the subplot of teaching the NGOs a lesson was absurd and moronic. The business people had "gone native" and aligned themselves with one of the many political factions in the area. Furthermore, the goal of damaging the NGOs was directly contrary to company policy. The business decision-makers responsible needed to be called home and reassigned to more menial work. In case you were wondering, the project was in an OECD country, not the developing world.

I will close this long discussion of Shaping with a short story: As I finished a day-long discussion of Shaping as part of a seminar on megaprojects, one of the attendees approached me and said, "I have been a business opportunity manager at ___ [one of the supermajor oil companies] for over 20 years. For the first time, I believe I actually understand what my job is." The lesson from that story is not that my megaprojects seminar is brilliant, although I do think it is pretty good. Rather, it tells us how underappreciated Shaping requirements are even in the most sophisticated industrial companies.

CHAPTER 9

Basic Data Are Basic

Behind the design of any engineered project is a set of parameters that govern the design.[1] These parameters express the science underlying the engineering design of the facilities that will be built. Like many in the industry, we call these parameters, taken together, the Basic Data. The Basic Data sit behind and govern the design. They tell the engineer what materials to use, how to size things, how to sequence things, and what things are dangerous. Because different functional groups are often responsible for the development of the Basic Data, those developing the design may be only dimly aware of how the Basic Data were generated and may be completely unaware of the Basic Data quality.

Erroneous and incomplete Basic Data are a proximate cause of many megaproject failures. Basic data mistakes are quite common, and as we will see, are quite devastating to projects when they occur. In this chapter, we address the following questions about the Basic Data:

- When should the complete Basic Data be available to the project team?
- What are the consequences of incorrect Basic Data?
- Under what circumstances are Basic Data most likely to be problematic?
- What are the *root causes* of most Basic Data mistakes?

[1]An important characteristic of the megaprojects that we are examining here is that almost all are engineering-intensive. Most of them require a high level of precision in the design and they are very unforgiving of engineering errors. In many cases, engineering errors and omissions render the facilities highly unsafe as many of them handle and process large quantities of explosive, flammable, or toxic substances. As a class, only pipeline projects and some renewables such as onshore wind require little de novo engineering.

Before addressing these questions, I would like to describe the Basic Data for different kinds of projects so that the reader appreciates the breadth and complexity of the issues involved. It is not my purpose to present anything like a complete set of Basic Data requirements. A complete Basic Data for a single megaproject could easily require as many pages as this book.

Processing Facilities Basic Data

Following are examples of Basic Data for a chemicals or physical process, relating only to the heart of the process:[2]

- Detailed product characteristics and specifications
- Reaction temperature and pressure ranges and tolerances
- Reaction yield data (including waste quantities and waste composition)
- Reaction products, especially side reaction products
- Production of impurities, recycle buildup potential
- Separation efficiency/completeness and problematic characteristics
- Particle behavior in processing (diminution, agglomeration, etc.)
- Heat (energy) and material (mass) balances for every step
- Vapor liquid equilibria (VLE) data for column design
- Set, control, and alarm points
- Hydraulic requirements for pumps
- Materials of construction test results
- Raw material composition and variability
- Scale-up effects as applicable
- And so on.

[2]Almost all industrial megaprojects entail chemicals or physical processing, even if the project's technology is not normally considered a "chemical process." For example, crude oil production involves the separation of water and gas from the oil, which in some cases is actually quite difficult and complex. Liquefied natural gas (LNG) involves primarily physical processing, with chemicals processing required for sulfur and other impurities removal and disposal.

All the preceding Basic Data need to be understood not just for normal operating conditions, but for startup, shutdown, and upset conditions as well.

If the process is commercially established, the Basic Data may be known and codified. If the technology is to be procured from a licensor, all of the Basic Data around the heart of the process should be provided or incorporated into the package that the licensor is selling. If the process is new, all of the preceding data and more will have to be developed by R&D, and because the process has not been commercialized previously, the data will remain somewhat uncertain until after a successful startup and initial operation. There may be 4 to 12 separate chemicals processes in a megaproject; the most complex we have seen has over 30. All of the preceding data will have to be provided or developed for every process. But that is merely the beginning of the Basic Data development!

Megaprojects often require substantial amounts of infrastructure development: ports, pipelines, roads and bridges, power plants, and so forth. Each one of these has its own Basic Data requirements, some of which may be very complex.

Let me give you an example that illustrates just how difficult the Basic Data requirements can be for an ancillary facility, a seawater cooling system. Many processes require large amounts of heat removal at various stages. If large amounts of fresh water are not available or its use is not permitted, seawater may be required as the heat sink for the facilities. Here are some of the data requirements for a seawater cooling system, with no pretense that the list is complete:

- Maximum total cooling load that will be carried by seawater system at any time
- Seawater hardness and variability of hardness (driver of scaling)
- Chloride content (a driver of corrosion and therefore materials requirements)
- Seawater withdrawal that will be allowable
- Seawater temperature
  - By season
  - With year-to-year variation
  - By water depth at potential intake points

- Organisms present in the potential intake water
    - Microorganisms will determine biofouling properties
    - And therefore, biocide selection and effectiveness
    - Macro organisms (shellfish, etc.) and potential for macro-fouling and plugging
- Biocide types and levels in effluent water that will be permit-able
- Byproduct formation from interaction of biocide (e.g., chlorine) with natural organic compounds
- Sea life kill that will likely occur and what will be permit-able and socially acceptable
- Discharge water temperature
    - By season
    - By facility loadings, and so on
- Discharge water temperature maximum that will occur and be permit-able
- Water intake and effluent locations that will be permit-able
- Other seawater cooling systems or other marine facilities being installed in the same area and their effect on all of the preceding

Behind many of these items there is a host of required science. Figure 9.1 shows the integration needed for industrial seawater cooling systems.[3] The chart is instructive because it shows how much has to be considered just to decide what kind of biocides should be used and in what quantities. If the science or the data are incorrect, the system will not work as intended and may not even work at all. This example is of an ancillary part of a development that may well be considered quite mundane, but turns out to be quite complex. Even worse than complexity, however, is the time that may be required to produce accurate data. Unless someone has been collecting seawater information in the exact places that you require, you may need at least a year to collect the data to design the right seawater cooling system. For example, seasonal variation in thermal layer boundaries

[3]*Design for Energy and the Environment,* Boca Raton, FL: CRC Press, Taylor and Francis Group, LLC, 2010, p. 229. Permission to use will have to be acquired.

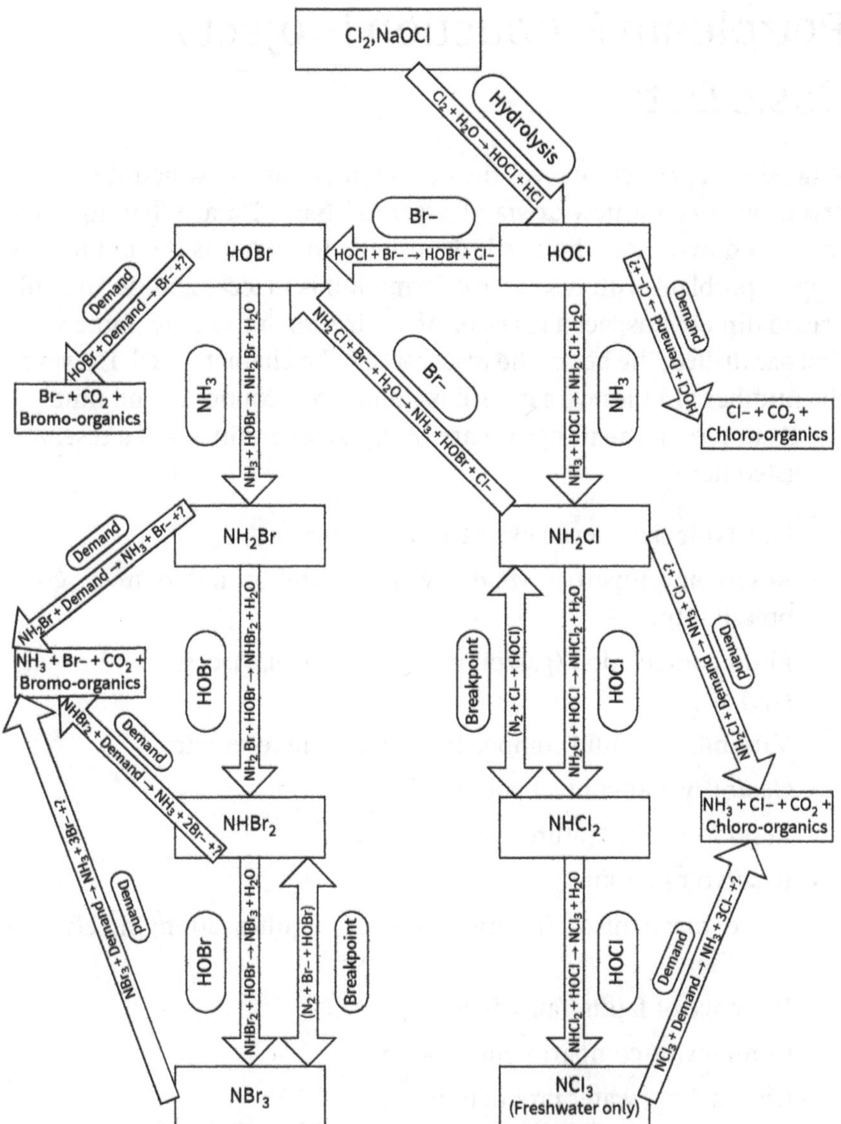

FIGURE 9.1 The Chemistry of an Industrial Seawater Cooling System

is quite common. If the intake is in what turns out to be the wrong water depth for part of the year, the fix may involve moving the intake many miles and getting permits to do so. Three megaprojects had seawater cooling systems that were so badly misdesigned that cooling could not be provided.

Petroleum Production Projects Basic Data

Whenever a project involves the development of a new petroleum reservoir, we open a new arena of essential Basic Data. What and how much is down there, how is it deposited, and what is around it? The biggest problem with reservoir information is inaccessibility. The only way to directly inspect a reservoir is by drilling into it. The more wells that are drilled, the better the reservoir can be characterized. However, the number of holes we can drill is limited by economics and time.

Examples of the things we are trying to ascertain about a reservoir are listed here:

- Reservoir size (aerial extent and thickness)
- Reservoir properties (porosity, permeability, net-to-gross, compressibility)
- Fluid composition (gas/oil ratio, impurities, viscosity and gravity, etc.)
- Variability in fluid composition across the reservoir[4]
- Gas/oil/water contact points
- Reservoir temperature
- Reservoir pressure
- Drive mechanism (reservoir energy, aquifer strength, etc.) or lack thereof
- Presence of faults/fault density
- Complexity, compartmentalization
- Channeling, water production
- And so on

---

[4]Crude oil composition and contaminants in natural gas, such as mercury, are not necessarily uniform across a single reservoir. It is quite common, in fact, that fluid characteristics in the flanks (edges) of a reservoir are substantially different than in the center.

Development of the Basic Data around a petroleum reservoir is the product of what is called the appraisal process. Appraisal is the next technical step after discovery. The data collection process involves seismic imaging, obtaining cores from wells, and getting fluid samples, and pressure and reservoir limits information from well tests. The data are then interpreted and synthesized into the Basic Data for the particular reservoir being developed and a comprehensive plan of how to drain the reservoir.

Reservoir appraisal can be time-consuming and expensive. But there is tremendous latitude around the amount of reservoir appraisal actually done. Generally, the extent of the appraisal process is a function of the expected size of the project that will be required to develop the reservoir; the larger the project will be, the more appraisal is justified to bring the project risk under control. But this rule of thumb is just that. We had one megaproject off West Africa in which the appraisal was limited to simple seismic imaging and the core from the discovery well. When this project was put into production, it produced for all of two weeks before flowing only water. It was a high-pressure pocket.

One of the most common sources of insufficient appraisal is a technical team's misplaced confidence that they understand a reservoir based on nearby producing fields. This has even occurred in oil sands development in which the reservoir is mined rather than pumped. One very large project assumed that all oil from Alberta oil sands would be the same, only to find that nature had failed to cooperate with people's assumption. Significant operability problems followed.

Basic Data Requirements for Minerals Developments

The Basic Data requirements for a minerals development are analogous to petroleum. Because exploitable minerals are usually closer to the surface and on land, the costs of the "appraisal" are usually much less than for petroleum in deep water. Nonetheless, there is a good deal of variability is how much is done, and depending on the project scope, will typically involve basic data collection aimed at defining the mining method (open-cut versus various underground methods) as well as the required metallurgical inputs to adequately process the ore.

Here are some of the data that should be acquired to classify the orebody and the overburden in terms of both physical properties for mine development and metallurgical data for associated processing facilities:

- Lithology and stratigraphy
- Physical properties and structures
- Wedge and slab formation
- Cavities
- In situ rock temperatures
- Metals content and metallization process
- Types of impurities
- Waste characteristics and volumes
- Particle sizing characteristics
- Heterogeneity
- Size, shape, and attitude
- Overburden features/properties/angle of repose
- Topsoil depth
- Weathered materials
- Groundwater location, sources, and character
- And so on

To be complete, many thousands of individual items may need to be filled in for the Basic Data that will underpin the mine and the processing. Especially important are data around the variability of the orebody as that will define the design envelope for the processing facilities.

Another Basic Data challenge unique to minerals development is that even after one has collected ore samples from many parts of the orebody and examined them, one does not necessarily understand how they will behave when processed. Minerals processing is very dependent on the physics of processing solids and each orebody is likely to behave slightly differently in processing. Those slight differences can make huge differences in plant reliability and process yields. Actual testing of material in the various process steps is very expensive, and therefore, routinely not done.[5]

Basic Data Requirements for Expansion and Modernization Projects

When I was a young man, I made the sort of mistake that only a young man would make: I agreed to fix a leaky pipe in the upstairs bath of a lady friend who owned a very old house. Four anxious days and 14 pipes later, I found myself completing the job in the basement. My lady friend was much more impressed by my sheer incompetence at having broken so many pipes than my devotion to her or attention to task.

Modifying and modernizing an existing facility is one of the most taxing of endeavors with respect to Basic Data development. For a greenfield development, those developing the scope have greater control and are more likely to know what they don't know. When modifying old facilities, you are heavily constrained by what is already there. The great challenge is to figure out what that really is.

The critical Basic Data problem for modernizations is trying to figure out exactly what is currently in place, its condition, and its performance. The Basic Data development often requires finding old plant records and documents that provide critical insights into what may lie underground. Maintenance records may (or may not) provide the condition of existing equipment. I once sat on a peer review panel trying to understand why a petroleum refinery modernization was overrunning so badly. The chief culprit turned out to be the number of pieces of pipe that had to be replaced while making 9,000 tie-ins of new equipment to old. I was reminded of that leaky bathroom pipe from hell.

Even with the new tools available, such as laser- and photogrammetry, the amount of work needed to understand the existing plant

[5]See E. Merrow, *A Quantitative Assessment of R&D Requirements for Solids Processing Technology*, Santa Monica, CA: Rand Corporation. 1986; E.W. Merrow, "Progress and Problems in Particle Processing," *Chemical Innovation, 30*, 34–41; and E.W. Merrow. "Linking R&D to Problems Experienced in Solids Processing," *Chemical Engineering Progress, 81*, 14–22.

may equal or even exceed the engineering work required for the new units. This is, in substantial part, a legacy of the industry's unwillingness to maintain true as-built drawings and design while making the inevitable thousands of changes to facilities over the years. It is also one of the key reasons why so many major plant modernization megaprojects fail.

What Are the Consequences of Basic Data Errors?

Over 10% of our sample suffered Basic Data errors or corrections to the data so late they could not be incorporated into the design. The differences in outcomes between projects with and without Basic Data problems are shown in Table 9.1.

TABLE 9.1

Outcome Variable	Projects without Basic Data Errors	Projects with Basic Data Errors	Statistical Significance of Difference
Average Production Months 7–12 versus Plan	76%	55%	.0001
Time Required for Startup (months)	5.8	17	.0001
Forecast Time for Startup (months)	4.5	5	Null
Cost Growth from Authorization (pct real)	21	19	Null
Slip in Execution Schedule[6] in Percent	23	29	Marginal
Percent of Projects That Were Successful	34	12	.0001

[6]Measured as actual time from authorization to mechanical completion divided by time forecast at full-funds authorization.

The differences shown in Table 9.1 are interesting both for what they show and what they do not show. The projects with Basic Data errors show large and statistically robust differences in planned versus actual production and in startup time. The differences would be still larger if we did not count resource projects with large downward revisions (greater than 25%) in the resource base as Basic Data failures. Many of those projects produced well in the early period, but the lives of the projects were cut short by the lack of resource.

Note, however, there is no difference in the expected startup times for the simple reason that the project teams were unaware of the Basic Data errors at authorization. However, in most cases, the Basic Data errors did come to light during execution, often in detailed engineering. But as the lack of difference in cost growth demonstrates, the project teams could do nothing about those Basic Data errors once execution had started. This is quite distinctly a megaprojects problem that we do not observe in smaller projects. When Basic Data errors come to light in detailed engineering in smaller projects, the projects undergo major scope surgery to fix the problems. In megaprojects, so many forward commitments have been made that such wholesale changes are not possible. Some of the projects slowed down to assess whether fixes could be made, but then continued on with the planned scope even though production problems were going to be inevitable.

About 12% of the projects with Basic Data errors were classed as successful projects. All of these projects were resource projects with large reserves downgrades that did not cause production attainment failure in the first two years.

When Should the Basic Data Be Complete and Available?

In a perfect world, the Basic Data would be available prior to the start of scope development, which we call FEL-2 or Select. The Basic Data constitute the foundation of the scope development team's effort. Realistically, if the Basic Data require much development, the middle

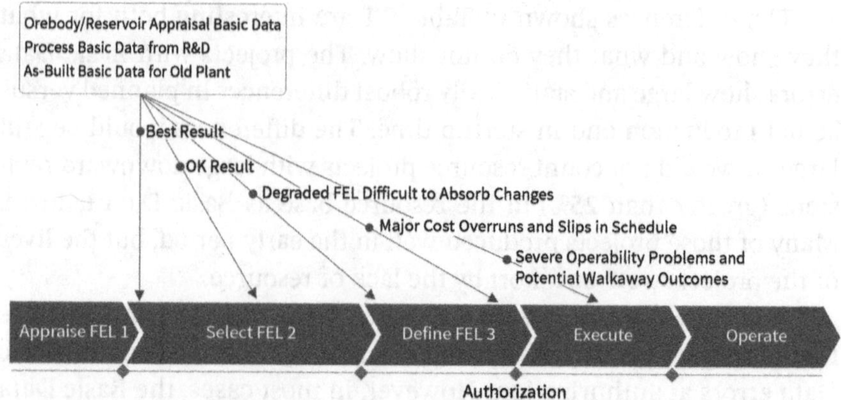

FIGURE 9.2 Timing of Basic Data Arrival Changes Project Results

of FEL-2 is about the best we are likely to achieve.[7] When significant changes to the Basic Data occur after the middle of FEL-2, there must be project consequences. What those consequences will be depends on how important the Basic Data changes are and how late they occur. Figure 9.2 illustrates what happens. If the Basic Data arrive early enough in Select that the design can fully reflect them, all is well.

Basic Data that arrive during Define disrupt the engineering work that is trying to put piping and instrumentation diagrams (P&IDs) in place and become a major distraction for the project team. Recall also from the discussion in Chapter 8 that Shaping should have come to closure at the end of Select (or put differently, the beginning of Define should await Shaping closure). If Basic Data arrive after the middle of Select, it will like delay the completion of the scope. If they arrive in Define, there is likely to be significant project cost growth. At best, that cost growth will occur prior to authorization, but it may well continue after authorization as well. If the changes are significant enough, the Shaping agreements may come unstuck and the project is now in serious trouble.

If the changes to Basic Data arrive after authorization, the project will very likely fail. The failure mode—cost, schedule, operability, or some combination—will depend on the particular situation.

[7]One of my colleagues who specializes in oil field development made an interesting comment here: *all* oil company work process maps look like Figure 9.2; appraisal is supposed to precede selecting the technology concept that will be used to develop the reservoir. In practice, however, appraisal almost always overlaps the Select phase and often continues into Define and Execute.

For example, in petroleum exploration and production (E&P), late data can sometimes be accommodated through a major change to the wells construction program, which will cause wells costs to overrun. For example, the location of the targets in the reservoir may have to change substantially due to new information about the reservoir. This may force the wells to be drilled at a higher angle and may complicate the completion of the wells. The cost of the wells may go up very substantially, but the change is accommodated. In a mine development, the analog may be a more expensive mining scheme or a major change to the ore preparation prior to processing. In modernization projects, the poor Basic Data usually result in cost growth and slip in schedule rather than production failures, but in chemicals, bad Basic Data from R&D often result in production disasters.

Sometimes, unfortunately, the Basic Data surprise simply cannot be accommodated and we find ourselves building the wrong project altogether. What then can result is a complete loss of the asset, which we call a walkaway, and 2% to 3% of industrial megaprojects fall into this sorry class. Basic Data errors are at the root of all of them. And, walkaways destroy businesses.

The timing of Basic Data completion can also affect the business decisions and the Shaping process for the project. When the Basic Data are incomplete, items are usually missing from the essential scope, which causes the cost and schedule estimates to be unduly optimistic. The rosy economics may even become a "reason" to fast-track the project, making the successful and timely completion of the Basic Data even less likely.

Under What Circumstances Are the Basic Data Most Likely to Be Incorrect?

There are a few situations that pose substantial risks of the Basic Data containing major errors:

- The use of new technology
- Situations in which the Basic Data are very expensive and difficult to obtain
- Inexperienced or relatively uninvolved lead sponsors

These situations should not be viewed as excuses for poor Basic Data. They are simply the situations in which errors are more likely to occur. Nor are these situations necessarily the root causes. We will discuss the most common root causes later.

New Technology

There is an old expression that certainly applies to incorporating new technology into megaprojects: "Try to make your mistakes on a small scale and to make your money on a large scale." New technology in a megaproject threatens to do the exact opposite. Any way you measure it, new technology increases project risks.[8] The mechanism by which risks increase is uncertainty, error, or tardiness in the Basic Data. For this analysis, I have selected the following scale as our measure of new technology:[9]

1. Conventional, "off-the-shelf" technology, widely deployed previously
2. First-time integrations of otherwise commercially proven technology
3. Minor modifications to existing technology; core technology is unchanged, but improvements are introduced
4. Major modifications to existing technology; core technology is modified
5. Substantially new core technology

A technology is considered core if it is central to the application. For example, a very innovative gas dehydration technology might be incorporated into the topsides of an otherwise conventional petroleum production platform. The dehydration technology would not be

[8] See E.W. Merrow, K. Phillips, and C.W. Myers, *Understanding Cost Growth and Performance Shortfalls in Pioneer Process Plant*, Santa Monica, CA: The Rand Corporation, 1981.

[9] More precise measures are available for various technology subclasses of megaprojects, such as process plants, offshore fixed or floating platforms, and so on. I chose this particular measure because it is available for all of the projects regardless of industrial sector or technology employed.

considered core because it is merely one of a number of steps in the overall process of separating impurities from gas, and other technologies could easily be substituted in the event of an unfixable problem with the new step. By contrast, an innovative mooring system for a floating platform would be considered core technology. A new chemical conversion process would be considered substantially new in a chemicals or petroleum refining facility.

Sometimes the technology per se cannot be considered new, but the Basic Data must be established anew anyway. For example, every new mineral orebody is at least slightly different than any other. The new match of ore to equipment and process creates Basic Data uncertainties that may require slight to major modifications of the processing kit to generate a successful project. Some ores, such as nickel laterite, for example, almost always generate processing surprises. In such situations, a failure to treat the situation "as if" it were new technology often leads to production failures. Most new matches of ore-to-process should include extensive testing of the ore in vendor facilities, and in some cases, may even require integrating piloting facilities to reduce Basic Data uncertainties to an acceptable level. Such piloting is often resisted because it is expensive.

How New Technology Affects Megaproject Results

New technology affects megaprojects results differently than smaller projects. In smaller projects, new technology use is associated with more cost growth and poorer operability.[10] For megaprojects, new technology mistakes degrade cost performance very little while destroying operability. This difference occurs because in smaller projects, when new technology generates late Basic Data, the team changes the design during execution. In megaprojects, wholesale changes in design during execution are usually impossible. If the team does not act on the information, no cost growth is generated, but operability is affected,

[10]When the Basic Data errors were not associated with new technology, the association with cost growth and schedule slip was very strong. Practices account for the difference.

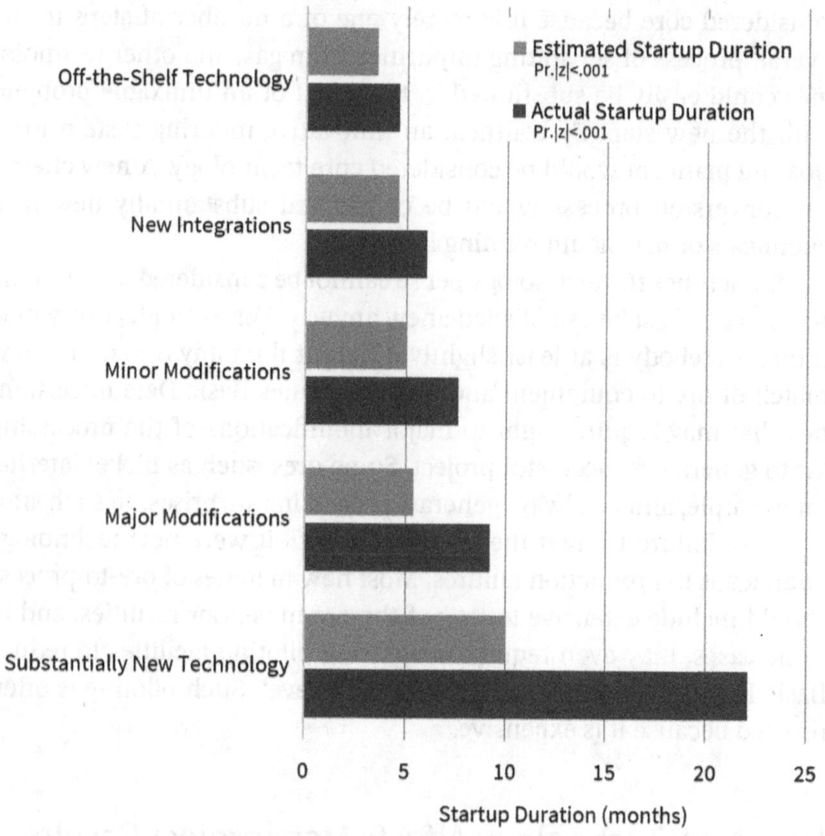

FIGURE 9.3 New Technology and Production Startup

often in devastating ways. Figure 9.3 shows the relationship between new technology and the difficulty of getting production started up.[11] The second bar is the time actually required.

Teams tend to be optimistic regardless of the level of new technology as shown by the forecast startup times. The teams' forecast was that each step on the innovation scale would add less than one month to startup time. The actual is closer to three months. But the increasing forecast times do tell us that the teams are aware of the higher risks as a result of greater step-out. Note the very sharp break as the

[11]*Startup* is defined as the period between mechanical completion of facilities (readiness to operate in principle) to steady-state, even if intended production rates have not been achieved.

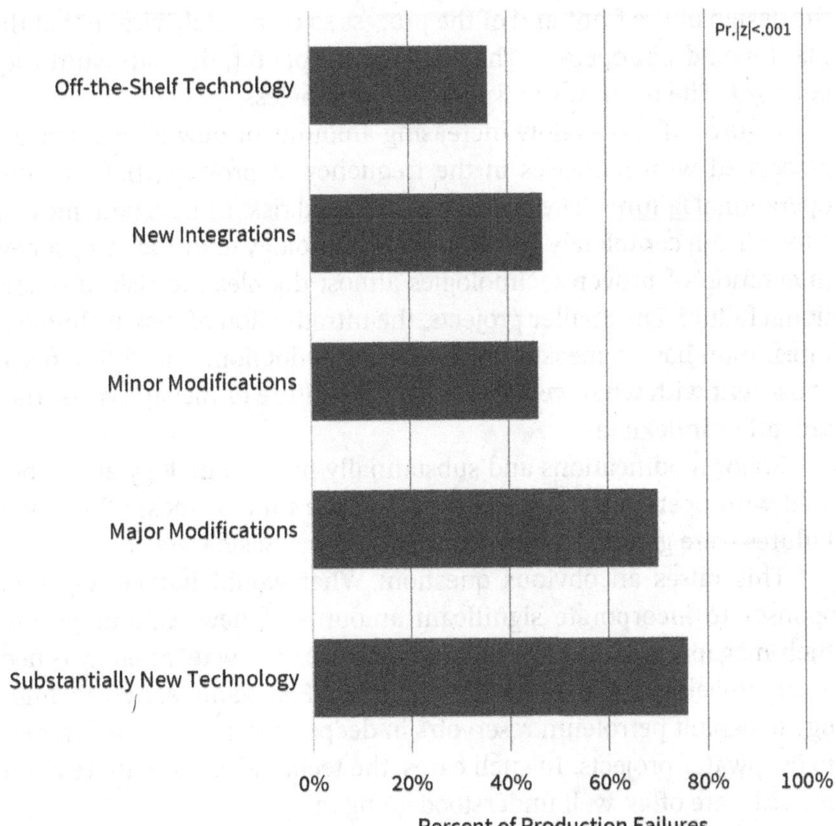

FIGURE 9.4 Operability Risks Increase with Technology Step-Out

technology becomes substantially new. The average startup time for substantially new technology projects is 22 months, and necessarily, the walkaway projects have been excluded as their startup times were infinite.

New technology simply not working as expected is not a surprising result. Often, however, the technology worked well, but other parts of the facilities failed. This happens when the new technology changes the Basic Data for the balance of plant in ways that were not obvious. Even more common is when so much emphasis is placed on the new technology that other things are neglected. For example, one quite innovative minerals-processing facility got the new technology heart of the process right, but got the ore characteristics essential to the design of the front-end of the process so completely wrong that the plant would not operate. That was the simple bit; the hard stuff they got right. The result was a walkaway nonetheless.

Figure 9.4 shows how increasing amounts of new technology are associated with increases in the frequency of projects that we label operational failures. The pattern of increased risk is important: moving simply from completely conventional technology to introducing a new integration of proven technologies almost doubles the risk of operational failure. On smaller projects, the introduction of new technology integration has no measurable effect on production. This difference is consistent with what we know about the nature of megaprojects: they are rather inflexible.

Major modifications and substantially new technology are associated with operational failures over half the time. Almost all of these failures were generated by serious gaps in the Basic Data.

This raises an obvious question: What would induce any sane sponsor to incorporate significant amounts of new technology into their megaproject? Most of the time, the use of new technology is necessary to being able to do the project at all. For example, new technology to exploit petroleum reservoirs in deeper ocean waters is inherent to deepwater projects. In such cases, the technology risks are real, but the risks are often well understood going in.

More problematic are cases in which the use of a new technology is expected to make an otherwise economically marginal project viable. Such situations are problematic because the economics are likely still not very robust, and new technology project results have to be substantially discounted for the risks. Highly successful new technology megaprojects do exist, but they are rare.

There are other problematic situations as well. In some cases, the business leadership is unaware of the amount of technology risk that is being taken by the project team. This occurs because the project team is concerned that if the business hears the words *new technology* the project will be killed because the business is considered highly risk-averse. Several of the walkaways had project teams that deliberately and carefully misled the businesses about the technology risk, claiming things had been demonstrated and proven when they had not.

One case was particularly instructive. This was a metal mining and processing complex exploiting an ore that was unusual from a chemistry standpoint. A technology team at the site had been working on the technology for many years and the commercialization of the technology was the only way to keep the site open. As a single owner project, there were no troublesome joint venture partners looking over their shoulders. The team carefully controlled and managed all information about the technology and the project. All reviews were carefully staged and dissenting views about technology readiness were never aired with anyone outside the team. (I doubt they were raised inside the team either, but we do know that a report by a consulting engineer that was very critical of the technology's readiness was made to disappear until it surfaced during the post mortem.) The only red flag that appeared on the front-end of the project was that the team leader was also the primary process developer. That is a conflict-of-interest situation because process developers are often deeply enamored of their technology "babies." The result was really ugly: the project cost more than doubled after the full-funds authorization; the process did not work when the project was ultimately completed (by a completely new project team); and the company closed the site permanently less than a year after the project was completed. There were two other cases that look almost identical to this one.

There are also instances in which no one involved on the project—business, project team, or technology developers—really understood the degree of step-out in technology that was being undertaken. This is easier than it may seem. Sometimes when making a number of incremental changes in technology, those changes interact to produce significant Basic Data surprises. Referring to Figure 9.4, this is why integrating known technologies in new ways can generate failures. Over a third of the projects that had only new integrations generated serious Basic Data errors and production failure followed. Two of these were minerals-processing facilities in which new control systems were being integrated as part of expansion projects. These projects were startup and operational nightmares.

No megaproject should ever undertake new technology unless that technology is necessary to the mission of the project. Discretionary use of new technology is admirable (and often profitable) in small projects, but it is begging for trouble in megaprojects. We had a number of megaprojects that were the result of major corporate efforts to make major advances in technology. Some of these bold efforts were the culmination of over a decade of development. Most of these programs did, in fact, move the technology forward, but all of the projects were failures and some were truly dramatic failures. In the worst case, it took so long to complete the very complex pioneering project, that more nimble competitors were able to snatch the technology via the contractors and get their less technologically aggressive projects online before the pioneer project was completed.[12]

The problem was not attempting to move technology forward; it was trying to incorporate a great many advances into a single large project. That rendered the project too complex to manage. A more sensible approach is to push the technology forward in pieces. For example, the first deepwater tension leg platform (TLP), Shell's Auger Project, was preceded by a pilot in the North Sea (Conoco's Hutton Project) that tested the drilling and production concept in shallow water (~500 feet). Auger did not also pioneer subsea (wet trees) in deep water. That was done by Petrobras. Later, combined subsea production and floaters in the form of spars, TLPs and Floating Production Storage and Offloading (FPSO) platforms would become commonplace, but not all at once. *The general principle is this: if a megaproject is to be used to move technology development forward, make the project as simple an application of the technology as possible.* Complexity and new technology interact in ways that are difficult to predict and likely to cause project failure. The lesson is not to avoid new technology; it is to keep it as simple as humanly possible.

In some cases, technologies may be acquired via license from technology development firms. These licensors sell packages that usually include the preliminary (basic) design for the technology. Generally, licensed packages have reliable Basic Data, but not always. Prudent sponsors will want to see the licensed technology in operation elsewhere

---

[12]There are some very interesting differences between industrial sectors in seeking competitive advantage via technological innovation. The chemicals and pharmaceuticals industries seek to put patent "ring-fences" around new technology developments to the greatest possible extent. The petroleum and minerals industries typically do not attempt to hold new technology close or at least do not appear to do a very good job of doing so. In minerals, intellectual property tends to be held by the supply chain, and in petroleum, intellectual property associated with facilities tends not to be tightly guarded at all, allowing the contractors to move technology from owner to owner.

and talk to those that have licensed before about how complete and accurate the data were that were provided by the licensor. Check for the number of prior licenses that have been taken out and actually operated successfully. Being number one or two is not safe ground for a megaproject. The most problematic aspects of licensed packages are often the data around the supporting utility requirements for the technology. The use of licensors also adds interfaces that have to be managed, and creates opportunities for disruption to schedule when the licensor's data are late. The use of licensed packages also increases the number of required engineering hours significantly—about 15% on average.

In offshore wind, there is a similar problem with the wind turbine suppliers. The owners adopt the latest and largest turbine as soon as it emerges and apply those turbines to very large projects despite the fact that the units have unknown reliability and maintenance costs. This dynamic is created by the reverse auction format followed in many of these projects, which renders them very low margin. The "latest and greatest" appear to improve the margins but any reliability problems can quickly make that margin disappear. The vendor guarantees are never enough to rescue the margin even if they are sufficient to bankrupt the vendors!

Expensive and Difficult to Obtain Data

Sometimes the Basic Data are simply very difficult to obtain and are always subject to uncertainty. For example, the characteristics of a petroleum reservoir constitute the most important part of the Basic Data for an oil and gas project. But because the reservoir is, by its nature, inaccessible, the data must be inferred and interpreted from measurements from seismic survey, appraisal wells, and well tests. The usual situation is that we have to make a trade-off between the cost and time associated with gathering information, and the certainty and completeness of the information. Judging that trade-off correctly is one of the hallmarks of successful petroleum production companies.

Skimping on the Basic Data development when the reservoir is small and the project to develop it will be small as well makes some economic sense. An extensive appraisal program for a small reservoir that is going to be developed with one or two subsea wells tied back to an existing host would make no economic sense. By contrast, skimping on the Basic Data development for a large reservoir that will require a multibillion-dollar project to develop is foolhardy unless some extreme constraints are in play. About 16% of the petroleum development megaprojects experienced a major reserves downgrade of 25% or more after startup. If the reserves downgrades were as a result of greater reservoir compartmentalization than expected or problems with petroleum flow, this translated to lower than planned production and economic failure of the project. Often, such projects end up requiring many more wells programs than anticipated or unplanned enhanced recovery schemes. In other cases, the reserves downgrade was based on a misunderstanding of the areal extent of the reservoir, and initial production was not seriously affected, although the project economics were eventually affected by less producible petroleum than expected. Although the projects with major downward revisions in reserves could be considered Basic Data failures, I did not classify the projects as failed projects unless they failed on one of the other dimensions, such as cost, schedule, or production in the first two years.[13]

In chemicals and minerals processing, the most common source of Basic Data errors derives from a decision not to pilot a new process or not to pilot an old process for a new chemical feedstock or ore. Prior IPA research has shown that fully integrated pilot plants are essential whenever the process is complex or whenever heterogeneous solids are being processed.[14] But a fully integrated pilot plant (i.e., a pilot plant that includes all processing steps in the same manner as the commercial design) is expensive, in some cases, amounting to 25% of the eventual cost of the commercial scale facilities. The businesses considering the pilot plant decision sometimes tell me that the cost of the pilot plant will kill the economics of the venture. To which I can only reply, "You have simply found an alternative way of saying the venture is uneconomic."

[13]Of course, the projects with major upward revisions in reserves could also be considered Basic Data failures as well, but are not classified as such. Ten percent of the petroleum projects had upward revisions of more than 25%. Those projects undoubtedly left some value on the table as well.

[14]See E.W. Merrow, "Bringing New Technologies to Market: The Process Industry's Experience," IPA 1995. Heterogeneous solids needs to be interpreted broadly. For example, the recycling of plastics, even if a single type is involved such as recycling of PET bottles, must almost always be considered a difficult feedstock because that feedstock will contain a great many unwelcome surprises from cigarette butts to chewing gum!

Inexperienced (and Occasionally Oblivious) Owners

Sometimes teams and their business leadership are simply oblivious to the risks they are running vis-à-vis Basic Data development. This occurs most often when the lead sponsor is either inexperienced with the type of project (i.e., lacks expertise), or in cases where the sponsor has turned leadership of the project over to a contractor. Of course, these situations are not mutually exclusive. Some examples should clarify what I mean.

In one case, a chemical company was sponsoring a multibillion-dollar grassroots complex using entirely conventional technology. Its chosen contracting strategy was EPC-lump-sum turnkey with penalties for late completion and a penalty for failure to operate that was a few percent of total cost—quite a sizeable penalty. Their experience with the core technologies was deep and everything was carefully defined in a performance specification. But this project required a seawater cooling system, which was entirely outside the company's experience. The complex was built on time and on budget without difficulty, and then took over two years to start up because the seawater cooling system did not operate properly. First, the seawater temperature had been mis-specified by the sponsor. (It had used old records of seawater temperatures in the area with no data of season-to-season variation.) Second, biofouling was severe. Third, the system was subject to repeated breakdowns of uncertain origin. Ultimately, the system had to be redesigned and rebuilt from scratch by another contractor. Four years later, the complex was up and operating as intended. Because the sponsor provided the seawater temperature data, adjudicating who was accountable for what was very difficult, and the contractor was hit with almost no penalty. The complex, which would have turned a nice profit, ended up net present value (NPV)-negative because of the delay in production.

Here is another example that would almost be amusing if it had not been so expensive. A joint venture was building a grassroots liquified natural gas (LNG) complex that required extensive air cooling. (LNG, of course, requires extensive heat transfer.) They secured the Basic Data for the ambient air temperatures and wind directions from the local weather forecaster. Guess what? In this case, even the weather forecaster didn't know which way the wind blows! The wind direction error, combined with inaccurate air temperature data, rendered the heat exchange inadequate to produce LNG anywhere close to capacity. Because of the plant layout, increasing the air cooler capacity is almost impossible so the complex's output is limited permanently. Unfortunately, in this case, 100% of capacity was forward sold with take or pay guarantees that obligated the sponsors to buy LNG on the merchant market to fulfill their obligations if they were unable to produce it. (They even sold their design margin, which is unusual, but the market was great at the time.) This was one very expensive Basic Data error. How could such a mistake occur? The company laid off almost all of its LNG-knowledgeable people after they had completed a prior project. There was nobody on the team who could signal the risk they were running by not verifying information acquired from a local source.

Root Causes of Basic Data Errors

The most important cause of Basic Data errors is the drive for speed. To paraphrase the Iron Law of Oligarchy:[15]

Speed Tends to Kill and Absolute Speed Kills Absolutely!

When pressure is applied to complete a project in less time than the normal gestation of the project, corners get cut. Project directors tend to cut the front-end of the project because only by doing so can they even imagine completing the project on the schedule that the business leadership wants. It is extraordinarily difficult to accelerate Basic Data development successfully. A good deal of Basic Data development is necessarily sequential and cumulative. Errors or faulty assumptions will tend to cascade through the basis of design. When there were Basic Data errors in a project, the time spent on front-end loading

[15]For those interested in trivia, the Iron Law of Oligarchy—Power tends to corrupt and absolute power corrupts absolutely—was coined by obscure Swiss sociologist Robert Michels and is found in his book *Political Parties*. The Iron Law is often misattributed to Niccolo Machiavelli.

Phases Two and Three (Select and Define) was a third less, even after controlling for project size and technology.[16] On average, the seven to eight months "saved" in front-end loading was given back roughly four times over; twice in execution and another two times in startup. It behooves project directors to show these results to their business leaders who want megaprojects accelerated.

The second most common source of Basic Data errors is miscommunication or noncommunication between functions. Sometimes what I thought I said is not what you thought you heard. If you and I speak different professional languages, it is all too easy for us to miscommunicate. I will never forget listening to an angry exchange between a reservoir engineer and a facilities project manager during a postmortem of a problematic petroleum production project. At issue was the rapid buildup of wax in the wells of a gas condensate reservoir. The reservoir engineer said, "I told you it was a high-pressure/high-temperature reservoir, why didn't you listen!" The project manager said, "You never said anything about wax—not a word!" At which, the reservoir engineer simply repeated what he had said before, but more vehemently; in his world the word *wax* was fully understood if the reservoir is high-pressure/high-temperature condensate.

Miscommunication across functions is common in all projects, but is it is especially common in megaprojects. There tend to be more functions involved in these projects. It is much more likely that the Basic Data require development, which in turn, requires more cross-functional communication requirements. The businesses tend to be much more involved in megaprojects, and many business people speak no project and many project people speak no business. As we will discuss in later chapters, project organizations and teams are rarely set up in ways that make cross-functional communication easy.

Finally, sometimes Basic Data errors occur because something was simply overlooked. This tends to be more common when the lead sponsor's personnel are not deeply familiar with all aspects of a project's technology. But that is the usual case with megaprojects. The volume, breadth, and depth of data that must be produced for a successful

[16]Result is significant Pr|t|<.03.

complex megaproject are breathtaking. Some things are inevitably missed, but most of those are small and can be rectified later. Missing something critical can and does happen. When the Basic Data needs of a project are not understood at the beginning of project planning back in FEL-1, when the opportunity Shaping process is just getting started, it sometimes turns out to be too late to get good quality data when the need is recognized.

The Basic Data Protocol as an Antidote to Failure

I believe that most, although probably not all, Basic Data failures are preventable. Surely those caused by excessive speed can be prevented if the right people can be persuaded that excessive speed is self-defeating. Nobody *wants* to fail.

The best way to prevent Basic Data failures caused by oversights is with a Basic Data Protocol that covers *all* aspects of a project's technology. Many companies maintain protocols or checklists for all of the primary technologies they employ. A Basic Data protocol goes a bit further than the standard Basis of Design document. First, it covers all aspects of a project, including parts that are not standard for the sponsor. That means that protocol development work is needed whenever a project's technology includes elements that have not been subjected to a Basic Data protocol before. Second, it is not enough to simply list an item and check it off later. There must standards of quality and there must be accountability for data accuracy and integrity. There must be a change procedure that provides notification of those whose design may be affected by the change.

The Basic Data Protocol is the technical counterpart to a project risk register:

- For each area of a project, the protocol includes what Basic Data will be required.
- What activities are outstanding that will be required to secure the data.

- The schedule for production of the data.
- Who (by name and function) is responsible for the production of the data and for informing the project team if any slips in schedule occur.
- Actions that will be taken (including slowing or halting the project) if certain Basic Data are not obtained by a critical milestone; in others words, is there a Plan B?
- As said earlier, projects should be data- and accomplishment-driven on the front-end, not calendar-driven. But if there is no management system in place to manage the Basic Data, it is almost impossible to be data-driven.

Finally, every company needs to educate those who make the important decisions in their megaprojects (i.e., the businesses) that getting the Basic Data right is essential to success. I will always remember the answer given to an executive's question about why don't we just design conservatively if the Basic Data are uncertain: "Because then we would have a conservatively designed, but still very dead, white elephant."

CHAPTER 10

Project Definition—Getting the Front-End Right

For want of a nail the shoe was lost.
For want of a shoe the horse was lost.
For want of a horse the rider was lost.
For want of a rider the battle was lost.
For want of a battle the kingdom was lost.
And all for the want of a horseshoe nail.

Because megaprojects are fragile, even little things matter. Let me offer an example of a seemingly trivial oversight in project preparation that brought down what could otherwise have been a great project.

The project was a greenfield chemicals joint venture megaproject executed in a nonremote, project-friendly area. The Shaping process developed without any problems and the scope was fully defined at closure. The project team did an excellent job defining the project. Our evaluation of its front-end work gave the team an almost perfect mark. Their undoing was the "almost." A single item was not completed before the project was tendered for EPC-lump-sum bids: a HAZOPs[1] evaluation of the design. The HAZOP, of course, not only finds potential hazards in the design, it also tends to find any errors and omissions in the piping and instrumentation diagrams. The team elected not to do HAZOPs because it decided to put the task in the requirements for the winning contractor. I believe that when the team made the decision, it already had a good idea of who the winning contractor would be and it knew the company to be a technically strong organization. It was considered a minor shortcut by the team, but the team members were pressed to meet their sanction date, and HAZOP is one of the very last tasks in FEL-3. So instead of a perfect 4.00 score on their FEL index, they received a 4.25.

Several months into execution, team members asked their contractor to show them the results of the HAZOP. The contractor responded that they didn't think the sponsors *really* meant for them to do the HAZOP so they hadn't done it. The owner team demurred, saying that the complex would handle huge hydrocarbon inventories and the HAZOP was not optional. So the contractor stopped work, performed the HAZOP, and found a significant number of errors that had to be corrected.

Because design had been progressing rapidly for several months with both the contractor and a licensor participating, the changes were very disruptive to engineering and engineering fell seriously behind. The engineering contractor had bid the project using the most highly respected international construction contractor in the region as its subcontractor. When informed that construction would have to begin nearly a year later than planned, the construction contractor voided their agreement with the engineering contractor, as they were permitted to do by their agreement. The construction firm had other projects to which it was committed that now conflicted with our project.

As a result, the lead contractor was forced go looking for alternatives and finally had to settle for a number of smaller construction firms, several of which turned out to be hopelessly incompetent. Construction hours spiraled out of control, overrunning the contractor's

[1]HAZOP stands for Hazards and Operability Study. It is a rigorous examination of the design, especially studying what happens when the plant is started up, shut down, or experiences an upset such as sudden loss of power.

bid estimate by over 25 million field hours! The whole project fell still further behind, and when the project was finally delivered, the result was a shoddily constructed, marginally operable complex. All this is despite the fact that the contract was a "lump sum turnkey" with penalties and was awarded to one of the world's premier engineering contractors. The plant took a year and half to start up, and in my opinion, will never operate satisfactorily unless it is thoroughly recapitalized. "All for the want of a horseshoe nail."

For a number of reasons, the sort of debacle just described would not happen on a smaller project simply because HAZOP was postponed. Because the engineering effort would be smaller, it would probably be possible to catch up. The market for competent construction firms would not be so constrained for a smaller project. And in the case of a smaller project, the HAZOP, which caused the problem to begin with, probably would have been executed by the team because it would not have been that time-consuming. Because megaprojects are fragile, they are terribly sensitive to seemingly small mistakes.

The definition of a project from the formation of the core scoping team to full-funds authorization is what we call the front-end loading (FEL) process. After 30 years of showing the data, badgering, cajoling, and whining to the industry about the criticality of FEL, I believe there is now virtual consensus among project professionals within the community of industries we serve that FEL is the single most important predictive indicator of project success. There are very few project professionals in the process industries who do not agree with the basic principle that definition and planning drive success, and those who don't should probably be in some other line of work. In over 700 megaprojects, only a few had project directors that considered FEL as not very important. All were inexperienced as project directors, which is unusual for megaprojects, and all were disastrous failures.

The basics of what later became the IPA FEL index were published in 1981.[2] Of course, the formalization of the process did not start there. Exxon Research and Engineering had a work process as early as the 1960s that, in structure, is very much like the stage-gated process that is

[2]E.W. Merrow, Kenneth Phillips, and Christopher W. Myers, *Understanding Cost Growth and Performance Shortfalls in Pioneer Process Plants*, Santa Monica, CA: The Rand Corporation, 1981.

now standard within the petroleum, chemicals, pharmaceuticals, and finally, minerals industries. I have encountered a number of "inventors" of the process over the years and I have never doubted that the process was invented in parallel any number of times. It is indeed such an obvious process that parallel invention would be expected.

We have succeeded so well in getting agreement that defining a project thoroughly is a good thing that we are starting to see a backlash of complaining that we have "too much of a good thing."[3] Of course, one can do too much FEL; it is perfectly obvious. That is why IPA has always spoken in terms of "best practical" FEL, not "best possible." As soon as the investment in planning gets large enough to create a forward-going economics trap, you are doing too much. For megaprojects with difficult Shaping situations, one also has to be aware of the problem of the FEL getting out in front of the Shaping negotiations and distorting negotiating position due to sunk costs. Yes, I know that sunk costs are sunk, which is to say should be forgotten. However, sunk costs are often still too real psychologically to be dismissed. Unfortunately, we are nowhere near the point of having too much definition for industrial megaprojects. Indeed, quite the opposite is true.

What Is FEL?

FEL is the core work process of project teams prior to authorization. The work process is typically divided into phases or stages with a pause for an assessment and decision about whether to proceed. The gate assessments should examine both the economic/business and technical aspects of the project at that point. Those decision-points are generally called gates. A basic rendition of the FEL process is shown in Figure 10.1. The number of gates in a system is not terribly important, although I believe that three is the minimum essential number to have a coherent process. There needs to be at least one gate at which the business case can be assessed; a gate when the scope is closed and the implications of the scope can be evaluated; and finally, a gate that

[3]See Nick Lowes and Jean Paul van Driel, "Too Much of a Good Thing?" *Petroleum Review*, June 2004.

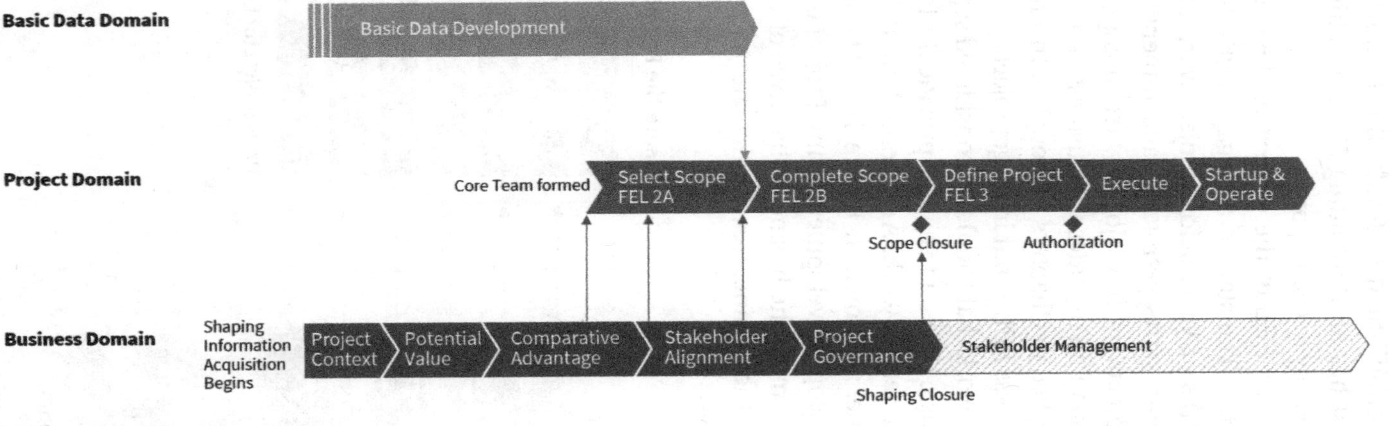

FIGURE 10.1 FEL in Context

triggers the full commitment of funds. But I know one (very good) project system that has an astounding 32 gates, although only a few are actually used as key decision points.

Figure 10.1 shows FEL in the context of the overall megaproject development process. The start of a megaproject's development often occurs many months or years before project work begins. Basic Data development usually starts petroleum and minerals projects, and is often the project precursor in major new technology developments in other industries. Shaping includes the business case development process and was described in Chapters 5 through 8. In smaller projects, we would call that process FEL-1, but in megaprojects, it is a large and very complex stream of work that should be considered separately.

Inputs from Basic Data and Shaping provide the foundation for the scope development team's work. An essential input from the business is the project frame, as shown in Figure 10.2. The frame constitutes the charter to the scope development team. Project objectives must be formulated so as to meet the business objectives of the capital spend. The more clearly the business can articulate its requirements and

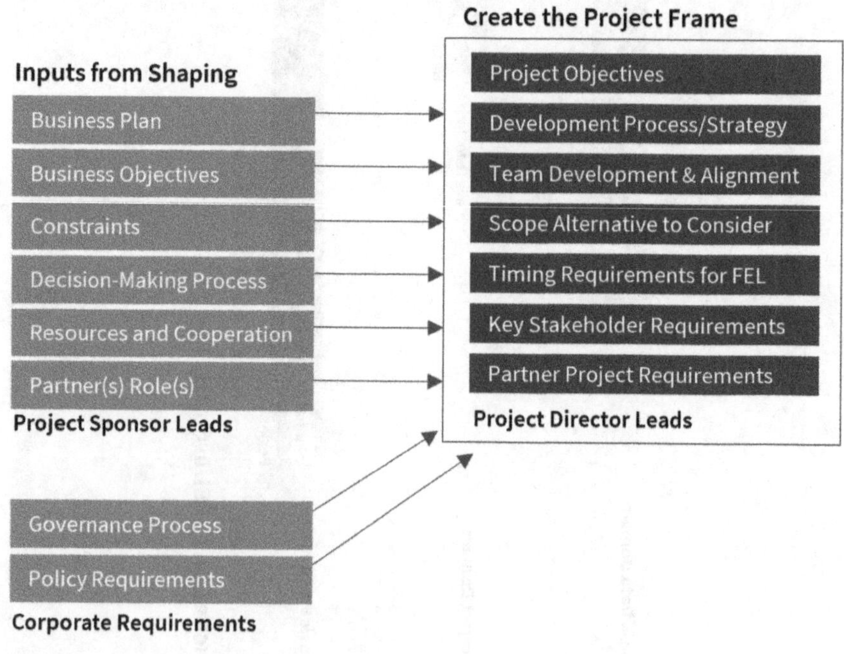

FIGURE 10.2 From Shaping to Frame

desires, the more straightforward the scoping team's work becomes. Of particular importance are any constraints on the scope that emerge from the Shaping process to that point. For example, if there is a capex ceiling for any partner, that is crucial information. If the Shaping/commercial side have made timing commitments, those need to be fully communicated. (Of course, it is true that those commitments should not have been made without vetting from the projects organization, but we all have to live in the real world.)

The business requirements must be consonant with corporate requirements. Corporate is responsible for providing and implementing the capital governance process (the subject of Chapter 15) and any other policy requirements. For example, there may well be requirements around environmental compliance, carbon intensity, and other sustainability issues from corporate. If the business requirements violate or push the scoping team toward violating corporate requirements, the conflict needs to be elevated very quickly. This problem is not hypothetical. We see it fairly frequently. For example, the business wants local environmental standards to be followed to save money while the corporate policy requires that more stringent standards be followed. Carbon intensity requirements have been established by a few of our clients and are in progress in many others. Those requirements will open up new problem areas for scope development teams.

One of the most important misunderstandings within industrial firms is the purpose of the gates in the work process. Many business professionals assume that because the engineering and project management organization is the steward for the stage-gated process, the process is structured to meet an engineering purpose. In fact, however, the gates serve, not engineering interests, but the interests of corporate management and the shareholders. The corporate purpose is to allow points in the development process for decisions to stop, recycle, or proceed to be made. The work process without the gates is a combined business/engineering process that starts out very heavily business-focused and acquires its technical and engineering focus along the way.[4] The engineers would gladly forego any gates and follow

[4]In resource development projects and projects incorporating new technology, the Basic Data development function is also very active early on.

a seamless process all the way through, but that would be a disaster for the corporation because corporate control of capital would be lost.

It is very important to the health of the corporation's capital program that those decision points in terms of the development of the projects are the same for every capital project brought forward to a gate. Without commonality of FEL requirements for all projects at each decision point, effective governance of the capital portfolio is not possible. The loss of governing control occurs because projects with different levels of FEL accomplished have cost estimates, schedules, and production performance promises of very different reliability and quality. As we will see, this general observation about all projects is especially applicable to megaprojects because megaprojects are extremely sensitive to FEL status.

In an effective megaproject development, there will be a lively interchange of information between those attempting to Shape the project and those responsible for developing the technical scope of the project. The information needs flow both ways. For example, for onshore projects, the scoping team needs access to the site of the project very early. The Shaping team has to ensure that access is available. At the same time, the Shaping team will be very anxious to understand the likely cost and schedule of the project, but unfortunately, until a basic scope is available, the early cost estimates and schedule forecasts really don't mean very much. Until the scope development gets to the "refine scope" stage shown in Figure 10.1, any cost estimated will tend to have a strong low bias unless analog benchmarks are available.

Cost estimates made at this point are little better than educated guesses because the physical scope that will be required to create a real project has not yet been defined. But guesses or not, there will be at least one cost "estimate" for the project. The problem with early cost forecasts is not just that they are usually too low. It is that they are too low by a completely unknowable amount. The cost number that was thrown out there might be 80% of the eventual project cost or it might be 30%. That means the early numbers cannot simply be de-biased by applying some factor. For example, doubling the early numbers would kill some very good projects, while doing little or nothing about the truly terrible ones.

The best approach at this juncture in a project is to take a set of projects that are broadly similar and ask whether this one has characteristics that would make it tend to be lower or higher than those projects on a capital cost per unit output basis. If, for example, your project is petroleum production, ask how much capital per barrel are we spending on projects with similar-sized reservoirs? Is this project in deeper or shallower water than those? Does it have easier or harder logistics? Is the resource owner easier or harder to work with? The same sorts of questions can and should be asked for minerals and chemicals projects. Nonetheless, the cost numbers at this early stage are not really estimates in the usual sense; they are, at best, indicators of cost. The same general rubric applies to schedules as well. At this point they are indicative only—and usually too short. Conceptual benchmarking, sometimes known as reference class forecasting, is very dependent on having appropriate analog data and making good decisions about what "appropriate" means.

The corporate governance problem is created when cost and schedule numbers from a project that is still early in gestation are compared with those from a project that has been fully and carefully developed. The fully and carefully developed project will often lose out because of the inherent low bias in the cost and schedule forecasts for a poorly defined project. Having the poorly defined project win out distorts behavior and encourages misrepresentation of projects by rewarding the poorly defined projects with money. If you create a situation in which liars tend to win, sooner or later that is all you will have.

It is very unfortunate that the gate to enter scope development is by far the weakest in most organizations. Too many projects pass through the gate without much assessment. This, in turn, creates too many projects in FEL-2, which consumes the most creative technical people in the organization. Often, they are doing work that has no possibility of becoming a real project. Because the "into scoping" gate is weak, a good many bad business ideas start scope development. Some of them inevitably become real projects. Unlike later gates at the end of scope development and at final investment decision (FID), there is nothing approaching an industry standard in terms of deliverables for the gate to start scope development. Businesses have been unwilling to subject themselves to the sort of strict standards that would make the gate meaningful and corporate management has often abdicated its role.

Megaprojects with very weak business cases are much more likely to be single-owner sponsor ventures or have a dominant lead sponsor and a small, passive co-sponsor. Joint venture partners seem to have the effect of checking irrational enthusiasm, perhaps because partners are more skeptical of the lead sponsor's prowess than that lead sponsor is. However, when the business case for a megaproject is weak, there are some telltale characteristics. First, the projects tend to enter FEL-2 (Scope Development) with a large number of possible options to be examined. That is highly problematic because prior research has shown that entering FEL-2 with more than two or three scope options results in FEL-2 not being complete when it is declared done.[5] This is not a necessary outcome, but an outcome that is generated by running out of time. To reiterate an earlier point: eventually the calendar will start driving a project team no matter how much time was promised at the start of an activity. Second, the projects with weak business cases are likely to come under intense pressure to cut costs during FEL-3. As discussed in Chapter 4, cost reduction exercises almost always result in failed megaprojects. And third, weak business cases are associated with aggressive schedules because a more aggressive schedule will make cash flow and NPV appear to be better.

Assessing the Scope Development Phases

We characterize FEL as having three big blocks of work. The first is getting the project established and adjusted in its site. Examples of the kinds of issues that need to be tackled are shown in Figure 10.3. For onshore projects, the labor supply is particularly critical. For offshore petroleum projects, this is just as important as it is for onshore projects and is, in some respects, more difficult. Offshore projects have to understand the site in terms of ocean floor and the metocean conditions.[6] When moving into new ocean territory, fully understanding

---

[5]Paul Barshop and Chris Farroknia, "Best Practice for Alternative Selection in FEL-2," Presentation to the 19th Annual Meeting of the Industry Benchmarking Consortium, March 2009. Available at www.ipaglobal.com

[6]Metocean = meteorological and oceanographic.

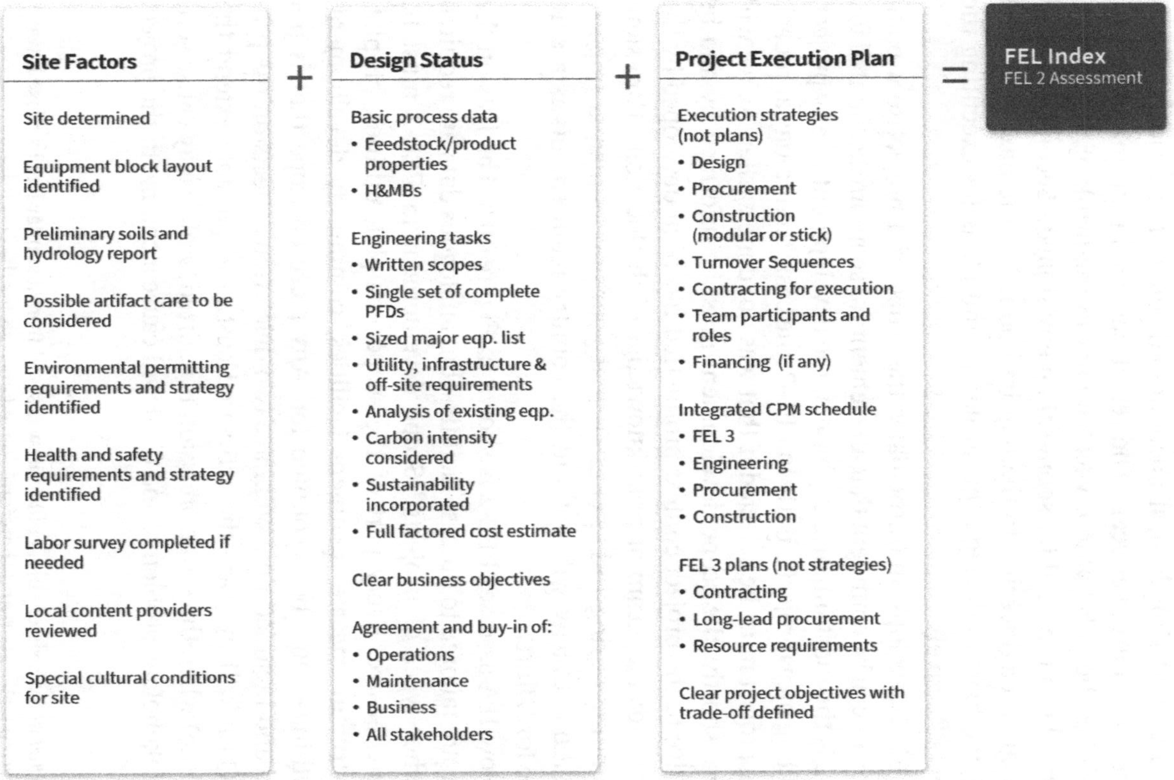

Site Factors

Site determined

Equipment block layout identified

Preliminary soils and hydrology report

Possible artifact care to be considered

Environmental permitting requirements and strategy identified

Health and safety requirements and strategy identified

Labor survey completed if needed

Local content providers reviewed

Special cultural conditions for site

\+

Design Status

Basic process data

- Feedstock/product properties
- H&MBs

Engineering tasks

- Written scopes
- Single set of complete PFDs
- Sized major eqp. list
- Utility, infrastructure & off-site requirements
- Analysis of existing eqp.
- Carbon intensity considered
- Sustainability incorporated
- Full factored cost estimate

Clear business objectives

Agreement and buy-in of:

- Operations
- Maintenance
- Business
- All stakeholders

\+

Project Execution Plan

Execution strategies (not plans)

- Design
- Procurement
- Construction (modular or stick)
- Turnover Sequences
- Contracting for execution
- Team participants and roles
- Financing (if any)

Integrated CPM schedule

- FEL 3
- Engineering
- Procurement
- Construction

FEL 3 plans (not strategies)

- Contracting
- Long-lead procurement
- Resource requirements

Clear project objectives with trade-off defined

=

FEL Index
FEL 2 Assessment

FIGURE 10.3 FEL 2 Assessment and Index

the metocean conditions can be quite difficult because there may be no records that cover the location adequately. For example, when BP pioneered the move into the area west of the Shetland Islands off the United Kingdom, it encountered some of the most difficult ocean conditions ever seen. The result has been that one of its vessels there, the *Schehallion*, was battered to the brink of destruction and has been replaced far sooner than envisioned.[7] Second, we need to progress engineering to the required point for the next gate. And third, we have to develop the strategies and plans for executing the project effectively.

FEL-2 develops and articulates the scope of a project to a point where we can be confident that all elements of scope are accounted for. FEL-2 is the most important phase in the development of any project, including megaprojects. Early in FEL-2, the basic technology approach to the project must be selected if that was not done earlier. As we will discuss shortly, the scope development must be informed by and be sensitive to the project context profile that has been developed by the country advance team or prior knowledge of the location.[8] For example, finding during FEL-3 (FEED) that your environmental impacts mitigation strategy will not suit the country requirements is a sure recipe for failure.

How IPA assesses FEL-2 is shown in Figure 10.3. The lists on the figure are tailored to process facilities, but analogous data are required for other types of projects.[9] Scope development in FEL-2 must be comprehensive. Every part of the scope—on-plot, utilities, off-plot, infrastructure, waste treatment facilities, community development, everything—most be accounted for. Any piece of scope that is not found and included now will have two deleterious effects on the project: (1) it will increase the estimated cost (and possibly extend the schedule) when the scope omission is realized, which may cause serious stakeholder problems; and (2) it will cause a change to the project

[7]The *Schehallion*'s sister ship, *Foinaven*, was saved from a similar fate because it was a converted icebreaker, and therefore, rugged enough for the conditions.

[8]See Chapters 5 and 6.

[9]There are separate FEL indices for petroleum production projects, mines and minerals, pipelines, and pharmaceutical facilities projects. Modifications are made to the diagrams shown for power projects.

at a time when change is disruptive. The heat and mass balances must be closed, the process flow diagrams must be complete, and every last piece of major equipment accounted for. The equipment list will then be priced and become the basis for the development of a *reliable* capital cost estimate for the entire project.

Site deliverables should include all relevant aspects of the context that have been learned in Shaping. For example, if the site may contain archeological value or artifacts of indigenous cultures, that needs to be included in the plan for the site development. The plot plan should be carefully considered in FEL-2. Plot growth in FEL-3 (and its equivalent of topsides weight growth in offshore projects) indicates that scope was missed or input from a critical function such as maintenance was inadequate. Site considerations may have to include local content requirements, which also have to be incorporated into the project execution strategy. Site conditions should also include any special circumstances that may be required for a labor camp, such as dividing the camp for cultural and religious incompatibilities. In today's world, engineering deliverables should include the carbon intensity of the project and related concerns such as circularity. And the execution plan must include the financing strategy if external financing will be employed. The more aspects of the project that are included in the execution plan, the easier risk assessment and management will be later on.

If FEL-2 is complete, then the cost estimate will be centered on the actual cost of the project in real (constant currency) terms.[10] Barshop and Giguere found that the most important single measure of FEL-2 closure is whether the process flow diagrams (PFDs) are complete. When the PFDs are complete, projects tend to experience no cost growth during FEL-3. When the PFDs are not complete, or when alternative scopes are still under consideration, significant cost growth occurs and the probability of project failure increases very significantly.

[10] Paul H. Barshop and Christopher Giguere, "Improving the Effectiveness of the Scope Development Phase of Front-end Loading," Presentation to the 16th Annual Meeting of the Industry Benchmarking Consortium, March 2006. Available at www.ipaglobal.com

The Dangers of Starting Scope Development Too Early

Scoping activities should not start until sufficient Basic Data are in hand to allow the work to proceed authoritatively. The desire to push a project into scope development prematurely is understandable—it appears to make something happen—but it damages the long-term prospects for the project. In order to start scope development, a scoping team needs the project frame from the business and a holistic understanding of the Basic Data. In resource development projects, the largest portion of those Basic Data will be the description of the petroleum reservoir or mineral orebody. As discussed in Chapter 9, the handover point from the Basic Data developers to the project scope developers is often hazy and inconsistent. If the reservoir or orebody appears to be large, that sometimes triggers a very early start to scope development because it is assumed that the project will surely result and there is a desire to declare commerciality in order to book the reserves with financial markets. In new technology process projects, the trigger to start scope development may be corporate enthusiasm rather than data availability. For example, we are currently coping with the fallout of a new technology de-carbonization project that was pushed along by corporate management looking to build sustainability credibility, only to realize in the middle of construction of the pioneer plant that a pilot plant was really going to be essential to establishing a reliable Basic Data.

I suspect that many people involved in the early stages of a project believe that there is not any downside to starting scope development early. After all, the sooner we get started, the sooner we will have a better sense of the cost picture for the project. I believe that view is mistaken on several grounds.

First, when the business case is not sufficiently developed to provide a clear frame for the scoping team, the first formulation of the scope may be far wide of what will later be considered an acceptable scope. The project may be larger or smaller than what is needed. It may be impracticable in the required time. Often, the project frame cannot be established for the scoping team until after a considerable amount of Shaping work has been completed. If we simply have no idea of what stakeholders other than ourselves are going to require, we lack the information needed to develop a scope for many megaprojects.

Second, starting scope development with insufficient Basic Data is always a mistake. When the Basic Data are insufficient to develop an accurate basic concept for the project, the scoping team will start making assumptions to fill in the missing pieces. Unless very lucky, some of those assumptions will be wrong, and the scope will later be seen as inadequate.

When the insufficiency of Shaping or Basic Data becomes clear during scope development, we start to make changes to accommodate the new information. What we rarely do, but should, is discard all of the work to date and start over. Changing the wrong scope with multiple patches rarely results in a scope that is as good as doing it right the first time. The first scope developed also has an "echo" in the final scope unless we start over; time is rarely saved.

If you recall the Shaping Nightmare that I described in Chapter 5, the project scoping was completed without anything known about the desires of the local community. The sponsors locked themselves into that scope despite violent opposition to aspects of it from the community. From the sponsors' point of view the scope was obviously correct for the project because it was low cost and effective. But that was not at all obvious to the local community and the resulting decade of dispute made the project a reputational disaster for the lead sponsor and uneconomic in the end.

At the end of FEL-2, we should have closure of the Shaping process, closure of the project scope, and cost and schedule forecasts that are reliable. By *reliable*, I mean that they are centered on what the eventual actual values are most likely to be and the distribution around the most likely value is known and real, not the figment of somebody's imagination. But the forecasts are not yet highly precise, which is to say, the distributions around both cost and schedule will typically be on the order of –15/+25 on a single standard error. At this point, the stakeholder-investors will have to make a decision about whether to do or not do the project. It is unlikely that any more information will be forthcoming. The last option on the project is about to expire.

Some will surely object at this point that the final decision has not yet been made. Full-funds authorization will not come until after the FEL-3/FEED/Feasibility phase is complete. Surely, we will get one last chance to decide on the project, making this end of FEL-2 decision less important! That interpretation of the FEL process is, I believe, profoundly incorrect. FEL-3 is necessary and important, but it culminates not in a decision about whether we *will* do the project, but a decision about whether we are *ready* to do the project.[11] The decision about whether the project should be done has to be made at the end of FEL-2. FEL-3 is far too expensive to be canceling projects after completing it. FEL-3 activities only become important to the decision about whether to do the project if FEL-2 activities were incomplete or otherwise defective. FEL-3 should not be important to the go/no-go decision.

There are occasionally other circumstances that will lead to a project cancellation when FEL-3 is under way or even complete, but they are peculiar and unusual. For example, recently a megaproject was killed after FEL-3 when one of the major investors suffered a reversal of fortune in its general business and no longer had enough money to proceed. The project will go forward at some point but another partner will have to be found. We know of a few projects that were canceled because an announcement by a competitor changed the market opportunity dramatically. Sometimes, megaprojects are canceled because the market for the product turns down sharply during FEL-3. However, unless something structural has changed in the market, a downturn should not cause cancellation unless the sponsors no longer have the cash flow or ability to borrow to sustain the project. Market timing should be irrelevant for megaprojects. By the time the project is up and producing, the market may well have changed again anyway.

Assessing FEL-3

FEL-3 is all about preparing to execute the project. FEL-3 is about filling in all the details. All the items that were rated as "preliminary" at the end of FEL-2 need to become "definitive" at the end of FEL-3. And *definitive* means complete and final. The framework for the FEL-3 assessment is shown in Figure 10.4.

[11]Often, even the question of whether we are ready to execute is moot because so many commitments have been made to so many parties that FID will take place whether or not we are ready.

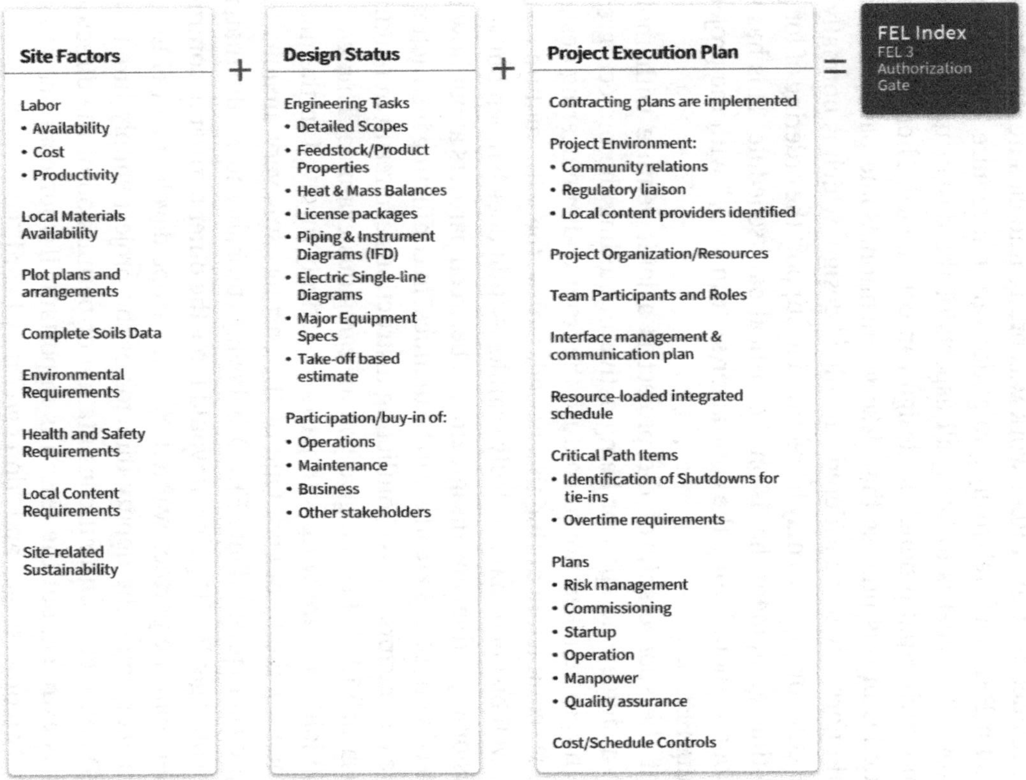

Site Factors

Labor
- Availability
- Cost
- Productivity

Local Materials Availability

Plot plans and arrangements

Complete Soils Data

Environmental Requirements

Health and Safety Requirements

Local Content Requirements

Site-related Sustainability

+

Design Status

Engineering Tasks
- Detailed Scopes
- Feedstock/Product Properties
- Heat & Mass Balances
- License packages
- Piping & Instrument Diagrams (IFD)
- Electric Single-line Diagrams
- Major Equipment Specs
- Take-off based estimate

Participation/buy-in of:
- Operations
- Maintenance
- Business
- Other stakeholders

+

Project Execution Plan

Contracting plans are implemented

Project Environment:
- Community relations
- Regulatory liaison
- Local content providers identified

Project Organization/Resources

Team Participants and Roles

Interface management & communication plan

Resource-loaded integrated schedule

Critical Path Items
- Identification of Shutdowns for tie-ins
- Overtime requirements

Plans
- Risk management
- Commissioning
- Startup
- Operation
- Manpower
- Quality assurance

Cost/Schedule Controls

=

FEL Index
FEL 3
Authorization
Gate

FIGURE 10.4 FEL 3 Authorization Gate FEL Index

When local content is an issue, understanding the capabilities of the local materials and service providers is an essential part of the site factors work. It needs to be addressed early enough so that the information can be included in any invitations to tender. Actually identifying local providers is an integral part of the project execution plan.

Provided that the FEL-2 work was brought to closure, the design tasks for FEL-3 are relatively straightforward but require a great deal of work. The goal is to bring all aspects of the design up to a level from which rapid production design can commence. There are some subtleties in this process that deserve mention. Some parts of what would normally be considered "detailed" design, which is normally a post-sanction process, may be required to support the ordering of long-lead time equipment that is on the critical path schedule. This has to be done without letting the contractor(s) "run away" with the project during FEL-3.

If the sponsorship of the project is a joint venture with more than a single lead sponsor being active in guiding the project, great care has to be taken not to confuse the front-end engineering design (FEED) contractors during this period. Unless the joint venture team is so well blended that it is truly seamless—that does happen but very occasionally—then any disagreements between partners about how to proceed with FEL-3 are likely to be manifest in conflicting instructions to the contractors. Those conflicting instructions can result in making a hash of FEL-3. Let me give you an egregious example. This was a 50/50 joint venture with both partners actively involved in the management of the front-end. One of the partners was very anxious for the project to proceed into FEED, believing (probably correctly) that, if they could get FEED going, it would force the other partner to commit earlier than the partner wanted. So with scope development (FEL-2) about half done, the deputy director of the project simply hired the FEED contractor without consultation or permission of the director! That is extreme, but the lesson is important: if your contractors are given two orders: "go" and "don't go," they heard "go."

The "best practical" rating for engineering design is what we call an "advanced study design." We are frequently asked how this translates into the more conventional measure of "percent design complete." I resist giving a simple answer because the two measures are related but hardly the same. Design complete is generally calculated as the portion of expected engineering cost that has been spent. That measure suffers a number of problems. It is a percent of what may be a completely fictitious denominator, as engineering costs tend to overrun more than any other single line item. Of even greater concern, the design may be advanced too far in some areas and barely begun in others, and the "design complete" number will sound perfectly reasonable.

The better way to measure is to ask what engineering tasks are complete. There are three tasks that, taken together, constitute the acid test of whether the design is ready for sanction:

- The Piping and Instrumentation Diagrams (P&IDs) are complete, reviewed, and approved as issued for design (detailed engineering).
- The major equipment specifications completed and the long-lead time items ordered.
- The cost estimate was developed with take-offs of all material quantities from the P&IDs.

If all three conditions are met, the design is very likely "advanced study." If "no," or the more common "well, sort of," is the response, the design is Limited Study and the project is not yet ready for sanction. Of the successful projects, 67% had achieved Advanced Study versus 39% of the failed projects. ($Pr>|X^2|<.001$).

Engineering is an area in which one can do too much prior to authorization. Our "best practical" rating of "advanced study" is substantially short of the "best possible" "Full Design Specification." An interesting aside here is that none of the successful projects achieved a full-design specification prior to authorization, but three of the failed projects did. These were projects in which the engineering effort continued despite major Shaping problems. The sponsors were overcommitted to the projects and continued when they should have quit.

FEED should be pushed further than it usually is. It is very helpful to require the FEED contractor on projects in which that contractor will continue into execution to create and sequence the engineering packages with input from owner construction people; from the contractor's construction organization if the contract is engineering, materials procurement, and construction (EPC) form; or from potential constructors and fabrication yards as a part of the prequalification process. We would also encourage a change to the rules of credit[12] such that the owner will only pay for *in-sequence complete, reviewed, and issued for construction* engineering work packages. One of the biggest headaches in engineering is the contractor's frequent desire to perform work out of the sequence that will support construction. Out-of-sequence work often causes rework and vitiates any attempts by the constructor to do comprehensive work packaging. Correct sequencing of engineering and the procurement that derives from it drive efficiency in construction and module fabrication. It is important to understand that most EPC firms are engineering driven, not construction driven.

Although FEED work is part of FEL, it is, in most respects, more akin to execution work rather than planning. The work is high-volume and massively parallel. What this means in practice is that FEED does not accommodate changes at all well. Significant changes during FEED slow the work and make it more likely that FEED will not be completed when we run out of time. Often on megaprojects FEED is being done for different scope areas by different contractors in different locations. Any change that triggers the need for change in packages being done by others becomes an opportunity for serious errors to be introduced.

The third big element of FEL-3 at authorization is completion of the project execution planning. The development of the execution plan should start with the project itself at the start of FEL-2. By the time sanctioning of the project is near, the execution plan should be quite detailed in all aspects. Many aspects of the execution plan must be decided no later than the start of FEL-3. For example, whether the construction strategy will be modules or stick-built should be made as early as possible in FEL-2 because it affects how the design will be developed in FEL-3.

It is tempting to postpone some aspects of execution planning on the theory that the needs are far enough in the future that there is

[12]The rules of credit are the formula on which the contractor will be paid as detailed in the terms and conditions of the contract.

plenty of time. This usually turns out to be a mistake. For example, it is very tempting to delay the first draft of the commissioning and startup plans until sometime during execution, especially on long projects. The fault in that logic is that the turnover sequences for megaprojects are often complex. The turnover sequence defines the order in which various units should be commissioned, started up, and turned over to operations. Most of the turnover sequences are required, not discretionary. After the turnover sequences are finally worked out, you may well realize that you cannot achieve the desired sequence because you failed to order a few pieces of long-lead time equipment way back in FEL-3. If the first draft of the turnovers had been drafted in late FEL-2 that would not have happened.

The local content providers need to have been identified and qualified well before any bid packages go out to prime contractors so the local content risk can be reduced in the eyes of the potential bidders. The outlines of the contracting strategy should have started back in FEL-2 because how and who is contracted to assist with FEL-3 will depend on how you intend to contract the execution. As discussed in Chapter 13, if the execution strategy is going to be lump-sum, hiring one of the desired lump-sum bidders to do the FEED work is not a good idea.

Especially for ventures in new geographies for the lead sponsor, the building of the operating organization must be planned during FEL. One of the sadder projects among our megaprojects was a grassroots refinery in which the project was done extremely well, being completed on time and on budget at a competitive cost. However, because the plant-manager-to-be did not believe the refinery could possibly be done on time, there was absolutely no operating organization to commission, start up, and operate the refinery when it reached mechanical completion. It took nine months to cobble together an organization to run a couple of billion dollars of investment that had been sitting on the ground rusting.

The most difficult single aspect of execution planning is the development of a high-quality schedule. Developing a good schedule is difficult not only because it simply takes a lot of work, but because too many companies no longer have the depth of planning and scheduling expertise required or the data needed to properly resource-load the schedule. Resource loading of the engineering and construction

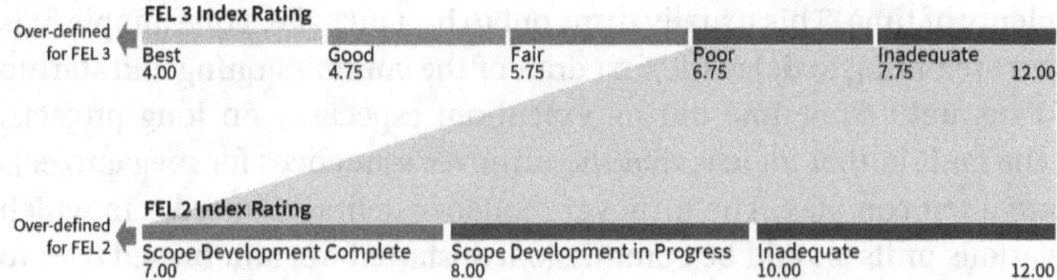

FIGURE 10.5 FEL Index Both: FEL 2 and FEL 3 Are Reported on a Single Scale

provides deep insight into whether the schedule you would like to meet is achievable by mere humans. We return to the importance of schedule later in this chapter.

The relationship of the measurement schemes for FEL-2 and FEL-3 is shown in Figure 10.5. The numbers shown are the points in the index where we break from one category to another. Both FEL-2 and FEL-3 are measured on the same scale, but with quite different expectations for how much work has been accomplished by the time the gate at the end of the phase is reached. Note that in both cases, it is possible to overdefine. Too much definition means that the project is no longer synchronized with other critical activities. For FEL-2, it means that we have moved into FEED (feasibility for minerals) before achieving Shaping closure. Recall that Shaping closure should coincide with passing through the gate at the end of scope development. Overdefinition for FEL-3 means that we have moved into execution of the project without passing through the sanction gate, which means we never stopped to check whether we were ready to execute the project.

"Best practical" FEL-2 is when the scope development is complete and all elements accounted for, all site elements are preliminary, and the pieces of the execution plan that will be needed for FEL-3, including the construction strategy and the basic contracting strategy, have been settled. If the project were authorized at that point, the FEL would be rated as "poor" with respect to sanction, although "best practical" with respect to Gate 2. In general, the costs to the end of FEL-2 are no more than about 0.5% to 1.5% of eventual total cost. If recycle has been necessary or if the Shaping process has slowed progress, the costs will be toward the high end of that range. If all has gone smoothly, the low end of the range will usually suffice. In any case, remember that none of the money spent in FEL-2 for either Shaping or project development is project investment; it is information acquisition money.

To go from the end of FEL-2 to a ready-to-sanction project is considerably more expensive: another 2% to as much as 4% of eventual total capital cost may be required to complete FEL-3. FEL-3 for a megaproject will always involve the mobilization of contractors to do the details of the site and engineering definition, and to assist in the execution planning. FEL-3 costs are and should be considered project capital investment.

Why Is Complete FEL So Important?

Once we launch the execution of a project, our goal is to maintain whatever business value has been created in the Opportunity Shaping and Scope Development processes. That means we have to deliver on whatever promises have been made in the authorization package that was reviewed and approved by top management, often including the main board of directors. Maintaining value means that the project will be on or close to its sanctioned budget and schedule and will produce as promised after startup. So let's review the importance of FEL to achieving those goals.[13]

FEL and Cost Performance

Figure 10.6 plots the relationship between the level of FEL that had been achieved when the project was given the go-ahead for execution

[13]The underlying relationships between FEL and project results have remained unchanged since the first edition, but some additional controls are necessitated by two changes (not good ones) in company practices. First, we have to control for the increased number of projects that stuffed massive amounts of money into FID estimates to try to prevent overruns. This was an inappropriate response to the very large overruns that were common in megaprojects in the first decade of this century. Much of those overruns were caused by escalation in addition to poor FEL. Second, more projects were subjected to cost-cutting after FID, which destroyed the quality of the front-end work and drove longer schedules. That effect, too, has been removed when examining the relationships.

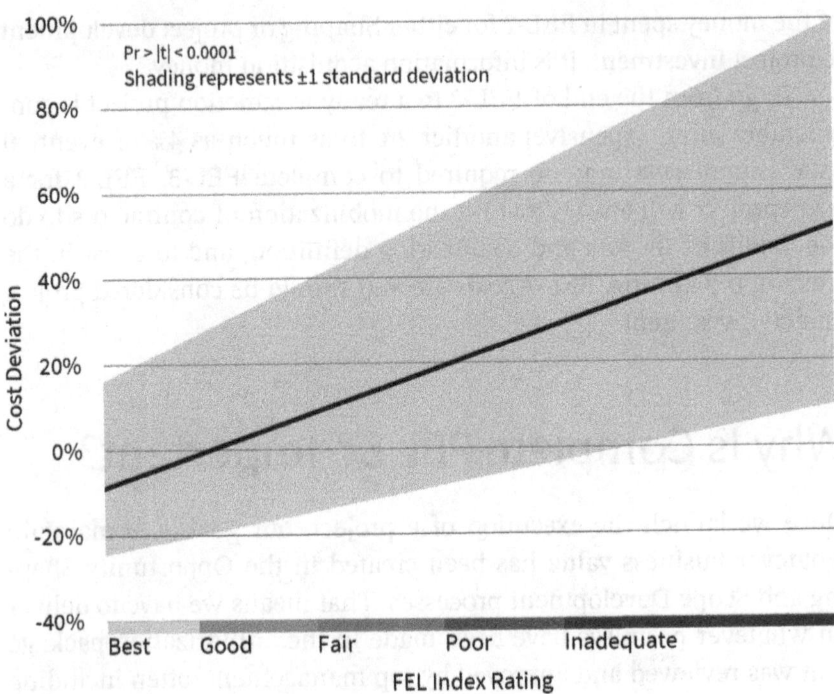

FIGURE 10.6 FEL Drives Cost Predictability

and how much growth in capital cost was seen, in real terms, to the end of the project.[14] The shading around the median trend line represents a standard deviation above and below the mean. Consider this chart in the context of risk assessment. If your FEL work is "best practical," you will on average underrun by a few percent. The distribution around that slight underrun is about –15% and +25%.

In this case, the reality is actually even better than the numbers appear. There were a handful of projects that were rated as "best practical" FEL but experienced huge (>70%) cost overruns for peculiar reasons. Two of the anomalous projects were overdefined, and Shaping problems caused major disruptions after authorization. In one case, an inexperienced project director ceremonially dropped

[14]Cost overruns are measured as the ratio of the actual total capital cost in inflation-adjusted, constant currency terms to the cost estimated (contingencies included) at full-funds authorization measured on the same adjusted basis.

all the project definition work in the waste bin after authorization saying that the project would be done "My Way!" As discussed in Chapter 4, a number of projects that were well front-end loaded projects were directed to undertake major cost-cutting after authorization, which made a shambles of the front-end work. When the outliers are discarded, the distribution around the slight underrun for best practically front-end loaded projects is about 10%. In other words, if the FEL is best, megaprojects are not particularly risky from a cost perspective!

By sharp contrast, if the FEL is "poor" at sanction, one is about equally likely to come in on budget or have a 60% (real) overrun. Now that is risky! If an outside observer—bankers please take note—is trying to understand the cost risk for a megaproject, the very first measure should be the quality of FEL. If the FEL is poor, the project is a bad bet to back. If the FEL is "best practical" the project is odds-on to be fine with respect to cost.

The same basic relationship between FEL and cost growth is found in all projects and is equally strong statistically. However, the slope of the relationship for megaprojects is over twice as steep as it is for projects of less than $250 million (2023 U.S. dollars). In other words, the same principles apply to all projects, but those principles are much more important for megaprojects.

FEL and Schedule Performance

Let's turn now to the risk of slipping our execution schedule[15] in Figure 10.7. The pattern for schedule slip is very similar to that for cost growth. The best practically front-end loaded projects usually achieved their schedules. When projects were rated "poor," they slipped by about 30%, which for the average project in our database means that first production would occur 13 months later than promised and 13 months later than the economic forecast for the project. Even more important from a risk perspective, the poorly front-end loaded project

[15]*Execution schedule* is defined as the point of full-funds authorization to mechanical completion (in principle, ready-to-operate) of all required kit. For petroleum production projects the period ends at first production.

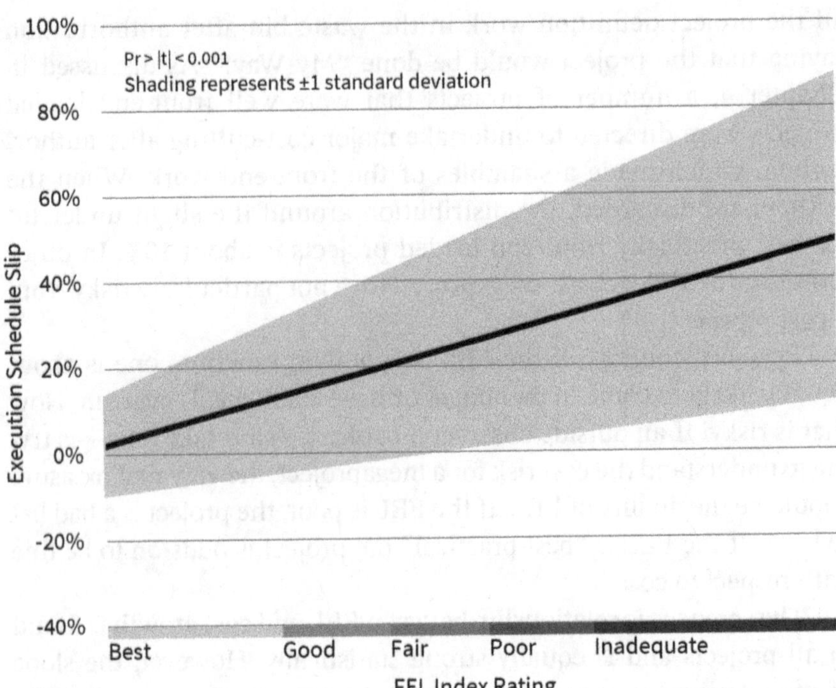

FIGURE 10.7 FEL Drives Schedule Predictability

is equally likely to be 26 months late to completion as to be on-time. Put in stark project management terms, if a project is "poor" on the FEL index at sanction, the only honest answer to the question: "When will this thing be done?" is a very unsatisfactory, "I have no idea."

FEL and Production Performance

The third big promise made at authorization and the promise on which all cash flow from the project ultimately hinges is operability. As described in Chapter 3, we classify a project as an operability failure if it has severe and continuing production problems into the second year after startup. The projects so classified averaged about 50% of planned production in months 7 through 12 after startup. The amounts spent to attempt to recover operability will never be known.

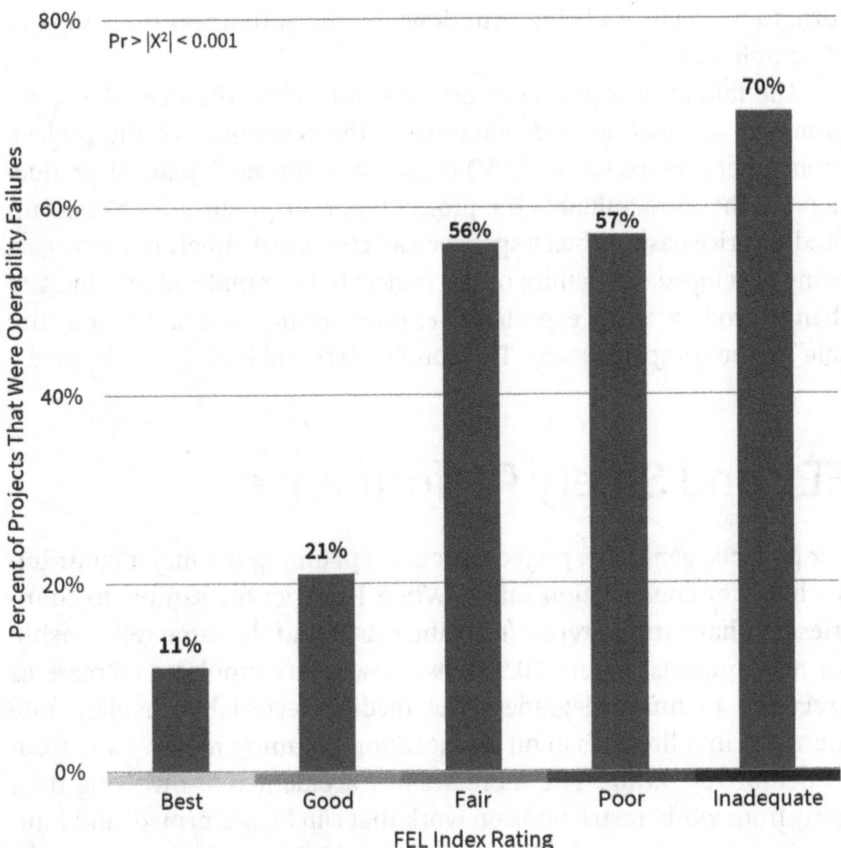

FIGURE 10.8 FEL Reduces Operability Problems

Figure 10.8 shows the relationship between the incidence of operability failure and FEL. When the level of FEL was "good" or better, the number of operability failures is under control. As soon as the FEL index moves into the "fair" range, operability collapses. Projects that did not achieve at least "good" FEL were odds-on not to produce close to expectations. There were a number of underlying causes of the operability disasters. Some were so schedule driven that corners were cut in both the Basic Data and the FEL. In some cases, the poor FEL triggered numerous changes during execution, and those changes caused quality to suffer. In some cases, poor FEL resulted in failing to fully understand the environmental permitting requirements, which led, in turn, to the facilities being shut down by the authorities for being out of compliance.

The failure of a project to produce at or close the rates that were promised at sanction is debilitating to the economics of the project. From a net present value (NPV) perspective, the early years of production are the most valuable the project will ever produce on a constant product price basis. When a sponsor's assets consist largely of the project being developed, the failure of the project to be completed on time and then to produce at the expected rates often means bankruptcy or a "fire sale" of the company assets. The bondholders and banks must be paid.

FEL and Safety Performance

For projects, generally, project execution planning is a major contributor to better construction safety. When I restrict my sample to countries that have strong reporting standards, I find the same relationship for megaprojects. Figure 10.9 shows how safety problems increase as execution planning degrades. The median recordable incident rate increases in a linear fashion as execution planning moves away from a "definitive" rating. The more serious accident rate involving days away from work, restrictions on work that can be performed, and injuries forcing a job transfer (the so-called DART rate) does not show an increase until execution planning degrades to "assumed." It then doubles. Both relationships are statistically significant.[16]

That better execution planning drives better safety should surprise no one. Better planned sites are more orderly sites. Better execution planning is associated with less aggressive schedules and much less schedule slip. When schedules begin to slip, safety begins to suffer. Projects with poor execution planning averaged almost a 30% slip in their execution schedules and almost twice as many recordable injuries

[16]Because safety statistics have a sharp skew that is difficult to transform, I employed a number of techniques to check my results including poisson regression, generalized linear model (GLM), and robust regression. All showed statistically significant results for both types of injuries. Although the statistical results are strong, I would not overinterpret the nonlinear result for the DART rate. Because the DART rate is more volatile than the recordable rate, the loss of observations is a potential problem.

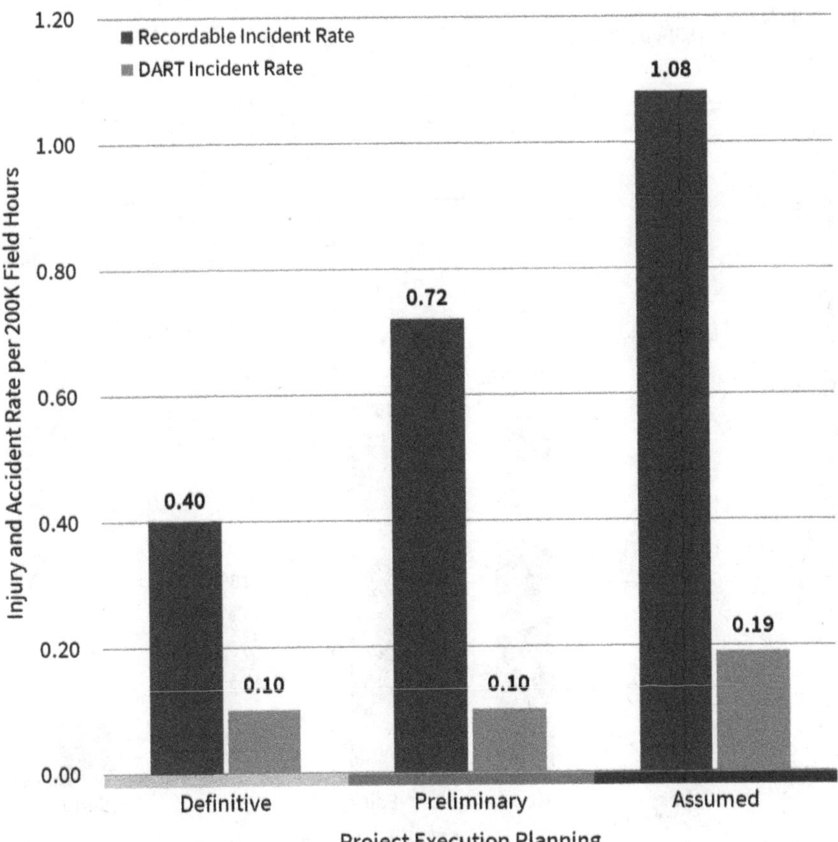

FIGURE 10.9 Execution Planning Improves Safety

than projects with "definitive" or "preliminary" execution planning. The DART injury rate correlates with execution schedule slip for countries with reliable reporting so strongly that nearly a third of the variation in serious injuries is explained by slip in the project schedule (Pr>|t|<.0001).

So, again, why is FEL so important? It is important because it is a prime driver of almost every project outcome that we care about: cost, schedule, operability, and safety. Figure 10.10 summarizes the relationship between the FEL index and successful projects. Almost two-thirds of the projects that achieved "best" FEL delivered what was promised at authorization. Among those projects that failed with "best practical" FEL, only a couple simply had bad luck. For example, one of them

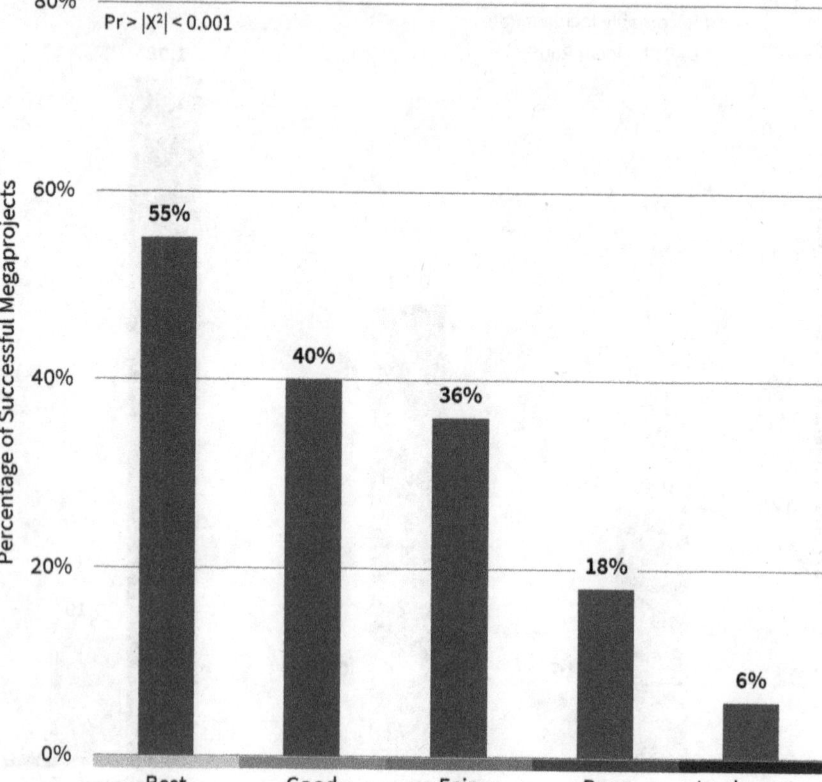

FIGURE 10.10 Relationship between the FEL Index and Successful Project

failed because a third-party (government) project did not get done anywhere close to schedule. Two suffered repeated failure of major equipment despite conventional technology and well-established equipment fabricators.

A few well-defined failures were very highly innovative projects that overran badly, but ultimately worked and proved the technologies, which may make money on future projects. A few others failed because they "gave away the store" to their lump-sum contractors because they were so anxious to get the projects done, and done on a lump-sum basis, they were willing to pay 50% and higher risk premiums.

As soon as the FEL index moves down to "fair," the success rate falls below one project in four, and at the worst level of FEL, success disappears altogether. Every relationship we have reviewed in this chapter holds for smaller projects as well. But in every case, the relationship is more dramatic and severe for the megaprojects than it is for their smaller cousins. This brings us once again to the peculiar bimodal character of megaproject results.

How Well Are Megaprojects Front-End Loaded?

Megaprojects are the most important projects in any industrial company's portfolio. When they succeed, the company is strengthened for the long-term. When they fail, massive amounts of shareholder wealth can be made to evaporate in a single project. Almost every project professional agrees that better, more thorough, FEL means better project results. Logic, therefore, would suggest that almost all megaprojects would achieve "best practical" FEL before the investors' money is committed. As Figure 10.11 shows, however, that is not the case. In fact, only one megaproject in five achieves best FEL, and as previously explained, that number is actually somewhat exaggerated by those who undid their FEL work early in execution. Half of megaprojects achieve "fair" FEL or worse. Fifteen percent of the megaprojects have a level of FEL that is the equivalent of a screening study, which is characteristic of projects just entering scope development rather than projects at full-funds authorization.

There are no statistically reliable differences in the level of FEL by industrial sector. Liquefied natural gas (LNG) is a little better than average, but not systematically so. Pipeline megaprojects are a little worse than average, but not systematically so. The real question is why isn't FEL much better than it is for all industrial sectors?

Why Isn't FEL Better?

The FEL story pulls together much of what we have discussed in the previous chapters of this book. While failing to do excellent FEL is a primary proximate cause of megaproject failures, it is a symptom of a

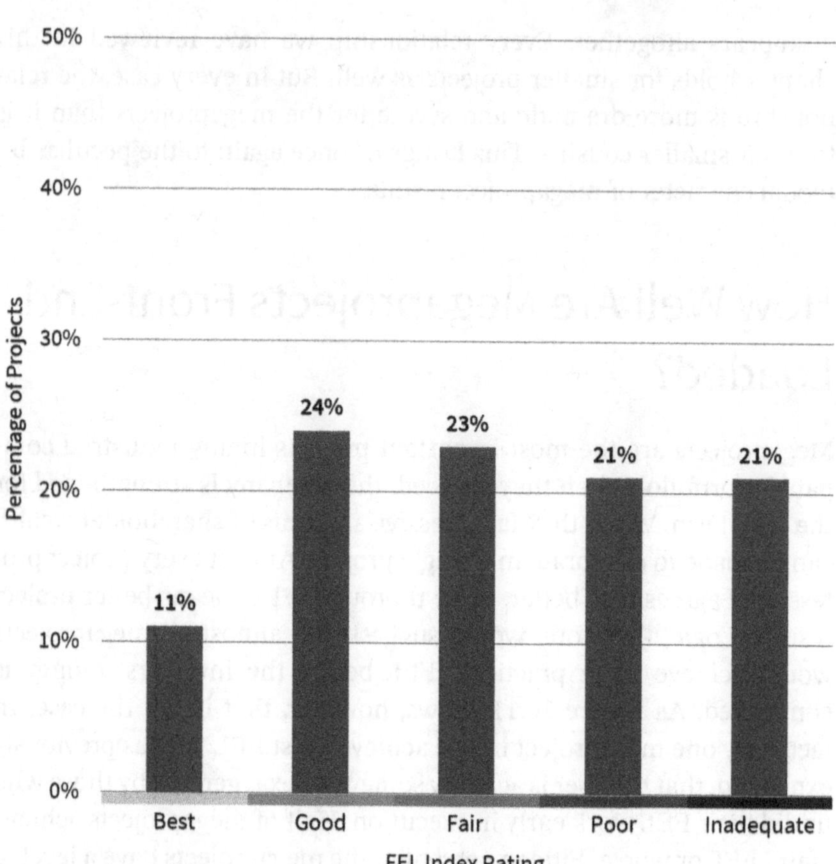

FIGURE 10.11 How Well Are Megaprojects Defined at FID?

set of deeper problems. The relatively poor FEL for megaprojects is an extension of projects generally. When looking at our overall database of over 14,000 projects, there is a systematic and undeniable relationship between larger size and poorer preparation. If we restrict our sample to only major projects over $100 million (2003 U.S. dollars) the result does not change.[17] Megaprojects are merely at the far end

[17]The statistical results here are overwhelmingly strong. When I regress the FEL index against the natural log of estimated cost (in constant 2023 U.S. dollars), the *t*-ratio around the coefficient is over 11, meaning that one would need to go 11 standard deviations to the left of the coefficient before the relationship disappears. The probability that the relationship could be generated randomly is vanishingly small.

of the cost spectrum and are, therefore, the most poorly prepared of projects on average.

What this means is that the more important a project is to the health of the modern industrial firm, the less likely we are to do the things necessary to make the project succeed. This perverse state of affairs starts with a lack of the people needed to do the work. The great majority of megaproject teams in today's world are understaffed. The challenging demographics of projects organizations were exacerbated by Covid and are unlikely to be corrected in the near future. IPA asks megaproject directors at the end of FEL whether they had adequate numbers of staff to get their work done. Sixty-one percent answered "yes" and 39% answered "no." When they answered "no," the FEL index was much poorer ($Pr>|X^2|<.0001$). But that is only the start of the problem. When the staffing was deemed adequate, 82% of the FEL teams were integrated. When the staffing was not described as adequate, only 25% of the teams were integrated. To some extent these two issues are tapping the same thing, but they are also tapping different realities as well. When the teams were not integrated, gaping holes were left in the FEL, whether or not there were enough people in total to get the work done. When the teams were integrated and the staffing was considered adequate, the average FEL was solidly in the "good" range. When neither condition was met, FEL was "poor."

But that is not the whole story. In Chapter 8, I discussed how having clear objectives and understanding the trade-offs among key outcomes was necessary to building strong teams. In Figure 10.12, we show that getting an improvement in FEL depends not only on understanding the trade-offs, which subsumes having clear objectives, but on team integration. When the team was integrated, understanding objectives and trade-offs drove much improved FEL. But when the team is not integrated, nothing helps. The team may perfectly understand what they are supposed to do, but if the team is not adequately staffed or is missing one or more of the functions on the team at the right time, the FEL effort fails anyway.

Late arrival of Basic Data also degrades FEL, and this effect is not washed out when we control for team integration and staffing adequacy. Part of the reason for this is that Basic Data problems are associated with the FEL duration actually being *shorter* than it would otherwise be. That result, in turn, is an artifact of Basic Data

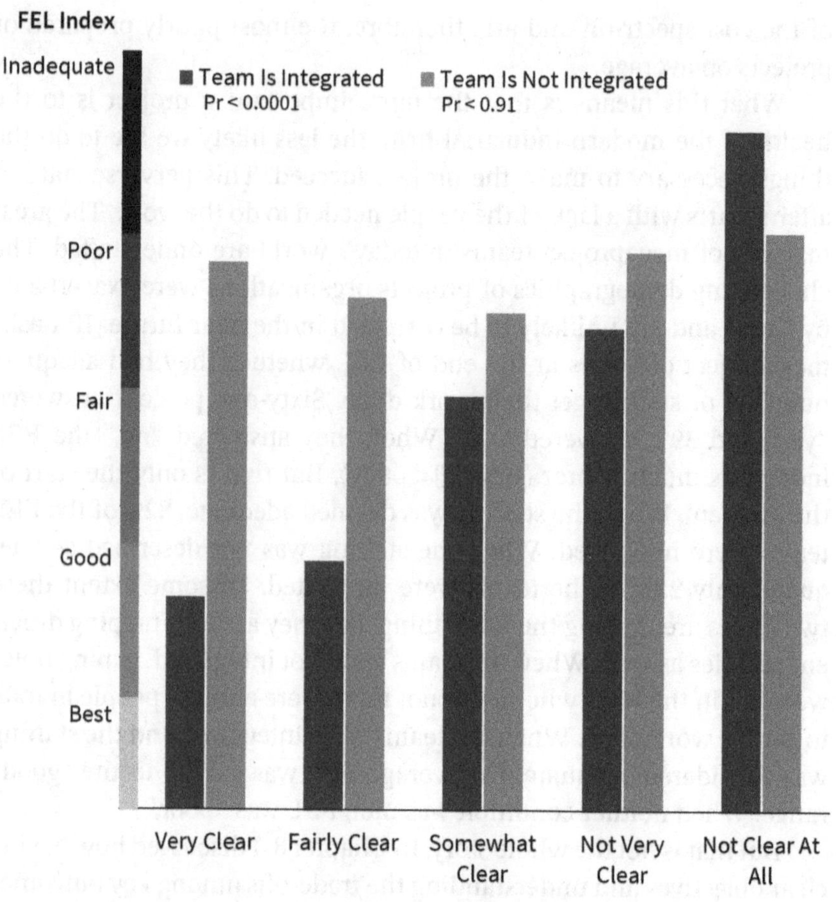

FIGURE 10.12 Team Integration Is the Critical Enabler

problems being greatly exacerbated by pressure to drive the FEL schedule. When the FEL schedule is being driven it is almost always because the entire project is being driven to be completed on a breakneck schedule. When corners are cut in Basic Data development, corners are likely to be cut in FEL, and every other measure of project quality as well.

Sometimes problems encountered in the Shaping process create problems in achieving "solid" FEL. When in a joint venture, which is the norm for megaprojects, partners may have very different ideas of what constitutes acceptable FEL. As the joint ventures are being formed early in Shaping, the businesses of the two (or more) partners may be discussing front-end work with little or no input from the project organizations. Because FEL issues are typically of low salience for business professionals, fundamental disagreements about how much FEL should be done or how long it should take may exist, but not surface. When they do surface, as they must eventually, it is far too late to realize that you have the wrong partner.

Often the formal joint venture agreements are very slow to materialize. Usually, prior to formal agreement on the joint venture, there is a certain amount of confusion about who is willing to pay for what. We often encounter cases in which one partner is paying all of the FEL costs because the joint venture agreement has not been signed. As the FEL continues without a signed joint venture agreement, the business folks in the lead owner can start getting very anxious about the amount of money that is at risk and start slowing spending.

Some partners use FEL as an integral part of their Shaping negotiating strategy. This may appear clever, but it really isn't. They want the other partner as much "out of pocket" as possible because it bolsters their position. This is not materially different than demanding an upfront cash payment, which is another negotiating ploy but one very easily recognized as such. Encouraging the other partner to go as far out on the limb in funding FEL as possible works because the two partners now have an asymmetrical loss situation in the event that the project does not go forward. The reason this strategy is not clever is because it encourages too little FEL to be done. The resulting losses associated with project failure make everyone a loser.

My very strong recommendation when in joint venture situations is to confront the FEL funding issue immediately when starting negotiations on the venture. Make the willingness of the other partner to fund FEL a simple matter of goodwill. If they are unwilling to fund their share, you must understand you are at an immediate disadvantage if you go forward in Shaping.

Sometimes insufficient FEL is done simply because the lead sponsor is excessively frugal (read: cheap) and doesn't want to spend the 2.5% to 5% required to get first-class definition of the project. We hear things like, "Why should it cost so much money? I once front-end loaded a big project on a napkin over a beer." If you are the project director, now would be a good time to post your resume.

More common, however, is that business management is driving the overall schedule for the project to first production. This is a problem we have already discussed in other chapters at some length, but one point needs to be revisited in this context: if, as the project director, you respond to overall schedule pressure by shortcutting work on the front-end, you are making a bad situation much worse. Poor FEL drives execution schedule slip, startup time, and poor operability. Most importantly, poorly front-end loaded projects end up being slower overall.

Finally, there is the belief in some quarters, even among some project professionals, that the amount of FEL required will be less for certain contracting strategies. In particular, there is a belief that if the project will be executed on an EPC lump-sum basis, the execution planning is not really needed or is not needed to the degree it is for other contract forms. Not only is the belief without empirical foundation, it is precisely wrong. FEL has more effect in restraining cost growth and schedule slip in lump-sum projects than it does in other contract forms. The reason is not hard to fathom. FEL reduces changes during execution. Owner changes during execution are major sources of profit for lump-sum contractors. You will get hit, quite appropriately, with the costs of the changes and the cost of the schedule delay that the changes cause. Then, at the end of the day, the project operability will suffer because changes degrade quality.

FEL and the Project Context

In the discussion of Shaping in Chapter 6, I said that the first step in a healthy Shaping process was to explore the attributes of the project context. That information is needed both by the business leadership, which are trying to make a difficult decision about whether to go forward into the Shaping process, and by the project team, which will need to mold their FEL activities to meet the challenges that the project context provides. The failure to fully explore the project context early in the evolution of the project puts the project team at a disadvantage. Before it can proceed, team members will have to find sources of information about the context or risk getting things terribly wrong.

There are three areas of the context that are particularly important for the project team to understand very early:

- Challenges of the physical location
- Availability and quality of the construction labor
- Permitting difficulties

I will discuss each of these areas in turn.

The Location: Dealing with Remoteness

We classify our projects into three groups: very remote, semi-remote, and nonremote. Very remote locations are more than 124 miles from any major population center (greater than 50,000). The actual projects in our database that are classified as very remote average 250 miles to the nearest population center.[18] Examples of very remote sites are around much of the Caspian Sea, the North Slope of Alaska, Central Africa, interior North Africa, much of Papua New Guinea, some parts of Australia, and more.

Semi-remote projects are closer to a major population center, but the population center is far too small to provide labor or large amounts of support to the site. For example, we would classify areas of Western Australia south of Perth as semi-remote, while interior areas north of Perth are mostly very remote. We classify most coastal sites along the Arabian Gulf as nonremote, but inland sites in some areas would be very remote.

Offshore petroleum development projects pose another sort of challenge to classify. Areas with extensive prior development are classified as nonremote. For example, most of the North Sea, the U.S. Gulf of Mexico, and much of offshore Nigeria, and more are classified as

[18]We are not entirely rigid about these definitions. For example, if the site is less than 124 miles from a population center, but is separated by 62 miles of dense jungle without access, we would classify it as very remote.

nonremote. However, the far northern frontier of the North Sea and the newly opened Atlantic margin are classified as very remote. If exploratory efforts are successful and they are further developed, they will be down-rated for future developments.

A little less than 20% of our sample are classified as very remote, about 35% as semi-remote, and the remainder as nonremote. The projects are roughly of the same size, with remote projects tending to be a bit larger. All three groups are widely scattered around the world, with every inhabited continent represented in all three groups.

What does remoteness do to the FEL effort? It makes it much harder. Table 10.1 provides some of the key differences in projects as a function of remoteness from population centers. The first thing to note is that teams are smaller. Holding size and complexity constant, the average core team for nonremote projects is twice as large as for very remote projects.[19]

When a project is remote, the cost of team members increases. People cannot be borrowed for short-term assignments from local facilities. And it is far more difficult to recruit team members for projects in very remote areas than nonremote areas. Potential core team members

TABLE 10.1 Remoteness and FEL Effort

Factor [20]	NonRemote	Semi-Remote	Very Remote
Core Team Size (number of people, FTE)	35	27	18
Integrated Teams	60%	55%	36%
Adequate Staffing	66%	65%	38%
Sponsor New to Region	9%	35%	57%
Problems with Government	11%	19%	30%
Major Infrastructure Needed	10%	36%	75%
Labor Must Be Imported	22%	45%	63%

[19]The differences in team size are statistically significant (Pr>|t|<.01).

[20]All numbers are percentages of sample except for the first row, which is number of people (full-time equivalent).

know that they are likely to be posted to the site for two to three years as the project progresses. Even if their families will be permitted to accompany them, that is simply not very attractive to many two-wage households these days. Because of the added cost, there is often pressure to keep team size down in remote projects.

Project directors must develop strategies for recruiting and retaining high-quality core team members for semi-remote and very remote projects or for any megaproject that may be viewed as undesirable employment for any reason. There are obvious things like premium pay, but money is a limited incentive. The corporation needs to support the project directors by providing clear signals that willingness to serve on these difficult projects will be career-enhancing.

One of the most common approaches to recruiting and retention for remote megaprojects is rotational assignments often in the form of alternating 28 days on and 28 days off. Each job is then shared with another person. Unfortunately, this approach is both very expensive and quite problematic in terms of effective teams.

The smaller team sizes are reflected in lower rates of team integration, especially for the very remote projects. One or more of the essential FEL owner functions is missing for about two-thirds of very remote projects. This result is merely echoed in the project director's assessment of the adequacy of the team size overall.

While the project team is shrinking, the amount of work and the difficulty of the work increase. As remoteness increases, prior sponsor experience in the area declines and the percentage of projects experiencing difficulties with the host governments increases. Problems with the host governments are things such as being unable to move material across ports, being delayed by local police looking for "consideration," delays in processing workers into the country, and endless spools of red tape. Very remote projects were more likely to be in politically unstable environments and have security concerns.

As remoteness increases, the chances that the project will be required to install major new infrastructure—roads and bridges, power, potable water, community development, even airports—increases. In and of itself, infrastructure is not a problem. However, it is not the type of scope that most industrial sponsors execute very often, so it is unfamiliar. Perhaps more importantly, infrastructure is traditionally a government responsibility or the responsibility of a government-owned entity.

When a project must provide infrastructure, it is likely stepping onto someone else's turf. In the worst case, part of the infrastructure will actually be developed and executed by the host government. Then the project has all of the concerns created by being dependent on third-party projects.

Finally, as remoteness increases, the chances rise that some or all of the labor will have to be provided from outside the country. Like infrastructure, that is not necessarily a problem, but it can be, especially if there are social and ethnic tensions that may be exacerbated by the imported labor or construction supervision.

The upshot of all this is that very remote megaprojects are front-end loaded significantly less well than less remote projects. Their average FEL at sanction is "poor." We left FEL-2 with open scope only 9% of the time for nonremote projects, but 35% of the time for very remote projects. This is another example of the glaring irrationalities we find in megaprojects. The more team size, team integration, and FEL are needed, the less we tend to do. The result is that only 2% of very remote projects succeed.

All outcomes tend to degrade as remoteness increases and degrade rather sharply for very remote projects. But the outcome that is glaringly poor for very remote projects is operability of plant. This difference, which is highly statistically significant, is true despite the fact that very remote projects employ less new technology than their non-remote and semi-remote counterparts. Sixty-percent of very remote projects were classed as operability failures versus about 30% of the remainder of the sample. In reading through the case histories, two things stand out. First, there were lots and lots and lots of quality control problems and the accompanying endless fix-it. Second, there were lots of infrastructure problems: poor power reliability, lack of water supply, and inability to get things to the sites in a timely way for repair.

Labor Supply Issues

By their very nature, megaprojects strain the supply of construction labor, particularly in the highly skilled crafts. Shortage of craft labor should be considered the norm, not the exception, for megaprojects.

In some parts of the world, severe shortages of labor are normal even for smaller projects, and from time to time, most parts of the world with significant construction activities have experienced shortages.

Determining the appropriate field staffing rates for megaprojects entails a complex optimization process that must juggle the following considerations:

- Availability by craft
- Productivity by craft
- Availability of craft versus wage rate
- Productivity of craft versus requirements (productivity tends to decline and may decline sharply as requirements increase)
- Availability and productivity versus the desired project construction schedule

It is the last item that is usually the most important consideration on megaprojects.

A labor shortage occurs when the numbers of qualified workers required to execute a given project in a given period of time cannot be found or cannot be found at prices the project can afford. As the schedule is shortened, the number of workers required at any given time increases rapidly. Just over 30% of megaprojects experienced labor shortages and those projects experienced a dismal 14% success rate, which is significantly poorer ($Pr|X^2|<.006$).

Labor shortages are only very rarely the root cause of megaproject failure. Rather, it is the recognition of the labor situation and how the project responds that determine success or failure. There are a set of front-end activities that relate directly to whether a project copes successfully with labor availability issues: the work of the country advance team in anticipating the labor situation; the use of labor surveys early in FEL; and the development of schedules with the number of craft required assigned to each task, which is called resource-loading. When resource-loading was completed as part of FEL, longer, more situation-appropriate schedules were set.

I will return to this subject in Chapter 14 in the context of execution. Some of the most spectacular megaproject failures have occurred when the labor situation interacts with project requirements and weak controls to produce a collapse of field progress.

Permitting Problems

The permitting process is a large part of the nexus between the project and the governments in whose jurisdictions the project will reside. Note that I use the plural here, because it is unusual that only a single government is involved. The central government will always have some role in authorizing megaprojects, but local and regional governments also often play a role, and in many cases, are more influential for your prospects than the central government.

In places with strong institutional environments, the permitting process is not only structured, it is bound by rules. If you fully comply with the rules, you will sooner or later receive your permits. Whether it is sooner or later depends very much on whether there is strong social support for the project or significant opposition. But even where there is strenuous opposition, if your project is fully within the rules, the permits will eventually be granted.[21]

It is also important to understand that a country may have a strong institutional environment overall, but the particular jurisdiction in which you want to execute the project does not. In those cases, the strategy should always be to try to get central government involvement, and in the best case, preemption of local prerogatives.

About 20% of the projects in our sample encountered significant problems in obtaining some or all of the permits that were required to execute the project. (Remember, many more megaprojects encounter permitting problems, but many of those are never sanctioned, and therefore, do not make it into our sample.) We say a problem occurs when a permit is denied after appropriate application or if the permitting authorities sit on the application for six months or more beyond the promised decision date. The effects of permitting problems on project results are summarized in Figure 10.13, and they are not pretty. The interior line shows the outcomes of projects that did not experience permitting problems. They were not all great projects but there are manifestly better on average than the projects that had permitting problems. Those projects averaged a 43% cost overrun

[21]When there is strenuous opposition in strong institutional settings, sponsors sometimes will elect to abandon the project because they believe there will be too much collateral damage to other things they may want to pursue or to their reputation.

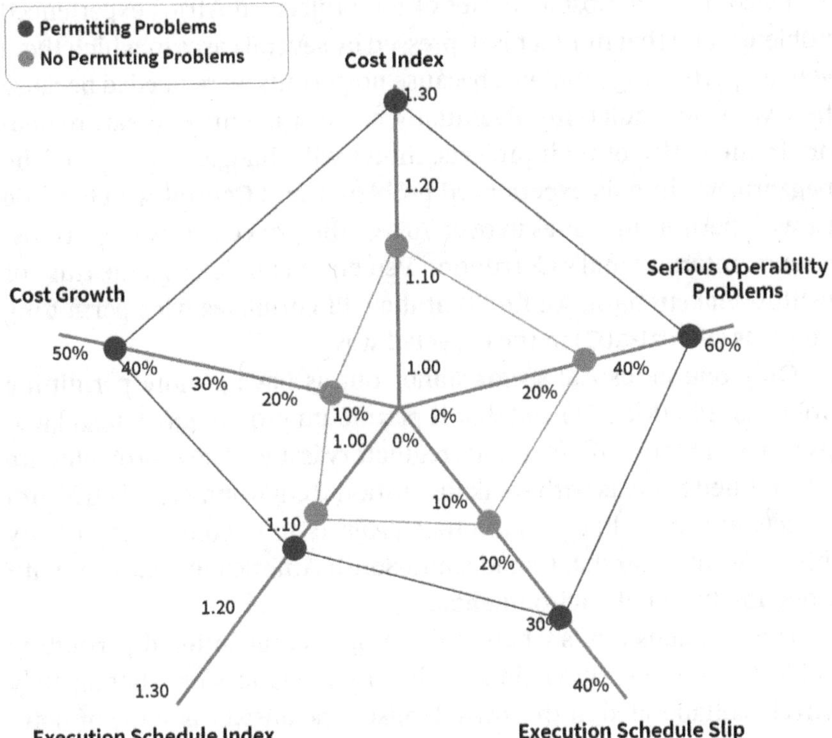

FIGURE 10.13 Permitting Problems Create Havoc

and 60% experienced operability problems. Note, they were about the same speed as the projects without permitting issues, but they had a very large slip in their execution schedules. What this tells us is that their schedules were much more aggressive than the projects without permitting problems. Again, speed kills.

Problems obtaining permits are not randomly distributed around the world. Less than 15% of projects in Europe, Australia, South America, Canada, or the United States experienced permitting problems. All the countries involved have (or did have at the time) relatively strong institutional frameworks for projects at the central government level. Permitting problems among the projects in the Middle East were almost unknown, with only a single project encountering difficulty. In most cases, the governments were sponsoring partners in those projects, which no doubt helps. But it is also true that the permitting frameworks in most of the Middle East are relatively clear.

By contrast, almost a quarter of the projects in Africa experienced problems, and that number is depressed by several cases in which there were no permitting problems because no permits were needed because there were no regulations. Eventually, as those countries create regulatory frameworks for their projects, things will change. Over 40% of the megaprojects in Asia experienced problems, and Central Asia tops the list with permitting issues in over 70% of the projects. If we use Transparency International's Corruption Perceptions Index as a measure of institutional strength, we find that the CPI correlates with permitting problems ($Pr>|z|<.02$) in the expected way.

Only one industrial sector stands out as having more permitting problems ($Pr>|X^2|<.01$) and that is petroleum production. One oil and gas project in four suffers serious regulatory issues. These problems are not confined to areas with weak institutional environments. Petroleum projects are more likely than other projects to encounter regulatory difficulties in Australia, Canada, and South America in countries with strong institutional environments.

The real question is whether the projects that suffered permitting problems were merely victims of the circumstances or whether they actively collaborated in this own demise. The answer is some of both. One element of FEL that we measure for every project is the level of definition of the permitting requirements and the actions that have been taken on permits. We expect the project teams to have explored the details of the permitting regime from an early point in FEL-2. We expect that the permitting process has been fully integrated into their FEL and execution schedule. We expect that a dialogue started with the regulators very early and that the discussions continued as the project evolved so the regulators would not be surprised by the scope and its implications when the permit applications were received.

For projects, generally, we consider a "preliminary" rating on permits to be the "best practical" status at authorization. This means that the team has fully explored the requirements and has submitted valid applications for all permits required. The rating only changes to "definitive" if the permits have been received or the authorities have signaled back that the applications are acceptable and the permits will be issued. That amount of assurance is not generally needed for projects, but it clearly is for megaprojects, even in areas with strong institutional settings. Figure 10.14 shows why.

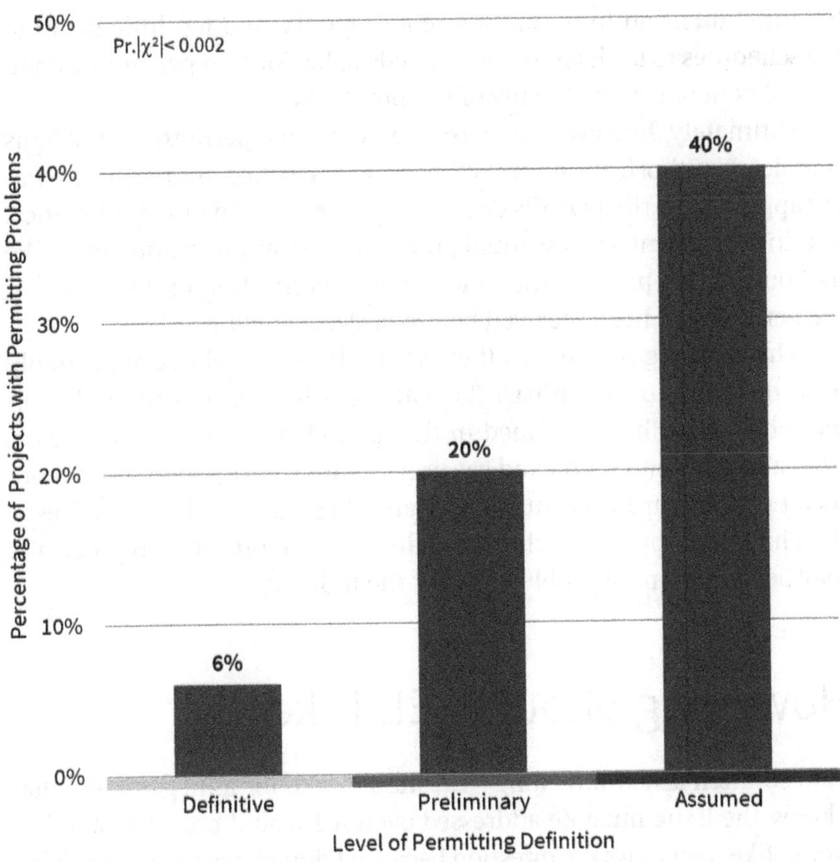

FIGURE 10.14 Permitting Definition Is Good Investment

When projects achieved a definitive rating on the permitting definition, they experience permitting problems only 6% of the time. When they had achieved what is "best practical" for projects generally, 20% had problems, and when they blithely assumed they would get their permits on time, the number jumped to 40%. The shocking thing is that 22% of projects overall and 28% of petroleum development projects were in that "assumed" category!

Projects that were "preliminary" rather than "definitive" were much more schedule aggressive ($Pr>|t|<.009$), and were much less likely to have done a thorough job on the development of the project schedule ($Pr>|X^2|<.0001$). So, one has to conclude that a good many of our permitting problems are self-inflicted. Too much drive for speed, too little attention to permitting requirements, and too little detail in the schedules to understand what needs to be done on permitting combine to generate a good many of the problems.

Ultimately, however, the best way to reduce permitting problems is to delay authorization until all necessary permits are received. Simply applying for the permits does not appear to make much difference. Making the permits an essential prerequisite to authorization does. We had only 3% of projects that encountered permitting problems when the permits had been received before project sanction.

The oil and gas sector's adherence to the advice above has actually been declining over the past 20 years (Pr.|t|<.01); it is the only element of FEL to have declined in that period. This may stem, in part, from a larger trend for oil and gas projects: they have experienced more social opposition in recent times than other industrial sectors due to the challenges posed by climate change. Therefore, securing permits may becoming more problematic for the industry.

How Long Should FEL Take?

I am so often asked how long FEL should take for a megaproject that I know the issue must be addressed even if I would prefer to skip it. I would like to dismiss the question because I don't have a very satisfying answer. The period in question here is from the formation of the core team to start scope development through the end of FEL-3 (FEED). If there were pauses during the process, for example, between FEL-2 and FEL-3, the hiatuses were removed in calculating the FEL duration.

There is no ideal duration for FEL except to say that it should end when FEL is completed to a "best practical" level. In other words, it is critically important that progress, rather than the calendar, determine how long FEL will be. The average project in our database cost about $4.6 billion in 2023 U.S. dollars and took 28 months in FEL. About 13 months of that time was in scope development,[22] and 15 months, in FEL-3.

[22]Recycled projects are not included, and any holds or pauses are normalized out of the data.

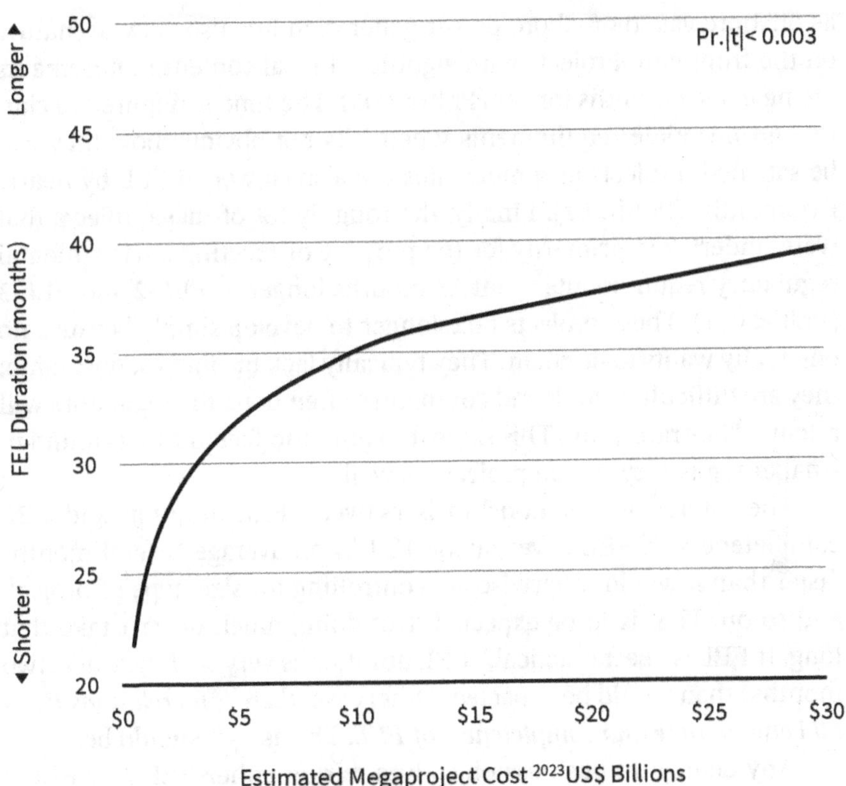

FIGURE 10.15 FEL Takes Longer for Larger Megaprojects

As expected and shown in Figure 10.15, the average FEL time increases as a function of project size.[23] The rate of increase is not terribly dramatic. There are no apparent "break points" at which the log-linear slope changes.

There are some significant differences in FEL time for different project situations. LNG projects take an average of nine months longer to get through the front-end (Pr.|t|<.02). LNG projects are often delayed on the front-end by the need to forward sell the product, and the sales deals are often complex and involve buyers sharing in project costs in some cases. Other large gas monetization projects, such

[23]I am showing the estimated rather than actual costs because those readers planning a megaproject's FEL might have some idea of the former, but little or no idea of the latter.

as offshore gas to on-shore power generation are also slow to mature on the front-end. Projects with significant local content requirements are nearly six months longer (Pr.|t|<.005). The time is required to clarify and negotiate requirements when it is not obvious how they can be satisfied. Projects at remote sites are also slower in FEL by nearly five months (Pr.|t|<.02). Finally, the roughly 5% of megaprojects that were undertaken primarily for the purpose of meeting environmental regulatory requirements spent 13 months longer in FEL-2 and FEL-3 (Pr.|t|<.001). These projects take longer to develop simply because no one really wants to do them. They typically lack business sponsorship; they are difficult to staff; and companies often hope the regulators will relent. (They rarely do.) This same dragging-the-feet in FEL is found in smaller regulatory-driven projects as well.

The interesting relationship is between FEL duration and FEL completeness. If FEL is very poor, FEL is on average several months faster than it would otherwise be, controlling for size, type of project, and so on. That is to be expected. Not doing much doesn't take that long. If FEL is "best practical," FEL duration is very *slightly faster* (two months) than would be expected. Otherwise, *there is no relationship at all between time and completeness of FEL.* This is as it should be.

Any change in business objectives during either FEL 2 or FEL 3 is associated with an average eight-month extension of the FEL duration (Pr>|t|<.007). Even with the delay, the objectives changes tend to degrade FEL quality and decrease the chances of success (Pr|z|<.0001).

Often the time required for FEL-2 (scope development) is very much a function of the progress and ease of the Shaping process. Where the Shaping process is smooth, FEL-2 proceeds as rapidly as the staffing of the effort permits. But if there are significant Shaping issues, FEL-2 should be slowed to stay synchronized with the Shaping effort.

The time required to execute FEL-3 (FEED) varies only slightly with the size of the project. About 15 months are required whether the project is large (>$5 billion) or smaller (< $2 billion). When projects are larger, the feed is often done by two or more contractors in parallel. Only when projects are extremely large (> $10 billion) do we see a statistically reliable relationship between size and longer FEL-3. Then the FEED duration increases to nearly 20 months.

There is one FEL factor that is associated with shorter FEL 3 durations: doing a poorer job on that critical permitting definition factor that we discussed earlier in this chapter. We "save" about two months as permitting definition degrades from "definitive" to "preliminary" and another two months as it degrades to "assumed" (Pr.|t|<.002). This underscores my earlier conclusion that time pressure was the driving force behind not doing an effective job in defining the permitting requirements. But if we encounter a permitting problem as a result of our shortcut, all of the "saved" time is given back plus a 50% penalty.

Sectoral Challenges to Good Front-End Work

Each industrial sector has unique challenges to preparing fully its megaproject for execution. We find almost no differences in the level of understanding of FEL between industrial sectors. Only renewables projects have significantly poorer FEL than other megaprojects, for reasons we will discuss shortly. Almost 100% of project teams understand the relationship between completing the front-end work and getting better project results. Almost all of the difficulties of completing FEL derive from the way that FEL work in a particular sector interacts with the other two work streams—Shaping and Basic Data development. I will discuss the sectors that have special challenges to the front-end shortly.

Petroleum Refining Sector

About 25% of the refining projects in our database are new greenfield refineries. Half of those projects are in the "best practical" or "good" group of FEL. By contrast only 27% of the remaining refining projects are "best practical" or "good" at FID. Those nongreenfields are expansion and modernization projects. The most common reason that the FEL was not complete for those projects is that critical Basic Data were late.

Expanding or modernizing an old petroleum refinery requires a very substantial data collection effort to understand the current condition of the facilities. The process, called the verification of as-builts, must start very early in FEL-2, and FEL-2 must be paced to accommodate the collection of the data. Unfortunately, it is the exceptional case in which the verification of the as-built condition of the refinery was started early enough and done well enough to support the FEED work for the project. This is the primary cause of the frequent failure of these projects. Other problems, such as insufficient refinery staff to support the project or lack of full cooperation between project and refinery, are real but workable problems. Lack of Basic Data cannot be worked around.

As logic would suggest, the element of FEL that does not get completed in nongreenfield refining projects is the critical engineering design status. Fifty-seven percent of the greenfield projects achieved "advanced study design" while only 39% of modernizations and expansions did. Only 22% of these projects ended up successful.

Mining

Overall, the mining sector does a reasonably good job in FEL, especially when one considers that mining projects have some of the most difficult Shaping problems of any sector. Most miners have learned through (often bitter) experience that Shaping and FEL are highly interactive for major mining projects. By their nature, mining projects are environmentally disruptive, and environmental permits are most often the biggest vulnerability in FEL. Mining projects also have a good many Basic Data problems, but those problems usually manifest themselves in poor operability rather than delays to completing the front-end. Mining megaprojects were also the least likely to be schedule-driven of any sector.

Liquefied Natural Gas

As noted before, LNG projects take a long time to complete the front-end, on average nine months longer than other equivalently sized megaprojects. Because product is forward sold, cost and schedule predictability generally have greater value for LNG than other megaprojects. One might reasonably hope that these factors would result in significantly better FEL by FID. In fact, FEL is very marginally better for LNG. In particular, FEED is more likely to be complete than other sectors. This results in slightly better cost and schedule predictability. However, the additional time available could have resulted in *much* better FEL, which would have resulted in more profitable investments.

Renewable Power Projects

We only have a handful of renewable power megaprojects in our data set, simply because we are very early in the development of these projects, which will become ubiquitous if the efforts to mitigate climate change gather momentum. The early returns, however, are not encouraging. These projects had the poorest FEL of any group of projects in the database at the start of detailed engineering. As discussed previously, these projects face very severe Shaping challenges and are often caught up in a "reverse auction" business model that forces very early commitment to the projects. Early commitment easily becomes an excuse not to complete the front-end work, which in turn, dooms these projects to fail.

Petroleum Development

As I mentioned in the "trends" discussion in Chapter 3, oil and gas development projects improved during the first two decades of the 21st century. The projects authorized after the start of 2016 and completed by 2023 were almost as successful as other industrial megaprojects. I was actually looking forward to substantially rewriting this section of the book for this edition. Then, I looked at the oil and gas megaprojects that were authorized after oil prices increased in 2021, and decided to leave the section unchanged. Why? Because all of the bad habits and practices that had led the petroleum industry's megaprojects to be so poor early in this century snapped right back when prices bounced back: the number of schedule-driven projects jumped and FEL plummeted.

There really can't be any question that the petroleum projects suffer more problems; the probability that the distribution of success that we see could be generated randomly is considerably less than 1 in 10,000. Figure 10.16 tells the story.

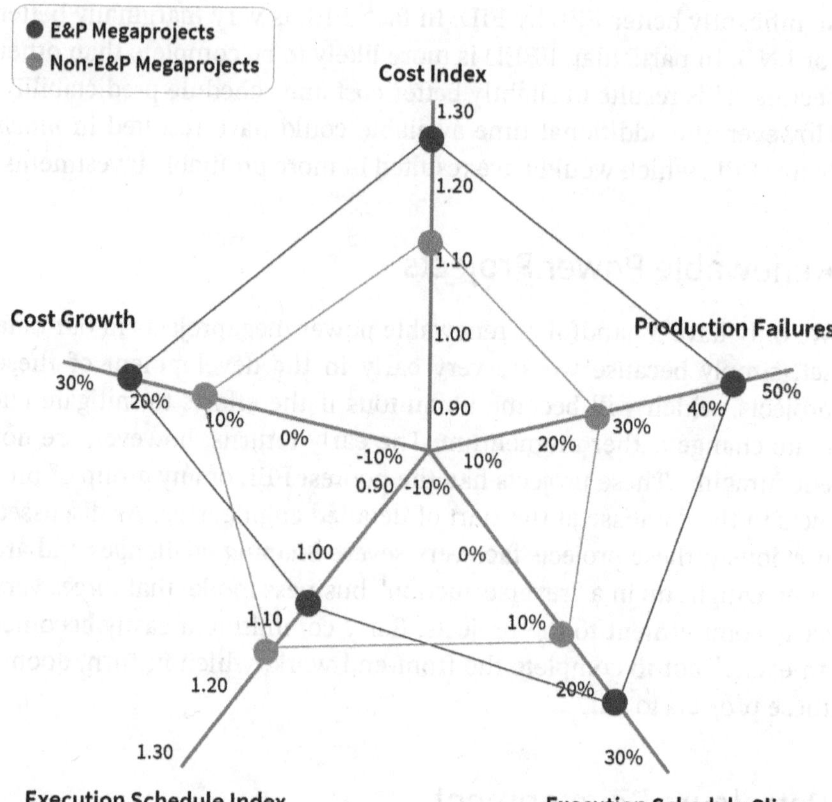

FIGURE 10.16 E&P Versus Other Megaproject Results

The average petroleum development megaproject is worse than megaprojects in other industrial sectors on cost overruns, cost competitiveness, production attainment failures, and schedule slip. The only measure on which petroleum projects look better is the measure of schedule effectiveness, and that is an important part of the story.[24]

One possible explanation of the difference in success rate could be simply that petroleum development projects are intrinsically more difficult than other megaprojects. But that hypothesis doesn't stand close scrutiny. Table 10.2 lists 11 factors that might reasonably be considered potentially problematic for megaprojects. Many of the

[24]The difference in schedule effectiveness is not statistically significant at a .05 cutoff probability value using a two-tailed test (Pr|t|<-.074).

TABLE 10.2 Difficulties and Success Rate

Area of Potential Difficulty	E&P Megaprojects	Other Megaprojects
Size (actual cost in 2023 U.S. dollars)	$5.1 billion	$4.6 billion
Average FEL-2&FEL-3 duration	29 months	30 months
Execution Duration	48 months	49 months
With Substantial New Technology	10%	6%
With Basic Data Problems	16%	18%
In Very Remote Locations	13%	15%
In Labor-short Locations	24%	34%
With Weather Problems	40%	44%
Lead Sponsor New to Area	23%	25%
Government Involved	35%	44%
Political Violence in Location	5%	9%

issues listed are, in fact, associated with poorer project outcomes. However, there is virtually no systematic difference between petroleum development and other megaprojects on any of the measures, and in a number of cases, the nonpetroleum projects look more difficult. Petroleum development projects are larger at the end of the day, but most of the difference is because they overran more. They took the same amount of time to execute. Even from a technology perspective, it is impossible to make a good case that petroleum development projects are more difficult. Both groups employ the similar amounts of new technology. Both suffer the same rate of problems with Basic Data. And the average engineering content of the nonpetroleum projects is much greater.

For petroleum projects, local content requirements are associated with a sharp increase in the instances of reported problems with host government authorities and an increase in permitting problems. For nonpetroleum projects, local content requirements were only weakly associated with an increase in problems with host governments and were associated with a *decline* in permitting problems. The results for the nonpetroleum projects fit with what many megaproject managers have reported to me: when properly managed, local content is often inexpensive and seems to reduce opposition to the project from the host government and other stakeholders.

One of the intriguing features of petroleum development megaprojects is the extreme separation between the successful and unsuccessful projects. As shown in Figure 10.17, the 22% of petroleum development projects that were successful were spectacularly so. They had no cost growth; they were inexpensive; they operated as planned with an average production in the first year ahead of plan; and they experienced no schedule slip whatsoever. The only respect in which they were less than extraordinary was in schedule performance, where they were merely average for projects with their characteristics. That one average result is, of course, no accident. The successful projects started execution with an average, meaning achievable, schedule and met it.

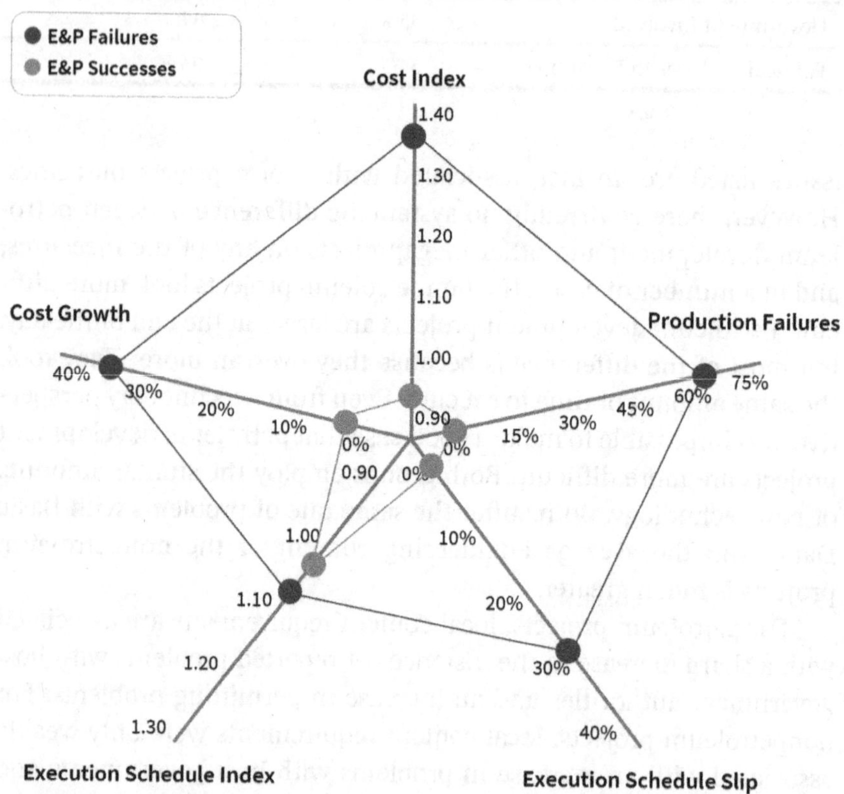

FIGURE 10.17 E&P Successes Versus Failures: Striking Difference in Performance

By very sharp contrast, the failures were dismal failures. They overrun their sanction estimates by over a third; they cost 36% more than they should have; two-thirds experienced serious production problems and they slipped their schedules by over 28%. The one outcome on which they fared reasonably well is schedule. There is no difference, statistically or practically, between successes and failures regarding schedule competitiveness. Again, this is no accident, and we will return to it shortly.

There are three big drivers of failure in petroleum development megaprojects. These three factors work individually and interactively to cause petroleum megaprojects to fail:

- The completeness of FEL at authorization
- Turnover in the project leadership
- Schedule aggressiveness

I will discuss each in turn.

Poor FEL Devastates Petroleum Development Projects

We have emphasized the importance of FEL for all projects, and especially, megaprojects, but it turns out that petroleum development megaprojects are even more sensitive to even small lapses in FEL than other megaprojects. Two dimensions of outcomes are particularly hard hit when the FEL is anything other than "best practical": cost overruns and production attainment. We measure FEL across three big areas for petroleum development projects: the reservoir, the facilities, and the wells construction. The combination of all three areas we call "asset FEL." In Figure 10.18, note that cost growth rises faster with asset FEL for oil and gas projects than for others. Note also that the relationship is stronger statistically as well.

Although E&P megaprojects tend to be less well defined than other megaprojects on every common measure, as mentioned earlier in this chapter, there is one measure on which exploration and production (E&P) projects are very noticeably deficient: definition of the permit requirements. Figure 10.19 contrasts the level of permitting definition

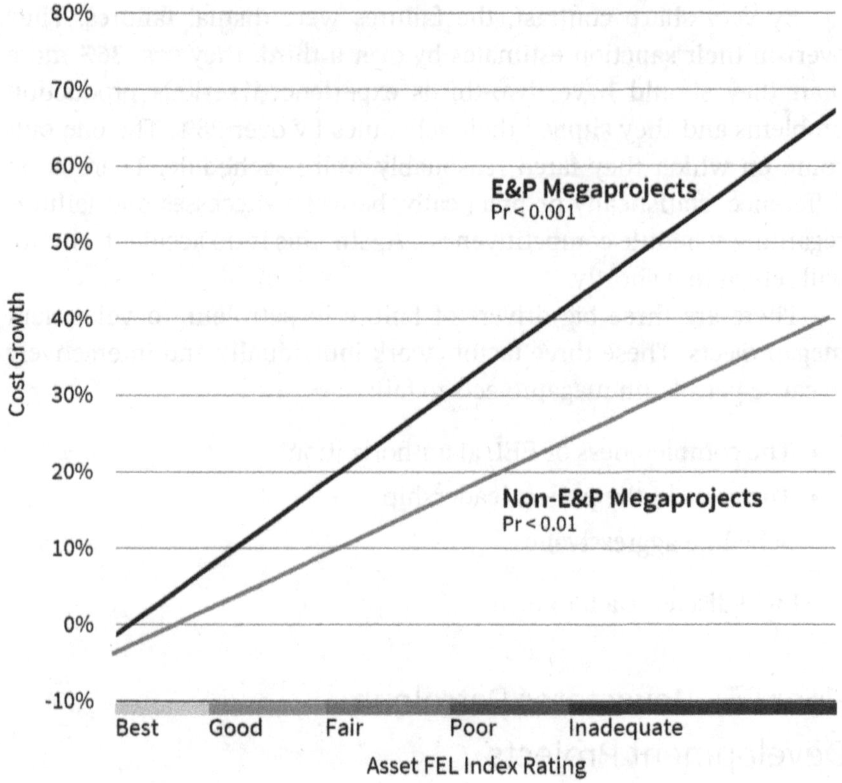

80%
70%
60%
50%
40%
30%
20%
10%
0%
-10%
Cost Growth
E&P Megaprojects
Pr < 0.001
Non-E&P Megaprojects
Pr < 0.01
Best Good Fair Poor Inadequate
Asset FEL Index Rating

FIGURE 10.18 Complete FEL Is More Important for Petroleum Development Megaprojects

for the two groups. The statistical test results show that E&P is clearly different along this dimension. A "definitive" rating on this variable means that all key permits that can be received have actually been received. "Preliminary" means that applications have been submitted and discussions have been held with the regulators about the requirements. "Assumed" means, literally, that the teams assumed that the permits would be forthcoming in a timely manner but at authorization had still not made application. Over 30% of E&P projects assumed that everything was going to be alright and only about one in five had permits in hand. By contrast, over a third of non-E&P projects had received their permits. In fact, many non-E&P companies refuse to sanction a project before the key permits are in hand. This bit of prudence is driven by the reality that permits are a signal that the government is on

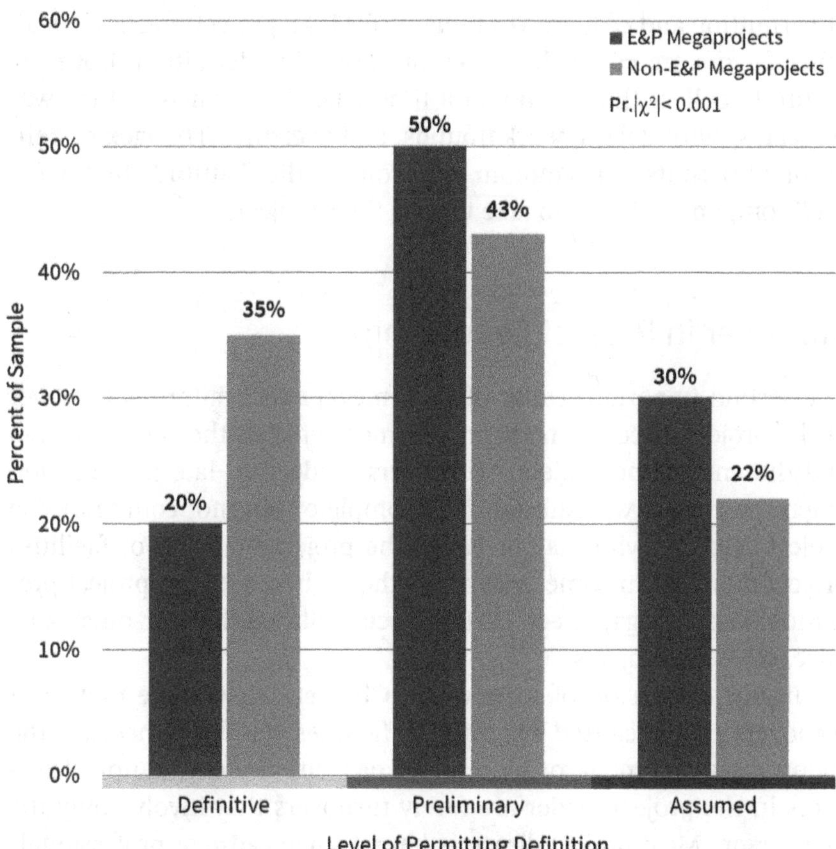

FIGURE 10.19 E&P Permitting Is Deficient

board with the project. Permits are almost never withdrawn after they are granted unless there is a clear violation of the premises on which the permit was granted.

I was so surprised when I saw the number of "assumed" values on this scale for E&P that I went back to the source material and read the analysts' notes taken at the pre-sanction interview. The attitude toward the permits was blasé; "they won't be any problem" was the most common comment from the teams.

Lack of definition around the permit requirements was associated with cost growth for all megaprojects, but was especially acute for E&P projects. Although part of this effect is explained by other factors, especially schedule aggressiveness, the link between poor definition of permitting and cost growth remains for E&P projects even when all other factors are controlled. Lack of permitting definition drove the failure to collect the permits in a timely fashion, which in turn was associated with delays, workarounds, and overruns. The lack of definition of permits is a symptom of a "roll-the-dice" attitude that many E&P companies appear to take toward their projects.

Turnover in Project Leadership

The second important cause of E&P megaproject failure is turnover of the project director one or more times between the start of FEL-3 and the end of the project. (Turnovers made very late in execution when the project was substantially complete were not counted.) The project director, who may be called the project manager or facilities project manager in some systems, is the highest ranking project professional on a megaproject. E&P projects replaced that person at least once in 54% of projects.

In our discussion of turnover in Chapter 11, we note that most turnovers are not caused by project difficulties, but by the needs of the sponsor, reassignment, or retirements or voluntary resignation. Turnovers in the project leader are rarely turnovers that involve only the one person. Most project directors have a small cadre of professionals with whom they work, and if the project director is reassigned, that cadre usually goes with him or her and a new cadre of people comes in with the new director. Turnovers in the project leader tend to damage all megaprojects, but they are devastating to E&P megaprojects. For non-E&P projects, the turnover of the project director was associated with a decline in the success rate from 62% to 39%. For E&P projects, the decline was from 48% to 7%! That's right, 93% of E&P megaprojects with a turnover of the project director failed.

Of course, turnover of the project director does not really explain all of those failures. Lots of bad things and poor practices tend to go together and reinforce one another. When project leadership turns over, FEL tends to be poorer, the team is more likely to be inadequately staffed, team integration is more likely to be absent, and the schedule tends to be more aggressive. However, even when all else is accounted for, turnover of the project director is still strongly associated with E&P project failure.

Why is project director turnover disproportionately damaging for E&P projects? Because E&P projects are usually organized in a manner that inadvertently renders the project directors critical to success, and therefore leave the project very vulnerable to discontinuity in that position. Most non-E&P projects are organized with all of the technical functions reporting directly to the project director. The only important functional interface is between the project and the business. While this interface is often fraught with difficulty, it is also often manageable.

Most E&P capital project organizations, and especially the large ones, are organized into at least three large technical functions: reservoir characterization and depletion planning, facilities engineering, and production wells drilling and completions. Even if E&P project teams describe themselves as integrated, the reality is that integration is fragile and depends heavily on the strength and whole asset view of the project director. Outside the project director, there is no individual with purview of all aspects of the development. There should be an asset development manager assigned by the business, but there almost never is. Therefore, that role falls inevitably to the project director.

In the parlance of organization theory, most E&P projects are weak to mid-strength matrix organizations. The functions maintain a fair degree of control of their personnel when they are assigned to projects. Very effective project directors pull the functions toward a "strong matrix" format. Most megaprojects that fail do so because of poor communication somewhere along the line. Weak matrix organizations are prone to communication failures and when the project director turns over, the disconnects between functions become acute. This is most often manifest in E&P projects in production attainment failures because production attainment success is most dependent on full functional integration. When there is no project director turnover, only 32% of E&P projects experienced production attainment failures. When the position changed hands, 60% did. For non-E&P projects, turnover of the project director was much less important to production attainment because all of the functions were more likely to have been fully integrated into the project team. This failure to strongly integrate the technical functions is the core pathology of E&P megaprojects.

Schedule Aggressiveness of E&P Projects

Another manifestation of risk-taking in petroleum development is schedule aggressiveness. Schedule aggressiveness is measured as the ratio of the promised schedule for execution time made at sanction to the industry average actual schedule for a project of that size and type—the "benchmark schedule." E&P projects are much more schedule-aggressive, on average, than non-E&P megaprojects. The average difference is 15% of execution time and the relationship is very powerful statistically (Pr|t|<.0001).

Schedule aggressiveness helps explain the failure of E&P projects to wait until permits were in hand to authorize the projects. More fundamentally, schedule aggressiveness is associated with Basic Data errors both for the reservoirs and for facilities. As discussed in Chapter 9, recovery from Basic Data problems is rarely possible.

One possible explanation of schedule aggressiveness is that projects primarily producing natural gas rather than oil are subject to commercial competition for gas sales. Project directors on gas projects often complain that those making the commercial deals did not consider project constraints when striving to close a deal, only to leave the project hopelessly schedule driven. By contrast, oil is purely a commodity and is only very rarely subject to niche market constraints.[25] The "gas hypothesis" for petroleum project schedule aggressiveness is flatly wrong. The oil projects are *more* schedule aggressive than gas projects by 13% (Pr.|t|<.021).

The argument against driving schedules for pure commodity projects was discussed previously, but is particularly compelling for crude oil projects. Schedule-aggressiveness damages every outcome except schedule itself, on which it has no effect. From a business perspective the strategy only has any merit in the odd case in which the arrangements with the resource owner have distorted the goal of configuring the project so as to maximize NPV.

One must remember that what appears totally irrational at the corporate level may be entirely rational at the individual level, which is the only level at which rationality actually applies. Much of the

[25]The only exceptions are when the crude in question is particularly difficult to process, such as highly acidic crudes that can be processed in only a few refineries.

schedule aggressiveness in E&P projects is driven by the desire of business unit leaders to meet production goals that are the basis of their incentive compensation. This often involves attempting to advance production from one or a number of projects. Let me offer an ugly but not terribly unusual example.

The project involved the development of an oil reservoir with expected ultimate production of 200 million barrels. The reservoir had no natural drive. Therefore, recovery depended on drilling water injection wells around the periphery of the reservoir and then producing wells toward the center. The project was a great success on cost and schedule up to the point at which drilling was set to begin. Then the business unit director ordered the team to drill the producers first and move up first production to fill a "hole" in the business unit's production profile. The team objected vehemently, citing the potential for reservoir damage. They were overruled. They drilled the producers and started production. With less than 50 million barrels produced, the reservoir collapsed and production was halted forever. The capital investment was suddenly deeply NPV negative.

Figure 10.20 summarizes the flow of problems on E&P megaprojects, and many smaller projects as well. The problems start with aggressive schedules and the difficulties of integrating functions that have strong separate identity. Both of these antecedents, separately and together, are associated with a set of decisions and conditions that depress the chances of success. Aggressive schedules mean that we are

Antecedents	Behaviors	Consequences
Aggressive Schedules Tenuous Functional Integration	Less Complete Reservoir Appraisal Poorer Front-End Loading More Difficulty Staffing the Project Higher Project Leader Turnover Poor Team Integration	+33% Cost Growth +37% Cost Effectiveness +30% Schedule Slip 48% Production Attainment 18 to 24 months after the promised date

FIGURE 10.20 The ABCs of E&P Megaproject Failure

less likely to start the project with a strong appraisal of the reservoir. This restricts the quality and completeness of the Basic Data package on which all else will be based. Schedule aggressiveness and difficulty integrating the functions generate poorer FEL. Schedule aggressiveness also makes projects less attractive to staff and to project directors who realize they have been set up to fail. The consequences are clear enough: a project failure rate of almost 80%.

A Final Comment on Megaproject FEL

The failure to complete FEL on megaprojects is costing industrial firms and their shareholders hundreds of billions of dollars of value. This has been understood for some time now, and yet, there are no signs of improvement. This can only mean that the business leadership of industrial firms fundamentally does not understand the relationship between FEL and success or that they have established incentive structures within the firm that render that understanding irrelevant.

I believe that those charged with the education of business professionals, especially in the United States and Europe, bear a good deal of responsibility for the failure of business professionals in industrial firms to understand the connections here. Curriculums that fail to fully distinguish between the management of commodity industrial firms and other types of manufacturing or financial services do not prepare business professionals to understand the essential roles of technical professionals to the survival of the firm. I believe that those who establish incentive systems with no accountability for capital stewardship by business professionals bear even more responsibility.

PART 3

People Do Projects

We have now discussed the three big streams of work that carry a megaproject from being an idea to a project ready to sanction and execute. If the three streams of work have been executed well with good flow of information between them, the project that results is very likely to be successful. Getting a megaproject from idea to authorization is almost always a multiyear endeavor, and occasionally, a multidecade endeavor. Now we turn our attention to the people who get the work done.

Projects are a purely artificial construct; there is not even an analog of a project in nature. Projects bring together purpose, technology, and people. Almost all megaprojects are actually performed by groups of people organized into a team, or more likely, a set of teams. Unlike projects, teams are not uniquely human. Many social animals form teams, usually for the purpose of hunting. People mostly form teams for sports and projects, the two most team-based activities.

In Chapter 11, I will first discuss megaproject teams, leadership, and team organization. The focus is almost entirely on *owner* teams and owner teams' strength. This focus will not surprise many in the industrial projects world, but it may feel misplaced by readers whose familiarity with megaprojects is through public infrastructure projects. Most public entities that invest in infrastructure megaprojects are what we, in the industrial world, would call very weak owners. Very few government organizations have the project staff needed to populate even a single megaproject, much less several at a time. As a result, government-funded megaprojects lean very heavily on contractors to develop and execute their projects with only minimal owner staffing. Most of the rampant pathology in public infrastructure projects stems directly from this fact. Weak owners do poor projects.

In Chapter 12, I will explore alternative ways of organizing megaproject teams. This is a subject that is rarely broached in smaller projects as they all tend to organize their owner teams in the same "line-of-sight" fashion. But megaproject teams are much larger and often need to become rather complex organizations to get all of the required work done. Chapter 12 also will explore the organization behind the teams because the quality of the team sometimes depends on the nature and effectiveness of the project organization that generated the owner team.

CHAPTER 11

Megaprojects Teams

A great deal has been written about teams and how teams can perform much better than individuals. There are books about team leadership, and on how to produce "high-performance teams," and how to motivate teams. I am sure that these books are right about lots of things (e.g., they mostly agree that good teams need good leaders), but I don't find much of what the literature has to say very helpful in understanding project teams, generally, and megaproject teams, in particular.

Unlike most other areas of business activity, functioning as part of a team is normal for project professionals. Virtually all of those in megaproject team leadership positions have a great deal of project experience, although often not on projects of the size and complexity of the project they are now undertaking. Personnel on megaprojects usually already understand what it means to be a team player: someone who freely takes on tasks in your area of functional expertise and then delivers those tasks on time with quality.

I see lots of problems on megaproject teams, but they rarely have their genesis in things like "bad team chemistry" or "lack of teamwork." You don't have to like the guy sitting next to you, but you do have to talk to him. Instead, the roots of problematic teams are almost always found in some of the fundamentals of the project itself and how it was Shaped.

I am going to start the discussion of teams by discussing a few conditions—precursors—that are necessary for effective megaproject teams.

- A proactive, hands-on stance toward the control of the project by the team

- Clear objectives for the team to pursue
- Project work process
- Team structure, by which I mean how the project team members report, also known as the strength of the matrix

I will then go through a number of key issues:

- Timing of team formation
- The size of the team
- Team integration—the involvement of all needed owner functions
- The degree of involvement
- Finding people
- Recruiting, absorbing new members, and shedding members
- Team leadership
- The importance of continuity
- The development of "robust" megaproject teams

I will conclude this chapter with a discussion of some team problems that are unique to megaprojects or particularly acute for megaprojects:

- Geographic dispersion
- The effects of "hybrid" (partially virtual) working
- Integrating joint venture partner personnel
- Interface management

These issues transition nicely to the next chapter, which focuses on different models of how to organize megaproject teams.

Team Precursors

Let's start our discussion of teams with the conditions that are prerequisite to building an effective project team:

- Understanding of the owner team's role
- Coherent project objectives
- Project work process

Owner Team Role

The first critical point in understanding megaproject teams is to agree on the role of the sponsor (owner) team. What does an owner team do that a contractor team could not do? Why do we need all of these people! As I think back on many megaprojects, I am sure that the business organizations did not understand the role of the owner team and I am not even confident that all of the teams themselves knew why they were there.

The role of the owner team is to generate comparative advantage for the sponsors. The team is where all of the owner functions come together to take the business opportunity and generate a project that is fashioned to the particular strengths and talents of the sponsor organization(s).

With very few exceptions, megaprojects are substantially unique endeavors. Each project tends to have a scope that is not duplicated anywhere else, even if the individual pieces of the technology are quite conventional. Similarly, every sponsoring company that will operate a megaproject is unique in a number of ways that are important to how a megaproject is configured. Different manufacturing/operating organizations have different preferences in terms of technology, control systems, sparing philosophy, maintenance approaches, product mixes, and operating philosophy. These differences have grown up over many years to be harmonized with the business organizations that run the company.

The development of the scope and preparation for execution of a megaproject requires the involvement and active cooperation of many organizations, both inside and outside of the lead sponsor firm. It would be easy to assume that gaining cooperation from outside organizations is the more daunting problem, but often it is the inside organizations that are far more problematic. One of the facts of life in the modern industrial firm is that various parts of the company often fail to cooperate with other parts. R&D or Exploration sees little benefit in cooperating with Engineering. Manufacturing or Operations see the businesses as the cost-cutting gnomes, and so on. So when a project leadership calls on the various functions to place people on a project team or to work differently than their norm to meet project timing requirements, the result is often refusal or simply being ignored.

This problem has always been present in large companies to some extent. Different parts of the companies, which we call functions, have different reporting lines, different measures of success, and different concerns. But over the course of my career spanning the last 30 years, the problems of functional cooperation appear to have greatly worsened. For example, it used to be that getting operations to provide feedback on the performance of a new project was easy. They were happy to provide the needed information, especially as it provided an opportunity to complain about what the engineers denied them. Today, getting that sort of simple cooperation may require going all the way to the top of the company and forcing the issue downward. Even then, simply ignoring a dictate from above is not unusual.

I believe the reason for the change in the level of functional cooperation is simple: relentless pressure on head-count has rendered most functional organizations unwilling to cooperate with others. This is especially true when another function is asking for high-quality personnel to be loaned, even if they are paying for 100% of the time. When companies do not cooperate internally, they become incoherent and they become easy prey for opportunistic outsiders. Many, perhaps most, of my client organizations—which are the "Who's Who" of the industrial world—are perched right on the precipice of incoherence. We will see this at work when we discuss contracting later on, but we see it all the time in assembling megaproject teams.

The owner project team has to knit together a host of functions to create a project that meets the needs of the company. This work cannot be performed by contractors for a number of reasons. Contractors, with very few exceptions, have almost no knowledge of operations. It simply isn't what they do for a living. Contractors do not understand the businesses of the companies they serve and have no need to do so. Finally, contractors do work for shareholders, but they work for *their* shareholders, not for owner shareholders. Only the hopelessly naïve believe that is not the case. The contractors are indispensable for the execution of megaprojects. Even the few owners that do essentially all of their project work in-house have to rely on contractors to execute their megaprojects. But they cannot substitute for owner teams.

Objectives Make Teams

As discussed in Chapter 7, the clarity of the business objectives to the project team correlates with key measures of project results: cost competitiveness (Pr>|r|.005), cost overruns (.03),[1] execution schedule competitiveness (.02), schedule slip (.003), operability (.008), and of course, success (Pr>|z|.002). Also, as the clarity of objectives as perceived by the project team declined, the number of dimensions in which the projects tended to fail increased (Pr>|t|.0001).

The key to the formation and development of effective teams is project objectives. What are the key characteristics of these objectives?

- The objectives need to be worthy. By *worthy* objectives I simply mean objectives that a project professional would be proud to pursue. I mentioned in previous chapters examples where the objectives were deemed not worthy. For example, putting the business's flagship technology in a position to be misappropriated. Or when the objective was to "crush" the nongovernmental organizations (NGOs). Another example involved the wholesale abuse of the terms of a production-sharing agreement between a national resource holder and an international oil company. The terms repaid the sponsor's capital first and then benefits of production were shared. The details of the arrangement made capital virtually free to the international company. The business director ordered that a design from a much larger project be copied because it would save time, even though it would cost much more than the appropriate technology would have. The project team felt (correctly) that it was exploiting the host country. Team members reported "it was so obvious what we were doing we had trouble looking our partners in the eye." The team effectively sabotaged the project until the business director was removed from the project, and ultimately, from the company.
- The objectives need to describe what will make the project a success from the viewpoint of all stakeholders, not just the lead sponsor(s). For example, if a specific number (or range) of direct

[1]After controlling for Corruption Perceptions Index.

jobs that will be created by the project was promised to the host government, that must be included in the objectives. Any agreements with NGOs around environmental or human rights compliance must be included. And any local content promised to the host government must be included. All of the key attributes that constitute success must be included.

- To the greatest possible extent, the objectives of the team need to provide insight into priorities among objectives, particularly the value of achieving a particular schedule.
- The objectives must be (seen as) *achievable* in principle by human beings with the time, money, and people available. The absolute guarantor of poor team morale and poor team quality are objectives that are simply impossible to achieve. When the objectives are viewed as unachievable, recruiting and retention of high-quality team members is understandably difficult. Some companies have adopted a strategy of setting "stretch target" objectives for projects. While that practice may have merit for smaller projects, it is a nonstarter for megaprojects. Megaprojects simply lack the flexibility necessary to achieve very fast schedules or very low cost targets.

Teams and Project Work Process

The third and final prerequisite to megaproject team effectiveness is the use of a systematic project work process. One of my colleagues has developed a "team functionality index" that measures the alignment of the team on a set of 27 measures. What he finds is that project team effectiveness only occurs when a strong and systematic work process is in play. This result should be expected.[2]

Work process tells members of the teams—most megaprojects have multiple teams—what work will be done, when, and in what order. The work process also is used by most teams as their key indicator of

[2]Robert S. Young, "Quantifying the Relationship between Project Team Functionality and Project Performance," *Proceedings of 2010 Annual Meeting of the Australian Institute of Project Management.*

whether they are making progress. It provides a common vocabulary for team members, and therefore, facilitates communication.[3] Having an established work process is so important to megaproject success that I would actively discourage a company from attempting to take a leadership role in a megaproject if it had not already developed and trained on a project work process.

Team Structure

Project teams are assembled from a large number of disciplinary skills. But those skills can be joined together in a number of ways. Figure 11.1 shows four different structures for project teams, all of which have been used in megaprojects. Each structure has strengths and weaknesses, but some are better suited to large complex projects than others.

Functionally based teams are not teams in the usual sense because the set of people doing the project work do not closely collaborate. The various skill sets required are housed in functional homes in the technical organization of the owner company. For example, within the engineering function, there will be subfunctions by discipline—civil/structural, mechanical, electrical, and so on. Work on a particular project is executed by members of the engineering subfunctional units as needed. Work is assigned by the functional leads and the functional leads will meet frequently to handle coordination. Collaboration occurs within functional units but usually not across functional units. Communication occurs up to functional leads, across to leads of another function, and then down to individuals working on the project within that function. There is no traditional project manager/director

[3]Unfortunately, in many companies, different functions employ different project work processes with different vocabularies. R&D, for example, may have a work process for bringing a development from a lab scale to ready-for-commercial-application that is structurally quite similar to that of the project organization, but because the vocabulary is different, communication is hindered. This problem is perhaps most severe in petroleum project development where the reservoir appraisal team, the facilities design team, and the wells teams are all working concurrently, but with work processes that do not communicate or even worse, with work processes that only *appear* to communicate, i.e., they use the same words with different meanings.

Function-Based System

Project work conducted within function

No real "project team," although coordinators may be assigned

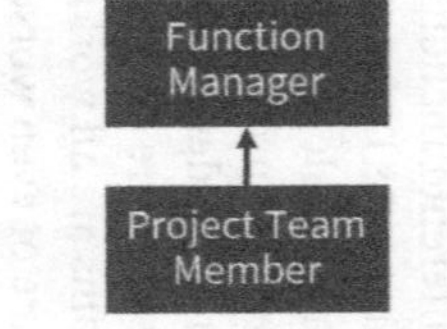

Expected advantages: efficient use of technical resources

Ensures strength in each functional area

Supports inexperienced personnel

Weak Matrix System
Function-Centered Matrix

Team performance measured by function

Dotted line report to Project Director

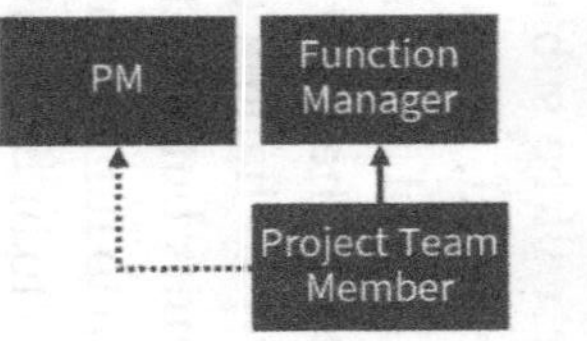

Easier to maintain functional strength

Functions assist in quality management of project work

Functions are responsible for work quality within functional area

Strong Matrix System
Project-Centered Matrix

Functions provide qualified people to projects

Primary authority vested in PM

PM

Function Manager

Project Team Member

Clear accountability lodged with project manager/director

Much faster decision-making

Requires stronger and more experienced people

Project-Based System

All functions report solely to PM

Little or no functional organisation behind individuals

Fastest, most nimble form of project team organization

Low-cost organization

There is no fall-back; the bench does not exist

No flexibility in portfolio size

FIGURE 11.1 Alternative Team Reporting Structures

in this structure, although an overall coordinator may be appointed who carries that title and is responsible for coordinating meetings of functional leads, and meetings with other parts of the company such as business or corporate leadership.

Fully functionally based megaprojects remind me of George Bernard Shaw's saying about dancing bears: it is not so remarkable that dancing bears dance well than that they dance at all! It is truly remarkable that megaprojects get done at all using this structure. Information flow is slow and strained. Issues that could have been resolved with a quick chat require documentation and quite formal communication through "channels." Functionally organized projects are very slow up to the point at which contractor(s) take over the execution of the project. Functionally based setups result in a project process on the front-end that is chopped into pieces with the work product of one functional group passed to another and another. The tendency for functional managers to withhold information is if they see it as beneficial to themselves or their function tends to permeate the projects.

Most functionally organized megaprojects are found in nationally owned companies. The functional organization is quite similar to a traditional bureaucracy, which is the standard form of government organization. The one clear strength of this structural form is that inexperienced personnel are "covered" by the functional group. Quality checking and assurance take place within the functional unit. Functionally based projects are unusual today for large projects, but were more common in times past and continue to be used for many small project situations.

Weak-matrixed teams bring together representatives of different functions, but do not fully second people to the project. The functions maintain control of which personnel to provide, performance review prerogatives, and the ability to rotate individuals in and out of their project roles. In a weak matrix structure, team members work *with* the designated project manager, but not *for* that project manager. In the simplest terms, weak-matrix structures make the project manager's job more difficult. If the project manager is blessed with excellent leadership skills, the weak matrixing will be no more than a nuisance. Unfortunately, excellent leadership skills are always in short supply.

In fact, all megaproject teams have some functions that are "weak-matrixed" into the project team. For example, if legal assistance is needed, it is essentially unheard of for a lawyer to report to the project manager rather than the function. Often, human resources is weak-matrixed;[4] sometimes, the procurement function is weak-matrixed; sometimes operations representatives are weak-matrixed. Each weak-matrixed element in a project team will tend to reduce the authority and control of the team leader—the project manager. Corporate management saying "Well, everyone should cooperate!" is equivalent to saying "Everyone should be good." Don't hold your breath.

In a fully **strong-matrixed structure**, all members of the project team are direct reports of the project manager/director. The project director will even evaluate the performance of lawyers and finance specialists working for the project. In the fully strong-matrixed structure the project director selects team members from the pool provided by the various functions and has the authority to go outside the company ranks if that is deemed necessary to getting the right person for a job. In those cases, the project manager even has the right (within reason) to deviate from the company's standard policies on remuneration and terms of service. In organizations with a tradition of strong matrix project management, it is quite normal for a project director to work with a preferred set of core team members on repeated projects.

The final structural type for project teams is the **fully project-based team.** In these cases, there is no "functional home" within the owner organization for project team members. Team members are part of a "standing" team that does repeated projects as a group. The only project-related functions within this setup are those that require some degree of independence such as estimating and environmental compliance. The "team only" structure is uncommon for established companies with a large capital portfolio. The most prominent example was the independent oil company Anadarko. The structure can be very effective, as was the case with Anadarko, but is also very dependent on careful team-member selection and retention.

The project-based structure is common in newly formed companies and "single-project" companies, that is, companies formed primarily

[4]Often, it is corporate human resources (HR) that provides services to projects, and that service is often a struggle. Recruiting project professionals is very different from HR recruitment generally and often not done at all well.

for the purpose of executing a single project. In these cases, of course, the team that is formed has no history of working together on past projects. Selection of personnel to staff these teams and steps to maintain team continuity of the team are essential to success. One also must remember that such teams will probably lack a common understanding of the project work process to be followed. "Green energy" companies pursuing wind, solar, hydrogen, geothermal, and carbon capture projects often have to form a megaproject team from a standing start. It is one of the most difficult aspects of creating a new company with a major project.

Key Team Topics

Timing of Team Formation

The core project team needs to be formed as soon as there is a reasonable chance that a project will develop. There is an understandable tendency to want to wait until "we are sure we have a project" to put the team together to save money. But early formation of the team ensures that there will be technical input available to business decision-makers from the earliest points forward. That technical input is very important early on because, in the process of starting the business deal, agreements may be made that greatly affect the ultimate viability of the project. Typically, early agreements that need technical input include:

- Site selection
- Technology and technology transfer agreements
- Timing for the project (often faster than practicable)
- Use of local content

The second reason to form the core team early is to be able to appoint the project director, who is very likely to be the only person in the entire sponsoring organization who may actually stay with the project from beginning to end. Between the time that the core team is named early in front-end development until the project is sanctioned, there will usually be a high level of turnover as personnel come on to the project, do their bit, and then move on to another project. Having the project director and a few of the director's reports on the project early helps to glue together the endeavor. The project director needs to develop a working relationship with the business director very early on because their relationship is among the most important for the project's success.

Team Size Matters

The most common attribute of megaproject teams is that they are too small at every point in the evolution of the project: from the earliest scope development to controls in the field in execution, we find that the most common set of initials on the organization charts are TBD[5] or a person named Vacant. Unfortunately, both TBD and Mr. or Ms. Vacant are hard to locate on the job and don't ever seem to get very much done. While it is true that their salaries are low, their cost to the company in the longer run is enormous.

How do we define the *core owner team*? The core team consists of "functional leads." The functions we count as part of the core team are listed in Figure 11.2. Forty-one positions are listed, some of which may have more than a single lead. For example, if a megaproject is composed of three subprojects, each of the subproject managers is a member of the core team. The core team, as the designation suggests, is a subset of the full project team. For a typical $2 billion project, the core team is about one-third of the total owner project team, if the project is fully staffed.

Complexity is the primary driver of the required core team size. Complexity has several dimensions. Oil and gas development megaprojects generally require larger teams because they are actually composed of at least three technical teams: the reservoir team, which is responsible for characterizing the reservoir and planning how to drain it; the facilities team, which is responsible for the development, design, and construction of the platforms or other facilities that will be needed; and the wells construction team, which will plan, drill, and complete the wells. Minerals mining and processing projects have analogous complexity.

[5]TBD=To Be Determined.

Business
- Project Business Sponsor(s)
- Lead Project Financial Modeler
- Supply Chain Lead

Project Management
- Project Director
- Project Managers
- Lead Interface Manager
- Information Management Lead

Project Controls
- Project Controls Manager
- Lead Cost Engineer
- Lead Scheduler/Planner
- QA/QC Manager

Procurement
- Procurement Coordinator(s)
- Supply Chain Manager(s)
- Materials Supervisors

Construction
- Construction Managers
- Labor Relations Specialists

Contracts
- Contracts Manager
- Change Order Specialist

Professional Services
- Legal
- Project-savvy Human Resources

Finance
- Economics and Investment Representatives
- Financial Advisors

Engineering/Process
- Engineering Manager(s)
- Discipline Lead Engineers
- Process Lead(s)
- Principal Geophysicist*
- Principal Geologist*
- Principal Petrophysicist*
- Lead Well Program Planner
- R&D Leads (where applicable)

Environment, Health, & Safety
- Environmental Lead
- Permitting Lead
- Safety Specialist
- Health Specialist
- Site Security Advisor (where an issue)

Operations/Maintenance
- Production/Operations Manager
- Operations Coordinators (each major area)
- Maintenance Representative

Local Government/Authorities
- Government/Authorities Relations Manager
- Government Liaison
- Customs Specialist

* Team members for mineral or petroleum development projects

FIGURE 11.2 Functional Leads in Core Team

In the case of new technology projects, regardless of industrial sector, a cadre of R&D personnel will have to be added, along with additional process design personnel.

A core team member who is often overlooked at the early stages is the information management (IM) lead. The IM systems that a project will employ and the requirements that will be imposed on contractors need to be decided as part of scope development. Waiting until FEED is too late because the provisions need to be in place in the terms and conditions for the FEED contractor. Information management is an increasingly important element in good project management.

The biggest driver of increasing core team size requirements is the number of subprojects involved in the development. It is not the project size per se that drives team size, it is the subprojects. For example, a \$2 billion LNG train addition at an existing site without new upstream gas supply requirements is a fairly simple project and can be handled by a core team of 20–35 people. Increasing the project cost by building two new trains instead of one does not increase the personnel requirements. Conversely, a \$2 billion grassroots chemical complex using new technology for one of the primary units may require 50% more people. The project will likely be broken into at least two subprojects, which increases the core team size by about 10–12 and an R&D cadre will be required that increases the core team by 5–10.

So what do the team sizes actually look like in megaprojects and what difference does it make? We counted the team size as the projects approached authorization and asked when the incumbents had been named. We also asked whether there had been turnover in the positions since the first person was named. Included in our count were any functional leads that appear in Figure 11.2. They were not counted if the position was vacant (TBD). No administrative personnel were included in our counts. If joint venture personnel were seconded to the project *and* had real jobs rather than oversight and liaison, they were counted. Independent contractors filling the positions were counted, but we noted they were not actually owner personnel. When an employee of one of the contractors working on the project filled the position, they were not counted.

After controlling for complexity, the degree of step-out in the technology, and being schedule driven, all of which decrease the chances of a successful project, each member added to the core owner team increases the probability of having a successful project by over 3% (Pr>|z|.02).

There are several compelling reasons why larger owner teams tend to deliver better megaproject results. Larger owner project teams are able to respond to crises in execution while smaller teams are not. Let me give you an example. This was an onshore oil field development project located right in the middle of nowhere (technical term). The terrain was rugged and the local population was generally hostile to the project because they had poor experience with prior projects. The area was also environmentally sensitive. In what is somewhat unusual for the oil industry, the lead sponsor decided to execute on an EPC reimbursable contract basis and forced a reluctant partner to agree.

The contractor got into serious trouble with the local population while building roads and transporting materials to the site. Whereupon the lead sponsor immediately replaced all of the contractor's field leadership with his own people. They were able to reassure the neighbors that the problems were over and proceeded to complete the project without incident. That was only possible because of an abnormally large sponsor team and the willingness to intervene quickly. Whenever I hear grumbling about a megaproject being overstaffed, I immediately think we might have a successful project on our hands here.

Larger teams on the front-end drive better practices. Larger teams are much more likely to have no key owner positions vacant. When there are no TBDs working on the front-end, we call the owner team "functionally integrated." All of the functions needed to fashion the project are present. In order to qualify as an integrated team, the functional leads on the team must be able to speak authoritatively for their function. For example, the operations member(s) of the team can make decisions on operational issues without checking back with anyone in higher authority. For a project of average complexity, the integrated core team was twice as large on average as the non-integrated team (Pr>|t|.03).

Integrated Teams Generate Better Projects

Developing an integrated team, one in which no key functions are in absentia, is the single most important project management practice for a megaproject. Unfortunately, less than 60% of megaproject teams in our database are integrated during front-end development.

All of the functions listed in Figure 11.2 are important, and missing any one of them can end up sinking a project. But some of the functions are critical to fashioning comparative advantage for a project. Chief among these are technology, scope developers (the process people), operations, and maintenance. These functions provide the input that makes the project distinctly reflect its primary owner. Of these, the function that is most often missing is operations.

Once, while closing out a failed chemicals megaproject, I asked the project director what he would have done differently. His answer was surprising in its simplicity: "I have thought about that question a good deal and the only thing I should have done differently is to have shut the project down when I couldn't get a single op rep [operations representative] during FEL-2. When they finally arrived during FEED, we had to make change after change and we were like a dog chasing its tail; we could never catch up. They might have fired me for shutting it down, but it would have been the right thing to do!"

Developing an integrated team might seem like an easy enough task, but it actually can be like pulling teeth. For example, a typical megaproject may need 3 to as many as 20 operations people during all of the front-end (Phases 2 and 3). Furthermore, these folks need to be the best that the operations department has. Operating facilities are short of people and have no doubt been "burned" while providing people for scope development for projects that were never authorized. Furthermore, under the best of circumstances, there is little or no benefit to the loaning organization.

Responsibility for team integration usually resides with the project director and their direct reports, the subproject managers. It shouldn't. Primary responsibility should reside with the *business* director, also known as the business sponsor. Business directors have more clout in most organizations than project directors. The operating organization often reports to the businesses, but never to engineering, as do most of the other functions whose people have to be pulled into a project. Gaining and ensuring cooperation in owner team development outside the project organization personnel should routinely be a business responsibility. The project director's responsibility should be to accurately develop the staffing requirements from nonproject functions,

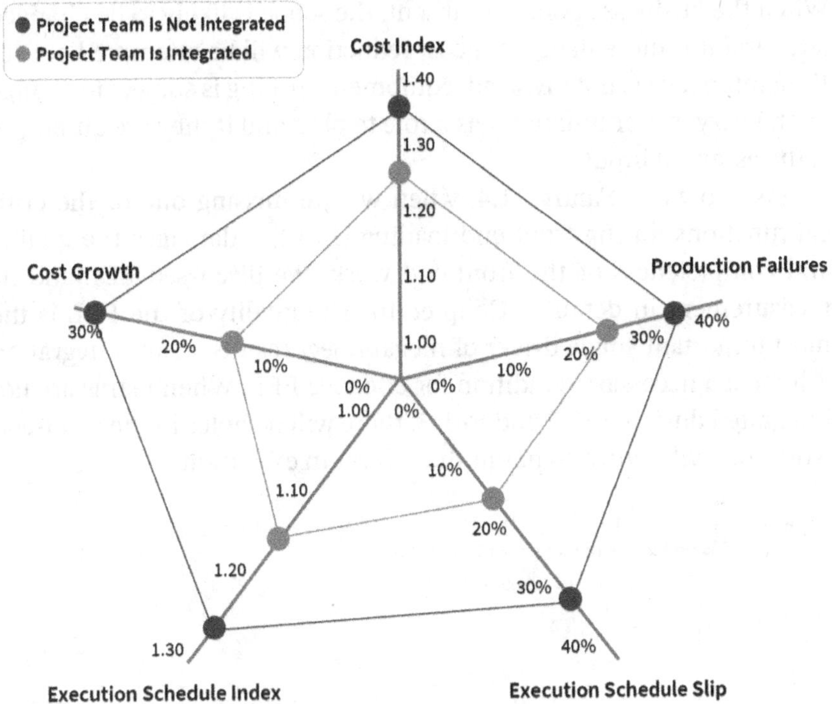

FIGURE 11.3 Integrated Teams Do Better Megaprojects

including R&D and reservoir/orebody, and make them known to the business director in a timely way.

I cannot overemphasize the importance of a functionally integrated owner team for a megaproject. First, as shown in Figure 11.3, projects have much better outcomes when all functions were actively involved. Every difference shown in Figure 11.3 is statistically robust. Only 23% of the projects that lacked integrated teams were successful versus 39% of projects with integrated teams.[6] (The 39% is not exactly heart-warming, which tells us that more than team integration is needed to produce successful projects.)

The effects of missing team members manifest in a number of ways. For example, when operations/manufacturing are not actively present in scope development, the scope may not be operable, or at a minimum will not be exactly what operations was looking to get.

[6]Difference based on Pearson chi-square test is significant at .001.

When the business sponsor is absent, the scope is likely to be changed later and it is more likely that cost reduction will be attempted at FID. If maintenance is not involved, equipment spacing is subject to change later. Every owner function has a role to play, and if they are absent, so is the essential input.

As shown in Figure 11.4, when we are missing one of the critical functions during front-end loading (FEL), it damages the quality and completeness of the front-end work. We discussed FEL and its measurement in detail in Chapter 10. The quality of the FEL is the most important single driver of megaproject results. Team integration is almost a necessary condition for effective FEL. When teams are not integrated during FEL 2 and FEL 3, there will be holes in the front-end work that will return to haunt the project in execution.

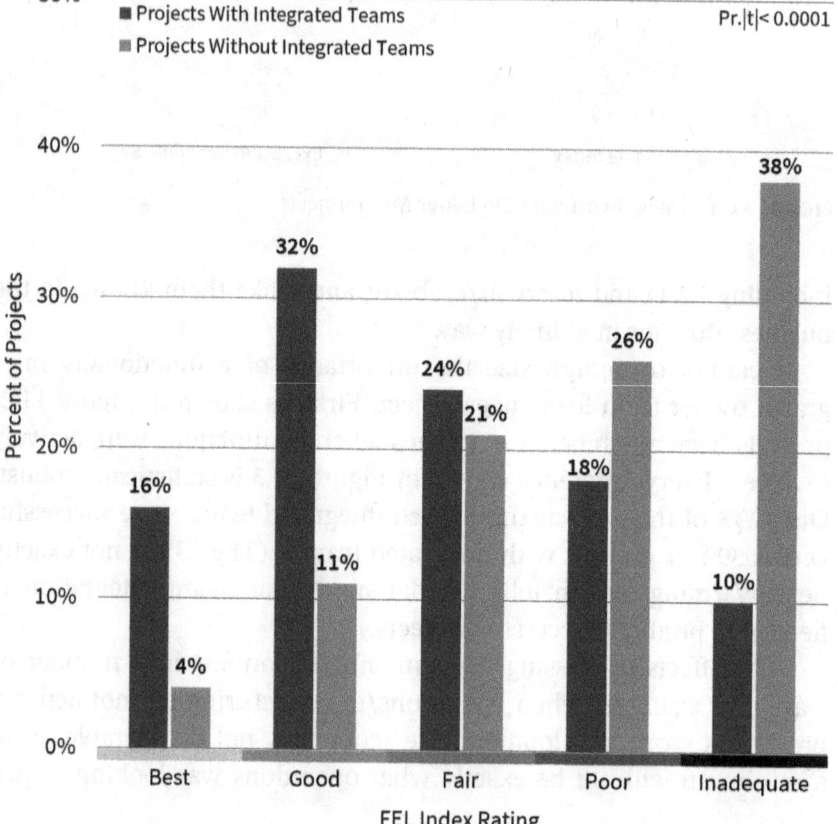

FIGURE 11.4 Integrated Owner Teams Do Better FEL

The two distributions of FEL work shown in Figure 11.4 are quite different; the chance they are drawn from the same population is vanishingly small. When FEL is "best practical" or "good," a project has a reasonable chance of success. Projects with FEL scores worse than "fair" have almost no chance at all. What is very peculiar is that almost all project teams in today's world know this to be the case, yet only one megaproject in seven achieves best practical FEL. That suggests that the decision to forego completing FEL is rarely a project team choice.

Previously I mentioned some of the functions, such as technology and process design and concept selection, that are essential for fashioning comparative advantage for the sponsor(s). There is another set of functions that are equally essential for reasons of moral hazard and control. Cost estimating, scheduling/planning, and controls in the field are all activities subject to conflict of interest when executed solely by contractors.[7] These functions, more than all the other traditional owner functions, have been subject to significant down-sizing since the mid-1980s in most companies in Europe, North America, Australia, and Japan. As a result, most megaproject sponsors have difficulty staffing these positions internally, and many have difficulty even supervising outsiders doing this work. I remember challenging one megaproject director at a major oil company about his need to staff the controls function for his project. He replied, "The 12 people needed to staff controls for my project would be more controls people than we have in the whole company around the world."

Team Integration and Owner Involvement

One of the surprising features of many megaprojects over the past 20 years is the low level of involvement in the project's execution by many of the sponsor teams. Over half of the teams reported that their intended (and actual) stance toward their project was to step back

[7]The insight that conflicts of interest are particularly acute in situations of team or joint production is hardly new. See Armen Alchian and Harold Demsetz, "Production, Information Costs and Economic Organization," *American Economic Review, 62,* 1972: 777–795. The sponsors-contractors relationship is simply a variant of the principal-agent problem in economics. It is very difficult, some would say impossible, to structure incentives in a way that eliminates the problem. This fairly obvious insight seems to have been lost on many sponsors.

and allow the contractors to do the project. In practice, what a passive stance means is that the sponsor team is not guiding the performance of the contractors at each step. They are not intervening actively when problems start to develop and they do not take responsibility for managing the interfaces, particularly the contractor-to-contractor interfaces on the project. They hold extended (owner and contractors) meetings less frequently.

Integrated teams were 60% more likely to take a highly involved and proactive stance than non-integrated teams. In part, this merely reflects the reality that non-integrated teams tended to be seriously understaffed. You can't be highly involved if you don't have the people. Also, because non-integrated teams were going into execution with much less firm information about the project from good quality FEL, they were often simply not in a position to take an active role.[8] For example, how can you take an active role in cost and schedule control if you do not have a high-quality, control-grade estimate and a resource-loaded schedule?

Interestingly, the level of owner involvement was unrelated to whether the execution was being done on an EPC lump-sum basis.[9] In fact, the "alliance" type reimbursable contractual arrangements were overwhelmingly associated with low levels of sponsor involvement. (We will return to this subject in Chapter 13.) However, taking a passive stance toward the execution of a project does suggest that the teams believed they had transferred execution risks to the contractors, regardless of the contractual approach taken.

Low involvement by sponsor teams is particularly prevalent in the petroleum industry. Almost two-thirds of the teams in upstream petroleum industry megaprojects took a "hands-off" stance toward their projects in execution versus 36% for the rest of the industry. The reader should recall from Chapter 3 that the petroleum industry production, that is, "upstream," projects also fared worst of any other sector

---

[8]Indeed, the FEL index is much worse on projects with low levels of owner involvement, averaging in the "poor" range on the scale shown in Figure 11.4. The high-involvement projects averaged in the "good" range. The difference (Pr>|t|) was significant at .0001.

[9]The chi-square probability was nonsignificant at .28.

in terms of failed projects. By contrast, over 80% of chemical industry project teams took a highly involved stance toward the projects.

There is a heavy price to be paid for being unwilling or unable to be proactively involved in the execution of the project. Only 16% of projects with low-involvement teams were successful. If the team was also not integrated, the success rate fell to a paltry 10%. And if the FEL index was not at least "fair," success almost disappeared entirely.

Where Do We Get All These People?

Adequately staffing industrial megaprojects in the early 21st century is one of the great headaches of project organizations. A number of factors have converged to make staffing extraordinarily difficult:

- There are more megaprojects than ever before.
- Twenty years of down-sizing of owner engineering organizations have left the cupboard empty.
- The aging of the workforce in the Organisation for Economic Cooperation and Development (OECD) countries has thinned out the remaining personnel and continues to do so as the baby boomers retire.

As a result, only a few megaproject sponsors around the world are able to adequately staff most their large and complex projects. Those are the companies that made a strategic decision during the 1980s and 1990s not to radically down-size their project organizations. Attempts by several large companies to significantly increase the ranks of their project organization in the past decade have largely failed. One company that succeeded in adding a large number of people in the past decade discovered that the people hired were of such low quality that they were forced to undertake a global purge of the poor performers.

Any thought that the contractor ranks can be used as a reservoir of talent for owners should be dismissed. The major international contractors from the OECD countries also face severe staffing problems. As a result, sponsors find themselves having to cobble together project teams and too often end up leaving critical positions vacant.

Individual independent contractors (ICs) and so-called "agency staff"[10] can usefully augment owner people. ICs and agency staff are often highly skilled, but they come with a problem: continuity. ICs need a steady stream of project work. What this means is they start looking for a new position about six months before the current position is due to expire, usually because the project is ending. When the market is tight, as it is going to be for the foreseeable future, they often leave their current position before the work is done. Staff from agencies are subject to the same limitation, as their employer will often want to move personnel to a more lucrative contract and substitute less skilled personnel. From the owner's viewpoint, this lack of continuity in functions such as cost control is a serious problem. When IC and agency controls staff leave early, the owner ends up with absolutely no idea of where the money went or why a schedule slipped. The sponsors then find themselves easy prey for spurious contractor claims because they have lost the people and the records necessary for claims defense.

If ICs and agency staff are going to be used, they must be contractually tied up for the duration of the project. For ICs, this means providing a significant (four to six months of salary) end-of-project payment. For agency staff, the situation is more difficult. Generally, owners will seek to tie particular agency personnel in their contract with the firm, but in my experience, this is rarely completely successful. I believe that bonus payments would be more likely to succeed, but have been resisted by owners.

The most common owner response to a lack of project personnel is to employ a project managing contractor (PMC). The PMC is usually hired to, in effect, replace most of the owner team. The PMC will engage the other contractors on the project and exercise cost and schedule controls in place of the owner. For companies hopelessly short of project management skills, the PMC approach is probably the only way they can act as lead sponsor for a megaproject. However, using a PMC is fraught with difficulties. When used in the traditional way, a PMC adds a thick additional layer to the organization, usually starting in front-end engineering design (FEED) (FEL-3). The use of

[10]*Agency staff* includes employees of specialist consulting firms. These firms offer services such as scheduling or field controls.

a PMC increases the cost of the project. The problem is less the cost of the PMC, although that can be substantial, and more the reaction of other contractors when a PMC is employed. Working for a PMC is viewed as a significant risk by other contractors. This is especially true because the PMC is usually now given a substantial piece of the engineering, materials procurement, and construction (EPC) work on the project. When that is the case, other contractors add an average 30% premium to their bids to account for the added risk. (That often results in the PMC being given even more of the EPC work at a price that is below the bids, but much higher than a competitive price.)

When use of a PMC is simply necessary, I recommend that the PMC be used as a source of personnel who will augment and complement the personnel of the sponsors. Control must be maintained by the sponsors if an effective project is going to result. Many contractors that act as PMCs resist this kind of fully integrated owner/PMC team because it reduces their control and profit opportunities.

Agency staff, ICs, and PMCs are nothing more than stopgap measures. If a company expects to be in a commodity business for the foreseeable future, then the process of rebuilding project management and other engineering disciplines from the bottom up is the only long-term solution. It cannot be done quickly and will provide little added value for at least five years, and not reach its full potential for a decade. However, it is the only viable route in the long term.[11]

If outside hiring is going to be attempted to fill in missing skills for a project or series of projects, specialized project resources recruiting talents are needed. Many human resources organizations are not geared to find and vet project skills. People who like to work on large projects are not looking for the types of positions that HR normally fills. They are often far more likely to be enticed by a really difficult and ambitious project than by a comfortable stable position behind a desk. If the HR organization is going to be used for recruitment of project resources, project professionals already on board should actively consult in the process. Hiring bodies is relatively easy; hiring skills is much more difficult.

[11] I should be clear that I do not expect more than a few companies to adopt such a strategy simply because it is a long-term solution. Among many of my clients, there is very little corporate interest in any long-term issues. Regrettable, but true.

Absorptive Capacity: A Key Dimension of Team Success

As I have stated several times now, projects teams are very peculiar organizations. They are deliberately temporary, which makes that recruiting task much more problematic and peculiar, and they are very dynamic. By *dynamic*, I mean that they add people—often in large numbers—at several points in the evolution of the project while shedding other personnel that have performed their tasks and are no longer needed or are no longer needed full-time. Figure 11.5 can help explain what I mean.

The team should be formed mid- to late FEL-1. The teams generally stay small until a decision is made to start scope development. Then the team may need to double, and then double again a few months later. Depending on the lead sponsor's capability, contractors may start to join the project early in scope development. If the owner has strong capabilities, the contractors may not mobilize seriously until the start of FEL-3 (FEED/Define or /Feasibility). When the contractor(s) join, there is another step change in team numbers. Members start leaving the team as early as FEL-3. In particular, it is important that the process designers have completed their work and will stop making changes as FEL-3 gets seriously under way.

Expansion of the team can give rise to a whole series of potentially deadly problems. The most common problem is that the person needed is simply not available when needed. Often, particular individuals are all but essential to moving a project forward. Sometimes, it is the particularly talented project director. More often, specific technology experts are needed for process design but are not available. And, of course, sometimes a great many people are not available because insufficient people exist in the company. Sometimes joint venture partners can be persuaded to part with skilled people even when they are not the lead sponsor. I always encourage lead sponsors to recruit joint venture partner people because I find it helps solidify the partners. It can also alleviate skill shortages.

One of the characteristics of front-end development work is that the schedules tend to be rather fluid. It is in the nature of scope development that it is iterative, and therefore, hard to precisely schedule.

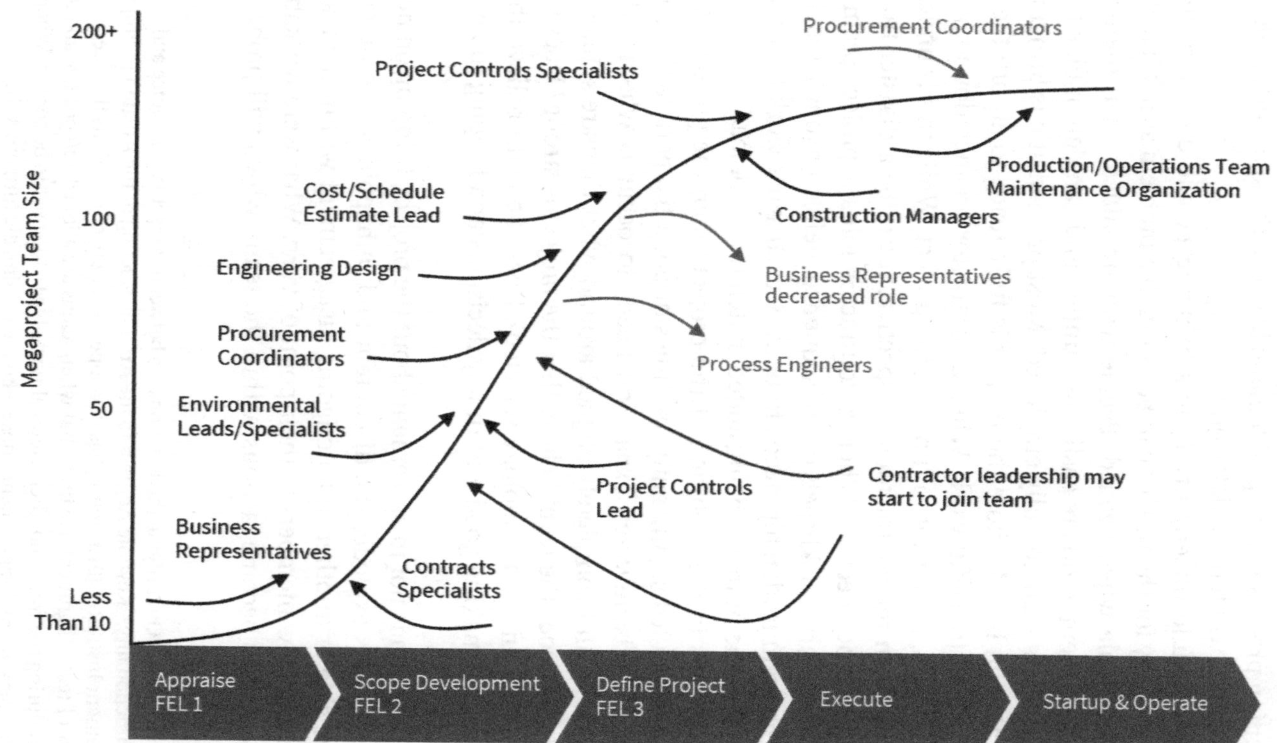

FIGURE 11.5 The Project Team Changes Its Size and Composition as the Project Progresses

Also, because the Shaping process is ongoing during scope development, work may need to be slowed or accelerated to meet changes in Shaping. Recall that letting the project development get out ahead of the Shaping process is very problematic because the sponsor's negotiating position will tend to deteriorate.

The schedule uncertainty fosters bringing people on before the project is ready for them. This can be as much a problem as not having people available when needed. People who are added when there is nothing for them to do are easily disgruntled and can demoralize the team members who are fully employed. Most problematic is bringing contractors on board before the project is fully ready to absorb them and put them to useful work. When a contractor organization joins a project in FEL, they want to run with the project. While this is understandable from the contractor's perspective, it can be a disaster from the project's perspective. When a contractor joins a project prematurely, work very quickly gets out of sequence. Before anyone joins the team, the team leadership needs to be very clear what work they will do, and that the numbers being added match the work load.

The points in the evolution of the project when the project team must be expanded significantly are times of potential peril to the project. The key issue when expansion needs to occur is whether the team is fully and completely aligned around what they are supposed to be doing. Does the team believe that the project is strong? Does the team believe in the technology selected? Does the team believe that leadership is making good and timely decisions and keeping the project moving?[12]

If the team is not in agreement about the project, bringing on new team members explodes the discontent and unhappiness. Those taking one side or another in an ongoing disagreement within the team will recruit new members to their point of view. What were workable disagreements become factions within the team, which will probably

[12]See Rob Young, "Quantifying the Relationship between Project Performance and Team Functionality," Keynote Address to the Annual Meeting of the Australian Project Management Institute, 2010. Young has developed a battery of questions that creates an index of team alignment. He finds that when teams are aligned and positive about a project during the front-end, their views almost always turn out to be correct. When team members are in disagreement, those who are pessimistic turn out to be correct.

require a change in team leadership to put right. Strong team alignment plus carefully worked out assignments for new members generate good absorptive capacity by the project team. In those circumstances, the new members help propel the project forward. If those two conditions are not met, the new members set the project way back.

One final note on adding team members: megaprojects often involve areas of scope with which sponsors are completely unfamiliar. That scope development is often given over to a specialist consulting engineering firm to develop without ever really integrating those people into the project team. That is a mistake because the communication between the team and the consulting organization will be weak and the opportunities for disconnects will be abundant.

The Role of Megaproject Team Leadership

I noted at the beginning of this chapter that the literature is in violent agreement that team leadership is important. I want to add my voice to that chorus, but I would also like to add some specifics about what constitutes leadership.[13] I have met a great many excellent megaproject directors, and superficially at least, they do not seem to have much in common. For every one that fits the mold of the strong military-type leader, there is another who better fits the mold of the quiet, thoughtful professor. I even know one megaproject director who started his major projects career as a "kick-ass and take-names" type, and then mid-career, completely switched to a "touchy-feely, team-building" type. And, he was equally successful in both modes! (He was nicer in the second incarnation, but generated respect in both.)

There are some qualities that go beyond the superficial that successful megaproject directors seem to share. First, they are generalists. Megaproject directors must often work closely with partners, regulators,

[13]For those keenly interested in the makeup of excellent megaproject leaders, see E.W. Merrow and N. Nandurdikar, *Leading Complex Projects*, Hoboken, NJ: John Wiley & Sons, 2018.

and politicians. They need to focus upward and outward, while the subproject managers can focus downward and inward. Most started their careers within the sponsor company outside project management. Many started their careers in the functions such as R&D, petroleum engineering, or geology, all of which are responsible for Basic Data development. Being able to reach across functions is a necessary quality.

Second, successful project directors are politically savvy within their own company organizations. They have a network within the company that can provide assistance when the project runs into difficulty. Especially important is the ability to get other functions to make good-quality people available when they are needed. This means that the successful project director often has friends and allies in the businesses or in the top management of the company. It is a shame that this is necessary, but it often is.

Third, they are good communicators and especially good at communicating upward. They tend to be able to take complex issues and simplify the decision-making of their business superiors. For example, they can explain in straightforward layperson's terms why the schedule acceleration desired by the business cannot be achieved without unacceptable sacrifice of cost or quality.

Whether a megaproject leadership is able to hold the trust of the project team depends, above all else, on their ability to insulate those at the working level from interference from outside the project. If people outside the project team do not cooperate with the project director, respect for their leadership erodes. Project professionals are willing to work on megaprojects because the projects themselves are interesting and exciting. If the leadership cannot keep the project momentum up, it is very difficult to maintain team morale. Only the very best project directors can succeed when the opportunity Shaping process is not going well.

The Project Business Sponsor

Recently, I was meeting with the executive committee of a large and prominent specialty chemicals company. We were discussing its upcoming portfolio of large difficult projects and the subject of the business sponsors for the projects came up. The question immediately arose, "What do you mean by the business sponsor?" My response, "I mean the person who is responsible and accountable for assuring you—the corporate leadership—that this project makes business sense, that there is a market for the product that will justify the cost of the project, and that at the end of the day you will be a stronger company for having spent this massive amount of shareholder money on the project." The CEO then said, "We don't really have such a position, but I think we really need one." My colleagues and I have had similar conversations a great many times over the years.

What Does a Good Business Sponsor Look Like?

The short answer to that question is: the ideal business sponsor looks like Ralph! So who is Ralph? In the earliest days of IPA, my colleagues and I encountered an executive at a chemical company named Ralph Kurland. Ralph oversaw the major projects in the company's commodity chemicals arm from a business perspective. Although he was truly brilliant and a good friend, I have often wished that we had never met him.

Ralph's experience included both operations and the business commercial side of chemicals, and for whatever reason, Ralph deeply understood how capital projects actually work. Ralph understood the role of the business sponsor to a tee: balancing capital cost and operations concerns while ensuring that everyone in the company cooperated to make his projects successful. Ralph understood that he had to get the deals done and the stakeholders all aligned before finalizing the scope. He understood that getting into FEED before closing the commercial deals was always a bad idea.

Corporate management worshiped him because his projects were uniquely successful—strong business cases with on-cost and on-schedule completions. Procurement cooperated because they knew that Ralph had the ear of the chair person even more reliably than they did. Project managers loved to work his projects because they would get the support they needed to be successful. Although a generation has passed since Ralph retired, no product manager who worked with him in their early years fails to mention him when I see them.

Ralph never forced the schedule, but because he made quick and authoritative decisions, his projects moved right along. Stage-gates really were there, but not really needed because Ralph saw no purpose in not doing good FEL. Ralph was his own effective governance machine. Alas, he also was one-off. Good business sponsors are really rare. For many years, Ralph was our model of how projects should work. If only we had business sponsors like Ralph, so many problems would go away. It took me almost a decade to realize that Ralph was unique, could not be duplicated, and was never going to be seen again. Some of my colleagues still pine for his return.

Ralph is missing because very few companies have a position or a career path for people like Ralph. Even petroleum development companies, which are voracious consumers of capital, rarely have a *business* position populated with people who look like Ralph. They sometimes have a position called "venture manager," but that position is staffed from the projects organization rather than the business. Several petroleum companies staff a position call "business opportunity manager," but that position is intended to find opportunities and shove them into FEL-2 (scope development) rather than act as a driver of good asset development.

Every megaproject needs a sponsor from the business side of the house. That sponsor needs to take on the project as the Shaping process is getting started and needs to stay with the project at least to FID.

I have a good friend who is a first-class megaproject director. He said that in 35 years with his company he had 30 bosses and only one of them was a really good business sponsor. The good business sponsor is always focused on the quality of the *business* asset that is being created, not solely on the project creating that asset. Figure 11.6 traces the sponsor's role throughout the project life cycle.

The work starts at a very intense level to lead Shaping and start the process of putting together the business case. When enough Shaping and Basic Data acquisition have been complete, the sponsor should lead moving the project into scope development. Until the basic scope is decided, the sponsor needs to continue to be very actively involved. For a megaproject, the business sponsor's role from inception to the start of FEL-3 (FEED) should normally be full-time. It is unfair to both the sponsor and the project for the sponsor to be forced to keep up with another job while shepherding a multibillion dollar venture forward.

Standard Industry Front-End Loading (FEL) Process

	Appraise FEL 1	Scope Development FEL 2	Define Project FEL 3	Execute		Startup & Operate
Gates		Is there a Business Case?	Is scope complete with business case still intact?	Is the project ready to Execute?	Is the project field-ready? (soft gate)	Handover
Sponsor Activities	• Identify need • Lead stakeholder alignment • Develop bus case • Develop options • Bring to Gate 1	• Guide (not lead) scope development • Ensure functional integration of team • Ensure consistency of scope and bus case • Complete stakeholder alignment • Close the deal • Present business case for sanction	• Manage the stakeholder alignment • Monitor progress • Intervene to assist when requested by project director • Ensure development of operating organization is progressing at pace			
Sponsor Level of Effort	HIGH	HIGH	MODERATE	LOW	MODERATE	

FIGURE 11.6 Sponsor's Role Is Accountability for Business Value of the Asset

A key sponsor role is to support the project director in all of those areas in which the project director lacks organizational clout: generating cooperation from weak-matrixed functions, properly staffing the operations roles, and dealing with as much of the organizational politics of the project as possible. If the business sponsor and the project director can forge a strong working relationship, the chances of producing a successful megaproject and business asset improve dramatically.

The Importance of Leadership Continuity

My final team topic is the importance of maintaining continuity of team leadership. Because project teams are temporary organizations with constantly changing membership, turnover in leadership positions is particularly damaging. Unlike permanent ongoing organizations, projects cannot have much in the way of institutional memory. Most damaging is the departure of the project director any time from FEL-2 through the completion of the project.

We have long noted the connection between turnover in the project leader and project problems for projects of all sizes. Some argue the causality is that project leaders are replaced when projects are going poorly. In fact, however, that is very rarely the way the causality flows. Only very occasionally are sponsor project directors replaced for (perceived) poor performance. It is usually much more mundane things like retirement, promotion, or some other form of reassignment that generates the turnover. Megaprojects are so long that maintaining continuity is difficult. Just over half (54%) of our megaprojects experienced a turnover in their top leader. Even worse, the great majority of those turnovers were not planned.

From a statistical perspective, the link between failure and turnover of the project leader is unmistakable. Even after controlling for every other factor that affects success, turnover of the project director is associated with a higher failure rate.[14] As Table 11.1 shows, every measure of project quality suffers when there is turnover.

[14]All differences shown in Table 11.1 are statistically significant at a probability of 0.02 or less. The same is true for smaller projects as well but the differences tend to be smaller.

TABLE 11.1 Failure and Turnover

Outcomes Measure	Without PD Turnover	With PD Turnover
Cost Overrun (pct)	13	26
Execution Schedule Slip (pct)	16	29
Projects with Poor Operability (pct)	22	33
Successes (pct)	45	23

How does the loss of the project director result in so much damage? Of course, some of the relationship between turnover and poorer projects is actually generated by other factors. Project systems that have less turnover tend to be better staffed and better managed. It is not surprising they produce more well-staffed projects, better team integration, better FEL, and better projects overall. However, even accounting for those things, we see the deleterious effects of turnover. The reason is that turnover in the project leadership becomes an opportunity for lots and lots of changes.

When the project leadership turns over, it seems to trigger a loss of memory among some functions and organizations bordering on total amnesia. Agreements between operations (manufacturing) and the project about design features come unstuck. The business may decide this is a good opportunity to add a product to the mix or otherwise change scope. And most importantly, every informal agreement between the project director and the contractors may suddenly disappear.

When there is a turnover of key leaders—the project director, the construction lead, or the lead engineer—the effect, in most cases, is that the position is, in effect, vacant for several months *even if the new person is on the job from day one!* That is because it takes several months for a new person to come up to speed fully. Still worse, moving a project director off a project often results in other members of the core team leaving as well to join the old project director on their new project.[15] This damages the old project still more.

[15]When the project director turns over, turnover of the construction manager doubles, and the chances of lead engineer turnover more than triples. This reflects the reality that a project director and a small set of key staff often prefer to do projects together.

I vividly remember a minerals megaproject in which the project director and the lead contractor project manager had a long a successful relationship doing large projects together. Because they had worked together and developed a good deal of trust between them, their current project was being done on a reimbursable contract basis with no penalties for delay. Because product had been forward-sold, it was, however, very important for the project to be completed on time. The project director was promoted to vice president and off the project, and all the informal agreements between the project director and the contractor disappeared without a trace. The contractor slowed down the project and then demanded an additional $100 million in fee to restore the original schedule. It may have been unethical and unconscionable, but it was effective; the sponsor paid and the project was completed on time. The lesson there is that trust is a very valuable thing. But like all valuable things, one should seek to economize on the need for it. All of the agreements should have been written down. Everyone should remember that projects have no institutional memory. The only effective memory is that of the project director and the other core team members who stay with the project throughout.

Continuity and team structure are intimately related. Companies that run functionally based and weak-matrixed projects tend to have very high rates of core team member turnover. Strong-matrixed projects have less, and team-centered structures typically have none. The other project characteristic that is closely tied to higher rates of turnover is if the project is schedule driven. If a schedule is set aggressively to meet some usually imagined market window, the effect is to burn out project leadership. The irony is that turnover of the project director is a primary driver of schedule slip in execution whether or not the project is schedule driven. Schedule-driven projects with no turnover come in close to industry average in terms of execution speed while those with turnover are 22% longer than average.

Robust Owner Teams

A robust owner team understands why the project is important and is confident of delivering a successful project. The team's stance toward the project is one of ownership. The contracting strategy does not affect the stance of a robust team—they will get their hands dirty on EPC-lump-sum contracted projects as readily as reimbursable ones. The robust team feels that the project director and business sponsor are keeping all the distractions and politics at bay so they can deliver the project successfully. They feel psychologically safe to be fully involved.

Megaprojects are long and always face obstacles. If the team gets discouraged, retention of team members quickly becomes difficult and recruiting new members, impossible. The role of leadership cannot be overstated. Leaders willing and able to listen, leaders with high emotional intelligence, and leaders who take accountability for decisions are essential to making megaprojects successful.[16]

Special Challenges for Megaproject Teams

Megaproject teams have some challenges that are unusual in smaller projects, among which are geographic dispersion and its cousin, hybrid team working; dealing with joint venture partners; and managing many interfaces.

Geographic Dispersion

Megaproject teams, especially during FEL-3 and engineering, are very likely to be spread out around the world. It is not uncommon for two or three contractors to be working on FEED and part of the sponsor team needs to be in each of those offices. Multiple contractors may do engineering and fabrication and construction, and again the team is dispersed out to many locations.

Geographical dispersion makes coherent management much more difficult despite all of the modern tools of rapid communication. The simple fact is that people sitting next door to one another can

[16]See E.W. Merrow and N. Nandurdikar, *Leading Complex Projects*, Hoboken, NJ: John Wiley & Sons, 2018.

communicate more easily than those separated by 5 to 10 times zones. There is really no solution to the problem because contractor availability and quality do not follow a simple geography. The more time zones and the more nodes, the greater the complexity in managing the team. The desire to minimize these often leads to suboptimal contractor selection by taking one that is local even if its skills and availability do not really fit the situation.

It appears that dividing up engineering into multiple offices complete with the use of low-cost engineering centers is a cause of late engineering. I say "appears" because the causation is very difficult to establish. Did we divide up engineering among more contractors because there was a shortage, which really caused the engineering to be late, or did the added nodes cause the tardiness? Or is it simply a matter of larger numbers of contractors, meaning more opportunities for someone to fall behind? Late engineering is one of the primary causes of project failure. We will return to this subject in Chapter 14.

The Effects of "Hybrid Teams"

After the Covid pandemic subsided, many project teams adopted a "hybrid" form in which some in-person work and some virtual work became the norm for project teams in some companies. As I write this in late 2023, we do not yet have enough data on megaprojects to conclude definitively that hybrid working is good or bad for the projects. We do, however, have sufficient data for smaller projects and fundamental logic to point the way: hybrid working is likely to make megaprojects much slower on the front-end and much harder to manage effectively in execution.

First, we know from prior research that teams produce better project outcomes when the team is co-located in the same building together. That alone would suggest that a team that is partly virtual would be less effective. Second, our research on nonmegaprojects shows that teams working in a hybrid mode are slower to complete front-end work.[17] Project managers report lots of frustration:

[17]Katya Petrochenkov and Charis Declaudure, "Project Team Ways of Working in the New Normal," December 2023. www.ipaglobal.com

reduced and unpredictable attendance at team meetings, decreased collaboration, less engagement, and "Zoom fatigue" as hybrid working requires that all meetings are both in-person and virtual. It is no secret that those attending a meeting virtually sometimes are less than fully engaged with the meeting. The often-heard "Would you please repeat the question" confirms that fact. The functions that are more often weak-matrixed into project teams, such as operations and procurement, are even more weakly matrixed in a virtual setting.

The overall effect of hybrid working by a project team in FEL loading is to weaken the authority of the project manager. Weakened authority is tantamount to morphing a strong matrix to a weak matrix, and making the already weak-matrix format unworkable.[18]

In FEED and project execution, the area of work most directly affected by hybrid or virtual working is the collaboration of the owner team and the engineering contractor(s). Like owners, most contractors have embraced hybrid working for fear of losing personnel. The effect is that contractor teams are not in the contractors' offices for in-person meetings with owners without careful pre-arrangement. Opportunities for spontaneous interactions are significantly decreased.

In the long run, I don't know how the "new ways of working" will work out. However, I am quite clear that projects are a highly team-based activity, and that working with team members virtually adds an additional layer of difficulty.

Integrating Joint Venture Partner Personnel

Joint venture partners can be a blessing or a curse. Partners that want their people assigned to the project only for purposes of oversight are clearly the latter. When a partner assigns people to the lead sponsor's team for the purpose of checking up, they are a drain on the resources of the team. The team spends its time answering their questions rather than getting useful work done. Some joint venture partners will insist that their personnel not be assigned regular team membership tasks.

[18]When the weak matrix form is weakened further it does not devolve to a functionally based structure. Functionally based approaches have a great many rules and procedures that govern how project work is carried forward. None of those essential rules exist when a weak matrix is loosened still more.

This is one of those issues that should be hammered out as part of the initial discussions between partners, not left to evolve on its own. Joint venture partner secondees should be fully and completed integrated into the project team. Where they have the experience, they should be given appropriate leadership positions. Joint venture partner personnel that have regular team positions gain a much deeper understanding of how the project is going. They are much less likely to be negative about the project team's performance because they have a deeper understanding of the issues than the "drop-in, drop-out" liaisons can.

Some of the most difficult joint venture situations are "equal partner" projects. In the case of equal partner projects, the project director will come from one of the partners and the deputy director from the other. They may even switch positions as the project evolves. These situations can be very difficult to negotiate unless the project director and deputy can genuinely cooperate.

When they cannot cooperate, we tend to see highly dysfunctional teams. Perhaps the worst example I have ever seen occurred on a recent project. A U.S. company and a national host company were 50/50 partners on a big complex project. The scope development was being done at the American company's location, and the process of creating a unified team had been working and working well for nearly a year when the new deputy director from the national company was introduced one morning to the collected project team. Instead of saying the usual pleasantries and words of encouragement, he said "I will now meet with *my* people," meaning, of course, those from his company. Twelve months of hard work on generating mutual understanding were wiped away with seven words.

The problem with 50/50 joint venture situations is that they beg for nobody to really be in charge. At the beginning of this chapter, I noted that strong project work process with everyone trained was an essential element in a successful megaproject team. There is a temptation in equal partnership ventures to try to "blend" the work processes of the two companies. Like most temptations, this one should be vigorously resisted. When work processes are blended, it ensures that no one knows what they are doing, rather than just half. There will be no training material available on this new hybrid process. Even worse, there really is a tendency to combine the worst features of both systems. Poor features of project work process do not occur randomly. They are there because somebody influential wanted them there. When the work processes are combined, those features are likely to survive for the same reason.[19]

Interface Management

Finally, megaprojects always contain a large number of interfaces. An interface occurs whenever independent or even quasi-independent functions or organizations come into contact. Interface management is an issue for even small projects, but it is a major issue for megaprojects. By the time a typical megaproject is completed, there will have been hundreds of organizations involved in varying degrees. In many respects, the task of megaproject management is a task centered around the effective management of the interfaces. The interfaces are opportunities for conflicts and misunderstandings to occur. The interfaces are the places where things tend to "fall between the cracks." As we will see in the next chapter, the team needs to be organized in ways that facilitate rather than hinder effective interface management.

Can Weak-Matrixed Teams Do Successful Megaprojects?

By definition, weak-matrixed teams have a significant number of team members whose cooperation is to a significant extent voluntary. Developing a large complex project without a strong authoritatively led owner team is exceedingly difficult because the requirements of the project have to compete with the interests of various functional leaders. If the functional leaders become stakeholders—that is, starting claiming some of the value of the project for their goals—the project is in trouble.

[19]See Phyllis C. Kulkarni and Kelli L. Ratliff, "Best Practices for Joint Ventures," presentation to the Industry Benchmarking Consortium Annual Meeting, March 2004. Available at www.ipaglobal.com.

When the team is not integrated (i.e., missing one or more critical functions) and not strong matrixed, decision-making slows down. Work is interrupted while negotiations proceed with:

- Procurement, looking for lowest cost
- HR, wanting to ensure that none of its rules are broken
- Another business unit leader that is an internal competitor for resources
- That head of the civil group who simply is an uncooperative person
- And so forth

There is no single voice providing direction. Decisions are made outside the team that affect the team's work that are not communicated to the team. Weak matrices weaken megaproject performance much more than simpler project performance because the matrix is always weaker for megaprojects to start with. Megaprojects always have a lot of centrifugal force working against them. If those forces get too great, the project flies apart.

In the megaprojects context, the role of the leader is to strengthen and tighten the matrix, and to keep everyone focused on the health of the project rather than other things. Extraordinary leaders can sometimes manage to turn even function-centered project situations into project teams that perform like a strong matrixed team.[20] Conversely, poor leadership can make a strong-matrixed team perform like a weak matrix.

[20]A fascinating case study of such leadership is found in Merrow and Nandurdikar, Chapter 8, 2018, pp. 150ff.

CHAPTER 12

Organizing Megaproject Teams

Whether we like it or not, organization is a necessary part of any discussion of projects. Teams do not spontaneously come together and everyone somehow magically knows what to do and when. Rather, individuals are drawn into a structure with reporting lines, rules, and norms.[1] It is important to understand that good organization does not cure poor project fundamentals. There is no perfect organizational form. Each approach to organizing a big project has drawbacks. Organizations always provide some opportunities for people to misbehave. Organizations will always have some features that retard rather than enhance the work process.

That said, some forms and approaches to organizations are clearly less damaging than others. Those better organizations:

- Define and communicate who is supposed to do what and when
- Hinder workflow as little as possible—never perfectly

[1]Behind every project, there is some form of project management organization that recruits, develops, and assigns individuals to projects. This book is not the place to tackle this huge topic, but it is a safe assumption that if the organizations behind the project cannot recruit, train, and qualify individuals to join the megaproject teams, the chances of success are greatly diminished. Pulling owner team members "off the street" rarely results in a successful project. Some megaproject directors can assemble an effective team from outside the owner company. But they can only do that if they have developed a network of very strong potential core team members whom they can pull into a new project.

- Put people next to each other that must communicate the most often
- Try not to have people who must cooperate intimately report up through different lines
- Above all else, better organizations will avoid incentives that are at war with the goals of the project[2]

As we think about the appropriate way to organize megaproject teams, one principle should stand above all the rest: the key to a successful project team is the flow of information to the right people at the right time. Remember that the entire front-end of a project and its engineering are nothing but information. Nothing physical happens until a shovel goes in the ground or the first steel is bent. Yet every project professional knows that by the time that shovel goes in the ground, the outcomes of almost every project are already determined.

Complexity Is the Nemesis of Megaproject Organization

If information flow is the key to good organization for all projects, it is doubly important for megaprojects. By their nature, megaprojects are complex and some of them are extremely complex. Complexity is the enemy of good flow of information. Let's consider the various types of complexity in megaprojects and how that affects organizational performance.

First, the Shaping process (described in Chapters 5 through 8) and all of the stakeholders and partners that are typical of megaprojects add substantially to complexity. Although the business side of

[2]This is the biggest problem of trying to do projects with functionally based teams instead of cross-functional teams. Each function has its own organization with its own organizational imperative to thrive and grow. When the project is handed to the functional organization to do its part, the work is interpreted in terms of the organizational imperative instead of what is best for the project. Most project systems around the globe discarded this approach about 40 years ago. A number of national petroleum companies continue to be organized in this fashion, probably as a legacy of being public organizations following the bureaucratic organizational model. It profoundly handicaps their ability to do large projects well.

the lead sponsor should take the leadership role in dealing with the stakeholders, their work involves a constant exchange of information to and from the project development team. If the stakeholders include joint venture partners, as they do about three-quarters of the time, that may add yet another set of tasks to be performed, especially if the partners want to oversee rather than contribute to the work. Often, the joint venture partners have very different project cultures, and may therefore require a lot of explanation for why the project is being developed and executed as it is. Occasionally, the joint venture partners deliberately throw "sand in the gears" because they have objectives that are not consonant with the lead sponsor's.[3]

Second, megaprojects usually have a number of distinct scope elements, and often, each major element becomes a subproject. For example, a gas to liquefied natural gas (LNG) development will usually have a gas production element with several scope elements, and of course, a facilities and wells construction component, a substantial pipeline project carrying gas to the LNG facilities, the on-plot gas plant and LNG plant, a supporting utilities project, and a major port project. Refining and chemicals projects often have several areas on on-plot scope, the supporting utilities, and various off-plot items such as ports and pipelines. Grassroots minerals projects have a mine development, processing facilities, and often a major rail or slurry transportation project, and finally, port facilities. The most complex megaproject we have seen was a project with 10 subprojects, each one of which easily qualified as a megaproject! Every subproject is an opportunity for something to go wrong. The organization must be structured so that the subprojects that need to talk to each other can do so easily at the appropriate times.

Finally, most of these projects have a number of contractors, often including multiple prime contractors responsible for different areas of scope and a host of subcontractors. Even more vexing, the

[3]We have seen this occur in a number of oil and gas developments when a partner in a development owns adjacent blocks. The partner may, for example, want its existing platform to be used as a host for the field instead of supporting a stand-alone development. Or it may wish to delay the one project so that another project, which would be more lucrative for themselves, can be developed first. These are example of Shaping issues that come to interfere in the success of the project development.

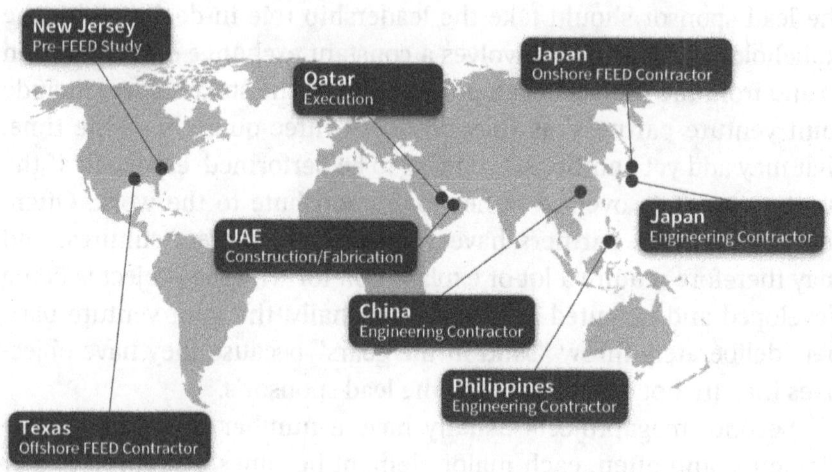

FIGURE 12.1 Scattered Team Members Increase Complexity

contractors are often scattered around the world. Figure 12.1 is a real example of the geographical complexity many projects suffer. The project shown has eight nodes, not including the lead sponsor's home office. In this case, as in many others, the coordination requirement is truly global.

Generally, responsibility for the equipment vendors will be left to the engineering contractors to worry about, so no owner team members are resident at vendors. However, if there is specialty equipment involved for which the sponsor is the expert, that generalization will not hold. During busy market periods, equipment vendors will almost always be on the critical path schedule not only with respect to eventual delivery, but with respect to the timely arrival of drawings that pace the engineering effort during FEED and early execution.

The Role of Organization Charts

Organization charts are really important and worthless most of the time. They are important because they can help newcomers to the team understand who is responsible for what. Even better if they indicate how communication should be effectuated. They are worthless most of the time because they are not properly maintained. When not fully maintained, the org charts confuse new team members rather than help them. If there are too many TBDs on the charts, then, of course, they are worthless except to remind everyone how understaffed the effort is.

I am always surprised at the number of org charts that are still maintained on paper in megaprojects. Or they have been transferred to electronic form, but very little of the data warehousing that is possible in electronic format has been used. Electronic org charts have the ability to provide a great deal of information to team members about who is doing what. They should be searchable by keywords so when someone needs to know with whom they should be communicating, the information is readily available.

Thinking about Organizational Approach

Of course, org charts, good or not, don't make much difference if the organization itself is a mess. So let's step back and think about the problems that megaprojects pose, and have that thinking lead us to how we should approach organizational design.

What characterizes megaproject organizational problems?

- The volume of work is prodigious.
- A large number of people must be effectively recruited, trained to some extent, and acculturated into the team.
- Much of the work must be executed in parallel.
- The work is heterogeneous, which requires people with different expertise, backgrounds, disciplinary language, and training.
- The heterogeneous functions must be working in parallel and constantly exchanging information about progress, setbacks, changes, and progress.
- In most cases, only the engineering and project management work is subject to disciplined and systematic work process.

- The cross-functional communication is retarded by lack of common knowledge, vocabulary, and shared worldview.
- Often, joint venture partners with different language and culture are an integral part of this mix.

As organizations get larger, communication within the organization gets progressively more difficult. In permanent organizations, the usual response to this situation is to progressively formalize and structure communication and develop layered roles and responsibilities. This is what we usually call bureaucracy. The bureaucratic form, although much maligned, is actually quite serviceable, which is why it is nearly universal. The bureaucratic form works in permanent organizations because the work is largely repetitive. But bureaucracy for a project organization is a killer because it is inherently slow, and the work is not merely nonrepetitive; you largely get only one opportunity to get something right. Large and complex megaprojects organized as traditional hierarchical organizations almost always end up getting bogged down and being restructured on the fly.

Structuring Megaproject Organizations

Most megaprojects are actually designed in largely the same manner as smaller projects, but with some accommodations. Most are set up in the "strong project manager" mode with a project director taking that lead position. Beneath the project director are a set of subprojects, for example, on-plot scope, utilities scope, and off-plot scope, each of which is organized as a traditional project with its own project manager, lead engineer, disciplinary engineers, and so on. Some activities can be centralized under the project director to gain economies of scale. Some activities need to be centralized to prevent chaos from breaking out. Human resources (HR) and procurement are usually centralized, and sometimes estimating and scheduling are also centralized.

This traditional structure only applies to projects in which most of the project work is executed by a project management organization.

So, for example, in petroleum production projects, only the facilities team is organized in this fashion under the single project director. The reservoir team that develops much of the key Basic Data and the operational plans for depletion of the reservoir and the drilling teams may be organized completely differently and are only rarely fully integrated into a single project organization with the facilities team. Note there is no compelling reason why they could not be matrixed-in the way others are. It just isn't done.[4]

Most of the way that petroleum projects are organized is merely a historical accident that has been institutionalized by turf-protecting organizational behavior. Teams should do projects; functions should provide the expertise to the teams. By organizing the functions as teams instead of organizing cross-functional teams, the petroleum industry inadvertently encourages poor alignment. The lack of functional integration that characterizes the oil industry, and to only a slightly lesser degree the minerals industry, comes with a very high price. It makes doing large complex projects particularly difficult because it maximizes the opportunities for the functions to be misaligned and misunderstand each other. It makes it possible for different functional elements to follow completely disjointed work processes. It also retards being able to accommodate new information, for example, from the reservoir engineers, quickly and easily. The unwillingness of the oil industry to organize its projects with a matrix that incorporates all of the functions into a single team is surely one of the root causes of its abysmal record on these large projects. One would imagine that a 78% failure rate would be a compelling rationale for change.

[4]I have heard lots of reasons that a matrixing of the reservoir function into projects should not be done, but the one I hear most is that doing so would lead inevitably to the weakening of the function. The function is so central to the success of an oil company, the argument goes, that its weakening would have catastrophic consequences. While I cannot agree to the inevitability of the argument, the weakening of the project functions over the last 25 years lends credence to the argument. We have seen instances in which full functional integration has occurred within petroleum development, but those have been mostly accidental as, for example, when the reservoir, facilities, and drilling functions are co-located in remote areas and integrate spontaneously. In those cases, markedly better project performance resulted.

Alternative Organizational Models

I see three basic models, but of course, with variations that should be applied to megaprojects as a function of their complexity:

- The traditional project model
- The hub and satellite model
- The organic development model

For purposes of applying the models, I am defining *complexity* in terms of the number of separate teams, not including the "center," or top management, that is needed to organize the project work.

1: The Traditional Model

If a project is large but simple, there are no particular reasons why the traditional model cannot apply. This approach works best with one or two teams reporting to a project director, who reports to the project business director (although these two should view each other as equals). The usual difficulties are the ones discussed in the previous chapter: not enough people and not enough cooperation from the non-project functions.

There are several important advantages to the traditional model. It is simple. Lines of authority are clear. Downward communication is easy and quick. Upward communication may suffer the same problems as any other hierarchical structure—unwillingness to communicate bad news—but the organization is small enough that upward communication can be encouraged. Decisions can be made very quickly by the project director as long as other functions and stakeholders are "well behaved."

If there are more than two or three subproject teams, the traditional model begins to falter because integration starts to become problematic. The need to manage the interfaces between teams (and the collections of contractors they will tend to bring along) becomes too big a job for the traditional project leadership. The project director now needs a coordinating team, and the coordinating team transforms the traditional model into a different model.

What happens too often is that the organization starts out as a traditional organization and then morphs into something like a model 2 organization without having been planned carefully at the beginning. Which activities end up where is a matter of expedience and reacting to what is not working rather than an articulated model. It is far better to assess the complexity of the venture at the outset and plan the model that is going to be needed because it helps the project director better anticipate staffing needs as well as the structure of the organization.

2: Hub and Satellite

When the project involves three or more teams with different scopes, I consider the project to be at least moderately complex. Command and control systems will begin to break down under the weight of the interface management and the sheer number of decisions being passed up to the project director to make. This prompts the need for a different model. That approach is usually the hub-and-satellite approach as shown in Figure 12.2. Each area is an area of scope. This should not be confused with a petroleum production project having separate teams

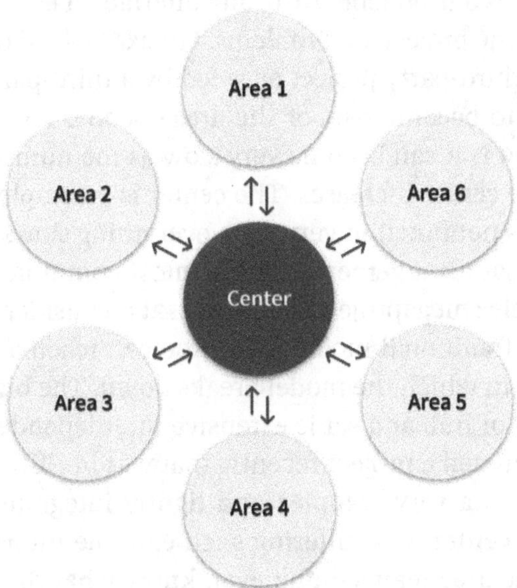

FIGURE 12.2 Hub and Satellite Model

for different functions. Each area team in a hub and sat has its own full scope of work to do.

Hub and sat is an improvement over the traditional command and control model in these situations for several reasons. First, the center's capabilities are beefed up. The safety program will be run from the center. Estimating, scheduling, contracting, and controls will likely be staffed at the center. Recruiting, training and orientation, and logistics will all be part of the typical center's activities. Often, some procurement activities, especially for long-lead items, may be included as well. Second, decision-making is pushed down to the areas for everything that does not have implications for other areas. And finally, the hub-and-sat approach may make geographical dispersion of the team easier to manage. Because each area is being managed largely as a separate smaller project, maintaining geographical cohesion by area is easier.

Hub-and-sat arrangements are not without problems. The boundaries for each area need to be very carefully drawn. As we say in New Hampshire, "Good fences make good neighbors." Hub and sat depends on having as few ambiguities about where one area ends and another starts as possible. Anything that must be managed as an interface between areas is a headache. Also, any interfaces between an area and scope outside the project are problems. For example, if one of the areas has to feed a third-party project or is fed by a third-party project, that interface has to become part of the area's scope. The other problem for hub and sat is it can become very slow as the number of decisions referred to the center increases. The center is a complex organization itself; if it does not function very well, everything slows down.

Hub-and-sat arrangements are the most common organizational form for complex megaprojects. Hub and sat is considerably more scalable than the traditional model, but it too can reach a point in terms of complexity in which the model breaks down. The biggest barrier to the scalability of hub and sat is extensive interdependencies between areas. We evaluated a project recently that was in FEL-2 (scope development). It was a very complex and tightly integrated project with 10 areas. The center was suffering such extreme information constipation that the area teams didn't even know what the cost estimates were for their areas because the center could not get the information out to them. Decisions that should have been turned around in a day or less were taking weeks. When hub and sat breaks down, our final model is the only viable solution.

3: The Organic Model

What I call the organic model is illustrated in Figure 12.3. This model seeks to maximize the number of decisions made at the teams' level by encouraging the teams to manage the interfaces between themselves and other teams that are affected by their decisions. I call this model *organic* because the development of the project occurs in much the same way as an organism develops. The center (brain) outlines the master plan and distributes the plan out to all of the teams to carry out. Surprises and changes are managed largely at the area level.

The keys to making this approach work are in those little stick-figure people shown in the diagram. Each team has one person, probably full-time, who is responsible for communications from and to the team. For example, if Area 3 makes a change that affects 2, 4, and 9, the Area 3 "integration manager" disseminates that information and gets the feedback from the teams affected. If Area 3's changes are not easily assimilated by the other areas, the areas get together and try to reconcile. The integration managers also meet regularly and with

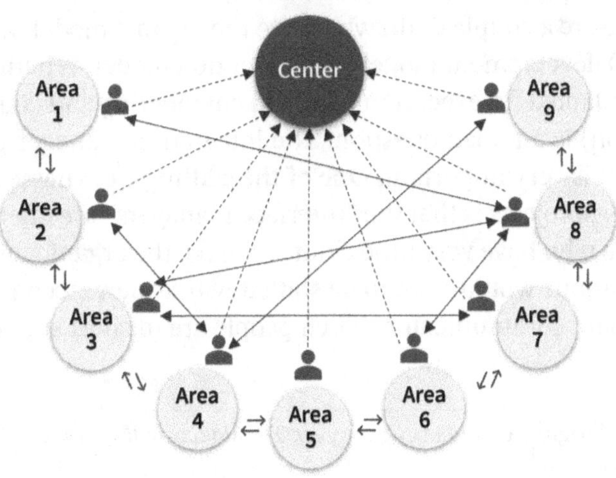

FIGURE 12.3 The Organic Model

the Center to be sure that everything is coordinated. The extremely complex project I previously mentioned moved to this sort of organization after it became clear than hub and sat would not go to scale. The change enabled them to move the project forward.

To my knowledge, this model was first developed and articulated by Alan Mullaly in the development of the Boeing 777, which would have to be classed as an extremely successful complex megaproject. The genius of the model is that it was designed to fit the problem, rather than trying to fit the development problem to an organizational model. Like many other complex megaprojects, the development of a commercial airliner involves a large number of concurrent development teams, each working on some piece of the airplane. The big problem is that, at the end of the day, it all has to fit together perfectly. Integration is the name of the game.[5] As the director of the 777 development, Mullaly called himself the "chief integrator."[6]

Like every other model, the organic model has strengths and weaknesses. When properly implemented, it can produce quality and speed in the front-end loading of the project. In the 777 case, the development time was cut in half from prior planes because the teams were able to work fully concurrently, making the necessary adjustments as they go. There were an astounding 200 concurrent design teams working on the 777 development. The model is clearly the most scalable of the organizational models we have seen.

There are a couple of drawbacks to the organic model. It is a better front-end development model than execution model. Whether it could even be adapted for execution (detailed engineering and construction/fabrication) is an open question. The integration manager position in each team is very important. One of the staffing weaknesses in a good many megaprojects is that the "interface managers" are often very junior people who have very little clout. To make the organic model work, these positions would have to be staffed with experienced people who are excellent communicators. Such people are in short supply.

---

[5]See Karl Sabbagh, *Twenty-First Century Jet: The Making of the Boeing 777*, New York: Simon & Schuster, 1995.

[6]Yes, it is very curious that this very successful model was not employed for Boeing's next airplane. Perhaps the explanation is that Mr. Mullaly had moved on to become the chief executive of the Ford Motor Company.

What about Programs?

Sometimes, the response to a megaproject being very complex is to transform the project into a program—a series of related projects executed over a substantial period of time rather than all at once. Sometimes the program format is used to spread the cost of what would have been a single megaproject over a longer period to conserve cash. Sometimes, the tightness of the engineering, materials procurement, and construction (EPC) market is also cited as a reason to go to a program format.

Whether a program is really a viable solution depends on whether the scope of the overall effort really is a single project both with respect to the logistics and with respect to the economics. When megaprojects are carved into pieces for whatever reason, the results have been miserable indeed. The sum of the program's projects surely cost much more than the megaproject would have. Even worse, some of the pieces of the program often end up stranded with no rationale because the pieces on which they depended were never built.

Programs should not be viewed as an alternative to a project organizational model. If phasing of a megaproject is desired, that can work as long as each phase is economically justified independent of the others. Programs only make sense when the work is actually programmatic in nature, which means that the various pieces are not intimately linked.

PART 4

Getting It Done

By the time a megaproject is complete, thousands of people and hundreds of organizations will have been involved with turning an idea into a major asset. Only a relatively small percentage of those people will be employees of the company or companies sponsoring and funding the project. However, as we have seen, that small group of owner people has outsized influence on whether the asset creation process was a success or a wasteful failure.

The vast portion of those working on our megaproject will be employed by the contractors and subcontractors who will render the design of the asset, procure equipment and materials from hundreds or even thousands of vendors from around the world, and physically construct the asset in fabrication yards almost anywhere in the world or at the asset's site or both.

This part deals with how the owner teams set about engaging the contractors that will execute the work to make the project, and then to the execution effort itself, and especially, the risk associated with the execution process. Contracting is, perhaps, the activity that project directors find most taxing, but doing it well is essential to a successful result.

In Chapter 14, I will turn my attention to understanding and managing execution risks. I refer to this as "residual" risk management as the primary risk management has already occurred or not on the front-end of the project. If the front-end has been done thoroughly and with quality, execution risk management is possible. If the front-end work is deficient, it is very unlikely that the project can be saved in execution.

CHAPTER 13

Contracting

If I had to select a few terms to describe megaproject directors and managers, *practical*, *hard-headed*, and *not given to magical thinking* would come to mind—except in one area: contracting. Contracting for the services needed to engineer, procure materials, and construct megaprojects is an area of intense disagreement and almost religious-like fervor among project professionals. Individual experiences with single projects, good or bad, come to shape views for a career. Every approach to contracting appears to have both ardent adherents and steadfast opponents. I do not expect the following discussion to change either of those groups, but I hope some facts will aid those still searching for what to do.

Contractors tend to do good projects well and bad projects poorly. By that I mean that contractors almost always succeed when the project has a strong business case, fully aligned stakeholders, bought-in sponsors, an integrated owner team, and best practical front-end loading (FEL). And when the sponsors are fighting among themselves, other stakeholders are sniping, the business case is marginal, the owner team is missing key functions, and the FEL is mediocre, the contractors always look moronic. We tend to exaggerate the importance of the contracting approach to project success or failure. No contracting approach guarantees success; most contracting approaches can succeed. Contracting is a second-order concern.

That said, some contracting approaches are fraught with more dangers. Some are unsuitable for certain situations. Some strategies work for some owner organizations, but will fail miserably for others because the strategy depends on owner strength. Some strategies will help a well-developed project deliver on its promise, but will fail on a project that is less well prepared. Every contracting approach brings with it uncertainty and possibility. Contracting is difficult, and it is situational. Perhaps that is why so many owner project and business professionals want to believe they have found *the* answer. In fact, however, *the* answer probably does not exist. There is, however, one rule that always seems to apply: if sponsors decide to engage in contracting games, by which I mean trying to get the better of contractors, they will always lose. Contractors always have been and always will be better at contracting games than owners. Their lives depend on it.

Before moving into alternative approaches, I need to address who should be involved in contracting decisions. The basic contracting strategy must be addressed as part of project Shaping. Disagreements among partners on this issue can be so violent that the project can come apart. The business leadership that will be fighting out any issues must be informed by its project management teams and the view of the project director should weigh very heavily in the discussions. After all, it will be the project director who must ultimately make the strategy work.

When it comes to the actual selection of contractors, that decision should absolutely be made by the project director and the team. Any involvement by business leadership in the selection of individual contractors is quite inappropriate and could be viewed as a breach of trust by partners. Any involvement of the lead sponsor's purchasing (procurement or sourcing) organization in the selection of contractors is likely to be catastrophic. The selection of the right contractor often comes down to the selection of the right contractor team. That needs to be a team that the sponsor team can work with creatively. Purchasing does not have to live with the selection made, and only rarely has the expertise required to even assist.

Contracting Approaches

There are four basic types of contracts for megaprojects with endless variations. I will define each and show the relationships between success and the use of the different approaches, and then discuss some fundamentals of successful contracting for large complex projects.

1. EPC Lump-Sum (EPC-LS) (Fixed-Price Contracting)

This most common form of megaproject contracting involves a contractor or contractors being responsible for engineering, procurement, and construction (EPC) for the whole project or for some portion of the whole project under a single contract. This basic form has a number of variations.

- **The traditional EPC-LS.** All parts of the project are under the single EPC contract, including installation for offshore projects. If commissioning and startup are included, the contractual form is generally considered "turnkey," which is to say that an operating facility is turned over to the owner/sponsors. The contractor will often subcontract for fabrication and/or construction, and for various other activities. The single prime contractor form is unusual for very large megaprojects because single contractors rarely have financial strength, enough people, and the full range of skills to devote to a very large EPC-LS without creating lumpiness[1] problems in their project portfolio. In some cases, contractors have formed joint venture consortia that offer a single EPC-LS contract for a large megaproject. These consortia often focus on a single technology package. The traditional EPC-LS form starts with front-end engineering design (FEED) being executed by a separate contractor, which is usually barred from bidding on the execution of the project. The FEED contractor and owner prepare an invitation to bid (ITB), which is sent to prequalified EPC contractors. After rounds of questions, bids are submitted and evaluated, and a winner selected.
- **Multiprime EPC-LS.** A second form of EPC-LS contracting involves multiple prime contractors reporting to the owner. Multiprime arrangements are common on very large megaprojects where single primes would be reluctant to take the risks associated with the whole project. Multiprime arrangements require a

[1]In this context, the term *lumpiness* refers to an unbalancing of desired portfolio risk profile due to a single element in the portfolio being unduly large.

good deal of owner competence to manage the interfaces between the contractors, but are otherwise very similar to the traditional model, involving separate FEED(s) contractor(s) and ITBs.

- **Conversion to lump-sum** is a strategy that starts the project with reimbursable engineering and procurement, and then provides an option for the owner and EP contractor to convert to a whole project lump-sum at some point during engineering, usually at second model review, which is typically about 65% detailed engineering complete. The EPC contractor on "convertibles" is almost always the FEED contractor, which eliminates the FEED-to-execution transition problem and the associated time requirements.
- **Design competitions (aka FEED competitions)** consist of the engagement of two or more EPC contractors to execute FEEDs in parallel, usually on a reimbursable basis with a cap, resulting in EPC-LS bids for the execution of the project. Like convertible contracts, design competitions avoid both the transition from FEED to execution and the long bidding process of the traditional forms. In a design competition, all FEED competitors are fully compensated for their FEED work.

2. Reimbursable EPC and EPCm

Under this form, a single contractor is responsible for all (or the great majority) of the project under a contract that reimburses the contractor based on the quantity of services and materials provided. The details of how the contractor is reimbursed are very important. Alternatives include a percentage fee, fixed fee, fixed fee and fixed overhead, and various incentive forms.

The key attribute of reimbursable EPC is that the engineering and procurement contractor controls the construction/fabrication as well. That provides both opportunity and lots of problems for the owner/sponsors. The precise manner in which the contractor is reimbursed interacts with the control of the field to determine the incentive structure under which the contractor actually is operating, which may be quite different from the incentive structure under which the sponsor thinks they are operating. We will return to this subject later. The fee structure for reimbursable contracts is very important and the subject of a great deal of misinformation.

Reimbursable EPC can also be operated with a multiprime arrangement, much like multiprime EPC-LS. Lump-sum and reimbursable EPCs can be run on the same project and are sometimes even run on the same site, but with generally very poor results. The poor results are driven by the fact that the reimbursable contractors are able to take away resources from the lump-sum contractors, resulting in (quite justifiable) large claims by the lump-sum contractors. In one case, a lump-sum contractor actually quit a major project under these circumstances, resulting in a complete disaster.

A hybrid of this model is EPCm—engineering, procurement, and construction management. In this case, the EP contractors hire the constructors/fabricators and manage their work. They may hire the constructors on any form of contract—reimbursable, unit rates, lump-sum or whatever, but the full costs of construction are passed directly to the owners without risk to the EPCm contractor(s). I group EPCm with EPC reimbursable for a very simple reason: they behave the same way. The key characteristic is that the engineering contractors control the construction activities.

3. Alliance Contracts aka Integrated Project Delivery (IPD)

Alliance contracting refers to a particular form of reimbursable incentivized contracting that was pioneered in the petroleum industry in the U.K. North Sea in the 1990s. It is not to be confused with long-term multiproject relationships between an owner and a contractor, which are sometimes also called "frame agreements." My use of the term *alliance* here refers to a grouping of all (or almost all) of the contractors working on a megaproject under a single compensation scheme. The grouping of contractors takes place for the particular project; this form is not to be confused with a contractor consortium or contractor joint venture. The primary goal of the alliance contracting approach is to align the goals of the contractors with those of the sponsors through a "shared destiny" approach. The schemes involve some form of bonuses or gainshare (usually in the form of splitting underruns among the sponsors and contractors) in the event that the project performs better than targets, usually on cost. In the event of an overrun, some alliance schemes have the contractors share some portion of that overrun up to some cap.

4. Split Form Contracting

Split form contracting refers to a strategy that involves reimbursable engineering and procurement, including, in some cases, the procurement of some lump-sum package items, followed by lump-sum contracts for construction or fabrication by constructors or fabricators that are independent of the engineering/procurement firm(s). The construction lump sums can be a single lump sum to construction management organization or a series of lump sums by craft discipline. However, the strategy does not apply in cases in which the engineering firms procure the construction or fabrication work. That strategy would be an EPCm arrangement. The key characteristic here is that the constructors/fabricators are independent of the engineering contractor(s), which is to say they are prime contractors to the sponsors.

Frequency of Use in Megaprojects

One of these four basic contract types, with variations, of course, was followed by all of the megaprojects in our database. Figure 13.1 provides the breakdown of the contract types in our sample. Lump-sum contracting in a number of variations is by far the most common approach to contracting large projects. Although EPC-LS contracts predominate, they are actually less common than in the 1990s. Some parts of the world, notably Canada and Australia, moved away from lump-sum contracting as their project markets heated up during the commodity supercyle because EPC-LS arrangements tend to become less cost-effective for sponsors (or even altogether unobtainable) when the market for EPC services is tight.

There are some differences in contracting strategy by sector, although some of the differences are better understood by location. LNG has more EPC-LS contracts than any other sector at 70%. Refining, chemicals, and petroleum production are all close to 50%. Mining projects are decidedly the most reimbursable of all sectors. Mining's favorite contracting form is EPCm at 72% of projects with another 1% executed on a reimbursable EPC form. There were no chemicals sector projects executed with an alliance type contract but every other contract type was found in all industrial sectors.

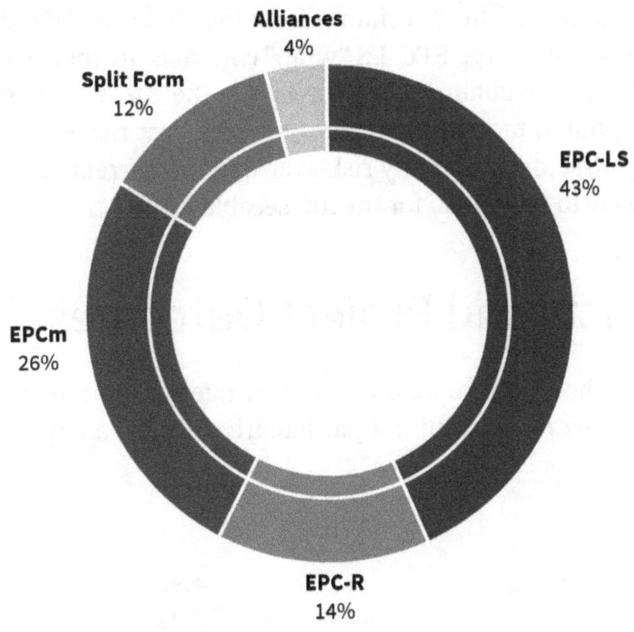

There were 1% of project contracting strategies that were so confused and confusing they could not be classified

FIGURE 13.1 Frequency of Contract Approaches

Contract type is, however, clearly influenced by geography. EPC-LS contracts dominated the megaprojects contracts in the Middle East (83%), South America (51%), Africa (53%), and Asia (48%). The dominance of EPC-LS in the Middle East is largely an artifact of the involvement by government-owned companies as sponsors or co-sponsors of projects in these areas. Governments tend to prefer whole-project lump-sum contracting the world over; nearly two-thirds of the projects in which the lead sponsor was a nationally owned company employed an EPC-LS contracting strategy versus about 34% of other megaprojects. Alliances were used predominantly in Organisation for Economic Cooperation and Development (OECD) countries, except Japan. The other contract forms were used in every sector and region at least on one occasion.

Using the final investment decision (FID) estimate as a measure of size, the reimbursable forms EPC-R and EPCm tend to be a little larger than average. This is a change from the 2011 sample and reflects a larger trend: very large EPC-LS "wrap" contracts are increasingly difficult for owners to obtain. Going forward in the 2020s decade, owners will have a much more difficult time shifting cost risk to contractors because contractors are highly risk-averse in the current environment and are likely to remain so for the foreseeable future.

Contracts and Project Outcomes

Figure 13.2 shows the success and failure rate for our four basic contract types. The results will not particularly surprise anyone who has

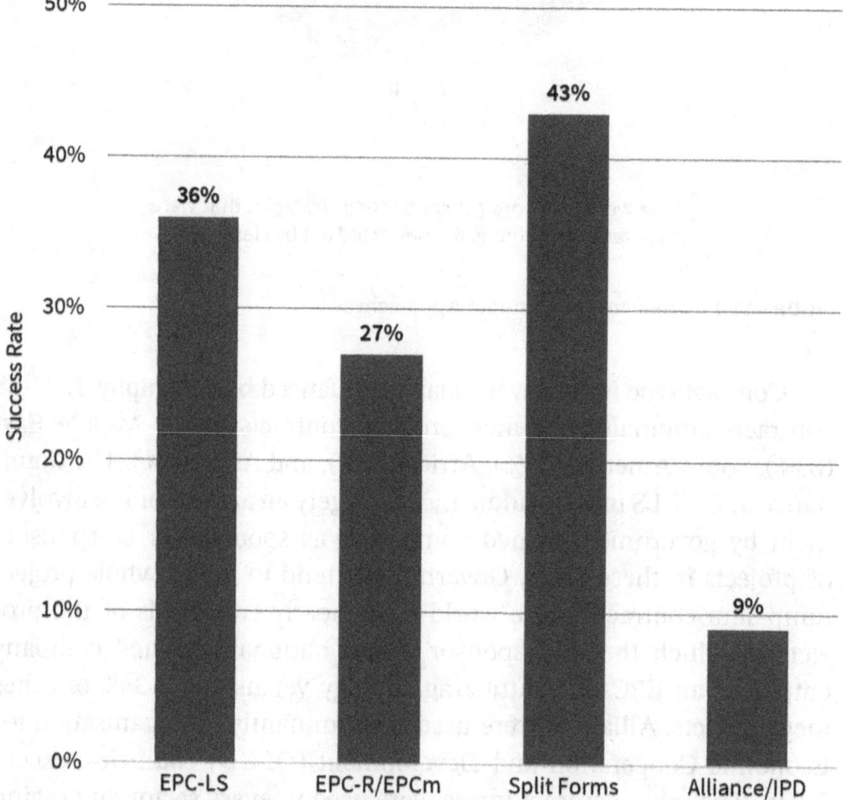

FIGURE 13.2 Success and Failure Rate for Contract Approaches

followed our research on contracting for industrial projects over the last 10 years. The lump-sum EPC projects had a success rate that was about average for the megaprojects overall. Given that they constitute over half the sample, that result is surely to be expected. The reimbursable projects fared worse than the lump sums. However, if we control for other factors that affect project outcomes, the reimbursable projects are not statistically different than the EPC-LS in terms of results. Reimbursable contracting is by far the most flexible approach for owners. The sponsors have complete control over schedule and quality. The greater control also, of course, implies a very "hands-on" approach to the project and many more staff.

In order to test whether contract type has an independent effect on project results, I first controlled for the completeness of FEL because it is a major driver of success and failure, and is far more important to explaining variation in success than contract type. Alliances and the split form projects are both statistically significantly different than the average in terms of success rate—split forms on the positive side and Alliance/IPD on the negative.[2]

The patterns of outcomes are different for different contract types. Figure 13.3 provides some greater granularity around the outcomes of projects by contract type. The EPC-LS contracts averaged only modest overruns of about 13%, but suffered an unacceptably high rate of failure in production attainment. The danger of this trade-off is inherent in lump-sum contracting. If the contractor is not in a loss position, quality will be reasonably good if owner controls are good. If the contractor is in a large loss position, quality will be poor. The high incidence of production attainment failure in the EPC reimbursable class was mainly driven by a higher incidence of the use of new technology and the higher use of reimbursable forms in highly remote locations. Those two factors together explain most of the differential production attainment failure rate. Highly remote locations are more likely to end up with reimbursable contract forms because obtaining cost-effective EPC-LS bids is difficult when the uncertainties around logistics are

[2]Results are based on logit regression z coefficient probabilities and are significant at less than 0.05.

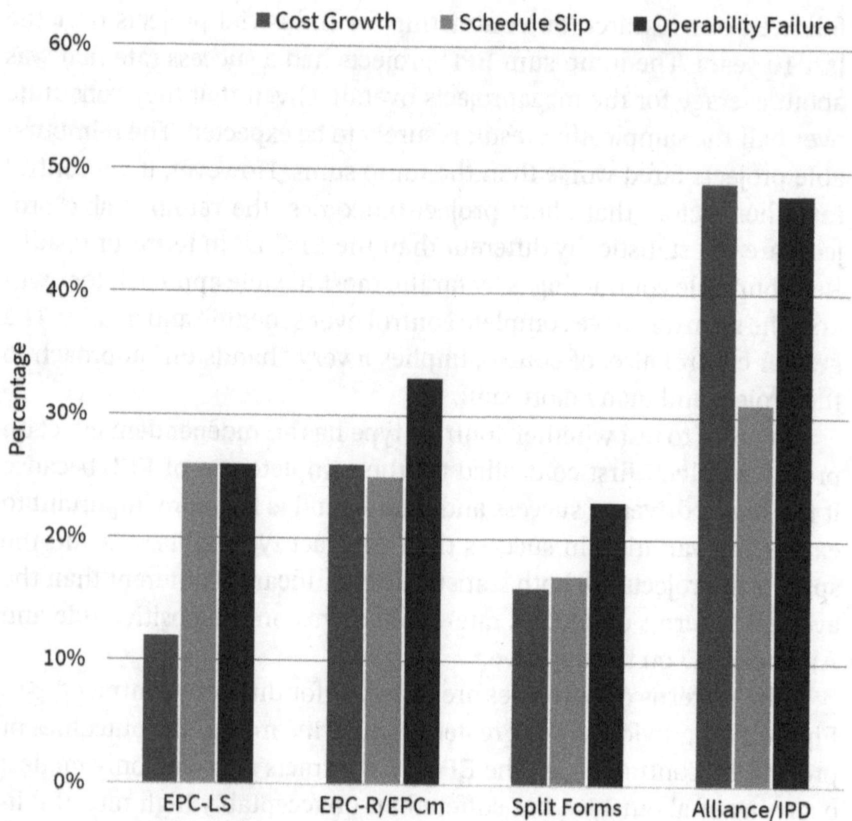

FIGURE 13.3 Outcome Differences by Contract Strategy (Percent)

high. The production attainment result is not a reflection on the use of reimbursable contracting; the reimbursable contracts were selected, in part, based on the uncertainty associated with the technology and location. The result does remind us about the importance of solid Basic Data.

The results of the alliance projects are really dismal with respect to every outcome, but especially cost overruns and production shortfalls. The average alliance project experienced over 50% cost growth and nearly 60% of the projects were production attainment failures. Only a few alliances were successful projects. Our results regarding alliance contracting flatly contradict the views of a number of published articles on the subject. Miller and Lessard, for example, believe that "Substantial gains in costs, schedules, and project delivery . . . can be made by the adoption of generative owner-contractor relationships," that is, alliance-type arrangements.[3] As I will discuss later, however, these arrangements actually increase instability in project execution. I would like to be able to report that this contracting strategy is dead, but that is not the case. It continues to be used, often by companies using it for the first time, and touted by academics. The form is also touted by associations that have both contractors and owners as members.

The split strategy projects fared by far the best of any contractual approach. One reason for this was that, for whatever reason, the split form contracting projects were the best FEL-loaded of any group; they averaged a "good" FEL index. However, excellent FEL was not the only reason for their success. Even after I control for FEL and team integration, the split strategy projects fared significantly better. I will discuss the reasons for their success later in this chapter.

Having now described the relationship between contractual approaches and project results, I want to explore the strengths and weaknesses of each approach, suggesting what promotes success with each strategy.

The Central Issues in Contracting Strategy

As we discuss contracting strategy in this section, there are three important considerations that need to be kept clearly in mind: the capabilities of the sponsors, the nature of the project, and the state of the EPC services markets. All three must be carefully and honestly assessed if a reasonable approach is going to result. The way these issues should push the contracting decisions is shown in Figure 13.4.

[3]Roger Miller and Donald Lessard, "Public Good and Private Strategies: Making Sense of Project Performance," in Miller and Lessard, op. cit., 2000, pp. 38–39.

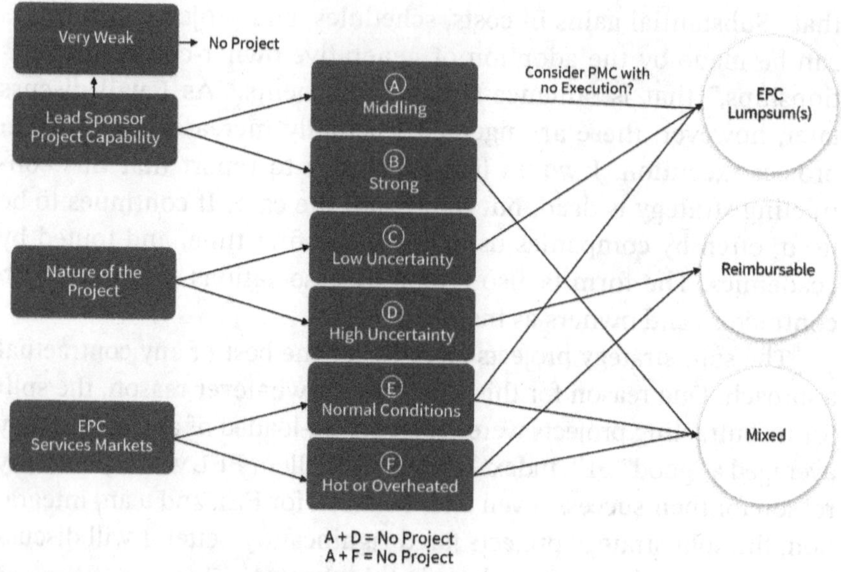

FIGURE 13.4 Considerations for Contracting Decisions

Sponsor Capabilities Influence Contract Approach

The following questions need to be addressed:

- Has the lead sponsor undertaken large projects before?
- Does the lead sponsor's business leadership understand the owner's role in project management?
- Does the lead sponsor have a mature project work process? By *mature*, I mean a work process that has been used many times before by the sponsor project organization that has trained its people on the use of the work process.
- Can the lead sponsor (with assistance from partners if they are willing) staff FEL with all of the needed functional leads?
- Can the lead sponsor develop a detailed estimate and schedule for a megaproject?
- Does the lead sponsor have a procurement organization that can order long-lead equipment during the front-end prior to authorization?
- Can the sponsor field a strong controls organization that can fully monitor and control engineering and construction?

If the answer to most of the questions is "no," the company is not ready to take on a leadership role for any megaproject. If the answers are mixed and "sort of" this should push the company toward an EPC-LS contracting strategy, perhaps with independent contractor support for certain missing skill sets. The focus will be on the preparation of a strong ITB package followed by strong quality assurance/quality control (QA/QC) in execution. These middling answers also make the use of a project managing contractor (PMC) more attractive, but as I will discuss later, projects with PMCs did not fare well. Sponsors that can answer all of the questions with an unqualified "yes" can employ whatever strategy they prefer.

The Nature of the Project

Some projects must carry more uncertainty into execution than others. New technology is one main source of uncertainty. Highly remote areas are another. Such projects are inherently more difficult. Greater difficulty translates into a higher incidence of late changes, especially during engineering. The probability of late changes influences the relative merits of different contracting strategies.

If change during execution is highly probable, even with excellent FEL, the contracting strategy is pushed away from EPC-LS and toward a strategy with reimbursable engineering. That is because changes rapidly undermine the cost-effectiveness of EPC-LS strategies. It does not follow, however, that construction or fabrication work must be reimbursable.

The State of the EPC Services Market

When the markets for engineering services, vendor-fabricated equipment, and craft labor are overheated, the chances of obtaining a cost-effective EPC-LS bid decline. The contractors view the circumstances as risky for them, and given the state of the market, they can afford to bid conservatively. If a lump-sum strategy is going to be pursued in a hot market, the sponsors need to remove as many of the risk elements from the contractor as possible. For example, prices can be indexed, currency risks hedged or otherwise reserved to the owners, and equipment ordered during FEL on owners' novation.

Nonetheless, if the markets are hot enough, it may become simply impossible to obtain EPC-LS bids or the bids may be high enough to render the project not economically feasible. If the sponsor group cannot manage a reimbursable format, at least for engineering, the appropriate action may be to cancel the project.

The current contractor market (2024) is generally not overly hot, but from a risk standpoint, it is behaving as though it were. Contractors in much of the world are dealing with very poor demographics that have produced too few engineers and other technically trained people. The major EPCs have dealt with the scarcity of people by moving large amounts of engineering to "engineering value centers" mostly in India. This has worked reasonably well, but has probably run its course. The so-called "engineering value centers" (EVCs) are now extremely busy, especially in India, and are not in a position to take on more work. The EPC contractors view the current environment, plus their own internal problems, as being too difficult for them to want to take on full project lump-sum work. Some of the contractors have formally announced they will take no further lump-sum work and others are declining to bid or bidding with large risk premiums. In some instances, the low bids are so high that the projects are not economically feasible for the owners.

For owners that have been dependent on EPC-LS as the strategy for their major projects, the current market constitutes a crisis. Many owners have turned to EPCm, on the advice of the contractors and ignorant consultants, not knowing that EPCm is a high-cost contract strategy. EPCm and EPC-reimbursable are the most costly strategies for owners, averaging 34% (26% median) above industry average cost in megaprojects. Most importantly, from a megaprojects perspective, EPCm and EPC-R do not scale well from an owner perspective. As projects get larger, the cost growth tends to increase for the EPCm and EPC-R forms for a number of reasons that are fully explored elsewhere.[4] By contrast, split forms and design competitions are not sensitive to scale in terms of overall effectiveness.

[4]See Edward Merrow, *Contract Strategies for Major Projects*, op. cit., pp. 92–105.

The Role of External Financing on Contract Approach

When banks finance projects, they routinely require that the project be contracted via EPC-LS and often even require that a single lead contractor be responsible for the entire project. These requirements as well as the behavior of government entities are the primary reasons that EPC-LS predominates in megaproject contracting.

It is very regrettable that banks insist on lump-sum contracting for two reasons. First, lump-sum contracting of very large projects can be expensive, and the larger the project the larger the penalty, especially when market conditions are tight. Second, EPC-LS contracting has absolutely no bearing on the risk profile of the project. Bankers, like some sponsor business people and lawyers, fail to understand that lump-sum contracts are not a ceiling on the cost of the project. Indeed, they are a floor on the cost because surely no less than the contract price will ever be paid. Furthermore, although cost performance is important, it is not nearly as important as operability, and when lump-sum contractors start to bump up against that contract "ceiling," the first thing to suffer is operability of the facilities. Given that banks are repaid via the cash flow from production, it behooves them to start understanding project risk at a first-principles level rather than the superficial.

What Drives Success and Failure in EPC-LS Contracting?

EPC-LS is a perfectly acceptable way to contract for megaproject execution. Many a successful project has been done using some form of this basic contract vehicle. There are some important pitfalls to be avoided, and there are some beliefs about lump-sum contracting among many sponsors that are actually quite wrong and tend to push us to make important mistakes. It is these pitfalls and mistakes we need to review as well as some creative uses of this vehicle. EPC-LS contracting is a risk-averse approach to contracting from the owners' perspective. Ironically, it is an approach that tends to work well only when inherent risk in the project is low anyway.

Some Key Pitfalls on EPC-LS Contracting

Much of the benefit of EPC-LS contracting derives from competitively bidding the work. The process of preparing the ITB, pre-qualifying a set of contractors that will be invited to bid, and then the evaluation of the bids themselves provide the sponsors with a great deal of information that can be used to help guide the project to success. The key to success lies as much in the process of competitive bidding as the results in terms of low bid value. The competitive bidding process provides the sponsors with excellent information about how much the project should cost if (and only if) they interpret the bid responses correctly. What this means is that there is very little value to sponsors in sole-source EPC-LS. Our research shows what others have shown as well: sole-source lump-sum contracting is an expensive option.[5]

Sole-source EPC-LS contracting sometimes occur because a technology license that the sponsor wants comes bundled with an EPC contractor. That arrangement is enormously bad for sponsors' wallets. Such tied-sale contracting arrangements clearly are a restraint of trade even if they are not universally illegal.

Other situations that generate sole-source lump-sums can be at least as bad. The worst case is when the primary FEED contractor is going to be allowed to bid the project in a lump-sum competition. This often has the effect of discouraging other qualified firms from bidding so the FEED contractor receives the project by default. Let me provide an egregious example.

The project was in a remote area that suffered serious security concerns. The FEED contractor, which was experienced in the area while the lead sponsor was not, carefully built the hourly labor rate. The labor would be sourced from an expensive area and the labor would

[5]T.C. Berends, *Contracting Economics of Large Engineering and Construction Projects*, Institutional Repository, 2007.

have to be flown in and out of the sites daily. The security costs would add greatly to the rate, and so on. The final expected hourly cost was well north of $100 per hour. The FEED contractor as he had fervently hoped was the only bidder; no one else was interested, primarily because the FEED contractor was being allowed to bid. The contractor then took home almost $100 on every hour as a low-cost source of labor was "discovered" and the local army was suddenly willing to provide security (for a small consideration), all of which resulted in an extra $500 million in profit to the contractor.

Still another route to the sole-source EPC-LS is the "convertible" lump sum. This form starts as a reimbursable engineering and procurement contract with an option to convert to lump sum at some point during engineering. In principle, there is nothing wrong with this approach and a lot to like. In principle, it means that almost all of the potential cost growth and schedule slip will have been discovered by mid-engineering, and there will be very little remaining risk to the EP contractor in taking the project on as a lump sum with a minimal premium.

In practice, convertibles usually turn out very differently. Because the owner expects the contractor to choose to convert, the owner is not prepared for any other outcome. The field controls organization needed to continue the project on a reimbursable basis is not there, nor has the sponsor done the things needed to bid the construction to a set of pre-qualified construction management organizations. The EP contractor, which is expecting to do construction on whichever basis it believes will be more lucrative, would not cooperate with another construction management organization anyway. If the contractor believes it can make more money through lump sum, it goes lump sum; otherwise, it stays reimbursable. It is one more contracting game sponsors can't win.

Design Competitions Provide the Best EPC-LS Projects

Design (or FEED) competitions provide some of the best and most consistently good performance of any contract type. They are highly cost-effective and cost-predictable and are schedule-effective, although still slip their schedules almost as much as other contract types. Only split forms are close to design competitions and split contracting is harder for owners to do.

First, let me clarify that, despite the name, design competitions are not usually about the development of alternative designs for a project. They can be on some occasions, but in most cases, the sponsor has fully defined the desired design during FEL-2 and the competitors are executing FEED based on that FEL-2 scope and working with the owner team to develop the execution plan for the project.

Design competitions produce superior results for several reasons. First, it is easier to persuade competent and qualified contractors to enter a design competition because they are, in effect, fully compensated for developing their bid on the project. Contractors spend a lot of money generating good quality bids for EPC-LS projects. That money is all "at risk" cost. For that reason, contractors often skimp on the quality of their bids on lump-sum projects. In design competitions, any temptation to skimp is removed as is the risk associated with the bid preparation. Second, design competitions eliminate one of the most vexing problems for owners: the endless back and forth about the inadequacies of the FEED work by the winning execution contractor. The review of the FEED work and requesting change orders for perceived or real deficiencies occupies the first three or four months of execution time in the traditional EPC-LS form. All of that disappears in the design competition because the winner cannot realistically complain about the inadequacies of their own work! Third, the winning contractor in a design competition fully understands the scope and the execution plan, having been fully and completely involved in both. And finally, the work from FEED to execution can proceed seamlessly, which makes the cycle time[6] competitive with any contract form.

There are some caveats needed for design competitions. First, the sponsor(s) must staff a team for each of the competitors during FEED. That is a problem for understaffed project organizations, but the upside is that design competitions do not have to be heavily staffed in execution. Second, three competitors are much better than two. Three competitors provide a lower cost project and protect again the

[6]Time from the start of FEL-2 to the end of startup.

circumstance in which one of the competitors drops out during FEED, leaving a sole-source situation. Third, all negotiations of terms and conditions for both FEED and execution (and startup if turnkey) need to be completed before the competition starts, not after the winner is selected. This prevents a delay and difficult negotiation just prior to the start of execution. All in all, however, design competitions are an effective way to secure a good EPC-LS project, often when getting a traditional EPC-LS would be impossible.

Schedule Incentives and Liquidated Damages

EPC-LS projects always include powerful incentives to minimize cost. Any money saved is profit earned for the contractor. However, the same structure creates incentives to float the schedule to whatever duration will assist in minimizing cost. Fortunately, good cost performance on EPC-LS correlates very strongly with good schedule performance ($Pr|r|<.02$) and less schedule slip (.01). The addition of incentives to achieve schedule have no relationship with better schedule performance. Directionally, the statistics point in the opposite direction! When schedule incentives were employed on lump sum, however, they were associated with an increase in the frequency of production attainment failures ($Pr|X^2|<.03$) in all industrial sectors. What is going on is quite apparent: at the end of the project, when contractors could see the possibility of gaining the schedule incentives by acceleration, they cut corners on quality so substantially that operability was damaged well into the second year after startup. Any time they shaved off the back end of the project was slight, but the damage to the project's value was huge. Schedule incentives should not be employed.

Sometimes schedule incentives have the effect of reducing schedule slip, but do so simply by lengthening the forecast schedules. The most extreme form of this game involves the FEED contractor insisting on a percentage of any sales of product that can be made due to early completion of the project. As FEED contractors, they are in a position to manipulate the schedule promised and then profit handsomely from his pessimism.

Liquidated damages (LDs) are a contract provision that imposes a penalty from the contractor if a project is late. In some cases, the penalties are quite substantial. LDs generally are not applied until a project is several months beyond the expected target completion date. Of course, LDs cannot be applied if the sponsors were responsible for the delay or if *force majeure* can be claimed successfully. LDs appear to have only a negligible effect on the low bids for projects, although they are so intensely disliked that some contractors may choose not to bid. In some cases, LDs are essential because there are very large downside consequences to the sponsors of the project being late. These circumstances include cases in which the production has been forward-sold with penalties for nondelivery and cases in which a large value stream is dependent on the completion of the project, such as a petroleum field's production depending on the completion of a gas plant. Unlike schedule incentives, LDs appear to work. The average schedule slip on lump-sum projects with LDs was only 6%. However, when I control for FEL, the relationship between LDs and schedule slip disappears.

Sponsors must understand that the schedule is the most common source of contractor claims. In some cases these claims are entirely justified. But schedule claims are a major source of abuse by contractors as well. There are so many forms of claims games relating to schedule, I cannot hope to cover them all. Fortunately, that has already been done.[7]

Taking the Very Low Bid

I have already discussed at several prior points what happens when a significantly low bid is accepted. (We defined a *significantly low bid* as one that is $100 million [2009 terms] less than the next lowest bid.) Acceptance of such a bid guarantees that the bidder does not fully understand the project or has made a disastrous bidding error. Either way, the sponsor will lose. Occasionally, sponsor greed drives acceptance of such a low bid. More often, however, the involvement of a government-related partner requires that any low bid will win.

All of the EPC-LS projects that were won on significantly low bids, $100 million or more below the next lowest bidder, failed. When the

[7]See James G. Zack, "Claimsmanship: Current Perspective," *Journal of Construction Engineering and Management, 119*, September 1993.

"winning" contractors realized the magnitude of their low bids, they immediately started to try to recover their losses. They floated the schedules longer to minimize costs believing (correctly in most cases) that they could avoid LDs. Even if the LDs would be triggered, the amounts of money contractors paid in LDs would be relatively unimportant in the scheme of things. The most damaging aspect of their behavior, however, was to cut quality corners at every opportunity. The sobering aspect of this is that the strength of the sponsors' controls organization for the project had no mitigating effect on the ability of the contractors to cut corners on quality when they were facing cost overruns on lump-sum contracts. The operability results were simply unaffected by controls for the lump-sum projects. (For nonlump-sum projects, however, higher quality controls in execution were clearly associated with fewer operability problems.) There is also no reliable relationship between "turnkey" provisions in the lump sums with regard to operability. The contractors on turnkey projects appear to be increasing their bids enough—about 5%—to absorb any losses associated with performance guarantees.

When EPC-LS contractors are facing a significant loss on a project, they routinely take several actions that further damage the project. They start squeezing their subcontractors and suppliers, and slowing down payment. That causes the subcontractors to go into defensive mode, looking for claims opportunities. Losing contractors will also start thinning out their management people on the project in an attempt to save money. This often extends right down to the general foreman level for fabrication or construction. The staffing levels need to be articulated down to the general foreman level in the bids, and then the sponsors need to try to hold the contractors to those levels as the project proceeds. I say "try" because it will be very difficult to do.

Acceptance of significantly low bids is so strongly associated with bad results, I believe that the procedure for handling them needs to be addressed between partners as a Shaping issue. If addressed as a Shaping issue that requires a full investigation of a seriously low bid, there will be at least some possibility of getting the bid rejected or allowing the contractor to amend. One might imagine that, given the overheated state of the megaproject market since 2003, no one will have to worry about very low bids. This is not so; serious bidding errors were made right through the boom market.

When Governments Control Contracting

In many countries in the world and for almost all nationally owned companies, the government controls the contracting process. In almost all cases, the government rules require competitive bidding of essentially all contracts. Often, as mentioned before, the rules will require that the contracts be lump-sum, fixed-price arrangements. In some cases, the rules do not actually stipulate that fixed-price contracts be let. However, they require specific government approval for all transactions over a certain amount. In one important case, the amount is $10 thousand. What that means is that the project would have to return to the government to secure approval every time it spent much of anything, which would be not only impracticable but wide open to abuse. The solution is to make a single expenditure for the entire project amount.

Governments almost always require that low bids be accepted. Acceptance of significantly low bids almost always triggers project failure. This means that pre-qualification of bidders is the most important single step in the contracting process. The pre-qualification process must not only be thorough, it must be done with an eye on the possibility that the government will seek to add bidders that for whatever reason it wants to win the competition. Remember, this is not just a "Third World" phenomenon. It happens everywhere.

The most important single change that could be made in the usual low-bid acceptance procedure is a provision for an investigation of any low bid that is substantially separated from other bids. The definition of *substantial* can be either a dollar amount (I would suggest $100 million) or a percentage amount (I would suggest 10%). Ideally, the investigation would enable the low bid to be rejected in the event that it is based on a misunderstanding of the requirements or an estimating error.

One common government provision that causes misunderstandings with bidders are rules forbidding anything but written communication between bidders and the project in the period between the issuance of the ITB and the award of the work. While this may seem reasonable to ensure a level playing field, it greatly hinders effective communication. Very early in project development, discussions need to start to amend these rules to allow a series of face-to-face (or telephone conference) meetings between the evaluation team and all of the bidders during the bid preparation. These occasions would allow the bidders to ask any questions in the presence of everyone.

There also needs to be allowance for the team to verify a bidder's representation of qualifications when questions arise during the bid evaluation process. One of our megaprojects failed because one of the bidders exaggerated their experience with the 3D CAD system. (They owned the system but had never actually used it!) When their bid was evaluated, some of the evaluation team raised questions about whether the bidder really understood the computer-aided design (CAD) system, but they were precluded from verifying the bidder's qualifications at this point. The result was that a critical part of the design was six months late, equipment was late being ordered, and materials were incorrect. The project spiraled out of control.

Some government rules around secrecy of company cost estimates have the ability to cause a significant amount of trouble. The government concern is that information about the estimate will be brokered to contractors and provide an unfair advantage. But in some cases, the secrecy provisions become absurd. For example, one national company keeps the sanction estimate secret from the project teams! The effect is that they have no idea of the relationship between what they are scoping and what things cost.

The usual assumption is that government rules are immutable and must be accepted. That is, of course, usually true. However, we did have a few projects that successfully argued with the governments for rules changes that would allow more flexibility. The project directors started discussions with the government about the contracting rules very early, sometimes over two years before the ITBs would go out. They made their successful arguments for greater flexibility by explicitly linking contract flexibility to more and more effective local content. In particular, what they sought was permission to contract directly for local content using whatever contracting vehicle would give the local provider the best chances to actually succeed in developing their skills rather than just dumping money into the local economy. These project directors got two excellent benefits from their persistence. They got high quality and inexpensive local content, and they took the local content requirements out of the ITBs for the international contractors in order to remove that source of very large risk premiums. The lesson is do not automatically assume that the government agencies will not consider strong arguments for added flexibility, especially when those arguments are couched in terms of their goals.

Creative Use of EPC-LS Contracts

When EPC-LS contracts are used, sponsors often feel that they have very limited control over the execution process. This view is reinforced by corporate legal staff that worry that any sponsor intervention in an EPC-LS situation will make it impossible to hold the contractor liable for poor results. (These folks believe in the myth of risk wholesale transfer, which I will discuss shortly.)

In fact, some of the most successful EPC-LS projects involved owners being "hands-on" in every facet of execution. The best EPC-LS projects were usually multiprime arrangements. This involved carefully carving out pieces of the project that could be executed almost as a parallel stand-alone project. Where I am from in the United States, we have an expression, "Good fences make good neighbors." This expression certainly applies to how the pieces of multiprime EPC-LS projects are defined. Parts of a project that are too intimately linked from either a design or construction perspective must be included within the same contract. Pieces that can be designed based on a requirements and specification statement without reference to the details of the design of other bits can be contracted separately. For example, onshore portions of offshore petroleum production projects are usually contracted with separate EPC-LS contracts. As long as the oil and gas composition data were correct from the reservoir appraisal, this arrangement usually works well.

A Good Example

One of the more ingenious uses of EPC-LS occurred in a chemical complex built in a developing country environment. The primary units consisted of an olefins cracker, a large power plant, and a number of olefins derivatives units. The cracker and the power plant were tightly coupled, feeding streams to and from each other, so they were grouped in a single contract. Each of the derivatives units were contracted separately, each with a different EPC-LS tender. The result was five prime contracts.

The contracting strategy was developed during FEL-2 as the scope was being developed. Knowing that the site offered some real challenges in access and logistics, they laid out the units so that separate access was available to each portion of the complex as they intended to contract it. The first task after site preparation was literally the construction of those "good fences." With five prime contractors and complex laydown and site logistics problems, most owners in this situation would have hired a PMC to keep track of everything and manage the interfaces. A PMC was considered but rejected because the PMC candidates wanted part of the execution. Instead, they hired a sixth contractor on a reimbursable basis with very clear rules about behavior—the reimbursable contractor was barred from hiring anyone who had ever worked for one of the lump-sum contractors on the project. The reimbursable contractor was assigned any tasks that "fell between the fences," such as logistics, canteen, and ensuring safe and timely movement of construction workers to and from the site. The reimbursable contractor also served another purpose: if one of the lump-sum contractors submitted a change order that the sponsor team thought was significantly overpriced, they refused the change, saying that they would have the reimbursable contractor do the work when the lump-sum contractor was out of the area. This had the beneficial effect of significantly moderating the prices on change orders from all five lump-sum contractors. The result was a highly successful project that could easily have become a nightmare.

The best EPC-LS projects had the characteristic of a hands-on sponsor team that would not let the contractors fail. In all of the lump-sum megaprojects, I cannot find a single instance in which the basis of a contractor claim was that the owner interfered when the contractor got into trouble on the job. There were cases of claims based on owner interference, but they were around issues such as the owner taking responsibility for managing the laydown yard, not intervention. Interference between contractors is one of the major sources of contractor claims.[8] Strong interface management, like that described in the preceding example, is what prevents those claims from materializing.

Interface management is one of the most critical jobs on any complex megaproject. The interface management effort needs to start as part of FEL-2 and continue right through the execution of the project. As discussed in Chapter 11, interface management is not a job for junior engineers; it is central to the success of the endeavor. One of the key mistakes made in EPC-LS projects is to imagine that because the contractors "are responsible for the execution of the project," the owner team size can be small. Owner team size on successful megaprojects is quite insensitive to contracting approach. What varies with the contracting approach is the content of what the team is doing, not the numbers of people required.

The Illusion of Wholesale Risk Transfer on EPC-LS Contracting

Most adherents of EPC-LS contracting for megaprojects argue that the contracting strategy effectuates significant transfer of risk and responsibility from the sponsors to the EPC-LS contractor. The facts, however, suggest that really is not the case. Some lump-sum prime contractors did indeed lose significant amounts of money on megaprojects in our set. However, those losses for the contractors did not translate into gains for the sponsors. Instead, those losses translated into facilities with an endless stream of operating problems.

Significant risk transfer from sponsors to contractors is structurally impossible. Contractors, including the very large contractors that take leading roles in megaprojects, are too thinly capitalized to survive wholesale risk transfer on large projects. During the period of overcapacity of EPC services between the mid-1980s and the early years of the 21st century, the contractors that had to take on significant

[8]See Robert Frank Cushman and James J. Myers, *Construction Law Handbook*, Vol. 2, pp. 967ff., Aspen Publishers Online, 1999. For a discussion of how the courts have treated the obligations of owners versus contractors in their obligations on subcontractor claims, see Michael C. Loulakis, et al., *Construction Management Law and Practice*, New York: John Wiley & Sons, 1995, pp. 357ff.

EPC-LS projects to have enough work mostly failed to survive. Many of those that survived were badly wounded, and all learned an indelible lesson: the failure to be carefully risk-averse will surely result in bankruptcy. The only cases in which major losses were sustained and high-quality projects resulted for owners involved large Japanese contractors. Those contractors were supported by large commercial banks that were part of their business consortia. They were, in effect, losing other people's money.

Risk transfer is possible on smaller projects because the contractor in a loss position can afford to complete the project with reasonably good performance without destroying his business. The value of preserving their reputation and the hope of future business make that calculation reasonable. On a megaproject, however, the losses are too large. When large amounts of money are involved, reputational risks have to take a back seat because the survival of the firm may be involved. Furthermore, because there are very few contractors that are capable of taking on megaproject leadership, industrial sponsors have very few choices. Every project in effect becomes a "one-night stand" because the downside consequences for the contractors are minimal. If industrial companies banned forever using contractors that have performed very poorly on megaprojects, they would quickly find themselves without contractors to hire. Even when contractors have behaved in utterly unethical ways toward an owner on a large project, they can be quite sure that more business will be forthcoming anyway. I can think of only a couple of cases in 30 years in which a major contractor has been effectively banned by an owner for poor performance. Those were by large national oil companies.

The simple fact that major risk transfer cannot take place on megaprojects should not lead sponsors to automatically abandon EPC-LS. EPC-LS arrangements have some important advantages in terms of project organization. EPC-LS reduces the number of interfaces that the lead sponsor has to manage. Often, the lead contractor in an EPC-LS strategy has developed working relationships with the organizations that will act as subcontractors for the project. The major contractors are often highly proficient at procurement and can orchestrate getting all of the various pieces of the project fitted together. EPC-LS may be the only realistic way in which sponsors with weak project organizations can have any hope of executing a megaproject successfully.

However, our findings have some important implications for how EPC-LS contracts should be approached by sponsors. If a sponsor is hoping for a bargain-basement price by using a lump-sum strategy, that hope will lead to trouble. Even when all works well, EPC-LS contracts do and *should* cost more than other contracting approaches. That is simply because the lead contractor is being asked to take on more work than in other forms. Also, there is some chance that an EPC-LS will result in a substantial loss to the contractor. (Remember, that does not necessarily mean a gain to the sponsors!) From the contractor's viewpoint, taking on a large EPC-LS is a bit like playing Russian roulette. Usually, there is no bullet in the chamber even if the project seriously overruns. That is because most significant overruns on lump-sum projects are accompanied by lots of changes that largely render the lump-sum nature of the contract moot. Once in a while, however, there is the unlucky spin and the contractor might get stuck with a catastrophic loss. The contractor wants, reasonably enough, to do everything possible to ensure against such a loss.

As a result, large EPC-LS bids will carry a risk premium over and above normal contractor contingency except when the market for their services is in a prolonged slump and they face the prospect of extinction without winning the project. Some owner companies, especially national companies in the Middle East, take a very hard "no change orders accepted" approach on their lump-sum EPC contracts, even when they, as the owners, have clearly made changes that should normally cause an increase in the contract price. Oftentimes, the courts of jurisdiction in any disputes are the home country courts, and hence, viewed as a home playing field advantage. In those cases, the companies are paying risk premiums of 25% to 40% over a "fair" contract price to the low bidders on the projects. Some of our "failure" projects in the Middle East came in on budget, on schedule, and started up appropriately but paid 40% more for the project than they should have.

Oftentimes, the underlying purpose of using an EPC-LS approach to contracting for megaprojects is not so much to transfer risk as to transfer *blame*. Under an EPC-LS arrangement, especially with a single contractor taking the responsibility, that contractor can become the designated scapegoat (the "one throat to choke"). A good many of the megaprojects built in the Middle East in the 1970s by Western contractors on reimbursable contracts overran hugely without any ability of the host governments to control. It soured the countries and their national companies on reimbursable contracting for a generation.

The Pricing of Risk in EPC-LS Contracts

The period of oversupply in EPC services for the global industrial megaprojects market came to an abrupt end in early 2004. The period of oversupply had extended over the prior 20 years, and that 20-year period significantly upset the power balance in contracting with a strong tilt toward the buyers. The effect of the imbalance was that owners could get almost any terms they wanted from contractors, many of which were struggling to survive. Many, of course, did not. This period saw a substantial concentration of the market for large industrial projects. By 2003, the top 10 international contractors controlled about 75% of the major projects market, up from roughly 50% a decade earlier. The concentration of the EPC market that can execute industrial megaprojects has not eased and may even have gotten worse in recent times. Some contractors, most notably Jacobs, have withdrawn from the industrial market, and other have veered away from lump sums and concentrated more on the publicly funded infrastructure markets rather than more onerous and engineering-intensive industrial projects work.

During the long period of oversupply, contractors were forced away from pricing risk as they bid on EPC-LS contracts and accepted more and more onerous terms for all types of contracts. During this period, it was very common for contractors to have to finance substantial portions of the project because the terms allow owners to withhold payments for relatively trivial reasons. Liability clauses were rewritten to make contractors liable for almost all mishaps, often even including cases in which the owner was found to be primarily responsible or even negligent!

When the market turned in 2004, contractors had accumulated 20 years of grievances. Those that survived had become very adept at avoiding potentially catastrophic risks. And as soon as market balance was restored, the major contractors started pricing risk back into their bids.

By examining the bids against the situation of the projects, we have isolated seven risk areas that contractors started to price in 2004. As the decade progressed, the risk premiums for these areas rose and peaked in 2008. They subsided some after the Global Financial Crisis and the 2015 decline in oil prices, but have roared back after the Covid pandemic shock. I will define each area and the rough amounts that have been added to base bids to account for the perceived risks associated.

Onerous Local Content Requirements. As discussed in prior chapters, local content requirements are nearly universal, even in areas that pride themselves as fully world open market. As I have also mentioned, getting local content into projects is simply business smart. Local content is associated with building local support for projects and with fewer hassles from opportunistic politicians. Local content is often considerably less expensive than alternative supply.

The problem with local content surfaces when there is a requirement that appears difficult or impossible to fulfill. In places without an industrial supply infrastructure, such as structural steel, pipe manufacture, high-quality equipment vendors, and engineering firms, relatively few inputs into industrial megaprojects can actually be supplied. The inputs tend to be restricted to nonengineered bulk materials and construction labor. Often, the local labor is not qualified for many of the key crafts such as alloy welding. For example, we had one megaproject in Central Asia that stipulated an astonishing 80% local content requirement for a petroleum development project and pipeline. There is not even basic line pipe manufacture in country!

Often, the host governments are trying to push the limits of feasible local content, which is understandable, but have trouble figuring out where that feasibility point becomes very expensive in terms of risk pricing. Not surprisingly, international company complaints are viewed as whining. In these situations, the local content requirements should be understood by the sponsors as a perceived major risk to lump-sum bidders. When local content is viewed as difficult to meet, contractors have added a premium of 30%–40% above the base bid for onshore projects. This addition has been so large that it has pushed away many sponsors from EPC-LS. For offshore petroleum development projects, the added premium has been around 15%.

Civil Unrest in the Immediate Area. For some obscure reason, contractors feel it is difficult to build a megaproject and dodge bullets at the same time. When there is shooting in the neighborhood, contractors are adding an average of 25%–30% to their bids.

Harsh Physical Environment or Climate. Contractors are perceiving projects in difficult climates as posing unknown risks that need some degree of cushion in their bids. Projects in remote desert areas, very mountainous areas, arctic areas, and tropical jungle areas are carrying risk premiums of 20%–25%. What the contractors are, in effect, saying is that there are so many unknowns in these areas that rather than trying to build the problems into the base estimates, they will simply put an additional premium on top. This is reasonable when one considers that developing a solid bid for a megaproject is an expensive proposition for contractors. In a period when they are receiving a substantial number of Invitations to Bid, the added time needed to explore all of the logistical challenges of harsh climates doesn't make economic sense. Our data on failure rates in very remote locations suggests that the additional premiums are founded in sound logic.

Political Instability. Political instability translates into logistical nightmares for contractors. They find that goods cannot be moved across ports. Visas are not being processed. Staff is being arrested by local authorities. Some nationals are now persona non grata. These sorts of hassles make getting a project completed in a timely way very difficult. While they may be the source of legitimate claims, that is not a welcome route for the contractor because the claims process is also risky. Areas of political instability are adding 15%–20% to bids.

An Unstable Regulatory Regime. Politically unstable areas also have unstable regulatory regimes, but I counted them under the prior category. Many quite stable political areas have regulatory problems. As discussed in Chapter 6, regulatory problems may be symptomatic of a weak institutional environment. In such environments, permits are highly political acts. But many areas with stable institutional environments have problematic regulatory regimes. In some cases, the regulators find themselves simply overwhelmed with the workload and cannot get permits issued in a timely or predictable way. In some areas, there are so many interveners allowed in the regulatory process that the timing of permits is utterly unpredictable. When contractors under EPC-LS are tasked with permitting, they look at this area as a source of delay, and therefore, risk, and are adding 15%–20% to the bids to cover.

High Potential for Craft Labor Shortages. During the middle of the last decade, craft labor shortages sprang up in a number of areas, including some that had never seen them before. Western Canada; West Australia, and then all of Australia; the Middle East; Central Asia; the U.S. Gulf Coast; and selected parts of Asia all found themselves unable to find enough qualified labor to get large projects completed on time. Labor shortages are a real and present danger to projects. The contractors were adding about 15% to bids in areas of labor shortage, which was probably not enough. In some of these areas, the contractors stopped bidding EPC-LS altogether.

Currency Exchange Risk. Essentially, every industrial megaproject spends money in a number of different currencies. Many contractors found themselves seriously hurt by currency exchange rate fluctuations in the 1990s as financial crises caused very sudden changes. Therefore, when risk pricing again became possible, the contractors attached a premium to accepting the currency risks associated with their lump-sum projects. The size of the premium averaged about 8%–13%.

I find two things astounding about this. First, the premium bid is far more than the amounts actually needed to go into currency markets and forward-buy the currencies in question, and thereby, fix their values. And second, why in the world are industrial companies passing currency risks to their contractors? The kinds of companies sponsoring these projects are quite sophisticated financially, certainly more so than many of the contractors. They should either accept the risk themselves or hedge the risks themselves rather than attempt to pass the burden along and get charged a hefty premium.

Other Areas of Priced Risk Transfer

The seven risk areas previously cited are not the only risks that contractors evaluate. There are a host of contractual provisions that carry real or perceived risks for contractors that are routinely priced into their bids. Among the most important are:

- Uncapped liability provisions. When liabilities are uncapped, such as being limited to insurance, contractors feel they are betting the survival of the firm on each large EPC-LS they undertake. In today's market, contractors will push hard for some limit to their liabilities on any lump sum.

- Definitions of what constitute *Force Majeure* events. In the wake of the Covid pandemic, the definition of *force majeure* has become central to many contract negotiations. Even if the definition of *force majeure* is clear and balanced, contractors are often entitled to no compensation for the high costs associated with suspending a project and remobilizing.
- Responsibility for consequential damages. Contractors do not want to take responsibility for consequential damages, such as lost profits, nor will they accept provisions that sneak consequential damages in through LD clauses. LDs for unexcused delay are usually accepted, and sometimes even embraced, by contractors if they limit liability.
- Payment provisions that make delay or withholding of payments easy. Contractors are thinly capitalized firms, that is, they lack a large asset base. This means that the cost of capital to contractors is generally considerably higher than the cost of capital to industrial owners. When the terms of the contract make withholding of milestone payments easy, contractors often find themselves financing part of a project. They used to view this as part of the cost of doing business, but no longer.
- Unclear provisions for processing change orders and schedule extensions. When the mechanisms for processing change orders and extensions are unclear (or simply do not work very well) contractors will almost immediately go into a defensive posture toward the owner and the project. An accumulation of unresolved change orders puts the contractor in a potential loss position that can quickly feel untenable.
- Ownership of float in the schedule. The lump-sum contractor's position is that any float in the schedule should belong to them. The owner's position is usually that the float should be jointly owned and available for use by either party. If the potential liquidated damages are large and kick in shortly after planned completion, the contractor is likely to fight very hard for float ownership.
- Broad definitions of gross negligence. There are generally two ways in which any contractual caps on contractors' liability can

be breached by the owner: a successful claim of fraud or gross negligence by the contractor. To make the lifting of liability caps easier, some owners have sought to redefine ordinary negligence into gross negligence in the terms of the contract. Expect vigorous opposition to this sort of language.

These provisions are contained in the terms and conditions in the contracts, and apply to all contract types. Although we have not measured the bid premiums from such onerous provisions, contractors do factor them into their bid decisions. In some respects, harsh terms and conditions are insidious; one common reaction of contractors to such provisions is to decline to bid or otherwise being involved in the project without explanation. This has the effect of shrinking the market that is already too thin. Harsh terms and conditions also start the contractors out in a defensive mode, which is not conducive to successful projects.

The Myth of the "A Team"

I was once having a conversation with the CEO of one of the top international contractors and the subject of incentive contracts came up. He asked me why so many owners seem to prefer them. I answered "Because they believe they will get the 'A team', that is, the best people the contractor has to offer." He laughed and said, "If they can figure out what the A Team is, they are welcome to them. But they have to tell me because I have been trying to find them for years!" I asked another contractor executive if he could name the "A Team" in his organization, and he said, "Sure, they retired two years ago."

There is an almost magical belief within the owner community that there are a set of much stronger project teams among the major contractors, which if they can be secured, will result in assured success. While, of course, there is variability in the competence of contractor teams, just as there is for sponsor teams, the A Team is a myth. As a sponsor you are much more likely to find yourself with an "A" team if your FEL has been excellent and all the owner functions were present and accounted for during FEL.

There are some attributes of contractor teams that do make a difference. First, all of the contractor lead participants should have worked for the contractor on at least one prior major project. If they have not, it is very likely that they cannot actually operate the contractor systems because they are not sufficiently familiar with them. One of the most common shortfalls of contractors is not that their systems are poor; it is that the people on the project don't actually know how to run those systems. Second, you would greatly prefer a group from your leading contractors that have worked together before as a team. The contractor project manager, lead engineer, disciplinary leads, lead cost estimator, lead planner/scheduler, and construction/fabrication manager, if they will be responsible for construction, should have experience together. The search for the mythical "A" team is a distraction from asking the right questions as you qualify the contractors. The issue is whether a potential contractor can and will field the right team for this particular project, and whether the contractor will give reasonable assurances that the team selected will stay in place.

Reimbursable Contracts Are for Higher-Risk Projects

Reimbursable EPC and EPCm contracts were used for a quarter of the projects in our sample. This contract form was used by every industrial sector and in every region in the world. Reimbursable approaches are most appropriate, and may even be essential, when a project is subject to significant uncertainties that will carry well into execution. For example, reimbursable contracts were twice as likely to be used in highly remote locations. Reimbursables were associated with greater use of innovative technology, and reimbursable forms were a little more common when projects were schedule-driven. Reimbursable contracts were much more common when local project markets were overheated. For that reason, reimbursable forms have been the predominant megaproject contract type in Australia, Canada, and Central Asia during the first decade of this century. Projects with inherent risks are tilted toward reimbursable forms because sponsors and contractors are much less likely to be able to agree on a lump-sum price when execution is uncertain.

Because of the economic inefficiency associated with risk transfer, real or imagined, from owners to contractors, the risk premiums contractors want for lump sum are too large for owners to swallow.

Straight reimbursable EPC contracts are very difficult for most sponsor teams to control. Very few owners have the very strong skills needed to prevent the reimbursable from becoming an open wallet that enables the contractors to charge many more hours than the budgeted ones for engineering and construction/fabrication. Most owners do not know, for example, what is an appropriate number of hours for various parts of the design. Most owners lack even basic understanding of megaproject construction management that would enable them to know whether the field is being properly managed or not.

The Use of Incentive Schemes

This lack of expertise has led many owners to attempt to mitigate the open-ended nature of reimbursable contracts through the introduction of incentive schemes. These schemes involve extra profits to contractors if the project underruns its budget, schedule, or other objectives as desired. Sometimes, the schemes involve extra payments for meeting the sanctioned objectives. Sometimes, they involve some form of penalties for disappointment such as "fee at risk" or "pain-sharing" approaches. The incentive schemes almost always applied to the prime contractors, which were the engineering and procurement organizations, and not specifically to the subcontractors that were used for construction.

None of the incentive schemes associated with reimbursable EPC contracts had any detectable effects on project success. They are a complete random walk. The success rate with incentives is actual lower than without, but not statistically significant. The only relationship that I am able to detect is that cost target incentives were associated with *greater* schedule slip and that finding is statistically marginal. Our findings flatly contradict case study findings by researchers such as Berends.[9] To be sure, there are some successful incentivized megaprojects; there just are not very many of them.

[9]Berends, op. cit., p. 128.

The incentive schemes suffer a number of defects. Most of these schemes were put in place with contractors that had also executed the FEED on the projects and had therefore had a primary role in the development of the sanction estimate. Knowing (or at least hoping) that the execution contract will contain incentives for underruns, these estimates characteristically overstate the bulk material quantities that will be needed to construct the facilities. Even slight padding of the bulk material quantities translates into a significant "cushion" in the estimate because the bulk material quantities are the primary drivers of engineering hours and construction hours. If all goes well, which is actually determined by fundamental things, the project then underruns, the contractor has "earned" a sizeable bonus, and the sponsors are pleased because they believe they have gotten a bargain. This leads some researchers and project directors to believe the incentive scheme has worked as well, when in fact, the result was created via creative estimating and the project is actually a bit more expensive than it needed to be.

Those are the good incentivized outcomes. In the much more typical case (about four times as likely), the project runs into difficulties. Those difficulties were usually due to the project fundamentals not being good. Then, instead of generating better outcomes, the incentives get in the way. Imagine yourself as the prime contractor expecting to make profits largely by earning incentives. You are now three months into execution and it is entirely clear that the project is headed for an overrun. You see this simply by observing the number of changes coming through the system. Now you are looking at three years more of an unprofitable project. How do you respond? You demand that the incentives be rebaselined. But if the sponsor agrees to that, the whole premise of incentives is undermined. If the owner refuses, then you, as contractor, view the best route to profits to be cranking in as many hours and as many change orders as you possibly can. You will try to make profits on field hours via hidden profit there. You are feeling ill-used and abused, and therefore, entirely justified in finding profit opportunities wherever they crop up. The relationship between owner and contractor sours, and the project becomes harder, not easier, due to the contract provisions.

Incentive schemes suffer an inherent logical problem: they implicitly assume that there is a great deal of money to be saved below the owner estimate during the execution of the project. But unless the estimate was padded, that just isn't true. Unusually efficient execution can save a bit if all goes well. But the idea that efficient execution can normally produce savings large enough to compensate contractors fairly is absurd. Execution is all about trying to hang on to the value that has been created. It is not about generating new value.[10]

I also have a nagging philosophical problem with the use of incentives in contracts, which goes beyond the simple fact that they don't work. I believe the offering and taking of incentives fundamentally disrespects the professionalism of contractors. What incentives are really saying is that "Because you, the contractor, won't do a good honest job just for your fee, I need to bribe you with some contingent money based on whether you actually show up for this job." Incentive schemes may reflect the broken state of relationships between sponsors and contractors in the process industries, but because they do not work and have so much potential for abuse, they have and will continue to make the relationships worse rather than better. The perceived need for incentive schemes was created by sponsors squeezing contractor fees during the 1990s down to a point where many of the contractors were no longer viable. Realizing that contractors with no hope of making a profit were without much incentive to do a good job, owners started to incentivize the contracts. The more appropriate course in a professional relationship would have been to simply restore a reasonable fee.

Controlling Contractor Hours and Fees on Reimbursable Contracts

Contractor hours can be effectively controlled by means other than lump sums or incentives. The most effective is the systematic reduction and then elimination of all profit potential as hours become excessive. The approach works in the following way:

1. Negotiate target hours for the major work tasks: detailed engineering, project management (if any), field engineering support,

[10]Those familiar with the project management literature will be reminded of the "influence curve," which dates at least back to the 1950s despite those claiming more recent paternity. The influence curve shows that the ability to shape the value of a project is high only when the rate of expenditure is low.

and commissioning and startup (if any). This will be a difficult negotiation, and the sponsor needs to bring as much data from prior projects to the process as possible.

2. The target hours, plus approved change orders (with hours, of course), will earn full overhead contribution and fee. The fee will stop when the target hours are reached in any category for that category. Alternatively, the fee will stop when the total ceiling is reached, unless that ceiling is raised by sponsor-generated change orders.
3. Another increment above the target, say 10%, will earn full overhead.
4. Above 110% no overheads whatsoever will be paid. The contractor will be paid only for their out-of-pocket costs.

This provides the contractor with:

- A guaranteed fee
- A cushion above the target on which they take no loss
- An incentive to never go more than 10% above the target because, at this point, they are foregoing other opportunities in order to complete your project.

This approach provides fair and balanced protection to both parties.

On reimbursable EPC and EPCm arrangements, the owner should want the contractor's profit to be made only in the contractor's fee. Unfortunately, that is often not the case, and unless the owners are careful, the fee may be but a small portion of the contractor's profit. Allow me a blatant example.

The project was a large onshore petroleum development project in a remote area. The project was technically straightforward. The big issue was going to be logistics and labor supply. Virtually all labor was going to have to be imported. The EPC contractor, as is often the case, executed FEED on the project. The project was estimated at $1.2 billion. When IPA evaluated the project prior to sanction, there were two problems. There was very poor granularity in the estimate, so it was difficult to conduct a sensible evaluation of the cost competitiveness of the project. Second, the EPCm contractor was only asking for a $10 million fixed fee. That was less than 1% of the total project!

It was particularly surprising to us because the contractor is well known throughout the industry for demanding high fees, so we were quite perplexed at the low fee and told the owner something was amiss. We were told, with a pat on the head, not to worry. Indeed, they were quite proud that they had managed to secure such a low fee.

The project was completed on time, on budget, with smooth startup. It was apparently a very successful project. When we conducted the closeout evaluation, however, nobody could produce a coherent breakdown of the total cost of the project. The first breakdown made no sense at all, and five iterations later, it still made no sense. The lead sponsor had hired a third-party controls firm to keep track of the costs, but had failed to ensure that the key people would remain with the project through closeout. We strongly recommended a complete audit of the EPCm's costs. And here is another problem: the sponsors had standard audit clauses in their contract with the EPCm for reimbursable contracts. But they had not actually used those audit rights throughout the project. When confronted with the demand for an audit, the EPCm contractor said, "Well, you can try, but because you didn't exercise any of the audit rights throughout the project, we didn't really keep a lot of the 'stuff.'" The attempt to audit the project was utterly hopeless.

That would have been the end of the story except that about a year later I ran into the EPCm contractor's chief estimator and controller on the project who was now working for an owner client of ours. I asked him how much the contractor cleared on the project over and above that $10 million fee. He chuckled and said "just over $250 million." They had made money on just about everything. Materials were marked up and every field hour generated a "fee' from the construction organization to the EPCm.

I would like to say that this story is genuinely exceptional, but I strongly suspect that it is not. If a sponsor is not in a position to carefully audit expenditures on a reimbursable contract, then sometimes money will disappear without a trace. Unexercised rights are lost no matter what the language of the contract says. Finally, third-party controls organizations can be very good, but they provide no benefit if they leave the project before the cost closeout reports are completed and all the loose ends cleaned up. Pay the contractors a good fee; audit to ensure that is all you pay!

Why Megaproject Alliances/Integrated Project Delivery Fail

If multiprime EPC-LS contracting thrives on the notion that "Good fences make good neighbors," alliance contracting believes in no fences at all. Alliance contracts are an extreme form of incentivized reimbursable schemes. The basic form is EPC reimbursable so the same set of contractors stay on the job throughout. The twist is that all of the contractors share in the incentive scheme, usually proportionately to their slice of the whole project's estimated cost. The underlying rationale for this approach is actually rather elegant. Most megaprojects necessarily involve a large number of contractors, subcontractors, specialty contractors, and vendors. As I previously mentioned, negotiating all of the interfaces among so many players is a major headache for sponsors in reimbursable formats, and is even a major problem in multiprime EPC-LS contracts. So, if we put everybody into a "shared destiny" pool, surely they will cooperate and manage the interfaces themselves. Even the sponsors will share in this pool. We are all in this together!

Unlike the rationale, the real world of megaprojects turns out to be quite messy. I have spoken to a great many contractors involved in alliance arrangements, and they have one thing in common: they privately despise the form passionately unless there is so much additional money in the owner's estimate that they cannot lose. They believe alliancing breaks the relationship between what they do and what they get paid rather than the opposite. Their point is simple: I may do everything right, but end up with nothing because some idiot somewhere else on the project made a mistake! Some specialty contractors, such as heavy lift and installation, will categorically refuse to participate in these schemes. It is the norm rather than the exception that the agreement on the incentive scheme in alliances was not finalized until well after the start of execution and sometimes years after the start of execution.

It was also thought by the designers of alliances that they would get the best features of EPC-LS with none of the drawbacks. The advantages of lump sum are: (1) the contractors manage their own interfaces, (2) the contractors will put that legendary "A team" on the project because it is their own money, and (3) the sponsors do not have to field as large a controls staff as on reimbursable projects because the contractors have no incentive to crank hours. The downsides of lump-sum are: (1) quality is always a problem, (2) a premium has to be paid for risk transfer that we usually never manage to actually effectuate, and (3) the contractor rather than the sponsor gets to keep any savings. With an alliance, the reasoning goes, the sponsor will get the "A team" because the contractors have the possibility of making a lot of money, the contractors will manage their own interfaces—just like lump sum—but the sponsor will get to share underruns, won't have to pay a risk premium because the basic form is reimbursable, and quality will not be a problem. (I have never actually heard the exact rationale of this last bit on quality.)

So, what do we actually get with alliances? We actually end up with some of the worst features of lump sums combined with the worst features of reimbursables:

- There is no evidence whatsoever that contractors assign more highly skilled and experienced people to alliances than to other reimbursables.
- In fact, what has been created is exactly the same incentive structure to skimp on quality that exists in lump sums, which is evidenced by the fact that alliances suffered the worst record of operability failures.[11]
- The interface management hypothesis is exploded by the fact that the contractors are actually *more* prone to fight among themselves, not less.
- As the data make very clear, there are rarely any underruns to divvy up. There were no underruns to share in over 85% of the alliance projects!

But none of the preceding problems are really the worst feature of alliances. The worst feature is the contract form actually makes it more difficult, rather than less, to resolve problems when they occur. Megaprojects are messy. There will be problems, even if everything

[11]The early burst of enthusiasm for alliance contracting ensued before the operability problems of many of the alliance projects were understood. Operability data are almost never made public voluntarily, especially when they are poor.

possible has been done to prepare the project. When a problem occurs, the contract should be pulled out of the drawer, dusted off, and read for assistance in resolving the problems. Alliance contracts, because we are "all in this together," do nothing to help us understand who is responsible and needs to step up and who is not. Alliance contracts are the epitome of "shared risk." "Shared risk" is shorthand for "it's nobody's responsibility." The typical alliance contract is so complex that it cannot be used to help settle disputes.

The alliance projects were understaffed by owners; in nearly two-thirds of the alliances, the project director described the project as insufficiently staffed. The alliances also had another feature that is characteristic of failure: "stretch" targets. More aggressive cost and schedule targets were set for the alliance projects than any other contract type. Part of the ethos of "alliancing" was that great things could be done via this new contract form. Alliance contracting is a bad idea that should be consigned to the dustbin of history for large industrial projects.

Contracting and Collaboration

As I suggested at the beginning of this chapter, contracting is where practical thinking often goes to die. There is a belief that permeates much of the discussion of alliancing and integrated project delivery as well as incentive contracting that if we could find the right contracting solution, problems of conflict and lack of owner/contractor cooperation would go away, or at least, be greatly mitigated.

There is a belief that different approaches to contracting can somehow resolve the fundamental problem, the principal/agent conundrum, that sits at the heart of every contract.[12] Some view different payment schemes for contracts as creating an adversarial versus collaborative environment for the project.[13] The outcomes of actual industrial projects, both very large and mid-sized, suggest that seeking

[12]Merrow, 2023, pp. 10–16 and pp. 150ff.

[13]See, for example, Thomas W. Grisham, *International Project Management*, Hoboken, NJ: John Wiley & Sons, 2010, p. 96; Phillip James Barutha, *Integrated Project Delivery*, Iowa State Department of Civil Engineering, 2018; or "Integrated Project Delivery for Industrial Projects," RT 341, Construction Industry Institute, 2019.

collaboration via contractual form is a fool's errand. We have actually seen some alliance projects that devolved into ugly acrimony, and EPC-LS projects that are characterized by owner and contractor working seamlessly to resolve problems. Conflict or collaboration are quite unrelated to contractor form.

When a project is set up for success by the owner, a collaborative work environment with the contractors is much more likely regardless of the contractual approach taken. Conversely, when the project is a mess from the start, smooth working with the contractors is very unlikely. With good leadership on the part of both the owner and contractors, good working collaboration is possible even when the project is struggling. But contract form plays but a minor role in the process. Contractual approaches that make risk assignment less transparent, such as integrated project delivery, actually add to the problem.

Why Split Form Contracting Succeeds

The orphan child of megaproject contracting is the "split" form, sometime also called the "hybrid" approach. It involves separate contracting of engineering and procurement services on a reimbursable basis followed by lump-sum construction or fabrication with a construction organization. This approach was least used, but was used at least once by every sector and in every part of the world. It was employed most frequently in petroleum development and in chemicals. As previously discussed, projects using this approach to contracting were much more successful than megaproject average.

To discover that the split form was more successful was hardly a surprise. Prior research involving over 2,800 processing facilities and petroleum developments around the world had established that the form was, by a substantial margin, the most cost-effective approach to contracting. Why does it work?

I believe there are several compelling reasons why the split contracting strategy is more successful than other forms. The split form breaks the contractual links between project engineering and construction or in the exploration and production (E&P) world among engineering and fabrication, installation, and hookup, and commissioning. Severing this link has a number of advantages. It reduces the engineering contractor's span of control, making the project more manageable. The focus is on engineering and engineering alone. It prevents the engineering contractor from devising their project strategy so as to make extra profits from nonengineering activities.

The split form removes any incentive of the FEED contractor, which is usually the engineering contractor on non EPC-LS projects, to pad the estimate or otherwise manipulate the incentive scheme. That frees up the use of incentives, if the owner so chooses, to be used for instrumental goals such as low engineering error rates and appropriate sequencing of design. It also frees up the use of instrumental incentives for the construction firm as well around issues such as quality and proper sequencing of construction completion so as to facilitate turnover and commissioning.

The split-form strategy improves the quality of the construction management because construction management must stand alone and not be subsumed by the engineering contract. It forces owners to know something about construction management because they are going to be selecting the constructor/fabricator rather than relying on the engineering contractor to either provide that skill set in-house or contract it with minimal owner input. Many of the world EPC firms are much better at EP than they are at C or Cm. Most of the EPC contractors are engineering-centric organizations that have relegated construction to second-class status. Projects, however, are done better when engineering is construction driven. The split form does not ensure that will occur, but it does prevent engineering from simply dictating how the project will be executed.

A split strategy makes it much more likely that construction or fabrication will not start until the engineering and procurement effort has progressed far enough and well enough that construction will not be slowed by late, inaccurate, and out-of-sequence design as well as late and out-of-sequence materials. I will return to this important subject in Chapter 14.

Finally, a split form strategy is associated with much better front-end planning. The FEL index for the split-form projects was far better than any other contract form ($Pr|t|<.001$). In particular, both engineering and execution planning elements were far superior when the split strategy was going to be employed. The reason for this link is simple: the split-form strategy must be planned early. The construction or fabrication contractors have to be pre-qualified, which forces the sponsor team to know (or learn) something about construction management.

Split Form Contracting and Understanding Construction Management

EPC contracting, both lump sum and reimbursable, has one very dubious virtue for sponsors: it enables them to contract their megaprojects while being almost entirely ignorant of what constitutes effective construction management (CM). When contracting EPC, sponsors usually get whatever constructors their engineering firm wants or can manage to get. Oftentimes the construction arm of that engineering firm we really wanted is far from first rate.

This book is not the place to discuss the intricacies of excellent CM. But sponsors must realize that excellent CM may be the difference between success and failure, and in labor short regions, it is the difference between success and utter disaster. If a sponsor is going to be capable of using the split-contracting strategy, the ability to select effective construction managers is essential.

I consider the following areas of knowledge to be the backbone of effective CM.

A Modern Safety System. Ideally, the CMs on a megaproject will employ a modern, positive-reinforcement based safety program and will work with the sponsor team to ensure worker safety. What we are actually seeing on too many sites, especially in low-wage regions, are systems designed to minimize accident reporting.

Sequencing of Design and Materials Delivery. The excellent CM can examine a project and explain, in detail, the sequences that must be followed in the delivery of design and the ordering and delivery of equipment and materials to the construction site. Proper sequencing will drive field labor productivity more than any other single item. The quickest way to depress field productivity is for workers to have nothing to do.

Materials Management. Megaprojects usually involve billions of dollars of equipment and materials. One of the most common problems on megaprojects is not being able to locate materials when they are needed for construction. Many a project ends up ordering items more than once because they can't be located, only to end up with millions of dollars of surplus material at the end of the project. At some sites, material walks off the site at the end of every shift because the laydown yards are not secure.

Materials management and all of the logistics that go with it are very complex systems for megaprojects. They may require modern technology such as radio frequency identification (RFID) and GPS location finders. Whether low tech or high, a great deal of skill and experience is essential.

Hiring Craft. The CMs on a megaproject absolutely must know how to acquire craft for the particular site. They must know the local norms. They must know what kinds of craft can be brought into a country or an area and which cannot. They must know where to source first-line supervisors. Conflicts between local labor and imported first-line supervision can shut down sites. In one of our projects, the animosity actually led to the murders of over 20 first-line supervisors.

Productivity Measurement and Problem Identification. Effective CM must know how to monitor productivity down to the gang level. Its systems must enable rapid aggregation of productivity so that the CM itself, at a minimum, knows what productivity looks like on a weekly basis. The effective CM has a system that immediately, not months down the road, tells it when an area is falling behind, and it can identify the problem as materials availability, changes, or craft skill immediately.

CM Staffing. The CM staff above general foremen should be at least 50% from the permanent staff of the CM organization. If more than half of the CM organization has been recruited from the street, you are not hiring a competent CM, just a collection of people.

CM Systems. The sponsor needs to understand what systems will monitor and report progress; how system completion and turnover will be ensured; how materials management will be done; how tools' quality, appropriateness, and availability will be ensured; and how work package planning will be done, including safety planning and backup task planning.

The Use of a Project Managing Contractor (PMC)

The PMC arrangement involves hiring a contractor that will act for the owner team or augment the owner team in managing the execution of a project. PMCs were employed by 15% of the projects in our sample, and were used with every contract type, in every region of the world, and in every industrial sector. Projects with PMCs were not substantially different than other projects. They were a little more likely to be onshore projects, but a good many of the PMCs were in petroleum development.

The projects that used PMCs were considerably more likely to fail than those that did not ($Pr>|X^2|<.03$). Their schedule performance and production attainment success were average, but their cost and cost growth performance were terrible. Projects using PMCs averaged a 40% real overrun and were highly uncompetitive in capital cost (+38%). They were a little poorer in FEL completeness at authorization, but that can account for only a small portion of the very high costs.

They were especially expensive when the execution contracts were EPC-LS and when alliances were used. I believe the reasons for these results are similar. The use of a PMC arrangement is met with great skepticism by the other contractors working on the project. The PMC is in a very powerful position to shape the destinies of the other contractors. If you believe that contractors don't trust owners, you are right. But they *really* don't trust other contractors! And if the PMC was also given part of the execution work on the project, as they were in a majority of cases, the distrust among the other contractors goes off-scale.[14] They believe the PMC will use its close ties to the owner and its position at the top of the project to make the execution of the project easier (and more profitable) for themselves and harder (and less profitable) for everyone else. As a result, on EPC-LS projects, the lump-sum contractors are bidding higher than you would otherwise expect.

Is this distrust justified? At least some of the time, the answer appears to be "yes." On some projects, the PMCs routinely disparaged the work of the other contractors to the owners. There were a number of complaints from other contractors about control of the laydown areas for construction. And in some cases, the PMC was quick to encourage the owner to replace execution contractors that were struggling . . . with themselves!

I am not sure that PMC arrangements can ever be used cost-effectively on large projects. I realize that this creates a real problem for some owners that simply do not have sufficient personnel to staff their megaprojects. If you have to use a PMC, I would make the following suggestions:

- Never allow the PMC to take any portion of the execution, and make clear to every other contractor that, under no circumstances, will the PMC be allowed to take on their work.
- Call the PMC something else: Owner Support Services, for example.
- If at all possible, seek to blend the PMC into the owner team with the owner team taking the key lead positions, such as subproject managers.
- Rather than using a Tier 1 international contractor for this role, seek out Tier 2 contractors or large contractors that do not take on EPC-LS international work. What is needed is a source of skills to support the understaff owner team, not an organization that will take over the project.

[14]There were even cases in which the PMC was contracted on a reimbursable basis for PMC work while executing work on an EPC-LS basis on the same project at the same site! This, of course, violates the first rule of sensible contracting.

Owners and Contractors Live in Different Worlds

Despite the fact that many owners and contractors spend large portions of their careers seated right next to one another, I am convinced that most owners and contractors fundamentally do not understand each other. In particular, I think owners imagine that contractors are like owners. I suspect most contractors think that owners are from another planet.

This was brought home to me a few years ago during a conversation I was having with the director of capital projects for one of the major international oil companies. This was no newbie; he had 30 years of project experience in petroleum development projects all over the world and a well-earned reputation for being deeply cynical. He said to me, "I just don't understand why these darned contractors won't take on any risk, and when they do, they can't manage it. It really irritates me!" I was so amazed at his naïveté that I was struck dumb. Those who know me will testify that doesn't happen often.

When it comes to perceptions of risk, owners and contractors live in completely separate worlds. As the expression goes: where you stand depends on where you sit. Owners complain that contractors don't want to take on any risk, which they equate to responsibility, and when they do, they want inordinately high prices for taking on the risks. Contractors believe that owners are pushing them to bet their business on every project and would push them into bankruptcy without a second thought.

The different views spring directly from the differences between industrial companies and contractors as economic entities. Owner/sponsors look at the world from the viewpoint of assets. Each project involves the creation of a new asset or the expansion and enhancement of an existing asset. How much cash flow the asset can generate relative to its cost determines the value of the project. Owner companies are judged in the marketplace by that calculus overall. Their balance sheets are "asset heavy."

By contrast, contractors are at the other end of the spectrum. They are almost devoid of physical assets. Their balance sheets are asset light and are asset light by design. Very few major contractors even own their headquarter buildings. Contractors earn primarily by the sale of services. They are judged in the marketplace by how well they avoid taking large equity risks as they earn fees from their services.

The difference between contractors and owners with respect to risk-taking can be illustrated with a simple mental experiment. Let's take, as an example, the average failed megaproject in our database. The project was estimated to cost about $4.2 billion in 2023 U.S. dollars. That average failure suffered a 33% overrun, roughly $1.4 billion. Now, let us suppose that one of the world's major contractors took the whole project on as an EPC-LS contract. If successful, the contractor might have hoped to earn about $200 million from the project, but it wasn't successful and it suffered a $1.4 billion overrun. If the sponsors were careful, the contractor's hope of recovering the losses via claims will be dim. Where does the $1.4 billion come from? It is deducted straight from the company's balance sheet. What would the effect be on a very strong contractor such as KBR or JGC or Aker? It would remove every bit of cash from their balance sheets and more! The loss would exceed the net profit for Fluor for 2022 by nearly 10 times! It would do the same to most other major contractors around the world. They would find themselves scrambling to find credit to avoid insolvency.

Now, let us suppose that the owners had to "eat" that $1.4 billion overrun. What results? The return on that asset would decline from about 15% to about 5%. That is a very disappointing result for the investment, but not catastrophic unless it was a very small owner. The $1.4 billion overrun, however, would be *added* to its balance sheet as an asset.

The economic differences between owners and contractors generate fundamental disagreements about how project risks should be priced by contractors. But in this regard, the contractors surely have the better of the argument. The first principle of risk pricing is that the price attached to a risk will be a function of the bettor's wealth vis-à-vis the size of the bet. In these bets, the contractor is almost always the poorer of the two parties to the contract and therefore *should* attach a significantly higher price to the risks that it takes on. Moreover, when taking on risks, it is economically rational for the contractor to seek to find ways of mitigating those risks.

Contractors equally do not understand owners' needs around creating operating assets. In my experience contractors focus too narrowly on meeting targets on cost and schedule, and attach little value to turnover sequencing and successful turnover of the asset to operations. These shortcomings should be expected given their orientation. Interestingly, construction organizations often appear more sensitive to the needs of turnover and commissioning than the engineering contractors.

Some "new and improved" approaches to contracting are based on the premise that, with the proper contractual structures, the differences between owners and contractors can be bridged and goals aligned. I believe, and the data strongly support, that the differences cannot be bridged. The contractual platforms such as alliancing are actually highly unstable because they cannot actually ensure that contractors will be fairly and routinely compensated for their work. Similarly, most incentive schemes are transparently easy for contractors to game, or again, end up failing to compensate contractors for their work.

Both owner personnel and contractor personnel come to work each expecting to do their best on their project. Both need to be compensated for what they do. At the end of the day, it is not at all clear that we should want contractors to "think like owners" or owners to "think like contractors." Owners need to focus their attention on asset health and quality. Contractors need to focus their attention on execution excellence. Owners and contractors are different. Understanding, appreciating, and supporting those differences are essential for successful projects.

CHAPTER 14

The Control of Execution Risk

The reader is about 90% through this book, and I am just now getting to project execution. Project execution is where 95% of the money will be spent, and typically, execution will occupy about 60% of a megaproject's total cycle time as measured from the start of scope development through startup. So why am I giving it short shrift? The answer should already be apparent: because very few projects actually fail due to problems that originate in execution. This is not to suggest that execution of a megaproject is easy; it is not. Rather, it is testimony to how good contractors, especially fabricators and constructors, have become at doing their work when it has been properly prepared.

If a project has been prepared well, execution is about maintaining the value that has already been created. It is about *active* vigilance and the willingness and preparedness to intervene. If a project has been poorly put together on the front-end, execution is all about damage limitation. Victory is snatched from the jaws of defeat in fairy tales, not in megaprojects. While it is possible to do everything right on the front-end and then snatch defeat from the jaws of victory, it is quite unusual.

Controls Must Start Early

The work that will become controls in execution starts back in front-end loading (FEL). The choice of the basic contracting strategy in FEL-2 starts to shape the kind of controls that will be needed in execution. Starting to shape the controls approach toward the end of FEL-3 is too late, but is the norm. I believe sponsors start to think seriously about control only in FEL-3 because they relate controls with construction or fabrication activities. In fact, it is far more important to be carefully monitoring engineering than construction! When problems start to show up in engineering, it actually may be possible to do something about them that will save the project. If the problems are not seen until construction, it is usually too late.

One essential element of planning how to control the project is to establish the project management information technology system and approach that will be used. Of highest importance is to plan for as much interoperability of IT systems as humanly possible. The IT systems requirements should be incorporated into the invitation to bids (ITBs) for EPC lump-sum (EPC-LS) projects and into the requests for quotation from all of the key vendors of equipment. Ideally, it would be possible to conduct all design reviews electronically, including reviews of vendor drawings. It is essential that the cost and schedule information provided by the contractors during execution be in a form that the sponsor's systems can use effectively. It should be mandatory that schedule updates be provided in their native electronic form and should be archived by sponsors for purposes of claims defense later.

The sponsors' rights to data and to audit must be established in the ITB and in the contract terms and conditions. Some owners believe that if they are pursuing an EPC-LS strategy, they cannot secure rights to data, to receive detailed reports, or to audit. That simply isn't true. Stipulate clearly what is desired in the ITB and in the resulting contract, and the rights are established. If (and only if) you exercise those rights immediately after the start of execution will you keep them. It is the sponsor team's responsibility to articulate the behaviors that it expects from the contractors and all others involved in the execution of the project. Those expectations should be communicated early and driven consistently. Getting the information that is needed to control the project is just one piece of that overall puzzle.

Full rights-in-data for reimbursable contracts are absolutely essential. Occasionally, a contractor argues that cost data are "proprietary" on reimbursable contracts. That is understandable and it does facilitate larceny. That any owner would ever acquiesce to those arguments, however, is utterly astounding. Without full rights-in-data, the sponsors will never know where the money went, only that there was an awful lot of it.

The owners' key roles in execution are to be constantly aware of exactly how the project is progressing, and to be prepared and willing to intervene constructively when problems occur. The only prudent position for sponsors is to assume that the contractors may not know how the project is going and may not tell you if things are going badly even if they know. Sometimes, the contractors' systems are not adequate to effectively monitor progress; sometimes, the people operating those systems are not operating them well. (Recall that this problem is to be expected if a large portion of a contractor's key people are "from off the street," that is, not long-time employees of the contractor.)

It is very common that when contractors find themselves in trouble, the last person to be informed is the sponsor's project director. The contractors will usually attempt to work themselves out of a problem before finally asking for help. To be forced to call the fire brigade when you have set your house on fire is embarrassing. It is often six months or more after the first signs of trouble actually appeared that the sponsor project team is informed. It is then certainly too late to fix any major problems. The house is going to burn down.

We had one case in which the contractor had gotten cross-wise with the government officials on securing work permits for personnel to enter the country to work on the project. Rather than bring the mess to the project director, the contractor attempted to get higher-ups in the ministry to "fix the problem," which made it worse. Only when the owner finally started to see positions going unfilled did the contractor admit the problem. The sponsor then worked with the government (with lots of apologies) to resolve the issue. By that point, the project was already falling behind.

On the positive side, we had a project in which the main contractor was having huge problems with the neighbors in an onshore petroleum development project. The sponsor's controls organization saw the problems immediately and stepped in to completely change the project's approach to environmental considerations and clearly saved the project. That is the owner's job and it doesn't make any difference what type of contractual arrangements are being used for the project. A project being EPC-LS is not an excuse for an owner team allowing the project to fail.

Priorities for Monitoring and Control

Priorities are, in part, a function of the type of contractual arrangements. For example, the emphasis required on cost is high for reimbursable contracts and less for EPC-LS contracts. The level of quality checking is very high for EPC-LS and for cost incentivized EPC and EPCm reimbursables. Quality control (QC) is less urgent when non-incentivized reimbursable and mixed approaches are taken, which is not to say that it is unimportant.

The variation in emphasis does not mean that concern and attention to go nil on any contract type. For example, on non-incentivized reimbursables, quality is still an issue. However, the incentives to cut corners are not as severe. One of the (many) problems with alliance contracting is that sponsors have not realized that the incentive structure in those contracts creates exactly the same situation in terms of QC as EPC-LS contracts.

After studying these projects for many years, I am convinced that once execution starts, which is really during front-end engineering design (FEED) and not post-sanction, the priorities overall and independent of contract type should be:

1. Safety
2. Schedule and especially whether the project is *on schedule*
3. Quality and how quality interacts with schedule
4. Cost

Safety must be No. 1 for several reasons. Safety is an ultimate value, not an instrumental one. The reason to be safe is a matter of human dignity, not a matter of saving money, having better morale, having fewer labor disruptions, and having a better construction or fabrication schedule. Those things happen too when safety programs are strong, but they are serendipitous, not the underlying reasons. Holding safety as a core value is essential because the contractors will be watching carefully to see whether the sponsor is willing to shortcut safety to serve an immediate purpose. Experience has taught contractors that too many owners don't really care about safety when it doesn't suit them. The sponsor team's dedication to safety sets the behavioral standard for everything else. The sponsor's requirement that all accidents, injuries, and near misses will be fully and openly reported reinforces the transparency that is needed for effective controls.

After safety comes schedule, not cost, even if the project is fully reimbursable. That order may surprise some readers given the emphasis I placed on capital cost in Chapter 8. After all, as Figure 8.2 shows, the first determinant of profitability is production attainment, followed by cost, followed by schedule as a distant third. Schedule is important in execution because, if the sponsor is watching it carefully, lagging schedule is the key leading indicator of trouble ahead. Slippage in the progress of detailed engineering should raise alarm throughout the sponsor team.

Every project director knows that as execution proceeds, all projects become schedule-driven. Cost comes to depend on meeting schedule because there is an optimal schedule that is an indicator of being on cost. Being rushed at the back-end leads to quality problems as well. Too often, however, the careful watch on schedule begins too late in execution because controls were not ready. Monitoring of engineering progress really needs to start in FEED and be fully mobilized at the outset of detailed engineering.

Whether detailed engineering is likely to slip should not be a mystery to project teams. Figure 14.1 shows the relationship between the completeness of FEL at sanction and slippage in the detailed engineering schedule.

Even when FEL is "best practical," engineering slip today averages over 24% (but only 10% at the median). For anything other than "best practical," engineering is likely to be very late. (We define detailed engineering as complete when demobilization of the full design team occurs, usually about 95% complete. Slip is measured as the ratio of the actual period from mobilization to demobilization divided by the planned time.)

Other factors contribute to slip in detailed engineering as well. Engineering for oil and gas development projects slips more than other sectors, probably reflecting the market situation for engineering

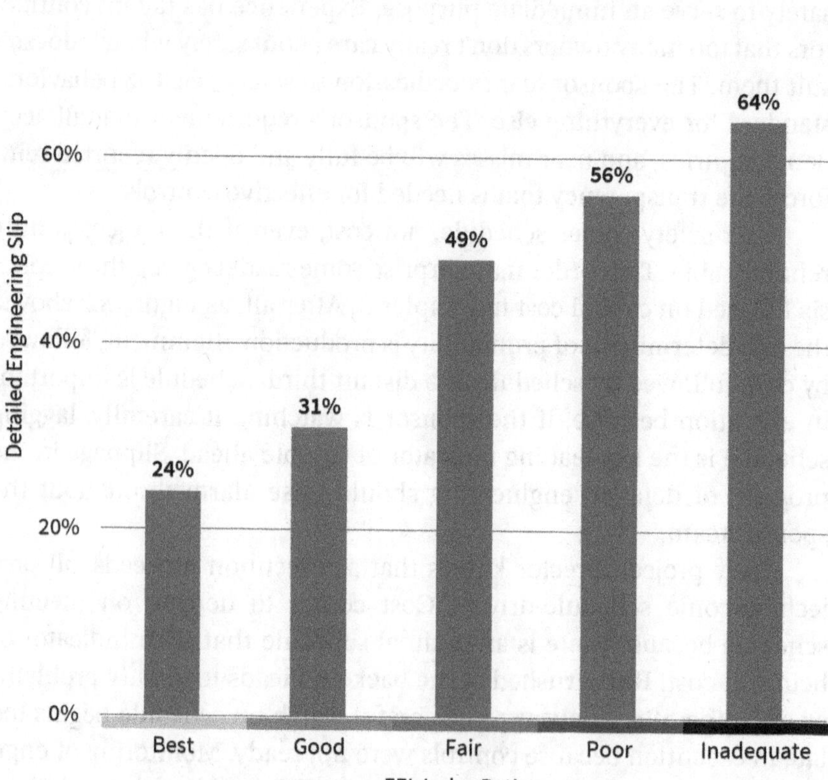

FIGURE 14.1 FEL Drives Detailed Engineering Slip

contractors in the sector. Slip in engineering is very responsive to whether the controls organization has been set up prior to the start of execution. When FEL and the IPA Project Controls Index are both "best practical," the median engineering slip falls to less than 2%. Good owner team development lowers engineering slip. Finally, the use of substantial new technology is associated with *less* engineering slip simply because we know to set more realistic engineering schedules when we are doing the engineering for the first time ever.

There was another surprise result as well. Projects based in Australia, both onshore and offshore, suffered very severe engineering schedule slips during the last two decades, even when all other factors are controlled. Australian megaprojects averaged a remarkable

68% slip in detailed engineering. Less than 5% of Australian projects delivered engineering on the planned schedule. This reflected the thinness of the Australian EPC market and the fact that most Australian projects are executed under EPCm contracts where there is no cost to the contractor in being late.

Although we did not systematically record it in the data collections, we know that late drawings from equipment vendors were another source of delay in detailed engineering. The problem with late drawings is particularly acute when the equipment is not standard. I encourage projects procuring difficult long-lead items to take a "co-engineering" approach to procurement. This entails separately paying the vendors for their engineering work, and even paying a premium for that engineering if the drawings are on-time. This approach appears to ameliorate this problem. Also, one consideration in the selection of vendors should be the compatibility of their information technology (IT) systems and their willingness to provide engineering work in a compatible system.

Slip in detailed engineering is an excellent indicator that the project is in the process of failing. If engineering is late, then procurement is late. If procurement is late, there will not be enough material to sustain the pace of construction or fabrication. In my view, late engineering is the last indicator that is still early enough to have much chance of being useful in changing the outcome markedly. *Even after controlling for the FEL index,* engineering slip is a predictor of success ($Pr|X^2|<.001$), cost growth ($Pr|t|<.001$), cost competitiveness ($Pr|t|<.001$), production attainment failure ($Pr|X^2|<.05$), and of course, execution slip ($Pr|t|<.001$), and schedule competitiveness ($Pr|t|<.001$) and procurement slip ($Pr|t|<.001$). Clearly, if engineering is slipping, the project is being lost. If the slip in engineering is discovered early enough and if there are contingency plans in place, the engineering schedule can sometimes be recovered. More often it cannot and then what is important is saving the project, not the engineering schedule per se.

It appears that most of the time, the sponsor team did not realize in real time that engineering was slipping. Several factors contributed to this problem. Sometimes, the owner controls organization was still in formation when detailed engineering was already under way. For this reason as well as control of front-end work, I strongly recommend that controls start at the beginning of FEED. By the time FEED is completed, the controls organization should be fully operational and its tools calibrated. If the FEED contractor is going to stay on as the prime contractor for engineering, then the controls are set. If not, the controls approach to engineering and the data that will be required of the contractors must be spelled out in the ITB.

Most owner controls organizations are better at monitoring construction progress than engineering progress. With modern design tools, the old-fashioned approach of counting drawings has no meaning. Unless the owner has set up the measurement system as part of the owner design reviews process, engineering progress is difficult to establish. Another very common problem was that reports of engineering progress from the contractors were not accurately discounted for design that had to be reworked because of engineering errors and omissions. When engineering quality was poor, progress was grossly overstated. Only design that has been reviewed, approved, and issued as final should be counted toward design complete. This is one of the ways in which quality control and assurance interact with schedule.

If engineering is late, the procurement of equipment and engineered materials will also be late. That, in turn, means that construction will either have to be delayed and possibly delayed quite substantially, or the cost of the project will fly out of control. *If the engineering is slipping, the sponsors must be willing to rework the schedule so that work in the field or in the fabrication yards and shops does not start prematurely.* The actual loss of time is not as bad as it looks because (1) the project would have slowed down in fabrication or construction anyway at a time when slowdown was really expensive, and (2) with more material and engineering available, construction is faster than normal. If the project has weather windows, a longer planned engineering period is just plain prudent.

Our experience with megaprojects says that sponsors fail to slow projects even when they realize that engineering is falling behind. What that actually means is that they had no backup plan ready for that event. Concrete plans on how to intervene in the event of trouble are what we call risk management! You must be willing to stop early because stopping later doesn't work. The need to slow a project when engineering slips is absolutely mandatory when the region is short of construction labor, a subject to which we will now turn.

Megaproject Survival in Labor-Short Environments

Almost a third of our megaprojects were executed in environments that were short of the craft labor needed to do the construction. In this respect, offshore projects are more fortunate than onshore. Except where local content requirements forbid it, offshore projects can move their fabrication site to where the labor is available. Onshore projects have the option of adopting modular construction, but modules only go so far in reducing the local labor requirement and introduce a new set of challenges in design and logistics.

We describe a locale as labor-short if craft labor cannot be obtained and brought to the site in the numbers the project requires given the schedule it has established. Almost all onshore megaprojects strain any local labor resources, but generally, labor can be brought to camps to supply the project. About a third of the time, that proves impossible and only 16% of those projects succeed. Some of the most spectacular failures among our megaprojects occurred in these projects.

During at least parts of the last two decades, we have seen severe labor shortages for large projects in Alberta, Canada; parts of Australia; the U.S. Gulf Coast; Central Asia; and much of the Middle East, especially along the Arabian Gulf. As the number of megaprojects is increasing again, we expect to see shortages recur in most of those areas in the next decade. In some areas, the labor shortages may even be worse than in the last decade as rapid economic growth in India makes surplus labor from the Subcontinent less available.

Labor shortages make the project environment especially fragile. If something goes wrong that bumps up the labor requirement, even modestly, the projects can go into a downward spiral in the field from which recovery is usually impossible. It is important to understand that the labor situation does not in itself cause projects to fail. But it does make failure easy.

The trigger that causes failure is the realization during field construction that considerably more labor will be required than expected. This situation is usually caused either by late and shoddy engineering that creates field inefficiencies, or in a few cases, by a mis-estimation of the labor requirements in the authorization estimate. When engineering deliverables are late, defective, or seriously out of the needed order, field productivity declines precipitously, which means that progress slows.

One reason this situation occurs is that owners have largely abandoned a decision-gate in their work process just prior to committing to field execution of the project. Owners often do not know that engineering has fallen seriously behind because they have no effective independent measure of engineering progress. They are, instead, relying on the engineering contractors' submissions of progress. The problem is that sometimes the contractors publish misleading numbers, or provide assurance they can catch up in time, or simply don't know themselves how far behind they have fallen.

The problem of late engineering became very widespread in the first decade of this century, and it is very likely to continue to be a problem for megaprojects going forward. The problem was exacerbated by the use of low-cost engineering centers in developing countries with ample supplies of engineers. Those centers are now essential for rendering at least part of the design for the great majority of megaprojects around the world, and they frequently do an excellent job. The problem we have seen with the use of the low-cost center, however, is that once engineering schedule has been lost, the time cannot be recovered. There are two reasons for this. Recovering schedule places a lot of stress on the interface between the contractor's home office and the center. Also, the work processes at most of the centers are quite linear. Doing work out of the planned sequence, which would be needed to recover schedule, would threaten to bring the whole process to a standstill.

Late engineering usually results in orders for engineered material, such as pipe spools, being late as well. That results in late and out-of-order delivery to the site. If the field is already mobilized, the situation usually goes from bad to worse. Because engineering is delaying field progress, engineering is progressively rushed as the constructors demand design so they can keep their labor busy. To save time, engineering quality control is often bypassed, which enables shoddy design to reach the field. Shoddy design in the field leads to field rework, which slows the project even more. Rework in the field is associated with safety problems, which slow work even further. And round and round we go. My attempt to illustrate this downward spiral is shown in Figure 14.2.

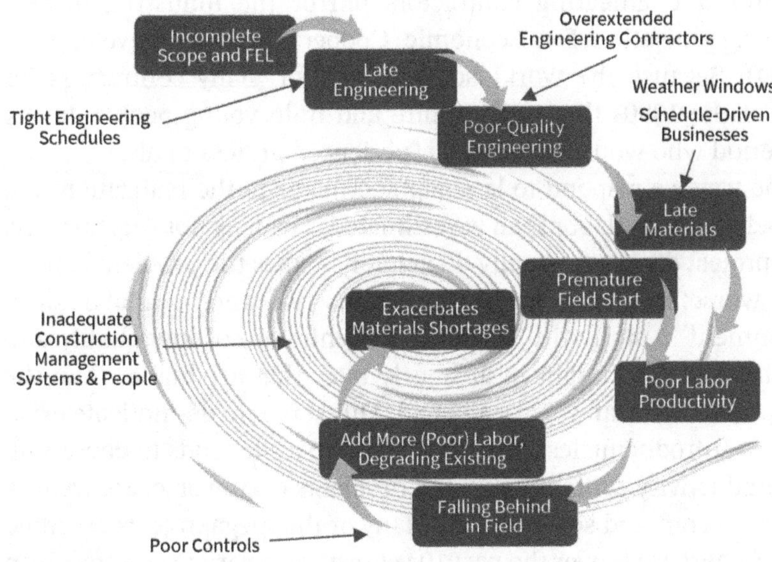

FIGURE 14.2 The Downward Labor Productivity Spiral

Of course, the most common reason that engineering falls behind right from the start of production design is that the front-end engineering was not complete. When the FEL engineering is not progressed sufficiently, the bulk materials (pipe, conduit, concrete, structural steel, etc.) cannot be measured accurately because the design will not support material take-offs. It is the bulk materials, not the equipment, that are the principal driver of required craft labor and the primary driver of engineering hours required. So we get growth in the bulk materials. There is more engineering to do than we had thought, so it falls behind, and when we get to the field, we discover that we never estimated enough field labor to start with. Things are often also complicated by seasonal weather windows that make the rescheduling of field start very difficult, and of course, businesses want to see "progress on the ground." On many projects, there is no float in the schedule that can be used because it was removed in the hopes of meeting the overly aggressive schedules with which we started the project.

Late engineering is also more common on large projects today because large engineering contractors are short of skilled and experienced personnel. The aging demographic profiles of the major megaproject engineering contractors mirror the industrial owners in the Organisation for Economic Cooperation and Development (OECD). Because the workload was light for many contractors for much of the 1990s they did not hire and train young people during that period who would be today's experienced professionals.

The way we respond to late engineering or to the realization that we need a lot more labor than we estimated is usually not very creative. What project directors usually do actually makes the problem considerably worse; they hire more craft. Because we were in a labor-short environment to start with, the craft they hire are of low quality and often have to be brought in at hourly rates that are higher than the more productive craft we already had. This serves to de-motivate existing craft. Introducing less productive craft to a site tends to depress all craft productivity, which makes the problems even worse. So, we hire even more craft and so on it goes. Many of the megaprojects executed in labor-short areas over the past 10 years have experienced some form of the downward labor productivity spiral.

A Truly Classic Example

Let me offer an example that is almost a checklist of what *not* to do in a labor-short environment. This was a difficult complex joint-venture project in a semi-remote area. It required a good deal of highly skilled labor, especially for high-alloy welding. I will start with the outcomes and then trace through how they got there. The total project was estimated to cost $5 billion. The project suffered a 50% (real) cost overrun and poor operability, although everything finally did get up and running for the most part. The overall execution schedule, by contrast, only slipped by six months. Field labor hours grew from just over 10 million hours to just short of 30 million hours, in a high-wage environment! How did they do it?

The business was clear from the outset that the project was to be cost driven. As a commodity-producing project, that is the almost always the right choice. As the project developed, however, the business pressure on the team to reduce costs not only continued; it increased. The team cut scope in one part of the project, but all of the cut scope came back later during execution as it became apparent that it was indispensable to functionality. In response to the cost pressure, the team made a classic error: it changed all of its estimating assumptions from "average" to "best-in-class." They assumed that equipment would be purchased at rock-bottom cost due to volume buying. They assumed they would be able to attract labor with minimum overtime. And they assumed that field labor productivity would be world class. The ratio of field hours to bulk materials was a full standard deviation below industry average. Their project management contractor (PMC) that was executing much of the FEL-3 work must have known better, but went along with the charade.

FEL-3 was declared complete with less than half of the piping and instrumentation diagrams (P&IDs) completed. As a result, the authorization cost estimate underestimated the bulk materials hugely because take-offs of the materials from the design were not possible. With no significant scope changes, concrete increased by a quarter; pipe, by over a third; instruments, by over two-thirds; and electrical quantities, by over a quarter. Now, the field hours to bulk materials ratio that had been merely heroic was totally unachievable. The team did resource-load the schedule at authorization, although exactly how they did that without quantities data is not clear. In any case, resource-loading a schedule based on a gross underestimate of quantities is a waste of effort.

The engineering was late; it had to be in that so much more work was required than estimated. Another project in the region had been counted on to provide a good portion of the project's craft labor supply, but it slipped, just as megaprojects have a tendency to do. The field started to fall behind almost from the moment it was mobilized. Nonetheless, labor productivity at that point was reasonably good.

Then the business and the project director made a fateful decision: we will not give on the schedule. In all fairness, this is a really difficult decision. Sometimes, salvaging the schedule is exactly the right move. Those are situations in which there is additional labor available, and the logistics and the materials available to install permit adding the labor to the site.

In this case, however, the labor was not available. It had to be recruited from thousands of miles away and its quality was not good. Productivity collapsed. For one large part of the project, welding productivity fell to over 20 hours per linear foot of pipe installed versus a norm of less than 4 hours per foot. Overall productivity was much worse than industry norms for the region, and by our estimate, about 10 million craft hours were wasted. But they got the project done and it sort of worked. However, $2.5 billion in shareholder wealth vanished in the process.

How to Survive

So, what is the antidote to the poison of a labor-short environment? I have found only two practices, which are intimately related, that reduce the odds of this situation developing. The first is to deliberately set more realistic execution schedules that reflect the actual field and labor supply conditions. The projects that were successful in labor-short environments set schedules on average that were 23% longer than a benchmark schedule for projects of their type and size. The failed projects set schedules that were 9% faster than the benchmark schedule. The difference is clearly statistically significant ($Pr>|t|<.003$). The second practice that counted was that the successful projects were much more likely to have developed detailed schedules as part of their FEL. Over 80% of the projects that succeeded in labor short environments had resource-loaded their engineering and construction schedules as part of FEL versus 29% of the failures ($Pr>|X^2|<.01$). None of the successful projects had only higher-level milestone-type schedules.

Figure 14.3 shows how developing more detailed schedules affects the chances of success when in labor-short situations. The projects that resource-loaded their schedules in labor-short environments succeeded 37% of the time. Those that did not almost always failed. While it is reasonable to protest that 37% isn't very good, it actually is a little better than megaproject average!

The Criticality of Complete Scheduling

Unfortunately, of all the execution planning tasks, the one that is most likely to be left undone is the fully integrated, networked, resource-loaded schedule. The pushback that we hear is primarily directed at the resource-loading of the engineering and construction or fabrication schedules as part of the FEL. The usual complaint is "Why should

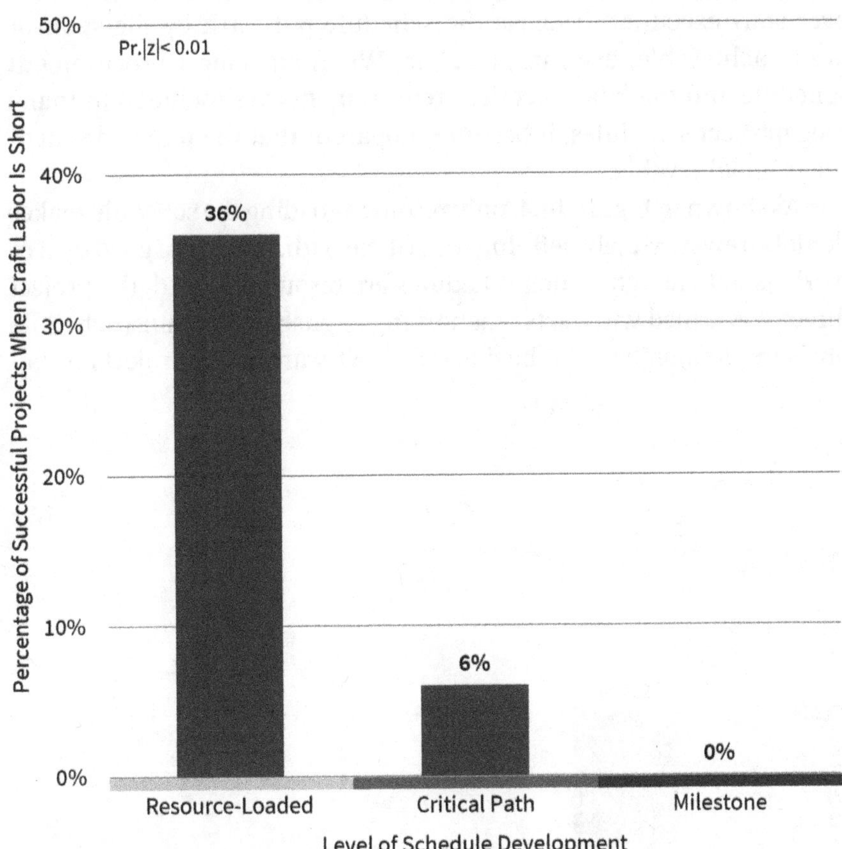

FIGURE 14.3 Scheduling Detail Is Critical in Labor-Short Environments

we resource-load the schedule when that has to be done by the execution contractors anyway? It just duplicates work!"

No, it really doesn't. First, some engineering, materials procurement, and construction (EPC) contractors create excellent resource-loaded schedules and many do not. They often do not resource-load the engineering schedule, and the engineering schedule turns out to be critically important for reasons previously discussed. Second, the reason that the sponsor(s) need to resource-load the schedule is to be able to evaluate whether the project is actually feasible as planned and whether the contractor they will be selecting to execute the project actually understands the job. Too many megaprojects fail before they ever start execution because the schedule put forth by the sponsor is not achievable, even in principle. When an honest procurement schedule and the labor resource requirements are included in many megaproject schedules, it becomes apparent that the targeted schedule is unachievable.

As shown in Figure 14.4, only resource-loading the schedule makes denial go away. Merely defining the critical path, which is a good deal of work, is not enough. When schedules are resource-loaded, the project director is armed with facts when trying to push back against schedule pressure. Remember, the businesses don't want these projects to fail

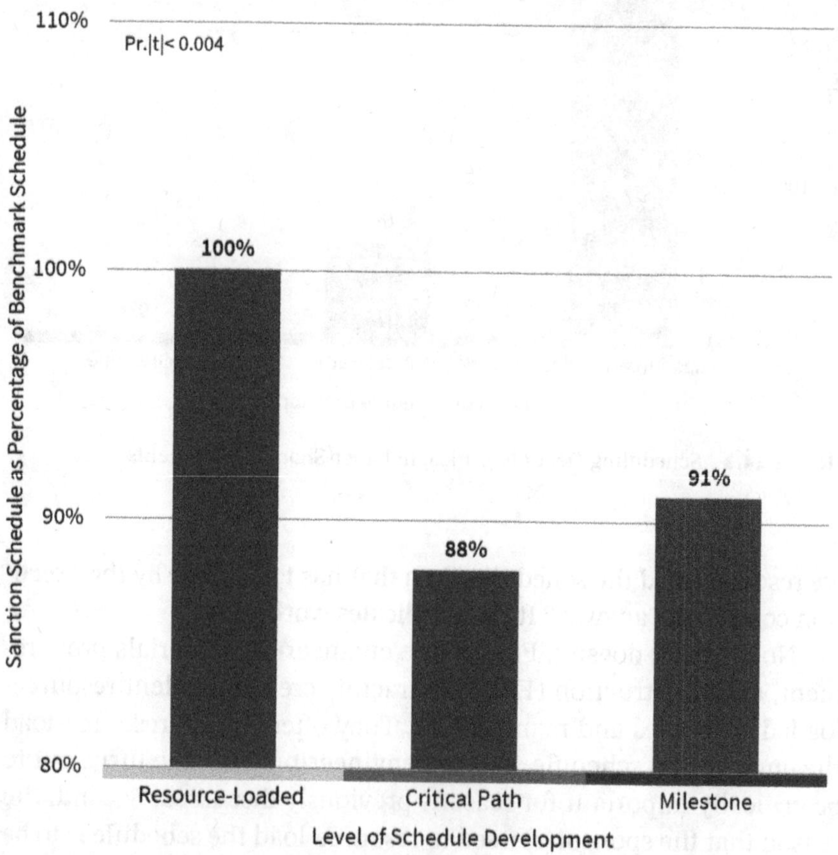

FIGURE 14.4 Resource Loading Is the Best Curb on Schedule Optimism

any more than the project professionals do. They just expect that the engineers will want to be too conservative. When confronted with the facts, they can usually be trusted to respond reasonably. Without the facts, it is just "our view versus their view."

Unlike many smaller projects, the schedules of megaprojects are typically noncompressible. For most projects, the execution schedule can be shortened significantly by addressing a relatively small number of items on the critical path. Usually, acceleration involves expediting a small number of major equipment items. If we are really in a hurry, labor can sometimes be profitably added to speed execution.

For megaprojects, however, the situation is very different. At any particular node in the critical path; there will not be one or a few items on or very close to the critical path, there may be 10 to 20. In order to achieve any acceleration at that node, all of the items will have to be successfully expedited.

A little mental experiment shows why that is unlikely to happen. If there is a (generous) 90% chance of expediting each item and there are 15 items on or close to the critical path at that node, the probability of gaining any schedule acceleration is $0.9^{\wedge 15}$ or about 20%, provided that the expediting of each item is independent of all others. That means I will spend a good deal of money and have only one chance in five of actually gaining any speed. (Note that if the chances of expediting 2 of the 15 items were actually 50% instead of 90%, the probability of gaining any speed falls to 6%.) Of course, I can simply remove all float in the schedule and pretend it will be faster, but given the fact that 78% of megaproject execution schedules slip, more float is needed rather than less.

Going the other route of trying to add labor to most megaprojects is a nonstarter. Most megaprojects struggle to accommodate physically and logistically the labor they plan to have and are in no position to add bodies. Megaproject schedules are solids; they cannot be compressed.

The situation with offshore projects that slip their fabrication schedules is often even more dire. Often the tow-out and installation of new production platforms must be scheduled more than a year in advance. The situation is frequently complicated by weather-window restrictions as well. When fabrication slips, tow-out and

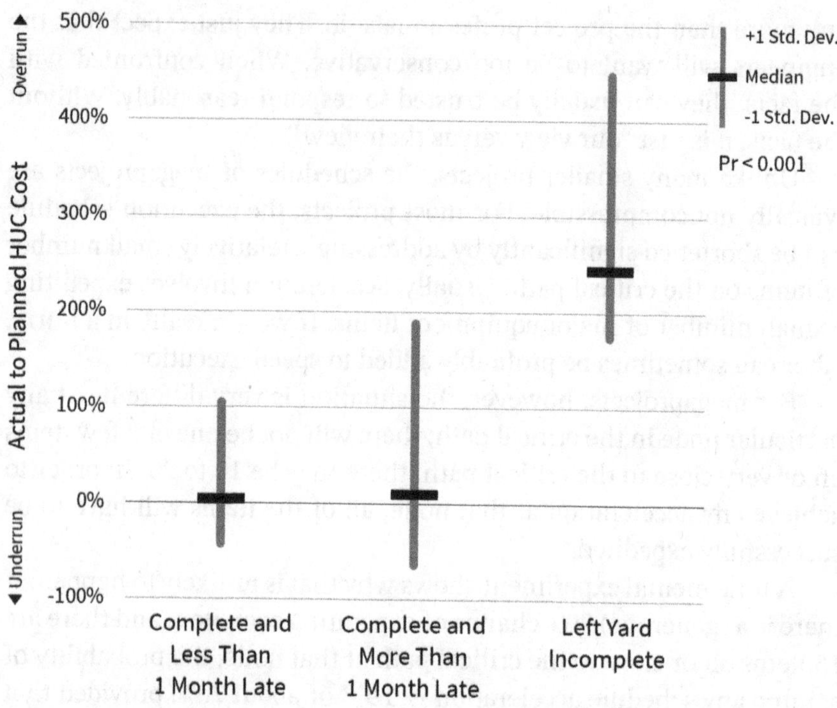

FIGURE 14.5 In Offshore Projects, Fabrication Work Carried Offshore Explodes Hookup and Commissioning Costs

installation cannot be allowed to slip, and fabrication work is transferred offshore. Figure 14.5 shows what happens when construction work cannot be completed in the fabrication yard and work is carried offshore.[1] The cost of commissioning the platform explodes as soon as work must be carried offshore. That is because, on average, each construction hour offshore costs four times what it would have cost back in the fabrication yard. If the execution of the project starts to slip in early engineering, there is often time to juggle the tow-out and installation dates to save a great deal of money. The projects that were forced to carry work offshore ended up with an average total facilities cost overrun of 47%.

[1]The figure is from "Hook-up and Commissioning: the Last Step to a Successful Project" by William Lamport and David Rosenberg, presented at the Upstream Industry Benchmarking Conference, November 2005.

Risk Management Practices

Almost all of the projects in our sample were subjected to a series of risk management exercises, starting in FEL. Because so many practices were applied to so many of the projects, it is difficult to explore the effectiveness of the practices statistically. Our research on the use of risk management practices on smaller projects suggests that there is value in things like brainstorming sessions for risks, SWOTs,[2] and so on. Our research around the use of peer reviews on smaller projects suggests they are of very limited use and may even cause harm by injecting too much conservatism into cost estimates.

Exercises that sensitize team members to potential problems down the road must surely be worthwhile. But we all must remember that the very basis of risk management is sound basic practice around things such as clear business objectives, team staffing and integration, and thorough FEL. In the absence of those things, layering on risk management practices is a futile exercise.

What I do not see in most risk identification, mitigation, and management exercises is a process for identifying the leading indicators of trouble, and then working through exactly how the project team will respond in the event that the problem starts to materialize. For example, very few projects had a backup plan for how to respond if the detailed engineering started to fall behind. Virtually none of the projects that needed to be ready to shift the start of construction, for example, were actually ready to do so. The right to intervene when engineering is falling behind must be stipulated in the contracts with the engineering and construction/fabrication firms.

I believe the way we approach risk management on megaprojects needs to be different than standard technique. I believe it needs to focus almost entirely on "what if" planning. Using real examples, how will we, as an owner team, actually intervene in the process if:

- The contractor is in violation of government rules around bringing people into the country?
- The businesses make a significant scope change during ______ (fill in the blank)?

[2]Structured brainstorming of Strengths, Weakness, Threats, and Opportunities.

- The government makes a rule changes around ________ (fill in the blank)?
- And so forth.

The focus traditionally is on identification of potential problems, entering those problems into a risk register, assigning a (usually junior) person as a "risk manager," and forgetting about it. Too often when a previously identified problem actually occurs, the project director and team are not prepared to respond because the response has not been worked through in advance.

Risk Modeling: A Tale of Two Practices

Two types of modeling are routinely practiced on large projects:

- Monte Carlo simulation of cost risk, usually with an eye to setting the appropriate contingency
- Probabilistic analysis of the authorization schedule to assess the reasonableness of the forecast time requirement

Although these practices appear similar, they actually have very different efficacy. Monte Carlo (and variations) simulation of cost is less than worthless; it actually does harm. Probabilistic schedule analysis is very useful.

Monte Carlo (MC) Cost-Risk Simulation Does Not Work

Sixty-one percent of the projects in our sample used MC simulation to model the probability that the authorization cost estimate would overrun (or underrun, but that is rarely an issue). MC is a simulation technique for aggregating a series of distributions of elements into a distribution of the whole. It was developed to shortcut the cumbersome mathematical task of summing distributions. There are several underlying assumptions for the accuracy of the technique, the most important of which is orthogonality, that is, every distribution must be independent of every other distribution or the interdependencies must be accurately modeled and incorporated into the simulation.

When MC is used to model cost risk, the procedure is first to develop the estimated cost of the project using normal practice for sanction estimates. Then, using a combination of team members and experts, a distribution is assigned around each element. For example, the cost of field labor (or any of its subelements) would be assigned an amount above and below the estimated value. The distribution might well incorporate both risk around changes (increases) in hourly cost and productivity. An interdependency with the distribution around bulk material quantities might also be introduced.

After all of the distributions around all the elements in the estimate have been assigned, the simulation routine is run that samples from the distributions randomly sampling as a function of the density of each distribution. The result from several thousand runs then forms the new composite distribution of cost risk. The contingency is set based on the probability of not overrunning that is desired, usually about 60% of not overrunning.

So does it work? In order for a risk modeling technique to be said to work, it must relate in a systematic way to the things that are first principles drivers of risk. As we have established, team integration, adequacy of team staffing, and, most especially, FEL are the primary drivers of cost overrun risk on projects. So if MC simulation is working, it should result in contingencies that correlate well with those factors. We would also hope that MC results would correlate better than when the technique was not used, or one might conclude it is a waste of time.

Lacking an integrated team adds to risk. When Monte Carlo is not used, project teams are reflecting that risk with higher contingency (Pr|t|<.0001). When MC is used, contingencies are actually *lower*, but the result is not statistically significant (Pr|t|<.08). There is no relationship between MC use and contingency when team staffing was not adequate. The real killer for MC comes from the relationship between contingency and FEL when MC is used. That is shown in Figure 14.6.

There are three relationships shown in the figure. The first is the actual relationship between cost deviation (the ratio of actual to authorization estimated cost) and the FEL index. The relationship is very strong and remains so no matter what other factors are introduced. It is a true driver of risk. The bottom line is the relationship

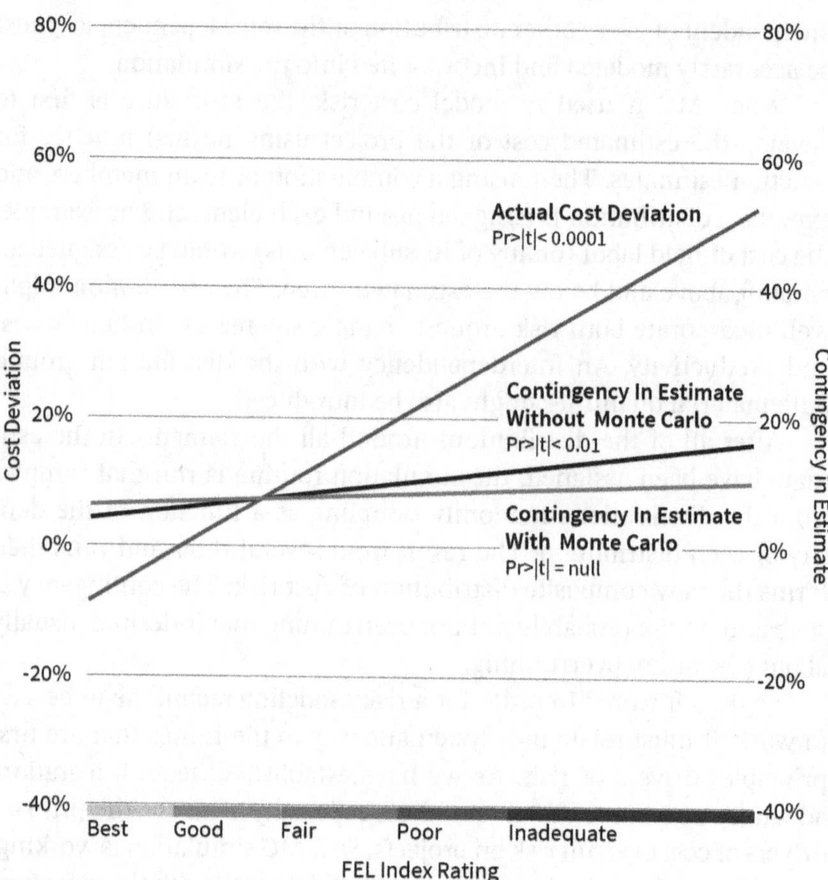

FIGURE 14.6 Monte Carlo Cost Contingencies Are Unrelated to Risk

between FEL and contingency when MC is employed. The line is flat. MC is producing an average contingency of 9% with a standard deviation of less than 4%, independent of any first principles element of risk. Remarkably, that distribution is normally distributed when we would fully expect it to be sharply skewed to the right. The average megaproject cost estimate when MC was employed overran by 21% with a standard deviation of 26% with a sharp right skew.

When MC was not used, teams are actually more sensitive to basic risks as they set contingency. A slope that is statistically significant at less than 1 chance in 100 does exist between contingency and the FEL index when MC is not employed. That is why I have to conclude that

MC actually does harm; it is not merely worthless.[3] The use of MC has no relationship to success of megaprojects or any of our other five figures of merit of projects: cost growth, cost competitiveness, schedule slip, schedule competitiveness, or production attainment.

So why is MC simulation so widely employed? I believe it is because it seems so plausible. The MC results have, to use Stephen Colbert's wonderful word, the feel of "truthiness" about them, that is, the sense of being true without any of the burden of actually being true.[4] After all, a "scientific simulator" generated these results, not mere humans! MC is also easy to use and has given birth to a substantial cottage industry that is deeply invested in the approach.

The reasons that MC fails are basic to the tool itself and its application to the problem.

- MC is merely a simulator that does an excellent job aggregating distributions. The problems start with the distributions themselves. Cost estimates rarely overrun because there were errors in getting the distribution around any individual element in the estimate right. Cost estimates overrun because the scope was not all defined, which means that the central value of every element in the estimate was wrong.
- The distributions used in the MC analysis are fabrications. By that I do not mean they are lies, but that they are made up—fabricated—by a group. They are not based on historically observed distributions of outcomes nor do they have any first principles basis. They are opinion. Behavioral research dating back to the mid-1950s and Ward Edwards' Engineering Psychology Group at the University of Michigan has shown that, when experts are asked to posit a distribution around some event, they will tend to make the distribution much more peaked and normally distributed than it actually is. That means that the distributions used in MC will actually tend to be systematically biased toward less variance. That is exactly what we observe in the data. Instead of a mean of 9% contingency with a near-normal distribution, we observe a

[3]These results hold for smaller projects as well.

[4]Until *truthiness* came along, I referred to the MC results as a thin gloss of scientific verisimilitude on pure BS. *Truthiness* is more succinct.

30% (9% plus the actual 21% overrun) mean with a sharply skewed distribution. Instead of a standard deviation of 4%, we should have seen a standard deviation in excess of 25%.

- The orthogonality assumption, which is absolutely central to the mathematical integrity of MC simulation, is grossly violated by the real world of projects, large and small. In projects, bad things tend to happen in groups, not individually, because projects are so tightly woven. Events that affect projects in major ways, such as scope changes, engineering errors, erratic business decision-making, or poor FEL tend to go together. Even when one of those things occurs individually, it tends to trigger a cascade of problematic effects. Defenders of MC will sometimes respond to this criticism by saying that the interdependencies can be modeled. That is pure fantasy.

Probabilistic Schedule Assessment Does Work

If MC simulation of cost risk is a complete flop, probabilistic evaluation of schedule has proven a useful technique for megaprojects. Probabilistic schedule assessment (PSA) involves examination of the elements on or near the critical path for a project and testing how varying the durations of critical elements changes the overall schedule duration. PSA is asking the question: how likely is it that everything will go according to plan?

The use of PSA at project authorization is associated with a 27% decrease in the amount of execution schedule slip by the projects (Pr $|t|<.001$). The use of PSA is helping project teams see that their chances of achieving the schedules that have been established are very poor. That then causes them to insert float at various points that are defined as low probability of achievement. Setting realistic schedules is associated with better overall results. The use of PSA is associated with a lower probability of production attainment failure as well as lowered schedule slip. More realistic schedules improve quality. Improved quality plays out in better operability.

Reading the Tea Leaves: Key Warning Signs of Trouble Ahead

The period from late FEL through early execution is a very busy period for project teams. It is easy for them to be too busy to be thinking about risk surveillance. But this period is about the last chance during which an impending disaster might be averted. To see if any telltale signs of trouble could be seen, I reviewed the project histories for any recurring events occurring from very late FEL through the first few months of execution that might have warned teams of trouble to come in time to make changes, especially in the schedule. I only list an event if it occurred in three or more failed projects and did not appear more than once in successful projects.

Changes

- Were any scope changes made during FEED? Scope changes in FEL-3 are strongly associated with detailed engineering being late.
- Has a change in the nameplate capacity occurred that was based on using up design margins in equipment? This is not "really" a scope change because it does not involve new equipment; it is merely using up all of the spare capacity in the specified equipment. This was strongly associated with startup problems.

Basic Data

- For E&P projects, are the seismic data (imaging of the reservoir) being reprocessed, even if there are assurances that "no changes will result"?
- Is a pilot facility still being run as execution is getting started? This is a killer.

Procurement

- Were the long-lead items actually ordered on time?
- Did the vendors provide a firm contractual commitment for delivery or a "target date"?
- Have any changes to long-lead items been required due to design development?

Contracting

- Was the licensing fee or contractor fee a "bargain"? For example, if a licensor is offering the technology for $1, it is because you are the guinea pig, not because they are generous. If the contractor fee request is abnormally low, it is because they know something you do not.
- Is the prime (or one of the prime) engineering contractors being asked to do something in a way that is not usual for them? For example, not subbing out part of the design? Or using an office that would not normally work on projects at your location?
- Are any of the engineering contractors balking at the terms and conditions for the contract? Remember, they all saw the terms and conditions as part of the ITB, so if they are not accepting them now that you are in negotiation, something else is going on. In most cases, it is wise to keep the second bidder "warm," even to the extent of some payment, until the deal with No. 1 is signed. (Keeping the second bidder warm also increases the chances that acceptable terms will be reached with #1.)

Shaping and Partner Issues

- Has an old and "put to bed" Shaping issue resurfaced at sanction time? For example, royalties, sharing of proceeds, environment, local content?
- Is a partner balking at sanction for whatever reason?

Early Execution

- Are the engineering contractors having difficulty mobilizing?
- Is the sequencing of engineering progressing as planned, taking rework into account?
- Have all the permits arrived?
- Is engineering have a high rate of rework?
- Are drawings from the equipment vendors arriving on schedule?
- Is there agreement and understanding between engineering and construction/fabrication contractors about exactly what the design submittals to fabricators will look like? How detailed will the drawings be?

If the answer to any of the preceding questions are discouraging, then engineering is probably going to slip, and the contingency plans that were made for that eventuality need to be put in motion. It is all too easy to hope that things will sort themselves out, but they almost never do. Now would be the time to slow the project by design rather than have it slow by default later on.

Maintaining Value

As the project progresses out of engineering and into construction or fabrication, the controls task shifts almost completely to preventing seemingly little things from becoming big problems. For onshore projects, the next critical juncture will be field mobilization. Some projects were tripped up by an inability to move workers in and out of the site each day. Long queues would develop outside the gates with waiting times of over an hour to get in. This problem is most likely to occur in low-wage environments where the numbers of people involved may be many thousands. But it has also occurred in Alberta and in the United States among megaprojects in the last decade. In high-wage countries, the labor absolutely must be paid for their waiting time or they will leave the project.

As construction progresses, the achieved labor productivity should be checked against the estimate basis continuously. If productivity is not as high as expected for the civil crafts, which are first on the job, it is very important to understand why. If the quality of the labor draw is not as good as expected, then there may be problems with labor quality throughout the job.

Often when there are labor productivity problems on a project, I hear both owner and contractor managements complain that the labor is unmotivated. Even if it happens to be true in a particular case, to frame the problem in that way is to lose the project. Labor productivity problems must be viewed solely as management problems. To do otherwise is to play the victim while the project suffers. In fact, most problems with labor productivity are problems of organization, materials management, first-line supervision, and basic labor skill. All of these problems are subject to management mitigation. It has been my observation that labor is often unmotivated at sites that are poorly run with insufficient materials available, and hostile first-line supervisors. Before even considering adding labor to the site to attempt to recover schedule, be certain that you understand the problem, and that additional labor will fix it rather than make it worse.

Finally, as construction or fabrication passes halfway, attention should turn to ensuring that the systems are being completed in the proper sequence for turnover to the commissioning and startup teams. This requires that the construction management organization will begin to switch its attention from maximum rates of materials installation back to the master schedule that dictates when various systems must be completed to have an efficient startup process.

The turnover sequences should have been fully developed during FEL with the operating organization that will eventually take over the facilities. As construction/fabrication proceeds, operator training and manual preparation must also be progressing on the venture side. Ideally, the same people who will lead the startup and initial operation of the facilities will be involved in the drawing review process in early execution and will be present as commissioning activities begin.

Megaprojects often take many months to commission and start up. Often, at remote sites the utilities are needed as early as possible to support construction. The utilities are almost always required to be fully operational and reliable before startup of any processing units begins. Waiting until mechanical completion of all units before beginning the commissioning effort will stretch out the total cycle time at a point that causes maximum economic damage because all of the investment is in place but not earning revenue. Unfortunately, that is often what actually happens because the utilities are often among the last units defined, engineered, and ultimately, completed.

PART 5

Finishing Up

In this final section, we address how corporate governance requirements shape megaproject outcomes and then address concerns for the future. More than anything else, I believe that governance is what distinguishes industrial projects from publicly funded infrastructure projects. Ironically, governments typically lack effective project governance structures because they do not generally embrace the project work processes that render effective governance feasible. It is governance that weeds out liars, opportunists, and dreamy optimists from controlling a project's fate.

With that said, there is some room for optimism in megaprojects. We are, in fact, doing them better today than 20 years ago. Our challenge for the future is that we will have to do them far better still if megaprojects are going to play their necessary part in preventing us from cooking our planetary home.

CHAPTER 15

Project Governance

Perhaps the single most important thing that I have learned during my study of large and complex projects is that they do not have to fail nearly as often as they actually do. Very few failed megaprojects simply experienced terribly bad luck that doomed their prospects. Overwhelmingly, there were errors and omissions of the owner sponsors of these projects that set them firmly on the path to failure. It didn't have to happen.

My colleagues and I have documented those errors and omissions over much of the last four decades to distill which practices are most destructive of shareholder value and which practices preserve or enhance value. By this point in the 21st century, almost all project professionals and most others engaged in industrial megaproject development and execution are fully familiar with the lessons contained in this book. Learning the lessons has, indeed, made a difference as the industrial megaproject success rate has more than doubled from the first five years of this century at less than 20% to over 40% in the most recent period. Although 40 is clearly better than 20, it is still far short of what is attainable if we simply do the things that we know we should do. So why don't we?

At the core, I believe the answer is poor project governance. Governance is just a set of basic rules that define which projects will be allowed to proceed and which projects will be denied. The purposes of governance are straightforward:

- Fund the projects with the best risk-weighted returns on investment.
- Eliminate projects that will create monetary and reputational loss.

- Thin and focus the project portfolio at various stages of the project maturation process so as to waste as few resources as necessary on hopeless projects.
- Encourage participants in the project development process to do the things that will enhance the company's capital productivity rather than erode it.

In short, governance is intended to ensure that a capital expenditure has a solid, well-grounded, and reasoned business case, and has been matured in a way that eliminates unnecessary risks and mitigates those that are necessary.

I believe that one has to conclude that the governance process for a good many industrial companies is not working very well. The evidence is compelling:

- Most megaprojects are noncompliant with governance rules at final investment decision (FID) and other decision points.
- A majority of megaprojects do not achieve even a "good" rating for front-end loading (FEL), much less a "best practical" rating.
- Many megaprojects scramble to get essential Basic Data before the end of FEED when they should have been available by early scope development.
- A great many projects enter front-end engineering design (FEED) with unaligned stakeholders, with partner disagreements, and other Shaping problems that should have been resolved or caused the process to slow until they were.

The upshot is that we get many more failures than we should have. And everyone needs to be clear: these failed megaprojects are gigantic destroyers of value. Industrial companies would be financially stronger and societies would be wealthier if these projects were more successful.

Why Is Good Governance So Difficult?

So why doesn't governance work better? There are still some pockets of ignorance, especially in newly formed companies, or new businesses, or companies doing their first megaprojects ever or first in many years. Fortunately, these situations are fairly infrequent. Unfortunately, many renewables and energy transition companies fall into one of these categories. But governance is a hit-or-miss proposition at a great many industrial firms that do megaprojects frequently.

Some academics, in particular, the Oxford School of megaproject study, believe that the problem stems primarily from the innate optimism bias of humans when faced with uncertainty. The optimism bias in decision-making is no doubt real and plays a role in making governance more difficult. So, too, does the problem of people being less than candid when it is in their interest to be so. The academics call that "strategic misrepresentation." However, a functioning governance process addresses both the optimism bias and lack of candor by requiring that the proper work be done so that optimism is squeezed out and lying becomes difficult, if never altogether impossible.

Probably more important than the human optimism bias or the (very human) tendency to prevaricate is the bias inherent in the project maturation process. Every project professional knows that early estimates and the schedules that accompany them will tend to be biased low. The bias is due to the very nature of the estimating process. I estimate the scope I see. I guess at the cost of the scope I *think* will be there but do see yet, and I estimate any other scope that is found later at zero. I can use conceptual benchmarking to de-bias when good analogs are available, but when they are not, the estimate is too low. Scheduling proceeds in the same manner. The problems of optimism and lying are *derivative* of this reality rather than its cause. If realistic and accurate early estimates and schedules could be developed easily, there would be little or no room for either optimism or lying.

The Role of Stage-Gates

The stage-gated process, which is employed by almost all industrial companies, was described in Chapter 10 and its importance for project outcomes was discussed. But the stage-gate process is also an integral part of most governance systems. Right at the core of portfolio management is the ability to compare projects in terms of their worth to the business. For the comparisons to be meaningful, one must know how mature a potential project is. The stage-gates provides a mechanism for facilitating better comparisons if all of a company's projects adhere to the process.

Even more critically, the stage-gates provide decision points at which governance must function. The pause points for decisions are standardized for maturity to make portfolio management more effective and because important questions are supposed to be answerable at each gate. At the gate to enter scope development, the questions are:

- Are enough Basic Data available to permit scope development to proceed?
- Is the business case sufficiently robust that scope development makes sense?
- Are there potentially killing Shaping issues that should be addressed before scoping starts?
- Is a functionally complete team ready to start scope development?

At the gate to enter FEED, the questions are:

- Now that the scope is complete, does the business case continue to be robust when viewed versus other possible projects to fund and the risk profile of the project?
- Are the Basic Data required for design complete?
- Is Shaping complete with stakeholders aligned around the allocation of project value?
- Is the project prepared to enter FEED and execution plan completion?

At the FID gate, the questions are easier:

- Are the Shaping, Basic Data, and business case materially unchanged?
- Is the project fully prepared to be executed?

The governance process is intended to ensure that all the answers to the preceding questions are positive. If an answer is not positive, the project should be paused until the question can be answered positively, recycled to an earlier point in the process, or killed. Actual behavior is quite different:

- The project is passed through the gate with an "understanding" that deficiencies will be immediately fixed.
- The project must be passed through the gate because commitments were made to others that make passage necessary.
- If things are really bleak, the project is "shelved." (Those metaphorical shelves can get very crowded.)
- Very occasionally, a project is actually killed.

The actual behaviors that we observe at gates renders the governance process highly political and responsive to how well the project advocates play the political game and who they know rather than the quality of the project being pursued. Although this process plays out for projects of all types and sizes, it is more common for megaprojects to be political than more routine projects. As an observation, the more complex the governance process is at a company, the more political it is likely to become rather than an application of rules to the situation.

Who Should Own Governance?

To answer the question of who should own the governance process, we need to ask who benefits from governance and who does not. On the negative side are the company's business unit professionals. Businesses like capital projects and the growth in their businesses that result. But they have no love of the governance process and generally consider it an obstacle to securing capital. Operations (production or manufacturing) have a small stake in good governance because facility quality is one of the elements included in the process. The projects organization has a moderately strong incentive to support the governance process because without a functioning governance process, it is very difficult to manage the project portfolio—far too many projects are in development relative to the number that can actually be funded.

The real beneficiary of governance is corporate management and the shareholders they are supposed to represent.

Corporate management is the only entity that is responsible for the overall health of the firm. One of the cornerstone measures of corporate health is return on capital employed (ROCE). Overspending on just a few megaprojects can significantly erode ROCE for all but the largest firms. Furthermore, corporate is responsible for capital allocation and budgeting, and when cash flow declines, it is corporate that must decide what to cut and how. Therefore, the capital governance process is either owned by corporate management or it does not work.

Alternative Governance Models

Over the years, we have seen a number of approaches to governance for major projects.[1] Despite the obvious fact that some approaches do not work as intended, changes in governance models are very difficult to do because those who have developed skills around managing within a given governance structure will fight hard to maintain the status quo. Some of the differences are by industrial sector, where companies clearly copy the governance approaches of sectoral colleagues whether or not they work very well. There are also big differences by size of firm and capital portfolio. For small companies with small portfolios, governance is usually conducted entirely within corporate management because every megaproject can have a material effect on company fortunes. The following models discussed only apply to companies with large enough portfolios that business units and projects compete for capital.

The Independent Project Review (IPR) Team Model

The IPR team model is most common in the mining sector. It entails creating a unit within corporate, often reporting to the chief financial officer, that deploys teams as required to conduct an assessment of a

[1]Governance of site and sustaining capital projects and other "less than major" projects is often handled as a budgetary process more than a governance process.

project's viability during the front-end. Often, the IPRs are conducted at the completion of a "study" phase, such as the end of the pre-feasibility study (roughly the end of FEL-2) or the end of the feasibility study (roughly the end of FEL-3). The review team will spend weeks with the study team assessing the completeness of the work and health of the project.

The IPR teams are usually multifunctional and include experienced project hands as well as financial experts, government relations, and others as appropriate for the particular project. They sometimes include Basic Data expertise such as geologists and other technical subject matter experts (SMEs). The teams are either standing teams or, more frequently, ad hoc teams assembled for a particular project.

When the IPR team has completed its work, it provides its findings to the CFO, the business leadership for the business unit in which the project is to be performed, and to the project team. The report then becomes an input into decision-making by the "investment committee" at the corporate level that will make the decision regarding the project's path.

Although understood as part of the process, the IPR approach is generally disliked by project (study) teams because the process consumes a great deal of time and energy, and would be classed as a "heavy" form of assurance. There are a number of problems with the IPR approach in addition to being consumptive of resources. The most pressing problem is that, for most companies using the IPR approach, the pre-feasibility (FEL-2) and feasibility (FEL-3) studies are not nearly of uniform quality and completeness. This means that the IPR team is constantly trying to compare apples and oranges, or as an IPR team member once told me, "Apples and oranges would be great; some of them aren't even fruit!"

The structural problem with the IPR team model is that it does not actually provide a decision. If the IPR team's approval of the study work was a necessary condition of the project moving forward, that would be governance. But, in fact, the IPR team's review is simply one input among many into the decision that is made behind closed doors of the investment committee or the board of directors. When governance is not transparent, no one involved in the process can learn what behaviors and performance are needed to secure approval. That benefits those who would prefer the process was political rather than principled.

The PMO/Value Assurance Unit Model

A second model houses the governance process ownership and the assurance process within the project management office of the projects and technology division of the company, or houses a stand-alone value assurance (VA) unit within the projects organization. This approach is common in the oil and chemicals sectors. This only works if the PMO is a corporate entity and does not work if each business unit has its own projects group.

In this model, the PMO or VA group is responsible for assessing deliverables at each gate—this process is tightly bound to the stage-gate process—and reporting or certifying that the project has achieved requirements. This information is then included in the gate-decision meeting as an input. The advantage of this model is that those doing the assurance reviews are much closer to the projects organization than an IPR team can be. Because the assurance group is part of the projects organization, there is considerable peer pressure to complete the work as required. The effect is to somewhat insulate the project work stream side of the governance process from politics.

There are drawbacks, of course. The deliverables required for a project to enter scope development are not the products of the projects organization; they are usually business unit work products. The business-to-scoping gate is the most routinely unguarded gate in stage-gate systems. In many systems, almost anything can be dumped into scope development with or without the needed Basic Data or any Shaping work accomplished. Recall the Shaping nightmare from Chapter 5, which was enabled by allowing scope development to proceed without any input from Shaping that would have told the scope developers that their highly cost-efficient scope was going to generate fierce local opposition.

The other problem is that this model is more about assurance than it is about governance. Assurance checks that the work required by the governance process is actually completed. Governance occurs in what is done with that information with respect to a project. The PMO/VA model tends to do a better job of assessing the quality and completeness of deliverables than the IPR approach, but that does nothing for the actual quality of decision-making, although decisions are usually more transparent than in the IPR team model.

The Steering Committee/Decision Review Board (DRB) Model

In this model, governance (gate) decisions are made by a "SteerCo" or DRB. Typically, this group is drawn from the executive levels of the business unit, corporate, projects, and sometimes production or manufacturing. The group is usually a standing group for the project, which is to say, it is intended that the same group members will see the project through from early gates to completion. This model is most often used in developing petroleum and chemicals, both commodities and specialties. This model is common in companies that are decentralized by business unit in which the IPR model is not used. The typical SteerCo or DRB will have five to nine members.

There are two very important drawbacks of this model, one practical and one structural. The practical difficulty is that all members of the DRB have very demanding day jobs as they are senior executives. What this means is that they have very little time to deeply dig in to understand what the health or pitfalls of a project might be at each gate. Getting behind the slick presentation to understand the project is difficult under the best of circumstances; it is impossible if there is insufficient time.

The structural problem is worse: this model is decision-making by committee. This ensures that decision accountability is diffuse, at best, and nonexistent, at worst. As one wag put it, "If we hold hands and jump off the cliff together, it wasn't my fault!" Unless a project coming to the decision-gate was grossly deficient in obvious ways, the DRB is very likely to allow the project through the gate. Because it is a group decision, no one is accountable when the decision is poor.

Sometimes, the SteerCo or DRB is deemed "advisory" rather than a formal decision group. This is a distinction without a difference. When a senior level committee is formed to review the progress of a project, that is, in fact, a decision-making committee. To overrule such a group would be career suicide for anyone else except the CEO.[2]

The Threefold Accountability Model

As is often the case, the simplest model is the best. In this model, there are only three players: the business sponsor of the project, the head of the projects organization (a corporate unit), and the decision-maker, a corporate executive. Because the project is a megaproject, the business sponsor may be the business unit leader and the corporate executive could be the CEO.

- The business sponsor certifies that the business case fundamentals are as represented in terms of expected returns, completed Shaping, and risk profile with the clear understanding that the returns on the project will be reflected in variable compensation (VC) for five years after project's completion regardless of their then position in the company.
- The head of the projects organization certifies that the project preparation and maturity fully conform to company requirements for the given gate. The head of projects understands that their approval of a project that was not in fact ready will be reflected in their VC.
- If the business sponsor and head of projects provide their okay to the project, the corporate executive certifies that the project fits corporate intention, portfolio, and policy and the project is approved.

[2]There can be very effective advisory boards established for difficult projects, but they do not look like DRBs; they are not staffed in the same way and they have a very different charter. Setting up an advisory board to review and assist a project team, especially when the project director is relatively inexperienced, can work very well if it is clear by charter and practice that the project team is free to reject any and all advice as it sees fit without repercussion. (It is best to add a requirement that recommendations be rejected in writing [with no copies to outsiders] in order to ensure that recommendations are actually seriously considered.)

All three players in this process have "pocket veto" authority, that is, if they do not affirm, the project cannot proceed: gates are closed by default, and opened only on affirmation of all three players. Sometimes, this model also includes a final agreement step by the executive committee or the board of directors, but if the model is established correctly, such a group can only stop a project, but not okay a project that has been stopped by one of the accountable players.

This model is the least commonly employed, but where it has been tried, it has proven very effective. The key, of course, is that accountability is only possible when the number of players is minimized and the decision-making authority of the players is clearly defined. Governance is necessary to accountability but is not sufficient. Accountability, ultimately, must work through the incentive system, and there must be consequences; no consequences, no governance.

Governance Is Important

Without an effective governance process, meaningful accountability for project outcomes is not possible. It is easy to make project directors or the heads of projects accountable in the sense of penalizing them when projects go poorly. But that is not the same as genuine accountability. When the business case for a project is weak, the project will usually be poorly executed because constant changes will be made to try to work around the weaknesses in the business case and Shaping. If the project was a bad fit with the corporate portfolio, that is not the fault of the business sponsor nor the project director. It is corporate's remit. Only if the project was not properly front-end loaded is the accountability on the project director and head of projects. The only way to make that accountability real, however, is with the pocket veto.

I am sure that many readers have heard groups within your organizations complain about how much they hate the "project process." Sometimes it is the businesses that complain; sometimes it is production; sometimes it is even the projects organization. After watching this play out for many years, I am convinced that the dislike is not for the project work process; it is for the governance process and the assurance process that accompanies it that is not working effectively.

When projects turn out badly, a common reaction is to double assurance. The process becomes progressively bureaucratic and cumbersome, and still poorly put together projects continue, so we *redouble* assurance. But if the incentive systems are not appropriate and if the governance process is not clear, no amount of assurance will ever fix the problem.

CHAPTER 16

Focus on Success

Nearly a quarter of the 21st century has already passed. As a global projects community, we are faced with the most daunting project challenge ever: to reinvent and redevelop the energy infrastructure of the entire world over the next 25 years. Megaprojects have always been important, but they have never been more important than right now. From the perspective of the number of megaprojects in front of us, the question of whether the governments of the world's nations get together to address climate change in a serious way makes no difference to the number of projects, only to their makeup. If concerted action does occur, we will see trillions of dollars devoted to low- and zero-carbon energy projects. If such action does not occur, which at the current time seems increasingly probable, we will see countless trillions of dollars poured into projects aimed at mitigating the consequences of global warming as massive dislocation occurs.

As a projects community, we need a real sense of urgency about the quality of our most important industrial projects, but it is my hope and expectation that those who have read the story of our past in this book come away with hope and confidence for the future. The fact is, as a professional projects community, we know what we are doing. We understand how to make these projects successful; we have doubled the success rate of these projects in the past two decades. We should be able to do so again in the next two decades. An 85% success rate in 2050 would make this a better world in which to live.

However, if we are going to be successful, we will need the help of others and we will need to make some important changes in how owner/sponsor organizations approach their megaprojects.

Address the Business-Technical Divide

The first, and clearly, most important challenge is to address the deep chasm of misunderstanding between business and technical professionals about how these projects should be developed, governed, and executed. The need for improvement lies on both sides of the divide.

Project and technical professionals generally are too reluctant to speak up when they see problems from the business side that will likely cause failure. When they do speak up, they too frequently do not articulate their concerns in a way that the businesses can readily assimilate. I often get the feeling when doing postmortems of the bad megaprojects that the technical professionals are more satisfied with having been right about an issue than getting the issue successfully addressed. Project professionals need to learn how to communicate in language that is clear and persuasive to their business colleagues. The attitude of "I could have told 'em if they had asked" is not acceptable.

The business professionals have to accept more than half the blame for this situation because it is the businesses that are genuinely in charge. To put it bluntly, too many business people making key decisions about these projects do not understand what they are doing. These big projects are very unforgiving. They must be prepared extraordinarily well, which takes both skill and patience on both the business and technical sides. Once set in motion at the closure of Shaping and Scope Development, they cannot be fine-tuned, speeded up, slowed down, or redirected, or realistically, even tweaked.

I am concerned that the businesses in some companies, especially big oil companies, will be convinced that none of these messages are aimed at them. They consider themselves project-savvy and far too successful to imagine that they are at fault. However, one does not achieve a 65% failure rate in petroleum development projects without a lot of large company projects included. Indeed, large company projects lead the way. And let's be candid, at $80+ per barrel, a lot of very bad projects make money. But they are still bad projects. And those bad projects are still eating away at the shareholders' capital and returns as well as the long-term sustainability of the firm.

I worry even more about the project savviness of executives in many renewables companies or arms of larger companies. Some of them strike me as far too cavalier about how difficult the megaprojects in their future are going to be. They have daunting Shaping challenges, often will require new technology, and the project groups of many of these organizations are hopelessly understaffed.

The first step to bridging the divide between the businesses and the project professionals is for the businesses to be far more inclusive of key project people in their initial development of the projects. Deals should not be struck without fully understanding the project consequences of how the deal is Shaped. Much more dialogue between businesses and project professionals is needed at every stage. The aura of distrust that now surrounds so many of the relationships between the businesses and the technical functions must be dispelled. Dialogue is the only way to do it.

Some observers of this dynamic between business and project professionals believe that the problems originate with the decline in the numbers of technically trained business people in industrial firms. I am not so sure. I see at least as many problems when the business people started as technical professionals as when they did not. Sometimes, I think "formerly technical" people need to be seen as being as "tough on those project people" as anyone else.

Instead, I believe that some of the problems originate in and are reinforced by business education curricula that emphasize financial savvy and de-emphasize the role of the technical functions in industrial firms. Surely a balance must be struck, but running a successful commodity-producing business is at least as much a series of technical problems about how to achieve the lowest possible cost of production as it is a series of financial issues.

The often covert hostility that has developed between business and technical professionals in industrial organizations is a first-order driver of poor megaproject outcomes. Bridging the divide will help restore a spirit of cooperation not only in the development and execution of the projects, but also more generally in the way the owner companies operate. The failure to bridge this divide threatens their existence.

Formalize and Institutionalize the Shaping Process

The need to Shape megaprojects is one of their nearly unique characteristics. Most sponsoring companies lack a systematic approach to Shaping that helps them ensure that the right things are getting done for every project. The Shaping process is what binds the project from the corporate boardroom to the production floor.

Every industrial firm has a strategy for how it will gain comparative advantage in a competitive world. That strategy includes technology, supply chain, and production assets. In successful firms, those elements are tightly woven together. The corporate strategy informs the businesses what sorts of assets in what areas of the world will be acceptable and desirable. The business goals for the projects define how the corporate goals around generating comparative advantage will be manifested in this project. And finally, the detailed business objectives define the project objectives that the team must meet to be considered successful.

Businesses need to think about and prepare for megaprojects differently. The Shaping process is how the sponsors' quest for comparative advantage is married to the messy real world of capital project opportunities. The Shaping process defines and then allocates the value of the project to stakeholders in a way that should be intended to create a stable platform from which the project can be developed and executed while bringing enough value to the sponsors to make the project economically worthwhile.

Shaping is clearly an art, but even art requires disciplined skill, practice, and process. Companies that develop the skills and processes to be able to Shape projects well will generate comparative advantage. But the ingredient that is most often missing is discipline. When it comes to capital projects, and especially to large capital projects, undisciplined is a fair characterization—just look back to Chapter 10 to see how many projects were woefully unprepared at full-funds authorization. Discipline is every bit as needed on the business side of these projects as the technical side, but we are not seeing it. The decentralized nature of many modern industrial firms, especially in minerals and petroleum, adds to the tendency to approach each new project with a new and hastily generated game plan.

The solution is not difficult, but by the nature of the problem, must come straight from the top of the corporations. Establish a standard work process for the Shaping of large projects, and then hold senior leaders in the businesses accountable for meeting the requirements that the work process entails. Governance of capital is a corporate responsibility, and that responsibility is being abdicated by a good many corporate managements.

Develop the Team Staffing Strategy

One of the big issues facing industrial sponsors going forward is how to staff the many projects that we would like to do. If the projects are too thinly staffed by sponsors, the data clearly indicate they will fail. Every company that hopes to sponsor megaprojects in the next decade needs to establish the approach they will take to staffing. There are several alternatives, none of which are truly ideal.

The first step is to take a complete worldwide (for global companies) inventory of the resources available. Most large companies that are even slightly decentralized do not really know what they have because important human resources that might be best employed corporately are locked up in business units. Highly decentralized companies usually are altogether in the dark.

The next step, obviously, is to compare the resources available and deployable to the intended large-project portfolio. When matching the portfolio to the skills available, it is important to be realistic about the staffing levels that will be required. Planning for skeleton staff is planning to fail. When the resources are insufficient to adequately staff the projects, some creative alternatives will have to be considered.

The first and most obvious alternative that should be employed whether or not other alternative staffing models are considered is a robust training program specifically aimed at the difficulties associated with megaproject management. The curricula should include training for *business directors and megaproject project directors together* as well as material for subproject managers and their reports, procurement/

supply chain, and finance and legal. (Finance and legal might best be trained with business and project directors.) The goal of a megaproject training program should be to take staff that has large project experience ($100 million) and prepare them for the special difficulties they will face on megaprojects. If a training program cannot bring enough people up to speed, then other possibilities might be explored as well.

A few companies have elected to develop long-term relationships with major international contractors to do their major projects globally. This approach has been used for smaller projects many times with mixed success. When used for large projects, these "partnership" arrangements have generally been disappointing. These arrangements tend to create very strong temptations for the contractor to use the partnership arrangement for purposes of developing people they have just acquired or to dump people who are not productive.

A few companies have established engineering centers in places like India to support their projects around the world. Some of these efforts have been clearly successful and help address the critical shortages of project management skills. However, these efforts have probably run their course as the surplus of skilled engineering personnel in places like India appears to have been exhausted.

Some of the critical skills, such as controls, quality assurance/quality control (QA/QC), and planning/scheduling might be acquired from other industries, such as transportation and infrastructure because those skill sets are largely transferable across industrial sectors. Third-party providers are also available for some of these skills, but with the caveat that they must be "tied up" for the duration of the project.

One alternative that needs to be fully considered is to trim the weakest elements of the large project portfolio to match the skill levels that can realistically be made available. While sponsoring companies are understandably reluctant to go this route, it would be far preferable to drop some projects that cannot be staffed properly than to thin out resources from across the portfolio and have a much higher large-project failure rate. Decentralized companies, that is, companies organized with strong separate business units, struggle to rationalize their portfolios. But they are precisely the companies that need it most. Decentralized companies suffer a disproportionate number of disastrous megaprojects.

Finally, all megaproject sponsors need to understand that there will be no bailouts of projects by contractors. The big contractors that can do this work are facing generally even more severe problems and constraints than the sponsors. The demographic crisis in technically trained people has arrived at arguably the worst possible time for humanity.

Remember, Front-End Loading (FEL) Is Still the World's Best Capital Investment

The investment needed in FEL is about 3% to 5% of total capital cost and about 30% to 40% of total project cycle time. The value of that money and time is huge; the projects with best FEL averaged over four times the net present value (NPV) per dollar of investment of all the rest of the projects. The projects that did not achieve at least "good" FEL were usually NPV negative.

If the FEL on your projects is other than "best practical," you need to ask why. The most common answer is schedule pressure, but there are other major contributors as well: unclear business objectives that fail to articulate what the business needs for success, the failure to secure cooperation from the nonproject functions, such as operations, and the lack of enough knowledgeable staff.

FEL is, above all else, a matter of discipline. In the best situations, that discipline is driven from the top of the organization through the businesses to the projects. Because the stage-gated FEL work process is a core business process, the businesses should insist on it. In any case, a technical authority sitting high in the corporate hierarchy needs to be in a position to stop poorly prepared projects before they incinerate shareholder wealth.

FEL is a matter of good corporate governance as well as a matter of project excellence. Without the level playing field that FEL provides, a corporation's portfolio of projects can never be truly coherent.

Corporate main boards of directors must insist on equally good preparation of all major projects.

Restore Professionalism (and Sanity) to the Owner-Contractor Relationship

The major international contractors are essential to getting megaprojects executed successfully. They are professional services firms, but they are not treated like professional service firms in today's marketplace. A normal market for professional service providers is that they are paid a fee for their services. If they are reputed to be extraordinarily good providers of services, they can command a higher fee than those considered mediocre. The highly skilled surgeon will have a more successful practice than the less skilled.

The owner community has de-professionalized the relationships between owners and contractors. The owners, through the ignorance of the businesses and purchasing organizations, have attempted to describe engineering and project management services as a commodity business that should be purchased primarily on price. In fact, however, only a small part of the engineering and project services, detailed engineering, even approximates a commodity. Indeed, EPC services should be primarily purchased based on quality, not price, because of the huge variability in quality contractor-to-contractor and project-to-project.

The misguided attempt by the owner community to de-professionalize engineering, materials procurement, and construction (EPC) services has resulted in pathological behavior that seriously damages major projects. Some of the contractors responded to the change in owner behavior and coherence by becoming almost nakedly predatory. Some have responded by becoming primarily defensive in their posture toward owners. Owners have responded by seeking to play incentive bribery games with the contractors, which cannot possibly work in the long term because the incentives will be gamed or the measures taken to prevent gaming will induce still worse problems.

Owners need to return to the basic notion that contractors should be paid for their work. If they do a good job, they need to be rewarded with a better chance of securing the next project. If they do a poor job, and do so systematically, they should disappear. To make that work requires a return to institutional coherence on the part of the sponsor community.

Toward More Successful Megaprojects

The industrial megaprojects executed over the last two decades or so have, taken as whole, been disappointing. It is important to remember, however, that there were also some genuinely brilliant successes. But those brilliant successes were not generated by geniuses; they were developed and executed by men and women who were careful, patient, cooperative, and committed to excellence. It is also important to remember that we have improved our performance markedly since the start of this century.

The next three decades of the 21st century will see more very large and complex industrial projects than at any time in history. The challenge for all stakeholders, sponsors, and contractors alike is to see that we generate many more successful projects in the next decades than we have in the last two. I hope that when it comes time for someone else to review the history of the next decade of megaprojects, there will be an even happier story to tell.

Glossary and Acronyms

Basic Data Also sometimes referred to as *Basic Data package*, the body of scientific information that underlies the design of facilities. The Basic Data for a megaproject would require many hundreds of pages to compile. The term is used in a number of places in the text and is the subject of Chapter 9.

Bias Mostly, we use the term *bias* in its statistical or mathematical sense in this book. For example, a set of estimates is biased if the average is not centered on the average of the eventual actual cost.

Cascading failure A cascading (cascade) failure occurs when a fault in a closely coupled network causes a widespread failure to all or a large part of the network. Cascading failures are the most common mode of failure in megaprojects.

Cost-Reduction Exercise A Cost-Reduction Exercise (CRE) occurs when the estimated cost for a project approaching authorization is too high for a gatekeeper to accept and the team is directed to reduce the estimate.

Endowment *Endowment* refers to size and quality of the business driver for a project. For example, for a minerals development project, the endowment is the quality and size of the mineral resource. For a chemical project, the endowment may be the size of a feedstock cost advantage, and so on.

EPC Refers to engineering, materials procurement, and construction—the three principal activities required to create a capital project. *EPC* also refers to the industry that provides these three services to capital projects. The firms in the EPC industry are called contractors, but not all contractors are EPCs; some provide only engineering services or only construction or fabrication services. In addition, *EPC* refers to a form of contracting for engineering, procurement, and construction services that has all three activities performed by a single contracting company or by a single consortium of contractor companies.

EPCm Stands for engineering, procurement, and construction management. EPCm is a contract approach in which a single contractor (or consortium) executes engineering and procurement and then manages, but does not perform, construction or fabrication.

Escalation *Escalation* is inflation in project inputs such as steel, pipe, hourly wages, and so on. If escalation exceeds background inflation, capital productivity in projects is declining.

FEED Stands for front-end engineering design. This term is used primarily by the oil and chemical industries for the third phase of FEL.

FEL Stands for front-end loading. This term refers to the work process needed to prepare a project for execution. FEL is generally organized into three phases: business case development, scope development, and project definition and planning.

Forward-selling Refers to selling the output of a megaproject before the project starts. Forward-selling is very important for liquefied natural gas (LNG), and in some cases, for metals. Forward-selling reduces some risks for the project sponsors on the commercial side, but often increases project risks because most forward-selling involves "take-or-pay" contracts. Such contracts obligate the seller to provide product to the buyer regardless of whether or not the project is operating at the agreed-on price. Conversely, the buyer is obligated to accept product at the agreed-on price.

IPA Stands for Independent Project Analysis, Inc., a global research and consulting company devoted exclusively to the understanding of capital projects and capital project delivery organizations in the petroleum, chemicals, minerals, pharmaceutical, and power industries. All of the data on megaprojects in this book resulted from IPA evaluations of the projects for their sponsors.

Local content requirements Local content requirements stipulate the value that must be purchased in country or the specific items that must be purchased in country. Formal local content requirements are a matter of law or written into contracts with the government resource holders. Informal requirements are enforced via the regulatory approval process or like means.

NGO Stands for nongovernmental organizations, including a range of public interest organizations usually devoted to particular causes that are often politically sensitive: environmental protection, protection of vulnerable native peoples, anticorruption, and the like.

Nonrecourse finance Nonrecourse finance is money lent (usually by a syndicate of banks) to fund a project without any ability to tap the balance sheets of the sponsoring companies. Nonrecourse loans normally have to be repaid from project cash flow only.

NPV Stands for net present value and is the time discounted value of a stream of production over the life of the project. Initial production always has the highest value in an NPV calculation. The rate at which the value of a unit of production declines is driven by the discount rate.

OECD Stands for the Organisation for Economic Cooperation and Development, an organization of countries with market-based economies, almost all of which are economically highly developed. Much of Western Europe, Japan, Canada, and the United States are among its 50 member states. The OECD designation is used as a shorthand for developed economies.

Permitting Refers to the process of securing various (usually many) regulatory approvals during the development and execution of the project. Permitting often governs the pace of the project.

PMC Stands for project managing contractor, which is a contractor hired for the purpose of largely substituting for an owner team. PMC arrangements are generally used only by owners with weak project organizations that cannot staff even all lead positions on the owner project team.

Project teams Refers to the groups of owners, individual contractors, and contractor personnel that develop and manage projects. In most cases, I refer to the sponsor's team as "the project team."

Resource holders The owners of natural resources that will be developed by the megaproject. Resource holders are usually governments.

Shaping The work required to understand the context for a project and its stakeholders, and then allocate the value to stakeholders in a way that is stable while still being profitable to sponsor/investors.

Sponsors Interchangeable with *owners*. Sponsors are entities, usually private firms or government-owned, that are seeking to develop and benefit from a megaproject. In most cases, the sponsors were also the monetary investors in the projects.

Stakeholders Individuals and organizations, including governments, that make an enforceable claim on some part of the project's value. Sponsors are stakeholders, but not all stakeholders are sponsors. NGOs and local communities, for example, are often stakeholders but rarely sponsors. The claim on value does not have to take the form of monetary payment. For example, environmental organizations may "take payment" in the form of a reconfiguration of a project that is (or is perceived to be) less damaging to the physical environment.

Team integration In IPA parlance, *team integration* refers to the owner team only. Team integration measures whether all required owner personnel by function were team members at the appropriate times in front-end loading and execution. Team integration is one of the most important predictors of project success or failure.

Index

P